PARLIAMENT

This collection of essays by leading academics, lawyers, parliamentarians and parliamentary officials provides a critical assessment of the UK Parliament's two main constitutional roles—as a legislature and as the preeminent institution for calling government to account. Both functions are undergoing change and facing new challenges. Part 1 (Legislation) includes chapters on Parliament's emerging responsibilities for pre-legislative scrutiny of government Bills and for evaluating proposed legislation against explicit constitutional standards. The impact on legislation of the European Union and the growing influence of the House of Lords are also examined. Part 2 (Accountability) investigates how Parliament operates to scrutinise areas of executive action previously often shielded from effective parliamentary oversight, including national security, war-making powers and administrative justice. There are also chapters on parliamentary reform, including analysis of the House of Commons 'Wright reforms', parliamentary sovereignty, privilege and the European Convention on Human Rights, Euroscepticism, and parliamentary sovereignty and the regulation of lobbyists.

The book will be of interest to anyone who is curious about the work of Parliament and is aimed at legal academics, practitioners and political scientists.

Volume 5 in the series Hart Studies in Constitutional Law

Hart Studies in Constitutional Law

Volume 1 The House of Lords 1911–2011: A Century of Non-Reform
Chris Ballinger

Volume 2 Parliament and the Law
Edited by Alexander Horne, Gavin Drewry and Dawn Oliver

Volume 3 Law in Politics, Politics in Law
Edited by David Feldman

Volume 4 Parliamentary Sovereignty in the UK Constitution
Michael Gordon

Parliament

Legislation and Accountability

Edited by
Alexander Horne
and
Andrew Le Sueur

·HART·
PUBLISHING
OXFORD AND PORTLAND, OREGON
2016

Hart Publishing
An imprint of Bloomsbury Publishing plc

Hart Publishing Ltd
16C Worcester Place
Oxford
OX1 2JW
UK

Bloomsbury Publishing Plc
50 Bedford Square
London
WC1B 3DP
UK

www.hartpub.co.uk
www.bloomsbury.com

Published in North America (US and Canada) by
Hart Publishing
c/o International Specialized Book Services
920 NE 58th Avenue, Suite 300
Portland, OR 97213-3786
USA

www.isbs.com

HART PUBLISHING, the Hart/Stag logo, BLOOMSBURY and the
Diana logo are trademarks of Bloomsbury Publishing Plc

First published 2016

© The editors

The editors have asserted their right under the Copyright, Designs and Patents Act 1988 to be
identified as Authors of this work.

All rights reserved. No part of this publication may be reproduced or transmitted in any form or by
any means, electronic or mechanical, including photocopying, recording, or any information storage
or retrieval system, without prior permission in writing from the publishers.

While every care has been taken to ensure the accuracy of this work, no responsibility for loss or
damage occasioned to any person acting or refraining from action as a result of any statement in it
can be accepted by the authors, editors or publishers.

All UK Government legislation and other public sector information used in the work is Crown
Copyright ©. All House of Lords and House of Commons information used in the work is
Parliamentary Copyright ©. This information is reused under the terms of the Open Government
Licence v3.0 (http://www.nationalarchives.gov.uk/doc/open-government-licence/version/3)
excepted where otherwise stated.

All Eur-lex materials used in the work is © European Union, http://eur-lex.europa.eu/, 1998–2015.

British Library Cataloguing-in-Publication Data
A catalogue record for this book is available from the British Library.

ISBN: HB: 978-1-84946-716-2
ePDF: 978-1-50990-645-1
ePub: 978-1-50990-644-4

A catalogue record for this book is available from the Library of Congress

Series: Hart Studies in Constitutional Law, volume 5

Typeset by Compuscript Ltd, Shannon
Printed and bound in Great Britain by
CPI Group (UK) Ltd, Croydon CR0 4YY

Foreword

LORD LISVANE, FORMERLY (AS SIR ROBERT ROGERS)
CLERK OF THE HOUSE OF COMMONS

In their Introduction, Alexander Horne and Andrew Le Sueur describe this book as having been written by both 'insiders' and 'outsiders'. This contributes to the great strength of the present work. It is pragmatic and practical—as such enterprises seldom are—and it also draws upon the wider context of academic study and public perception. Its combination of authors gives it what my farmer neighbours would call 'hybrid vigour' and its insights and analyses are both refreshing and challenging.

And the publication of this book is especially well timed. We are increasingly seeing our constitutional arrangements modified by a process of experimental surgery on a long-suffering patient, usually following insufficiently exacting examination and diagnosis. Work in progress includes patchwork devolution, including the complexities of English Votes for English Laws (and a situation where recent polling suggests that only one person in five believes that England has had a fair devolution deal); proposals for a British Bill of Rights; and the possibly seismic result of a referendum on the United Kingdom's continued membership of the European Union. This wide-ranging survey will be an essential source book for anyone seeking to understand or influence events.

In his wise consideration of the relationships between the organs of the State, Sir Stephen Laws challenges the orthodoxy of separate and tidy responsibilities. The will of Parliament is indeed something expressed at the prompting of the Executive rather than being some magical emanation, and it is reasonable to question its nature. A government with a Commons majority ('one is enough'!) which can convince its back-benchers issue by issue can do pretty much what it likes, especially if it ignores gypsy's warnings coming from the House of Lords. Laws suggests that it is for each House to define its role in the scrutiny of legislation. As someone who spent his career in the service of the House of Commons, and now finds himself on the Cross Benches of the House of Lords, this is a view that I applaud—and it has a particular resonance, perhaps, in the aftermath of the tax credit furore (something that I regard as primarily a failure of business management rather than the transgressing of some profound constitutional principle).

The Laws analysis rightly emphasises the importance of effectiveness: does this work? Does this deliver what is expected and required? This prompts thoughts about the nature of legislation as a regulator of society and its behaviours. Are we too focused upon statute? If you are running a restaurant, you may be dimly aware of the health and safety regime put in place by primary legislation. You may even be aware of relevant statutory instruments (but probably not). What matters to you is the local authority's guidance on, for example, how many washbasins you must have. We are increasingly regulated by guidance, often with only a quasi-legal status, and we have not yet quite come to terms with the problems of scrutiny and consistency that that poses.

This is close to the territory bravely explored by Andrew Le Sueur in his examination of automated decision-making, and the problems of effectiveness and legitimacy it raises. As the capabilities of central and local government shrink in response to economic austerity, and automation becomes more and more attractive, this is a scrutiny challenge that Parliament must confront, but one for which I sense that it is not quite ready.

If AJ Balfour was correct in his assertion that 'democracy is government by explanation' then he ought to approve of the concept of pre-legislative scrutiny (PLS); but I suspect that AJB's idea of explanation was to volunteer such explanations as he thought appropriate, rather than being closely examined on his proposals. Jessica Mulley and Helen Kinghorn rightly identify the great merit of draft bills: that Ministers have much less political capital tied up in them and are readier to accept evidence-based change without loss of face. But Mulley and Kinghorn are also realistic about the extent to which the pressures of the legislative timetable militate against the process: governments' (often wholly imaginary) need to demonstrate grip and activity; and the lack of time necessary to do a comprehensive and professional job of scrutiny.

PLS is part of the search for better ways of legislating. The myth of 'line-by-line' scrutiny in the Commons has been thoroughly exploded yet the phrase is trotted out again and again. The dynamics of the Lords, and the lack of programming, allow more exacting (and, for the Executive, less controllable) scrutiny, authoritatively charted by Philip Norton. However, it is reasonable to ask if there are better ways of going about the process. I have a hankering for the Victorian practice of a motion for leave to bring in a bill, allowing consideration of the need for legislation rather than immediate examination of detailed provisions. (There would, of course, need to be a significant gap between the granting of leave and the bringing in of a bill—something which the pressure of time might not allow.) And if we are to engage Parliamentarians more directly in what they are authorising, what about purposive clauses, which would express the elusive 'will of Parliament' and which might make the process of judicial interpretation both easier and more widely comprehensible?

Jack Simson Caird and Dawn Oliver grasp the nettle of better scrutiny through the establishment of legislative standards ('legisprudence') founded on the work of the Lords Constitution Committee. I must declare an interest as a member of the Lords Delegated Powers and Regulatory Reform Committee, which has also been in this business. It may be too much to hope that the use of such standards within government would survive the pressures of political expediency, but the articulation, and wide acceptance, of what constitutes best (or even acceptable) practice should encourage better scrutiny.

But I suspect that we have a way to go yet. The rising threshold between primary and secondary legislation, where statutory instruments are increasingly used for matters of policy and principle which should be the subject of primary legislation, and receive the appropriate examination and challenge, is a worrying phenomenon. And in the present Parliament there has been no shortage of Ministerial pronouncements to the effect that this or that bill 'sends a message', something which is emphatically not the purpose of legislation.

The magisterial review of Parliament's engagement with national security issues by Alexander Horne and Clive Walker, and Arabella Lang's fascinating study of Parliamentary examination of treaties, in effect give 'two cheers' for what Parliament has done and is doing, while offering tempting glimpses of what more could be done.

But here, and in Richard Kelly and Lucinda Maer's shrewd study of Parliamentary reform and accountability, we run up against two powerful limiting factors. First, the shrinkage of central government has dramatically reduced the resources with which the Executive can respond to the scrutiny and questioning of Parliament. In effect, the raw material of scrutiny has become rationed. And second, the currency of Parliament, and especially of the House of Commons, is one of time and political attention, a currency for which no quantitative easing is available. This has, for example, been one of the reasons for the disconnect between an effective European scrutiny system, broadly complementary as between the Houses, and the wider political process, as Paul Hardy recognises in his survey of Parliamentary engagement with EU matters. It is also the reason why there is as yet no sign of a House of Commons Business Committee and voteable agenda; it is difficult to imagine a government, except *in extremis*, being willing to give up the control which Balfour effectively completed more than a century ago.

The examination by Alexander Horne and Hélène Tyrrell of human rights issues will be an essential *vade-mecum* in the debate on a British Bill of Rights, just as Gavin Drewry's level-headed analysis of the UK's engagement with the EU will be for the referendum debate. Horne and Tyrrell's examination takes them into a fascinating discussion of parliamentary sovereignty—a concept I have always been uneasy with (as opposed to *legislative* sovereignty)[1]—and privilege.

I plead guilty to the charge, in Oonagh Gay's compelling study of ethical regulation, of opposing the codification of privilege (in my evidence to the Joint Committee on Parliamentary Privilege),[2] and I am delighted that the Joint Committee decided against codification. As Horne and Tyrrell point out, defamation remains a problem (which would not necessarily have been solved by codification). The Joint Committee's suggestion of guidelines to ensure the fair treatment of witnesses

---

[1] See Robert Rogers and Rhodri Walters, *How Parliament Works*, 7th edn (Routledge, 2015) 169–71.
[2] HL Paper 30 and HC100 of Session 2013-14, Memorandum No 9 and QQ191–37.

was welcome, and most select committees are courteous and fair to those they examine. A very few are not; and, for example, the administration of the oath to one witness in the last Parliament, without notice, was a most regrettable lapse of fairness. It is up to select committees, especially in the Commons, whether there is greater pressure for a right of reply to criticism in Parliamentary proceedings, with all that that might imply.

Every subject dealt with in this excellent collection of studies is a moving target. Some are moving faster than others. But every one of those subjects has benefited from expert and insightful treatment. In the uncertain and unpredictable context of constitutional and Parliamentary development, this book is an essential companion.

Robert Lisvane
January 2016

Acknowledgements

The editors would like to thank the UK Constitutional Law Association, the Study of Parliament Group and University College London (who respectively funded, organised and hosted a round-table discussion in April 2015, which informed a number of the chapters contained in this volume).

We would also like to express our gratitude to all at Hart Publishing who assisted with the genesis and production of this book. In particular, thanks go to Mel Hamill; Tom Adams; Richard Hart; Rachel Turner; Bill Asquith; Emma Swinden and Annie Mirza.

Finally, our thanks go to our respective spouses for their patience throughout the process.

Contents

Foreword v
Acknowledgements ix
List of Contributors xiii
Table of Cases xvii
Table of Legislation xix
Breaking News xxv

1. Introduction 1
   Alexander Horne and Andrew Le Sueur

   ### Part 1: Legislation

2. What is the Parliamentary Scrutiny of Legislation for? 15
   Sir Stephen Laws

3. Pre-legislative Scrutiny in Parliament 39
   Jessica Mulley and Helen Kinghorn

4. Parliament's Constitutional Standards 63
   Jack Simson Caird and Dawn Oliver

5. European Scrutiny 89
   Paul Hardy

6. Legislative Scrutiny in the House of Lords 117
   Philip Norton (Lord Norton of Louth)

   ### Part 2: Accountability

7. Parliamentary Reform and the Accountability of
   Government to the House of Commons 139
   Richard Kelly and Lucinda Maer

8. The Regulation of Lobbyists 161
   Oonagh Gay

9. Robot Government: Automated Decision-Making and its
   Implications for Parliament 183
   Andrew Le Sueur

10. Parliament and National Security 203
    Alexander Horne and Clive Walker

11. Parliament and International Treaties 241
    Arabella Lang

12. Sovereignty, Privilege and the European Convention
    on Human Rights 265
    Alexander Horne and Hélène Tyrrell

13. Euroscepticism and Parliamentary Sovereignty:
    The Lingering Shadows of *Factortame* and *Thoburn* 291
    Gavin Drewry

Index 311

List of Contributors

Gavin Drewry is Emeritus Professor of Public Administration at Royal Holloway, University of London and an Honorary Professor in the Faculty of Laws at UCL. He is a former Chair of the Study of Parliament Group and is a long-serving member of the Council of Administration of the International Institute of Administrative Sciences. He is also a Fellow of the Academy of Social Sciences.

Oonagh Gay, OBE, worked in the House of Commons Library for 30 years, until her retirement in 2015. She was Head of the Parliament and Constitution Centre and was a former Chair of the Study of Parliament Group. She has written extensively on issues around parliamentary reform, parliamentary standards, electoral law, public administration and devolution. She was joint editor of *Conduct Unbecoming: The Regulation of Parliamentary Behaviour* (London, Politicos, 2004).

Paul Hardy practised as a barrister for eight years before working in the European Commission for a four further years. He was Counsel for European Legislation in the House of Commons from 2009 to 2014, when he became the EU Legal Adviser in the House of Lords.

Alexander Horne is Deputy Legal Adviser to Parliament's Joint Committee on Human Rights. Since joining the House of Commons in 2003, he has worked in a variety of roles, including: Legal Specialist to the Constitutional Affairs Committee; Legal and Senior Policy Adviser at the House of Commons Scrutiny Unit; and Senior Researcher at the Parliament and Constitution Centre. He was also the Legal Adviser to the Joint Committee which examined the Draft Voting Eligibility (Prisoners) Bill. He is a Teaching Fellow in Public Law at UCL and was a former Official Secretary to the Study of Parliament Group. He is joint editor of *Parliament and the Law* (Oxford, Hart Publishing, 2013).

Richard Kelly is Senior Researcher at the Parliament and Constitution Centre in the House of Commons Library.

Helen Kinghorn is Assistant Counsel at the Office of Speaker's Counsel at the House of Commons. She read Law at Gonville and Caius College, Cambridge, was called to the Bar in 2006 and practised as a self-employed barrister until she joined the House of Commons in 2012 as a Legal Specialist. She has worked with a number of House of Commons and Joint Select Committees, including on pre- and post-legislative scrutiny inquiries, and drafting private members' Bills.

Arabella Lang is a senior researcher at the House of Commons Library currently specialising in international law and human rights. She has a Master of Research degree with distinction in law and human rights from Birkbeck, University of

London, a Certificate of Postgraduate Studies in violin from the Royal Scottish Academy of Music and Drama, and a first-class degree in law from the University of Edinburgh.

Sir Stephen Laws, KCB, QC (Hon), LLD (Hon), joined the Office of the Parliamentary Counsel from the Home Office in 1976. He remained a member of that Office, involved in the drafting of legislation, until his retirement from the Civil Service in 2012. From 2006 to 2012, he was First Parliamentary Counsel and Permanent Secretary, with responsibility for leading the Office and for the Offices of the Government's Parliamentary Business Managers. From 2012 to 2013, he served as a member of the McKay Commission on the Consequences for the House of Commons of Devolution. He is Senior Associate Research Fellow at the Institute of Advanced Legal Studies, Honorary Senior Research Associate in the Politics department of UCL and Honorary Fellow of the University of Kent Law School, as well as chairing the Advisory Board for the National Archives' 'Big Data for Law' project.

Lucinda Maer is Head of the Parliament and Constitution Centre in the House of Commons Library. She is a member of the Study of Parliament Group Executive Committee.

Jessica Mulley has been a Commons clerk for a little over 20 years, working both in procedural roles dealing with business in the Chamber and as clerk to various select committees. From 2012 she led the Scrutiny Unit, providing specialist support for select committees and for joint committees conducting pre-legislative scrutiny. She has lectured on pre-legislative and other forms of parliamentary scrutiny at a number of UK universities and regularly contributes to parliamentary strengthening internationally.

Philip Norton (Lord Norton of Louth) is Professor of Government and Director of the Centre for Legislative Studies at the University of Hull. He was elevated to the peerage in 1998. He is a member of the House of Lords Select Committee on the Constitution and served as the first Chairman of the Committee when it was appointed in 2001.

Dawn Oliver, FBA, QC (Hon), is Emeritus Professor of Constitutional Law at UCL. Her special interests are in constitutional reform in the UK, law and politics, and Parliament. She was Honorary President of the Study of Parliament Group 2010–15. She is joint editor of *Parliament and the Law* (Oxford, Hart Publishing, 2013) and of *The Changing Constitution* (8th edn, Oxford, Oxford University Press, 2015).

Andrew Le Sueur is Professor of Constitutional Justice at the University of Essex and a member of the Jersey Law Commission. He has served several stints as specialist adviser to select committees in both Houses of Parliament and was the legal adviser to the House of Lords Constitution Committee 2006–09.

Jack Simson Caird is Lecturer in Public Law at the University of Sussex. He is also Academic Secretary of the Study of Parliament Group. In 2014, he completed his doctoral thesis, 'Identifying the Value of Parliamentary Constitutional Interpretation', at Queen Mary, University of London.

Hélène Tyrrell is Senior Research Officer at the University of Essex and Teaching Associate at Queen Mary, University of London. She holds degrees from the University of Durham (LLB (Hons) 2007; MJur, 2009) and Queen Mary, University of London (PhD, 2014).

Clive Walker is Professor Emeritus of Criminal Justice Studies at the School of Law, University of Leeds, where he has served as the Director of the Centre for Criminal Justice Studies and as Head of School. He has published extensively on constitutional law, civil liberties, terrorism issues. In 2003, he was a special adviser to the UK parliamentary select committee that scrutinised what became the Civil Contingencies Act 2004, from which experience he published *The Civil Contingencies Act 2004: Risk, Resilience and the Law in the United Kingdom* (Oxford, Oxford University Press, 2006). His recent books on terrorism include *Terrorism and the Law* (Oxford, Oxford University Press, 2011) and *The Anti-Terrorism Legislation* (3rd edn, Oxford, Oxford University Press, 2014).

Table of Cases

A v Secretary of State for the Home Department [2004] UKHL 56 231
A v UK (2003) 36 EHRR 5 285
AXA General Insurance v Lord Advocate [2011] UKSC 46,
    [2012] 1 AC 868 267
Animal Defenders International v UK (2013) 57 EHRR 21 285
Benkharbouche v Embassy of Sudan [2015] EWCA Civ 33,
    [2015] 2 CMLR 20 90
Brasserie du Pêcheur v Germany and R v Secretary of State for Transport
    ex p Factortame (Joined Cases C-46/93 & C-48/93) [1996] ECR I-4845 301
British Railway Board v Pickin [1974] AC 765 285
Carltona Ltd v Commissioners of Works [1943] 2 All ER 560 190
Cheney v Conn [1968] 1 All ER 779 268
Commission of the European Communities v UK
    (C-246/89R) [1989] ECR 3125 300
Costa v ENEL (Case 6/64) [1964] ECR 585 297
Council of Civil Service Unions v Minister for the
    Civil Service [1985] AC 374 250
Edinburgh and Dalkeith Railway Co v Wauchope (1842) 8 Cl & Fin 71 285
Factortame Ltd v Secretary of State for Transport *see* R v Secretary
    of State for Transport ex p Factortame
Firth and others v UK [2014] ECHR 874 .... 277, 278
Francovich and Bonifaci v Italy [1991] ECR 1-5357, [1993] 2 CMLR 66 301
Frodl v Austria (2011) 52 EHRR 5 275
Google Spain SL, Google Inc v Agencia Española de Protección
    de Datos, Mario Costeja González (C-131/12) [2014] WLR(D) 202 111
Greens and MT v UK (2010) ECHR 182 .... 267, 272,
                                                                                                                                273, 278
Guardian News & Media v Incedal and Rarmoul-Bouhadjar
    [2014] EWCA Crim 1861 228
HM Treasury v Ahmed [2010] UKSC 2 231
HM Treasury v Ahmed (No 2) [2010] UKSC 5 231
HP Bulmer Ltd v J Bollinger SA [1974] Ch 40 .... 296, 297
Hirst v UK (No 2) (2005) ECHR 681 .... 48, 267,
                                                                                                                            271–75, 289
Hoon v UK (App No 14832/11) (2015) 60 EHRR 163, 286
Jackson v Attorney General [2005] UKHL 56, [2006] 1 AC 26 .... 265, 293
Karàcsony and others v Hungary (App No 42461/13) [2014] ECHR 939 287
M v Home Office [1994] 1 AC 377 277
McGeoch v The Lord President of the Council and another [2013]
    UKSC 63, [2014] 1 AC 271 .... 269, 277, 282
McHugh v UK (App No 51987/08) ECtHR, 10 February 2015 .... 277, 278
McLean and Cole v UK (2013) 57 EHRR SE95 279

Moohan v The Lord Advocate (Scotland) [2014] UKSC 67 267
NS v Secretary of State for the Home Department (Joined Cases
  C-411/10 & C-493/10) [2013] QB 102 305
Pepper v Hart [1993] AC 593 285
Prebble v Television New Zealand Ltd [1995] 1 AC 321 285
R v Chaytor and others [2010] EWCA Crim 1910, [2010] 2 Cr App R 34 285
R v Incedal *The Times*, 27 March 2015..228
R v Jones [2006] UKHL 16, [2007] 1 AC 136 218
R v Lyons [2002] UKHL 44, [2003] 1 AC 976 268
R v Secretary of State for Employment ex p Equal Opportunities
  Commission [1995] AC 1 ....295, 301
R v Secretary of State for the Home Department
  ex p Brind [1991] 1 AC 696 268
R v Secretary of State for the Home Department
  ex p Oladehinde [1991] AC 25 195
R v Secretary of State for the Home Department
  ex p Simms [2000] 2 AC 115 ....86, 276
R v Secretary of State for Transport ex p Factortame (No 1)
  [1990] 2 AC 85 ....90, 266, 291–310
R v Secretary of State for Transport ex p Factortame
  (No 2) (C-213/89) [1991] 1 AC 603 ....90, 266, 291–310
R (AB) v Secretary of State for the Home Department
  [2013] EWHC 3453 (Admin)..11, 305, 306
R (Chester) v Secretary of State for Justice [2013]
  UKSC 63; [2014] AC 271 ....269, 277, 282
R (Evans) v Attorney General [2015] UKSC 21,
  [2015] 2 WLR 813...293
R (HS2 Action Alliance Ltd) v Secretary of State for
  Transport [2014] UKSC 3, [2014] 1 WLR 324.................................. 11, 274, 285, 297,
                                                                                                                                304, 307–10
R (Reilly) v Secretary of State for Work and Pensions
  [2012] EWHC 2292 (Admin)...83, 84
R (Reilly) v Secretary of State for Work and Pensions (No 2)
  [2014] EWHC 2182 (Admin), [2015] 2 WLR 309 85
R (on the application of SG and others (previously JS and others) v
  Secretary of State for Work and Pensions [2015] UKSC 1 268
R (on the Application of Shrewsbury and Atcham BC) v Secretary
  of State for Communities and Local Government [2008]
  EWCA Civ 148, [2008] 3 All ER 548 194
Scoppola v Italy (No 3) (2010) 51 EHRR 12 275
Simmenthal II (C-106/77) [1978] ECR 629 ....298, 300
Smith v Scott 2007 SC 345 277
Thierry Delvigne v Commune de Lesparre Médoc and Préfet de la
  Gironde (C-650/13), [2015] WLR (D) 402 284
Thoburn v Sunderland City Council [2002] EWHC 195 (Admin),
  [2003] QB 151 ....285, 291–310
Tyrer v UK (1978) 2 EHRR 1..281
Van Gend en Loos (Case 26/62) [1963] CMLR 423...297

Tables of Legislation

UK Statutes

Act of Settlement 1701	309
Act of Union 1707	309
Anti-terrorism, Crime and Security Act 2001	234
Armed Forces Act 2011	205
Armed Forces Acts	205
Bill of Rights 1688	303
art 6	205
art 9	11, 158, 163, 284–86
Bribery Act 2010	163
Child Support Act 1991	39
s 50A	193
Civil Contingencies Act 2004	57
Claim of Rights Act 1689	309
Constitutional Reform Act 2005	18, 309
Constitutional Reform and Governance Act 2010 (CRAGA 2010)	241, 244, 250–63
Pt 2	10, 247
s 2	268
s 22	257
s 23	248
s 25(1)	248, 258
Counter-Terrorism Act 2008	231
Counter Terrorism and Security Act 2015	229–31
s 1	228
s 44	237
ss 44–46	209
s 45	237
s 46	236, 237
Criminal Justice Act 2003	231
Criminal Justice (Terrorism and Conspiracy) Act 1998	230
Dangerous Dogs Act 1991	27
Data Protection Act 1998	
s 12	9, 184, 195
s 12(6)(b)	196
Data Retention and Investigatory Powers Act 2014	237
s 7	225, 237
Department of Justice Act (Northern Ireland) 2010	233

European Communities Act 1972 .... 266, 276, 291, 294, 302,
    306, 307, 309, 310
    s 2(1) 91, 284, 292
    s 2(2) 91, 292, 303
    s 2(4) 91, 292
    s 3(1) 301
European Parliamentary Elections Act 1978 248
European Union Act 2011 248
European Union (Amendment) Act 2008 248
Equality Act 2010 128
Extradition Act 2003 128
Financial Services (Banking Reform) Act 2013 61
Fixed-term Parliaments Act 2011(FTPA) 80, 145
Forfeiture Act 1870 271
Freedom of Information Act 2000 181
Government of Wales Act 1998 303
Government of Wales Act 2006
    s 81(1) 268
House of Lords Act 1999 129
Housing Act 1996 187
Human Rights Act 1998 .... 11, 64, 75–77, 266, 276,
    284, 289, 303, 309
    s 2 .... 268, 272
    s 3 267
    s 4 267
    s 10 271
    s 10(1)(b) 271
    s 10(2) 271
    s 19 .... 75, 85, 236
Infrastructure Act 2015 18
Inquiries Act 2005 128
Intelligence Services Act 1994 .... 204, 225
    s 10 .... 221, 222
International Criminal Court Act 2001 249
Jobseekers (Back to Work Schemes) Act 2013 83
Justice and Security Act 2013 .... 10, 204
    s 1 222
    s 3 222
    s 3(3) 222
    Sch 1, paras 4–6 222
Justice and Security (Northern Ireland) Act 2007 233
Legal Aid, Sentencing and Punishment of Offenders Act 2012
    s 85 178
Legislative and Regulatory Reform Act 2006 128
Life Peerages Act 1958 .... 117, 129
Local Government Act 1972
    s 111 194

Localism Act 2011
  Pt 1 194
Magna Carta 309
Mental Capacity Act 2005 128
Merchant Shipping Act 1988 298
Modern Slavery Act 2015 54
  s 53 51
Northern Ireland Act 1998
  s 24(1)(a) 268
Northern Ireland Act 2009 233
Official Secrets Act 1989
  s 1(1)(b) 223
Parliament Act 1911 81
  s 2(1) 265
Parliament Acts 1911 & 1949 ....20, 265
Parliamentary Constituencies Act 1986
  s 4 237
Parliamentary Standards Act 2009 ....147, 151
Peace Preservation (Ireland) Act 1875 207
Perjury Act 1911 288
Petition of Right 1628 309
Police (Detention and Bail) Act 2011 84
Prevention of Crime (Ireland) Act 1882 207–208
Protection of Person and Property (Ireland) Act 1881 207
Prevention of Terrorism Acts 1974, 1976, 1984 209
Prevention of Terrorism Act 2005 ....230, 232
  s 13 234
Prevention of Terrorism (Temporary Provisions) Act 1974 230
Prevention of Terrorism (Temporary Provisions) Acts 1974, 1975 208
Prevention of Terrorism (Temporary Provisions) Act 1989
  s 27 209
Protection of Freedoms Act 2012
  s 57 232
Public Bodies Act 2011 126
Regulation of Investigatory Powers Act 2000 225
Representation of the People Act 1981 208
Representation of the People Act 1983 271
Representation of the People Act 1985 271
Scotland Act 1998 303
  s 57(2) 268
Septennial Act 1715 81
Security Service Act 1989 225
Serious Crime Act 2015 18
Social Security Act 1998 184
  s 2 .... 9, 188, 193, 195, 198
State Immunity Act 1978 90
Terrorism Act 2000 ....231, 232, 235
  ss 21–32 233

s 40	233
s 126	209
Terrorism Act 2006	231, 232
Pt 1	209
s 36	227
Terrorism Prevention and Investigation Measures Act 2011	234
s 20	209
s 21	234
Terrorist Asset-Freezing etc Act 2010	231
s 31	209
Transparency of Lobbying, Non-Party Campaigning and Trade Union Administration Act 2014	162, 173–79
Pt 1	173
Pt 2	173, 181
s 1	174
s 3	177
s 3(3)	174
s 4	177
s 5	177
s 7	177
s 9	177
s 12	178
s 12(1)	178
s 12(2)	178
s 12(3)(a)	178
s 12(3)(b)	178
s 12(4)(a)	178
s 12(4)(b)	178
s 14	178
s 18	178
s 21	178
s 22	178
Sch 1	176
Sch 2	177
Value Added Tax Act 1994	175

Statutory Instruments

Civil Procedure Rules (SI 1998/3132)	
Pt 68	297
Homelessness (Suitability of Accommodation) (England) Order 2012 (SI 2012/2601)	187
art 2	187
art 2(c)(i)	188
art 2(d)	188
Registration of Consultant Lobbyists Regulations 2015 (SI 2015/379)	179
Supreme Court Rules 2009 (SI 2009/1603)	
r 42	297

Other Jurisdictions

Australia

Independent National Security Legislation Monitor Act 2010 227

France

Constitution 1958, art 53 253

Germany

Basic Law, art 59(1) 253

Republic of South Africa

Constitution 1996, art 231 253

Treaties and Conventions

Arms Trade Treaty 2013 242
Athens Convention relating to the Carriage of Passengers and their
  Luggage by Sea 1974 242
Biological and Toxin Weapons Convention 1972
Convention on the Prevention of Terrorism 246
Convention on the Rights of Persons with Disabilities 246
EU Charter 306
  Art 51 306
European Convention on Human Rights (ECHR) 10, 265–90
  Art 6(1) 11, 286
  Art 8 75
  Art 32 269
  Art 46 .... 269, 272, 278, 279, 289
  Art 46(1) 272, 279
  Art 53 269
  Art 65(2) 289
  Protocol 1, Art 3 .... 269, 271, 278
  Protocol 11 270
  Protocol 15 .... 249, 270
  Protocol 30 307
  Protocol 30 Art 1(1) 306
Hague Convention on the International Protection of Adults 2000 249
Rome Statute of the International Criminal Court 1998 249
Treaty on European Union
  Art 5 99
  Art 6(1) 306
Treaty on the Functioning of the European Union
  Art 267 (ex Arts 234, 117 EEC, EC) 297
Treaty of Lisbon 2009 .... 95, 101, 103

European Legislation

Directives

Dir 80/181/EEC Metrication directive 302
Dir 95/46/EC Data Protection Directive, Art 15 195

Draft Bills

Care and Support Bill 74, 155
Communications Bill 2002 .... 49, 50, 56, 59, 133
Constitutional Reform and Governance Bill 256
Constitutional Renewal Bill 241, 250, 251, 254, 255, 257–63
Counter-Terrorism and Security Bill 229, 230
Crime and Courts Bill 67
Communications Data Bill 50, 54, 56, 59, 133
Dangerous Dogs (Amendment) Bill 52
Data Protection Bill 195
Deregulation Bill 50, 51
Enhanced Terrorism Prevention and Investigation Measures Bill 43, 47, 48, 229
Energy Bill 53
European Communities Bill 294, 304
Finance Bill 118
Fixed-term Parliaments Bill 67, 81, 82, 125, 135
Health and Social Care Bill 125, 152
House of Lords (Expulsion and Suspension) Bill 126
Investigatory Powers Bill 2015 225
Jobseekers (Back to Work Schemes) Bill 84, 86, 87
Justice and Security Bill 67
Lobbying Bill 61, 181
Local Audit Bill 40
Marriage (Same Sex Couples) Bill 2013 123
Modern Slavery Bill (2013–14) 5, 46, 47, 49, 51, 54, 55
Parliamentary Voting System and Constituencies Bill 125
Prevention of Terrorism Bill 2005 ....135, 230
Protection of Charities Bill 48, 49
Protection of Freedoms Bill 2010–12 155
Public Bodies Bill 2012 .... 67, 125, 135
Small Charitable Donations Bill 2012–13 155
Social Security Bill 193
Transparency of Lobbying etc Bill 2013 ....73, 181
Video Recordings Bill 256
Voting Eligibility (Prisoners) Bill 2012 .... 43, 48, 54, 275, 276, 281, 289
Water Bill 2012–13 52
Wild Animals in Circuses Bill 148

Breaking News

As always, the moment that a manuscript has been completed and signed off by the authors, it seems to be in need of some updating. The constitution does not stand still. In spite of the significant reforms in recent years, there always appear to be new changes to digest.

Before the book went to print, the editors took the view that it was worth highlighting five of these developments. The first are changes to the Standing Orders of the House of Commons made on 22 October 2015 to allow Members from England, or from England and Wales, to give consent to or veto legislation which affected only those parts of the United Kingdom. This followed from a Conservative Party manifesto commitment to introduce 'English Votes for English Laws' (EVEL) as an attempt to answer the longstanding 'West Lothian Question'. Under EVEL, the Speaker must certify any Government Bills (or elements of Bills or proposed amendments), which, in his opinion, relate exclusively to England (or to England and Wales) and are within devolved legislative competence. Motions giving consent are decided by Members from the relevant parts of the UK before Third Reading. Certified Lords amendments and statutory instruments also require consent under the process. The Speaker issued the first certificate under the new Standing Orders on 28 October 2015 in respect of the Housing and Planning Bill. The impact of this change on the legislative process will no doubt be watched with interest by Parliamentarians and constitutional lawyers alike.

The second change relates to an issue highlighted in chapter 12: namely a minister's duty to comply with international law. Until October 2015, the Ministerial Code referred to an overarching duty on ministers to comply with the law including international law and treaty obligations. The new version of the Code, published on 15 October 2015, omits reference to the final words, simply noting a duty to comply with the law. This has proved controversial and led the former Treasury Solicitor, Sir Paul Jenkins, to write to a national newspaper accusing the government of showing 'contempt for the rule of international law'.

The third event was predicted in chapter 10. On 2 December, the Government returned to the House of Commons with a new resolution to permit air strikes on Islamic State in Syria. The Government won the eventual vote by 397 to 223. This acceptance by the Government of the need to return to Parliament underpins the convention that the deployment of UK troops must usually be subject to a vote in Parliament.

The fourth development is the publication of the Strathclyde Review (otherwise titled *Secondary legislation and the primacy of the House of Commons*) in December 2015. The review was established after the Government's defeat on secondary legislation relating to tax credits in the House of Lords on 26 October 2015.

The recommendation, by Lord Strathclyde, (as the title of his report suggests) would appear uncomplicated: he advocated a new process, set out in statute, for the Lords to ask the Commons to think again about a statutory instrument. The Lords veto over secondary legislation would be removed. In his words, 'this would provide the government of the day with a degree of certainty, while maintaining for the House of Lords a simplicity of procedure in keeping with already established procedures for other forms of legislation'. However, this would be, in effect, a diminution of the powers of the House of Lords: in the event of a further Commons vote to approve a statutory instrument, the new procedure would enable the Commons to play a decisive role.

The fifth issue relates to the Government's long awaited Bill of Rights. Although a consultation paper had been expected in the autumn of 2015; this did not emerge. One potential reason for the delay became clear on 2 December when the Lord Chancellor gave evidence to the House of Lords Constitution Committee. During the course of his evidence, Michael Gove admitted that he expected that any consultation document would not appear until 2016. But he also floated the idea that the UK Supreme Court might be made, by a British Bill of Rights, into what he called a 'constitutional longstop' court. This idea appears to be aimed at dealing with matters relating to EU law (and potentially judgments of the European Court of Justice).

Alexander Horne and Andrew Le Sueur,
January 2016

1

Introduction

ALEXANDER HORNE AND ANDREW LE SUEUR

And so let us beginne, and, as the Fabrick takes its Shape in front of you, always keep the Structure intirely in Mind as you inscribe it. (Peter Ackroyd, *Hawksmoor*, 1985)

I. THE SCOPE AND PURPOSE OF THE BOOK

THIS BOOK PRESENTS a baker's dozen of essays about the UK Parliament's two principal and overlapping responsibilities—enacting legislation and holding the executive to account. The contributors are 'insiders' and 'outsiders'. The insiders—a former First Parliamentary Counsel,[1] officials from the House of Commons Library,[2] parliamentary lawyers and a member of the House of Lords—draw on deep and broad professional experience to provide fine-grained explanation and analysis of the dynamics of Parliament's work.[3] The outsiders are academics, who look at Parliament from the disciplines of law, public administration and government.[4]

The authors were not confined by any particular straitjacket of method or approach. Some chapters include historical surveys of the subjects they tackle; others concentrate on developments during the 2010–15 Parliament; some are primarily forward-looking and examine what could or should happen in the future. Several chapters use case study methods to focus intensively on particular episodes and seek out generalisations from them. Contributions were finalised during September 2015 (and we have sought to ensure that material is up to date to that point). Tantalisingly, an array of further important and interesting developments was at that date starting to unfold after the May 2015 General Election—including proposals for 'English Votes for English Laws' (EVEL), the operationalisation of the Conservatives' manifesto pledge to 'scrap the Human Rights Act' and enact

---

[1] The Office of the Parliamentary Counsel is responsible for drafting all Government Bills.
[2] The House of Commons Library provides impartial information and research services for Members of Parliament and their staff in support of their parliamentary duties.
[3] All write in a personal capacity; their views do not necessarily reflect any 'official' view in either House.
[4] Lord Norton counts twice as both a parliamentarian and an academic.

a British Bill of Rights, further devolution of powers to Scotland and Wales, and the legal framework for the in/out referendum on continued membership of the European Union.

This collection of essays follows on from an earlier book in Hart Publishing's Studies in Constitutional Law series by Alexander Horne, Gavin Drewry and Dawn Oliver (eds), *Parliament and the Law* (2013). Whereas that book considered how the law applies to Parliament, this book examines the effectiveness of Parliament in the law-making process and its scrutiny of government. Both functions are undergoing significant change as Parliament faces new challenges. The book does not set out to provide a comprehensive textbook-style account of Parliament's work. For readers wanting a more systematic approach, we recommend Michael Zander's *The Law-Making Process* (7th edn, Hart Publishing, 2015), Robert Rogers and Rhodri Walters' *How Parliament Works* (7th edn, Routledge, 2015) and Philip Norton's *Parliament in British Politics* (2nd edn, Palgrave Macmillan, 2013) as useful starting points. And for readers interested in delegated legislation, the Hansard Society published an important piece of research in December 2014: Ruth Fox and Joel Blackwell, *The Devil is in the Detail: Parliament and Delegated Legislation* (Hansard Society, 2014).

Looking across the 13 chapters as a whole, two broad clusters of research questions recur.

First, against what measures should the effectiveness of Parliament be measured? As Stephen Laws puts it in Chapter 2: 'How can you tell whether Parliament is doing a good job at scrutinising legislation? What would constitute a good job?' Some chapters are imbued with realism about Parliament's constitutional purpose. Only if it is understood that government (not Parliament) is the author of legislation and policy, with Parliament having a secondary role as critic, can a true-to-life assessment of Parliament's strengths and weaknesses be made. As several chapters discuss, the critic's role is of fundamental constitutional value in providing political legitimacy for government-led law-making and action. Better—though not necessarily more extensive—use of pre-legislative scrutiny (Jessica Mulley and Helen Kinghorne in Chapter 3), more consistent and structured use of constitutional standards in scrutinising legislation (Jack Simson Caird and Dawn Oliver in Chapter 4), the House of Lords' engagement 'in the politics of justification rather than, as is possible in the Commons, the politics of assertion' (Philip Norton in Chapter 6) and greater parliamentary involvement in treaty-making (Arabella Lang in Chapter 11) are all offered as contributions to the legitimising role that Parliament can fulfil as it debates and scrutinises often highly partisan government proposals and acts.

A second type of research question is about how Parliament's effectiveness in its roles could be improved. Almost all chapters either assess previous reforms or advocate new ones, or both.

The book is divided into two parts, reflecting its title—Part 1 on legislation and Part 2 on accountability. But it will immediately become apparent to readers that improvements to the legislative process discussed in Part 1 are often designed to enhance accountability; while some of the issues dealt with in Part 2, could have an impact on the legislative process. These matters are necessarily intertwined.

II. OVERVIEW OF PART 1: LEGISLATION

The advice set out at the start of the chapter, taken from Peter Ackroyd's novel *Hawksmoor*, is aimed at the architect, but it might well apply equally to those who produce legislation. As GC Thornton argued, the drafter is an architect, an expert, a specialist—and well he or she needs to be. The complexity of the modern legislative process can be demonstrated by the fact that the Cabinet Office's recently updated *Guide to Making Legislation* (July 2015) now exceeds 300 pages. It includes detailed information on a whole variety of issues, such as: delegated powers; devolved powers; compatibility with the European Convention on Human Rights; impact assessments and explanatory notes. Continuing the analogy, if the drafter is the architect and the Government is the client, providing the policy to be turned into law, what does that make the modern backbench parliamentarian? Perhaps a surveyor, looking for faults and defects in the fabric of the legislation: a scrutineer as much as a law-maker (or, as Laws puts in Chapter 2, Parliament's role 'is that of critic not author')?

The Government has itself acknowledged, through its good law initiative,[5] that people find legislation difficult to find and understand. Reform has the potential to engage people in the democratic process and also to improve the quality of legislation. Parliament has a role to play and reforms can be seen—from the introduction of pre and post-legislative scrutiny committees, the pilot 'public reading' of Bills (designed to give members of the public the opportunity to provide their views on Bills before they are made into law) and even more limited reforms, such as the useful 'track changes' versions of Bills available on the UK Parliament website (which show the effect of any amendments made at Committee Stage in the text of the Bill).

A. Chapter 2: What is the Parliamentary Scrutiny of Legislation for?

Part 1 of the book commences with a searching examination by a former first Parliamentary Counsel of the purpose of parliamentary scrutiny. Laws considers the assumptions that are made and that should be questioned by anyone who is proposing to look into the value and efficacy of the parliamentary scrutiny of legislation. He asks: 'How can you tell whether Parliament is doing a good job at scrutinising legislation? What would constitute a good job? What, even, in this context do we mean by Parliament?' His premise is that, in practice, 'it is the

---

[5] www.gov.uk/guidance/good-law.

Government not Parliament that is legislating'. He challenges what he regards as a 'distorting' myth that 'the political leadership, when it comes to legislation belongs to Parliament, rather than to the Government' and rejects the notion of 'Parliament as the steward of a settled constitutional system'. He argues that it is misleading 'to assert that Parliament has a special role as guardian of the framework or parameters of the system, and so has functions that are independent of the responsibility of the Government for how the system is operated in practice'. He also rejects as misleading the idea that 'the Government governs with laws made by Parliament: that legislation is actually the principal tool by which the Government governs the country'; legislation, he argues, 'is often no more than an incidental aspect of policy implementation'. Rather, Parliament's principal function 'is to provide political legitimacy for the implementation of what usually begins as a partisan proposal'. These factors compel the conclusion that it must be for each House to define its own role in the scrutiny of legislation. As 'critics rather than authors' of legislation, the two Houses should be 'selective about how they carry out their function of legislative scrutiny'. Laws advocates adopting a sampling process, which is 'an accepted and effective form of quality control in other areas'; this might include focusing on 'constitutional propriety'[6] and 'technical quality'. In relation to scrutiny of policy, Laws calls for greater awareness 'of the different aspects of the policy that are always going to be available for analysis', arguing that the emphasis will change from Parliament to Parliament, from Bill to Bill, so 'Parliament needs to be willing to change its methods of scrutiny according to the factors that politics demands should be given the most attention on a particular occasion'.

B. Chapter 3: Pre-legislative Scrutiny

Mulley and Kinghorn look at pre-legislative scrutiny (PLS)—the 'occasional, additional stage of parliamentary scrutiny of government proposals for primary legislation'. They note that the 'near-universal consensus of the late 1990s that PLS would be a good thing has been largely unchallenged since and lent some credence by experience' over the past 20 years. They suggest that the 'pattern of Bills selected for PLS often bemuses' and highlight the recommendation in 2013 by the Political and Constitutional Reform Committee (not accepted by the Government of the day) that government should be required to publish reasons for not producing a particular Bill in draft for pre-legislative scrutiny. They consider the pros and cons of different types of committee for undertaking PLS—House of Commons departmental select committees, other established specialist committees, ad hoc committees from one House, and joint ad hoc committees with membership drawn from the Commons and the Lords. One distinctive feature of the PLS process, they

---

[6] See Simson Caird and Oliver in ch 4.

note, is that officials from bill teams attend committee meetings on a 'speak if spoken to' basis to deal with queries as they arise. The chapter demonstrates how 'prior and concurrent activity within and without the executive' can shape every aspects of a committee's PLS scrutiny, as in the case of the draft Modern Slavery Bill. It also examines how PLS committees are staffed, including from the House of Commons Scrutiny Unit and outside specialist advisers. The authors identify success stories where PLS worked well, but also highlight instances in which it had less impact (which may occur where Bills are too large in scale, are 'portmanteau' Bills covering several distinct topics, where the government's policy or the drafting is not sufficiently developed and where there is insufficient time for the committee to complete its work). Echoing insights by Laws in Chapter 2, Mulley and Kinghorn argue that the 'role of PLS in building political legitimacy around a set of legislative proposals should not be underestimated', but they also argue that PLS holds out the 'potential, not always exploited in practice, for parliamentarians to influence the scope, direction and emphasis of legislation far more fundamentally than is usually achievable through Parliament's more long-standing law-making processes'.

C. Chapter 4: Parliament's Constitutional Standards

Simson Caird and Oliver make a case for 'substantive parliamentary constitutional standards' being used during the legislative process. They advocate the use of a code of the *general* constitutional principles that emerge from reports on *particular* Bills by the Joint Committee on Human Rights, the Delegated Powers and Regulatory Reform Committee (DPPRC) and the House of Lords Constitution Committee.[7] They acknowledge that not everybody agrees that scrutiny based on constitutional principles is an unmitigated good and should be heightened—political constitutionalists may see such a development as undermining 'effective and responsible government' and some take the view that 'the elected government must be able to gets its legislative business through'. The authors admire the increasingly effective scrutiny of Bills in the House of Lords, which is 'a success story of Parliament in the twenty-first century thus far' (a point that Lord Norton returns to in Chapter 6), which they contrast unfavourably with the House of Commons. They concede, however, that: 'The House of Lords' lack of democratic legitimacy means that the Lords' ability to defend constitutional values is limited by their own and others' recognition of the primacy of the House of Commons.' After an account of several other calls for statements of legislative standards to be adopted, the authors turn to their project (with Robert Hazell) of extracting general standards from the House of Lords Constitution Committee reports and organising them into a

---

[7] Which they have already produced: see J Simson Caird, R Hazell and D Oliver, *The Constitutional Standards of the House of Lords Select Committee on the Constitution* 2nd edn (London, UCL Constitution Unit, 2015).

code. They note that the Constitution Committee 'frequently refers to its previous reports and builds upon earlier analysis of particular norms. Thought of in these terms, the Committee's output can be understood as a form of "legisprudence"'. Many of the norms, they argue, are 'not inviolable rules', but 'rather they identify legislative choices that demand specific forms of justification from government'. Justification is of particular importance 'in the context of bills that seek to achieve significant constitutional change'. They conclude by saying that the development and use of a code of substantive constitutional principles of the sort they advocate 'will serve to enhance the legitimacy of the process of enacting law with constitutional implications by moving away from governmental cultures of resistance and authority towards compliance with parliamentary requirements for justification, legitimacy from which both government and Parliament would benefit'.

D. Chapter 5: European Scrutiny

Hardy notes at the start of Chapter 5 that despite the evolution of the European Union (from EEC to EC to EU), the main characteristics of the scrutiny systems put in place in the House of Commons and the House of Lords have remained in essence the same—'a largely documents-based approach with a scrutiny reserve preventing ministers from agreeing to proposals in the Council (of Ministers)'. This, he argues, may not last in the face of calls for significant reform. He provides a detailed 'insider's' account of the work of EU committees in both Houses and analyses the strengths and weakness of the processes. The system in each House is different: the Commons has one select committee to scrutinise all EU documents, whereas the Lords has a total of seven select committees that focus only on sifted documents.

A strength of the Common's scrutiny system is, Hardy argues, its breadth. He notes that in the 2010–15 Parliament, the number of the debates on the floor of the House on European documents increased considerably. This was a consequence of two factors: the committee became more active in recommending debates and 'new procedures for debates on reasoned opinions and opt-in decisions meant more documents were debated on the floor of the House, despite the Government's refusal to list all of them for debate'. Breadth of remit, however, also brings with it a weakness in that few of the documents can be scrutinised in depth. Finding ways to 'mainstream' scrutiny of EU proposals in the work of other Commons committees has unfortunately been elusive. Hardy's experience supports the conclusion that 'European Committees are composed of MPs who rarely participate because they have little or no expertise in the subject matter to be able scrutinise the Government's policy, and are unfamiliar with the procedures'. The strength of the Lords' scrutiny system is its size: sub-committees 'are able to build up expertise' and, like the Select Committee, are relatively well-staffed. This enables engagement with a wider community of stakeholders. The sifting process frees up time for sub-committees to conduct inquiries in addition to the weekly scrutiny of documents, with the resulting reports now accompanied by sophisticated media campaigns. Hardy concludes by questioning the 'received wisdom ... that the systems of scrutiny in either House complement each other well: the Commons does breadth, the Lords does depth'.

E. Chapter 6: Legislative Scrutiny in the House of Lords

Lord Norton's chapter offers a rich analysis of the dynamics of legislative scrutiny in the House of Lords. Norton argues that 'procedures may be seen as necessary but not sufficient for the House to affect significantly the content of legislation'; the 'dual aspect of composition (the political and the individual) provide the sufficient conditions'. He provides a detailed analysis of how procedures differ in the Lords and Commons in relation to both Bills and secondary legislation, and in respect of post-legislative scrutiny. His conclusion is: 'There are greater opportunities for members [in the Lords] to participate, primarily in Committee, yet it is not just the process that is particular to the House, but also those who participate.' Turning to the composition of the House, Norton contends that there are two dimensions: 'the political and the individual'. In relation to the political dimension, the exclusion of over 500 hereditary peers by the House of Lords Act 1999 'effectively transformed the House into a House predominantly of life peers and one in which no one party held a majority', with the effect that 'whichever party is in office, it cannot carry a vote relying solely on its own party members in the House'. Echoing one of the themes explored by Simson Caird and Oliver in Chapter 4, Norton shows how, in the Lords, the Government has to 'engage in the politics of justification rather than, as is possible in the Commons, the politics of assertion'. In relation to the individual dimension, he notes that while the Lords is one of the busiest legislative chambers in the world, 'unlike the Commons, membership is not seen as a full-time occupation', so it may be described as a House of 'experience and expertise'. The composition of the House, he argues, 'creates an environment conducive to constructive engagement and consensus'. Turning to impact, he says that the Lords 'is important both in terms of its unseen and its seen impact'. In conclusion, he identifies 'pressure to strengthen further the means of scrutiny'—in particular, enhancing how the House deals with secondary legislation and introducing evidence-taking committees to scrutinise Bills that start in the Lords.

III. OVERVIEW OF PART 2: ACCOUNTABILITY

The general concept and practice of government accountability to Parliament has been the widely debated in recent years in Parliament and in academic circles. A particularly valuable academic contribution is by Nicholas Bamforth and Peter Leyland (eds), *Accountability in the Contemporary Constitution* (Oxford University Press, 2013).

8 *Alexander Horne and Andrew Le Sueur*

Part 2 of this book contains chapters whose main focus is on Parliament's role in scrutinising areas of executive action. Some of these areas, such as national security[8] and international treaty-making,[9] were previously shielded from effective parliamentary oversight; others have yet to catch the attention of parliamentarians.[10]

A. Chapter 7: Parliamentary Reform and the Accountability of Government to the House of Commons

Richard Kelly and Lucinda Maer's chapter focuses on parliamentary reform and the accountability of the Government to the House of Commons, and, in particular, the responses to the MPs' expenses crisis of 2009 and the recommendations of the Wright Committee that sought to empower backbenchers. They analyse the operation of the new Backbench Business Committee to schedule non-ministerial business and the election of select committee chairs by the whole House. Despite a commitment in the 2010 Coalition Agreement, a House Business Committee was not established due to the lack of consensus about its feasibility and scope. Also on the modernisation agenda were ways of achieving better public involvement, including an e-petition procedure and a public reading stage of Bills. The authors conclude by saying that: 'The Wright reforms themselves may not have *directly* increased accountability, but they empowered backbenchers to better hold the government to account and provided a new framework for parliamentarians and the public to have access to the parliamentary agenda.'

B. Chapter 8: The Regulation of Lobbyists

Back in 2010, when he was still the Leader of the Opposition, David Cameron warned that lobbying was the 'next big scandal waiting to happen'. At the outset of Chapter 8, Oonagh Gay notes that receiving payment for lobbying—seeking to influence decisions made by public office holders or officials—and being lobbied has been the subject of some regulation for 30 years in Parliament. As she explains, the 'concern is that parliamentarians who act as lobbyists offer some form of privileged access to governmental or legislative processes'. During the 2010–15 Parliament, several Members in both Houses found themselves the subject of sting operations by investigative journalists; some were subsequently exonerated, while others were found guilty of a breach of parliamentary rules. Against this background, Gay's chapter provides a detailed analysis of the codes and rules adopted in each House and examines the scope and implementation of

---

[8] See Horne and Walker in ch 10.
[9] See Lang in ch 11.
[10] See Le Sueur on automated decision-making in ch 9.

Part 1 of the Transparency of Lobbying, Non-Party Campaigning and Trade Union Administration Act 2014, which came into force in April 2015, which regulates the activity of multi-client lobby firms.

C. Chapter 9: Robot Government: Automated Decision-Making and its Implications for Parliament

In Chapter 9, Andrew Le Sueur calls for Parliament to take seriously the implications of administrative automated decision-making by government, a type of decision-making that looks certain to increase as government becomes 'digital by default' and technologies become more sophisticated. Apart from section 2 of the Social Security Act 1998 on 'Use of computers', neither the statute book nor parliamentarians have systematically addressed the constitutional implications of automation in the public sector. Le Sueur asks and seeks to start a debate about the answers to six basic questions: (1) Can automation enhance compliance with the rule of law? (2) Will automation lead to a shift from administrative discretion and professional judgment by officials to rule-bound decision-making? (3) What is the legal basis for automated decision-making? (4) Does automation involved delegation of executive power to a computer? (5) Should there be a right to object to decisions being taken by automated means, like there is in the private sector under section 12 of the Data Protection Act 1998? (6) Should there be no-go areas for automation?

Le Sueur argues that these and other issues related to automation call out for a select committee inquiry, either by the House of Commons Public Administration and Constitutional Affairs Committee or the House of Lords Constitution Committee. A useful outcome of an inquiry along these lines could be political impetus for the development of standards, either in the form of a good practice guide (for designers and operators of automated systems, as has been adopted in Australia) or a statutory framework, or both. Further, he suggests, Parliament should be considering automation issues when examining Bills and secondary legislation—and he provides a framework for doing so. More broadly, he discusses how Parliament could learn from the new styles of thinking emerging from the Cabinet Office's Government Digital Service unit ('service patterns', 'user focus' and 'breaking down silos') in developing its roles in the legislative and accountability processes. Finally, the chapter confronts the most basic of questions—what do we mean by 'the law': 'So here is a radical proposal: we should treat "the app" (the computer programmes that will produce individual decisions) as "the law".'

D. Chapter 10: Parliament and National Security

In Chapter 10, Alexander Horne and Clive Walker explore Parliament's responsibility for holding the Government to account on national security matters. There is, the authors explain, a long history of Parliament and its select committees taking an interest in both military matters and national security, which they trace from the immediate aftermath of the Glorious Revolution (in relation to military matters) and the last quarter of the nineteenth century (in respect of counter-terrorism). Accountability practices are diffuse and the authors focus on three case studies from the 2010–15 Parliament: (1) whether a new convention has been established that Parliament needs to be consulted when the Government wants to deploy armed forces; (2) the Intelligence and Security Committee set up by the Justice and Security Act 2013; and (3) parliamentary scrutiny of counter-terrorism legislation. Drawing out generalisations in relation to counter-terrorism legislation, the authors suggest that 'affirmation is more often given to "process legitimacy" rather than to "output legitimacy"'; on the whole, Parliament's work 'cannot be claimed to have produced frequent or substantive alterations to government stances'. In relation to the new war powers convention (which has become an issue of pressing contemporary concern due to the Syrian crisis) and the reformed arrangements for supervision of the intelligence and security services, there is evidence of a commitment to further openness.

E. Chapter 11: Parliament and International Treaties

Arabella Lang considers the new powers conferred on Parliament under Part 2 of the Constitutional Reform and Governance Act 2010. The new role 'looks muscular' (Parliament may indefinitely delay the ratification of a treaty by government), yet neither House has passed a motion objection to a ratification, there have been few debates on treaties, there is a question mark over whether the Government's limited duties can be enforced, and the Act 'does nothing new to help Parliament actually scrutinise treaties effectively'. Lang argues that it is hard to see how much difference the 2010 Act has made in practice. She explains and assesses a range of possible further reforms: there are international precedents for giving Parliament a greater role in the ratification process; there would be mechanisms for enabling a greater number of debates and votes; the 21-day sitting period specified in the 2010 Act could be extended; the arrangements could additionally be widened to cover currently excluded treaties and 'treaty-like documents'; new institutional mechanisms could be established, such as a select committee on treaties; and opportunities for parliamentary scrutiny could be brought in to the earlier stage of negotiation of treaties.

F. Chapter 12 on Sovereignty, Privilege and the European Convention on Human Rights

Alexander Horne and Hélène Tyrrell's chapter examines the impact of the European Convention on Human Rights (ECHR) on parliamentary sovereignty and privilege. They point out that the disquiet about the influence of the Strasbourg Court is not matched by the statistical record: relative to the number of applications made, the number of judgments against the UK is small. But few issues better highlight the tensions between Parliament's sovereignty over the domestic legal order and the international obligations under the ECHR than the saga surrounding the (dis)enfranchisement of prisoners, which they explore in detail.

Moving on to parliamentary privilege, the ECHR can also have a potential impact on the internal operations of Parliament. The authors discuss how, unlike the domestic courts, the Strasbourg Court is not constrained by parliamentary privilege and the prohibition on questioning or impeaching parliamentary proceedings under Article 9 of the Bill of Rights 1688. They flag up the possibility that the absolute immunity granted by Article 9 in defamation cases may come to be regarded as disproportionate and consider the reach of Article 6(1) ECHR over parliamentary disciplinary proceedings and any sanctions imposed.

G. Chapter 13: Euroscepticism and Parliamentary Sovereignty

In the final chapter, Gavin Drewry engages with the impact of the UK's membership of the EU on parliamentary sovereignty, reaching back to the litigation sagas of the Spanish trawler-owners (*Factortame*) and the metric martyrs (*Thoburn*) to shed light on the underlying political dynamics of the Eurosceptic cause. Moving closer to the present day, he looks at Mostyn J's judgment in *R (AB) v Secretary of State for the Home Department*[11]—in which a claimant had sought to assert a right (to the protection of personal data) not available under the Human Rights Act 1998, but contained in the EU Charter of Fundamental Rights—and the subsequent political response. More recent still, he ends by considering the implications of the UK Supreme Court's judgment in *HS2* (about the intended use of the parliamentary hybrid bill procedure as the statutory basis for authorising the successive stages of the proposed 'HS2' high-speed rail network).[12]

---

[11] *R (AB) v Secretary of State for the Home Department* [2013] EWHC 3453 (Admin).
[12] *R (HS2 Action Alliance Ltd) v Secretary of State for Transport* [2014] UKSC 3, [2014] 1 WLR 324.

Part 1

Legislation

2

What is the Parliamentary Scrutiny of Legislation for?

SIR STEPHEN LAWS

I. INTRODUCTION

Is the parliamentary scrutiny of legislation effective? How can it be improved? These are legitimate and frequently asked questions.

The consensus for most who seek to answer them is that parliamentary scrutiny is not effective enough, or at least that there is room for improvement. In the House of Lords, the view that the scrutiny of legislation in the House of Commons is often incomplete and inadequate[1] is used to vindicate the role that the Lords adopt for themselves. Many different suggestions for improvement have been made, and plenty have been implemented and are thought to have been beneficial.

There are few (if any) human institutions that are incapable of being improved; so I am not going to question the consensus. But nor am I going to embark on yet another attempt to answer the questions, or indeed many of the further questions I shall pose below. Rather, this chapter (which will be confined to primary legislation) is intended as an examination of the assumptions that are made, and should be questioned, by anyone who is proposing to look into the effectiveness of the parliamentary scrutiny of legislation or to suggest improvements to it.

The premises on which the effectiveness of parliamentary scrutiny is criticised and on which suggestions are made for its improvement are often left implicit and not discussed. They need more attention. In particular, what is the parliamentary scrutiny of legislation for? How can you reach conclusions about the ways to improve a process without a clear idea of what the process is supposed to achieve? The fundamental purpose of the parliamentary scrutiny of legislation may not be as obvious as it is often taken to be.

This chapter is based on the inferences drawn from a 37-year career of involvement in the legislative process. It is not based on any other form of empirical research. Rather, my ambition for what, I happily concede, is only a

---

[1] See, eg, HL Deb 16 May 2006, col 131 (Lord Forsyth); HL Deb 25 February 2010, col 1112 (Lord Alderdice).

piece of armchair analysis is that it will provide an initial orientation for those who want to study the legislative process. I hope it will help them, or perhaps provoke them, to question where exactly they are starting from, and to form a clearer idea of whether that is the right place to begin.

II. MEASURING SUCCESS

When I was the First Parliamentary Counsel, I needed to devote a great deal of energy and thought both to how to measure the quality of legislation and to how to assess the contribution to its quality that was being made by the Parliamentary Counsel. I needed to be able to test whether our standards were being maintained and to secure, so far as possible, that we were doing everything we could to enhance the value of our contribution. I was required, and obviously wanted, to be able to prove—by more than mere assertion—that the Office of the Parliamentary Counsel represented good value for money.

This proved to be one of the more difficult aspects of the job. This was not because it was in any way difficult to get the answer that I hoped for and needed. Fortunately, there were plenty of people involved in the process who would willingly offer their subjective endorsement of the excellence of the Office's work. But, while it was difficult otherwise to get an objectively measurable answer, the logic of what was needed to get an objective answer was straightforward. First, I needed to be clear about what our role was. Second, I needed to be able to define what difference our carrying it out was supposed to make. Lastly, I had to find a way to measure how good we were at making that difference.

The Parliamentary Counsel are only one of the participants in the process of producing legislation. Compared with Parliament, their role is narrow and relatively easy to define. Nevertheless, it was still difficult to find a way to obtain unambiguous and objective evidence about how well it was being carried out, and it was definitely extremely difficult to do so against any useful timescale. There is potentially a very long delay before any departure from the best might emerge. A problem with an Act might not appear until a case years after the Act became law. Even if we assumed, for the purposes of testing our performance, that the role of the Parliamentary Counsel was to give effect to the intentions of those instructing us—a considerable oversimplification—it was often just as difficult to identify those intentions in retrospect as it sometimes is for the courts to find an intention for Parliament in the words used by the drafter.

What is needed to show that legislation has been well made is that notoriously difficult thing: the proof of a negative, in this case, that things have not gone wrong. The most effective legislation is often the legislation that produces a desired behaviour change without any need for litigation or numerous prosecutions. When an Act is criticised as being ineffective or unnecessary because, for example, it has resulted in only very few prosecutions, that fact is at least as likely to be evidence of its success as of its failure.

Even when things can be shown to have gone wrong, there is then the further difficulty of identifying exactly what caused them to go wrong and of sharing out the responsibility between the different participants in the process of production. Nor is it always straightforward to develop a clear understanding of what 'going wrong' entails.

Inevitably, there were some who suggested to me that if clear answers could not be found, it was better to stop asking the questions.[2] That is a counsel of despair and is also not practicable if you are seeking to answer the questions in order to know the answer when you yourself are asked them by more persistent questioners.

There is a similar problem for Parliament. How can you tell whether Parliament is doing a good job at scrutinising legislation? What would constitute a good job? What, even, in this context do we mean by Parliament? These are questions asked not only by students of Parliament but also, in a different way, at regular intervals by the electorate.

III. DIFFERENT SCRUTINY IN THE DIFFERENT HOUSES?

The question of what institution is being referred to when it is the functions of Parliament that are being considered can sometimes be suppressed in discussions of parliamentary scrutiny. Is parliamentary scrutiny something that needs to be carried out to the same extent by each House in parallel? Or should the scrutiny by each House be different, so that each complements the other? If the latter, in what respects? Are different forms of scrutiny required in the different Houses for different sorts of Bill? Incidentally, many of the questions about the different roles of the two Houses in the scrutiny of legislation are also relevant to any proposal for reforming the House of Lords.

When the House of Lords is described as a 'revising chamber', is that intended to give it a different role: one that would supplement, rather than overlap, the role of the Commons? Or is that description something that, without adding anything, is made only for the purpose of subtracting from the role of the House of Lords particular aspects of the more extensive scrutiny that it would fall to that House to carry out if it had the same role as the Commons?[3]

Is it, perhaps, appropriate for the role of each House to be determined on a case-by-case basis according to what has or has not been done by way of scrutiny

---

[2] Something Lord Irvine of Lairg had suggested in relation to something that subsequently became a concern of mine as a member of the McKay Commission: the West Lothian Question (*Daily Mail*, 17 July 1999). I am delighted that the Parliamentary Counsel Office, with its 'Good Law' project, is continuing to ask these questions and has made real progress with finding at least some answers to it: see www.gov.uk/guidance/good-law.

[3] For a view from the House of Lords about what this means, see the *Report of the Leader's Group on Working Practices* (26 April 2011), ch 3, paras 70–74, available at: www.publications.parliament.uk/pa/ld201012/ldselect/ldspeak/136/13606.htm.

in the other House? Or, as is often assumed, is the adoption of that approach by the Lords a symptom of the inadequacies of the scrutiny carried out in the House of Commons? The Parliamentary Counsel have a principle they call the 'four eyes principle': every draft produced by a drafter should be read and subjected to review by another drafter—a second set of eyes. Is that the principle that should govern the relationship between the two Houses? Or should other considerations determine the different roles of the two Houses? Is the ideal the same form of scrutiny by each House, but from different perspectives, deriving from the different compositions of the two Houses? Or is the ideal a difference in the forms of scrutiny by each House that would itself determine the most appropriate distinctions in composition?

How, if at all, do any assumptions made about the role of each House fit with the fact that, for most Bills at least, it is possible for the first House to be either House? Although it is more usual for the House of Lords to be the second House on a major political Bill (and it is either impossible or very unlikely for it to be the first House on a Bill dealing with financial matters), it is by no means exceptional for a very important or high-profile measure to begin its passage through Parliament in the House of Lords.[4] What does that say about the notion of a 'revising chamber'?

IV. DEFINING PARLIAMENT'S ROLE AS THAT OF 'THE LEGISLATURE'

The uncertainty demonstrated by questions about the different roles of the two Houses in the legislative process is only one aspect—a consequence rather—of a much more fundamental, false and usually silent assumption frequently underpinning attempts to examine the nature and adequacy of the parliamentary scrutiny of legislation.

Any description of the constitutional institutions of the UK is likely to draw on the classic distinction between the executive powers, the legislative powers and the judicial powers. This distinction is linked to the doctrine of a separation of powers that is found in the structure and theory of many modern constitutions, including, of course, the constitution of the USA. It is a doctrine that is assumed by many—in my view, wrongly—to be the essence of constitutionalism. Whatever the inherent virtue of that doctrine, however, it is a model that seems to me to fail on just about every front as an accurate descriptive model for the UK constitution. I say this despite the various things that have been done in recent times apparently for the purpose of moulding our institutions to fit it better.[5]

---

[4] In the 2014–15 parliamentary session, the Bills for both the Infrastructure Act 2015 and the Serious Crime Act 2015, which were substantial measures in the Government's legislative programme, began as Bills first introduced into the House of Lords.
[5] Including, of course, the Constitutional Reform Act 2005.

My further view that the separation of powers also fails as an accurate description of what the UK constitution should be is, perhaps, better discussed at another time and in another place.[6] Suffice it to say, in this context, that any analysis of the UK constitution is likely to be misleading if it assumes that it is possible to allocate different discrete areas and degrees of influence to different institutions. The institutions of the constitution are, in my view, better analysed as different forums for the exercise of political influence by individuals and groups of individuals on each other. So, their different compositions and manifestations are better seen as establishing and defining the qualification and different degrees of legitimacy for the influence exercised by their members, rather than as descriptions of collective bodies with accumulated powers that are supposedly vested exclusively in particular institutions, as such.

However, under the supposed model of the UK constitution based on a tripartite separation of powers, the Queen in Parliament is invested with the legislative power. It is then assumed that the legislative power is to be exercisable, in practice, by the two Houses in accordance with the constitutional laws and conventions governing the relationship between the two of them.

The assumption that the legislative function belongs exclusively, or even only primarily, to the two Houses is then assumed to make them ultimately responsible for every aspect of the legislation they pass. This means that any discussion of the effectiveness of parliamentary legislative scrutiny—or of ways of improving it –proceeds on the premise that anything that goes wrong with legislation is ultimately Parliament's responsibility. It is assumed that there is an obligation on Parliament to do everything possible that would improve the quality of legislation. Parliament must deal with every respect in which the quality of legislation falls short of perfect.

This way of looking at things leads to a consideration of parliamentary scrutiny that obeys the following logic. First, it sets, or presupposes, a test of good legislation, then it decides what would produce better legislation and, finally, it draws conclusions about what Parliament should do to ensure that better legislation is produced. This is not, it seems to me, the only or necessarily the best way to look at the matter, although it can still lead to interesting and useful proposals.[7]

Proposals that adopt this logic implicitly require Parliament to reform itself to match its supposed all-embracing function. They tend to exclude the possibility that Parliament should itself determine its role in the legislative process according to what it—or rather each of its component Houses—is best qualified to do or is

---

[6] The arguments I would use would be based, to some extent, on the analysis set out in my evidence to the House of Commons Parliamentary and Constitutional Reform Select Committees inquiry into a written constitution. See http://data.parliament.uk/writtenevidence/committeeevidence.svc/evidence-document/political-and-constitutional-reform-committee/consultation-on-a-new-magna-carta/written/17085.html.

[7] See the work of the Hansard Society in A Brazier et al, *Law in the Making* (London, Hansard Society, 2008); and R Fox and M Korris, *Making Better Law* (London, Hansard Society, 2010).

most capable of doing. At the very least, they imply that any approach based on priorities is necessarily a compromise with the ideal. The ideal, it is assumed, is that Parliament does everything within its power to make legislation better, however impracticable that is in practice—and however much distraction it provides from doing what Parliament can do best.

The premise is that the role of the House of Commons, for example, is permanently fixed by the unwritten constitution's supposed classification of that House as part of the legislature. It might seem more democratic, however, to assume that the role of that House should be dependent on the different composition of the House produced from time to time by the electorate and on the political influence that is in practice required of members of that House by the mandate given to them by the electorate.

Is it the case that the electorate is expected to choose its representatives against a clearly defined and unvarying job description? Or is the job of those who are elected better described, both in practice and in principle, by reference to what those who elected them would like them to do? Perhaps the answer has to lie somewhere between the two, but, like any drafter who has spent a career with the freedom and responsibility provided by parliamentary sovereignty, I am sceptical about any analysis that assumes that some parts of a conceptual structure are fixed and unalterable. Lawyers who practise law outside the Office of the Parliamentary Counsel have to work with the law as the fixed point when solving a problem. Parliamentary Counsel are used to dealing with problems every part of which is a moving part or at least a moveable one. A similar approach is required when considering the role of Parliament and how well it carries it out.

The premise that Parliament is the nation's legislature and is vested with exclusive legislative power is based on what is manifestly a myth. Even disregarding the frequent delegation of legislative power to members of the executive, Parliament clearly does not have exclusive control of the legislative process. Neither Parliament nor its membership has any significant practical power, independently of government decisions, to initiate legislation that stands any chance of actually becoming law. In practice, Parliament's role in relation to legislation is reactive rather than proactive. It responds to legislative proposals put forward in a fully drafted form by the executive.

The notion of Parliament as the legislature rests on one constitutional fact: the political reality that a majority in the House of Commons has an ultimate veto over legislation and that there is a legally defined, but qualified,[8] veto for the House of Lords. These powers of veto necessarily also involve an incidental power to withhold consent to legislation in the absence of specified amendments. In purely practical terms, however, if legislation is proposed that the Government does not want passed, or if it wants to see a proposal amended in accordance with its wishes, it has mechanisms available to it that are just as effective as the veto

---

[8] By the Parliament Acts 1911 and 1949.

given to each House. Further, even the theory reinforces the practical position. Legislation requires not only the agreement of the two Houses but also the consent of the executive power in the form of the Royal Assent, given, invariably these days, on the advice of ministers.

The Westminster constitutional model vests the executive power in those who can command a majority in the elected House. This is not designed to produce a separation of powers, but, instead, tends to avoid the sort of deadlock a true separation of powers would sometimes involve. Our constitutional arrangements ensure that the Government has the initiative on the introduction and passing of almost all legislation. That is guaranteed by the Westminster model, together with the rules of order in the House of Commons and the political inhibitions in the House of Lords that derive principally from its unelected status.[9] If legislation passes in a form that is contrary to the wishes of the Government, it is only because the Government has felt a politically induced need to withhold from using the mechanisms at its disposal to amend it or to block it. The only way legislation can be forced through against the wishes of the Government is by building an irresistible political consensus to which the Government must accede. In practice, the Government needs, willingly or sometimes unwillingly, to collaborate with the creation of all new law. It is politics, not law, which in practice enables the influence of members of the two Houses sometimes to prevail over the influence and wishes of those in government.

Even after recent reforms,[10] the Government retains effective, practical control over the parliamentary time that is required to get government or other legislation through the House of Commons. Convention in the House of Lords requires the Government to be granted the time reasonably required for the purpose of getting its legislation through that House. This also means that the Government can, in practice, deny sufficient parliamentary time to any legislation that is not acceptable to it. The members of each House do collectively possess a theoretical veto over all legislation and in practice have the potential to deny or to exhaust the time the Government needs to get its legislation through. On the other hand, the Government always has the opportunity to find more time by sacrificing lower priority items or, usually, and subject to the risk of taking political damage for doing so, of using its majority in the Commons to force legislation through more quickly.

Nevertheless, while this puts the Government in the driving seat when it comes to legislation, it most definitely does not prevent the members of both

---

[9] In addition, the rules of financial procedure in the House of Commons, particularly Standing Orders 48 and 50, together with the Commons' financial privileges that govern relations between the two Houses, further limit the power of members of either House, other than as members of the Government, to initiate legislation with significant financial implications.

[10] Principally those resulting from recommendations of the 'Wright Committee', the House of Commons Select Committee on the Reform of the House of Commons, *Rebuilding the House: Implementation* (HC 2009–10, 372) to give effect to the principle set out in para 22 for the enhancement of the House's control of its own agenda, timetable and procedures. See further ch 7 below.

Houses from having very considerable influence over the detail of legislation and, in my experience, also over what the Government chooses to ask them to pass. The Government, when it is considering what to legislate on, is subject to considerable inhibitions that cannot always be seen from outside and are often impossible, or at least very difficult, to measure. Governments feel considerably constrained by apprehensions about triggering an unwelcome controversy—with the concomitant risk of unnecessarily expending precious political goodwill—and by the desire to avoid wasting valuable parliamentary time required for other parts of its programme.[11]

The opportunity for Parliament to initiate and pass legislation without the agreement—or at least the acquiescence—of the Government is, in practical terms, non-existent. Private Members' Bills or Private Peers' Bills are, for practical purposes, no more than petitions to the Government to allow the law to be changed. Governments may agree more or less willingly—according to the political pressure they come under—to the enactment of laws that have been proposed from the backbenches, but government acquiescence is the very least that is required for them to succeed.

V. LEGISLATION AS A TOOL OF GOVERNMENT POLICY

None of this is necessarily a bad thing. This system suits an analysis of public policy-making that recognises that neither legislation in general nor any specific proposal for new legislation is self-contained and independent of the otherwise coordinated, day-to-day processes of government and public administration. It fits with the notion that the responsibilities of national political leadership are rightly borne in practice exclusively by the elected government rather than shared with Parliament, and that Parliament's influence is more properly and effectively exercised in scrutinising the discharge of those responsibilities, and in holding to account those required to discharge them.

All this also fits with the practical reality that the Government's annual legislative programme, which is announced in the Queen's Speech, needs to be an integrated whole. In practice, it is conceived as a coordinated combination of proposals for implementing the priorities for the Government's policy programme. Governments are elected to effect change—to make things better, by whatever test for 'better' they set for themselves—and the legislative programme results from the decisions that have to be made about the relative importance of whichever of those changes require legislation in order to be implemented. The programme may also

---

[11] See the research being carried out by Professor Meg Russell of the UCL Constitution Unit, which she suggests is leading to the conclusion that Parliament is more influential over legislation and other matters than conventional wisdom normally assumes, and that that influence is increasing: www.ucl.ac.uk/constitution-unit/research/parliament/legislation and www.ucl.ac.uk/constitution-unit/constitution-unit-news/141014.

have to be supplemented by changes that are needed to respond to unanticipated events. But this does not affect the need and ambition of every government to ensure that all parts of its programme are at least mutually compatible, and preferably mutually reinforcing.

It is a myth to suggest that political leadership, when it comes to legislation, belongs to Parliament rather than to the Government. This myth distorts a proper view of legislation and so of its scrutiny. It involves an assumption that legislation is somehow a precursor or precondition for the formulation and implementation of policy rather than part of the process by which the Government gives effect to the changes it desires and to the policies it has already decided on.

It is this myth that also leads to two further inconsistent assumptions about what legislation is for. Each is used in a separate way to argue for more power for members of Parliament in each House to initiate legislation. But both assumptions are false.

The first assumption is that there is one relatively settled or permanent set of rules, enshrined in law, that provide the framework and invariable context for the activities of the people and of government. On this basis, Parliament is then the guardian of these rules with the exclusive power to change them and for this reason needs, it is assumed, to be separate from those, including those in government, who are subject to them.

This way of looking at things is sometimes encouraged by the way in which the preoccupations of the practising legal profession create a tendency to look at legislation as principally a mechanism for tinkering with a system for resolving disputes between legal persons. In fact, most legislation is about creating incentives to legal persons to change their behaviour and about doing so in a way that it is hoped will not give rise to disputes. When legislation is directed at dispute resolution rules, it is usually only if that is regarded as a good way of incentivising a behaviour change. Changes to civil law are a relatively inefficient way of doing that. Furthermore, the principles of stability and predictability, which are essential to a system of resolving disputes about things that have already happened, have a different sort of relevance in relation to legislation which is directed at incentivising changes in future behaviour. When, for the purpose of bringing about change, legislation changes the rules of the relationship between government and the people (as it must very often do), it creates an inevitable tension with the values by which a dispute resolution system is assessed.

It is misleading, though, to assert that Parliament has a special role as guardian of the framework or parameters of the system, and so has functions that are independent of the responsibility of the Government for how the system is operated in practice. On that hypothetical view of the way in which the constitution works, the focus of Parliament, when considering legislation, would not be on the immediate, short-term implementation of policy, but on the integrity of a stable and predictable system within which executive action will be used to manage things and to effect change.

Of course, the long-term effects of legislation are an important consideration. They are important both for Parliament and for the Government. But, in practice, they are not in fact the principal focus of political debates on legislation in Parliament, even in the House of Lords. A description of our system of scrutiny that relied on that assumption would be based on a fallacy. Parliament is just as focused on the short-term policy implications of change as the Government, and wishing it otherwise would not turn Parliament into the guardian of the long term or provide a check on the perceived short-term preoccupations of the executive. Indeed, the responsibilities of office, together with the benefit of advice from a permanent Civil Service, probably have a tendency to induce more attention on the long term by the Government than might be expected from a more specifically political forum such as Parliament.

Treating Parliament as the steward of a settled constitutional system is misleading in another way. In practice, governments are constrained from legislative action by the need to expend political goodwill and use up parliamentary time in getting a Bill through. However, it would be wrong to infer from the existence of that political constraint that the constitutionally required way to decide policy is to begin by making selections from the options that are legally possible without legislation. There is no rule of life, or of the constitution, forbidding politicians from thinking outside the box until they have exhausted the process of thinking inside it.

Policy formulation should start with what ideally the Government would like to do to implement its political mandate, and in my experience it usually does. It is only when that is known that the analysis moves on to whether what would be ideal can be done within the existing law or whether, instead, it requires the law to be changed. It is only after it is known what legal change would be needed to achieve the Government's objectives that the Government can consider whether changing the law for that purpose is both desirable and politically possible. And it is only then that long-term considerations about the likely effect of the required change on the system as a whole can be taken into account—and, to the extent that they might be adverse, balanced against the short-term benefits of the policy in hand. There is a stage when the process of deciding whether to legislate involves assessing whether a legislative solution would be beneficial, but it is a stage that comes, or at least should come, after reaching an understanding both about what a legislative solution could achieve and—with a reasonable degree of precision—what it would look like.

Sometimes, maybe often, governments know in advance that legislation on a particular topic is likely to be impractical or a low priority, and then they have to rule out the legislative options early on. That does not mean that non-legislative solutions are inherently more constitutionally virtuous than legislative ones. The tests are entirely pragmatic. Non-legislative solutions are just easier and quicker to implement in practice, and they allow legislative activity to be concentrated on the cases where it will do the most good. Governments rightly prefer policy options that do not require legislation, but they do so because the benefits resulting from them are going to be seen earlier and because the incidental effects of non-legislative change, though never entirely certain, are usually easier to predict.

The financial and other costs of producing, implementing and communicating legislative change also tend to be higher than in the case of non-legislative change. It is for these reasons that legislation is seen as best left for cases where legislation is the only route for implementing the policy. Legislation is best confined to cases where the risk of creating unintended consequences is least. For this purpose, unintended consequences consist not only of the risks arising from any failure to predict practical effects—something which is an inherent risk with all structural change—but also from the risks to the ultimate policy that would flow from the possibility of being required to accept unexpected or unwanted amendments in Parliament.

So it is a myth that Parliament, when it legislates, is setting a neutral framework for policy decisions to be made by, for example, the Government between permitted options. Governments seek legislation to do particular things and to have particular effects, not with a view to securing an impartial and balanced matrix for decision-making. Parliament has to, and does, consider proposals for legislation in that context.

Occasionally legislation may be proposed to produce a system the operation of which, it is assumed, will produce better practical effects just because of the theoretical virtues of the new system. However, it is a very risky form of legislation where the benefits are expected to arise simply as the necessary consequence of the virtues of a new system, but without any clear idea about what the intended benefits will be or any analysis of why they would be benefits. All legislative drafters know that the most difficult sort of legislation to draft, and the most difficult to get right, is legislation that seeks to be impartial or neutral as regards how it will be used, or otherwise as regards its likely practical effect. The most daunting instructions are those that require the drafter to ensure that all options are left open.

The natural instincts of Parliament and of the courts are to seek to produce greater certainty from any vagueness. There is a tendency in both to be suspicious of words that are all-encompassing, words that end in 'ever', such as 'whatever' and 'howsoever'. The tendency is to seek to limit them by amendment in Parliament and, in the courts, by construction. Any attempt to cover all the options is likely to run the risk of suggesting one option or range of options as the most likely or dominant one. Any attempt to put other options in play will shift the balance in favour of those over others about which the legislation is less specific. Listing all the options will risk omitting one and may well give undue prominence to one that the Government thinks too unlikely to want mentioned, even though it may not want totally to rule it out. Legislation ceases to be impartial as to its effects the moment it has to be applied in practice. For these reasons, the process of legislation usually requires, and necessarily involves, a commitment to the immediate short-term goals, without, of course, losing sight of the long-term consequences of changing the rules to achieve them.

The second false assumption about Parliament's role in relation to legislation is that the Government governs with laws made by Parliament: that legislation is actually the principal tool by which the Government governs the country. How, it is sometimes asked, could a government govern if it could not get its legislation through?

This second assumption is as misleading a description of what happens in practice as the first, with which it is arguably inconsistent. The Government requires support in Parliament to give it political legitimacy for what it decides to do, but most government decisions do not need legislative approval. Legislation is not the principal tool for governing the country or even for implementing policy change. Most government activities can be carried on, and a great deal can be changed, without any need to resort to legislation other than of the purely formal sort referred to in the next paragraph. As explained above, legislation, in the sense that it is usually understood, is the tool used by government only for implementing its priorities for change and only where they cannot be implemented except by changing the law.

Legislation can only be regarded as a necessary and important tool for running the country insofar as the Government's decisions on supply and appropriation are formally encapsulated each year in legislative instruments. The principal tool of government for executive action and the implementation of change is the use of public money. Legislation, other than the formal legislation dealing with supply and appropriation, is often no more than an incidental aspect of policy implementation: for removing any legal vulnerabilities of the change required by a particular government policy. Often the core of what is wanted, which may be decisions about spending, will not be expressly dealt with in the Bill itself and may not even be within its scope.

'Parliamentary government' and parliamentary influence over policy would not be strengthened by giving Parliament more control over the initiation of legislation. It would only provide a more effective means for Parliament to transfer power from the executive (which is politically accountable to Parliament) to the judiciary (which is not). Proper government requires mechanisms to balance the many priorities that compete for attention at any one time. The legislative process in Parliament and decision-making in the courts are apt for dealing with only one matter at a time.

Achieving a policy objective by means of legislation sometimes involves legal coercion, but more often it involves the exercise of a discretion: with the intention that the change that achieves the objective will be produced only indirectly by provisions affecting, for example, the identity of the decision-maker or the parameters for that person's decision-making. This is another respect in which legislation and the day to day management and leadership of public affairs are entwined and cannot practicably be divided between different, mutually independent institutions.

Legislation is used most often for filling the gaps in a policy scheme for change rather than for authorising it in all respects.[12] Nevertheless, it is the frequent desire

---

[12] See S Laws, 'Giving Effect to Policy in Legislation: How to Avoid Missing the Point' (2011) 32 *Statute Law Review* 1, 6.

of Parliament to debate the wisdom of the scheme itself, coupled with the desire of the Government to get the benefit of a symbolic, parliamentary endorsement for its proposed policy change, that often results in legislation being proposed and framed in a way that at least suggests that the whole scheme depends on it. This approach then has the consequence that the legislation is treated by Parliament as if it did.[13]

VI. PARLIAMENTARY SCRUTINY AS A MEANS OF LEGITIMISING CHANGE

In this context, there is one further issue that those who wish to consider the effectiveness of the parliamentary scrutiny of legislation need to take into account. That is the extent to which any perceived need for Parliament to ensure the quality of legislation is actually only incidental to a more important objective of the legislative processes of Parliament.

At least one important function of Parliament in relation to legislation—maybe its principal function—is to provide political legitimacy for the implementation of what usually begins as a partisan proposal. The passage of legislation through the processes of the nation's principal institution for democratic debate is what turns a controversial political proposal into something authorised or required by law, and it does this by putting it in a form that can be accepted as a general rule by law-abiding members of society and applied by an impartial judiciary. So the constitutional processes for passing legislation for implementing a controversial policy proposal are, and need to be, processes that will work in practice to turn something politically contentious into something that attracts greater public acceptance and adherence.

Often when legislation is expedited, what are subsequently seen as technical deficiencies in the legislation resulting from undue haste in its preparation may be better seen as the failure of a rushed process to provide the legislation with sufficient legitimacy to make it effective in practice.[14]

There may be a similar difficulty in achieving legitimacy for a policy proposal where the legal changes that are needed to implement it and the substance of the proposal for which political legitimacy is sought have only a relatively loose or indirect connection with each other. This explains why Parliament and the

---

[13] See Evidence to the House of Lords Constitution Committee inquiry into the pre-emption of Parliament, www.parliament.uk/documents/lords-committees/constitution/preemption/PPEvidence.pdf, 93, para 4; and the oral evidence at: www.parliament.uk/documents/lords-committees/constitution/preemption/PPEvidence.pdf, 78–92.
[14] The Dangerous Dogs Act 1991 is often cited as a notorious example of how a rushed Act was defectively drafted, although it is difficult to identify exactly what drafting defects this criticism is based on. It may be that this Act stands better as an example of this phenomenon: that rushing through the Bill resulted in an Act that lacked sufficient legitimacy to command the respect it needed to work in practice.

Government will often collaborate in the scrutiny process to ensure that the endorsement is seen as covering more than just what is legally necessary.[15]

This is also the reason why legislation relating to a particular topic sometimes needs to be more specific about the most controversial aspects of the legislation. There may be a temptation to think that a Bill may pass more easily, and the law appear more impartial, if the provisions that are most likely to be criticised on political grounds are left more opaque. But it is the most controversial provisions which, for legitimacy purposes, need to be the least opaque.

As I have said, most legislation is designed to effect change by providing incentives for changed behaviour, either directly for legal persons generally or indirectly: by affecting a particular category of them, very often public sector decision-makers. The most usual form of incentive is probably a provision modifying the context in which discretions are exercised. Even the apparently most direct means of influencing behaviour, the creation of a criminal offence, is likely to be effective in practice only to the extent that it changes the context in which the police and prosecuting authorities exercise their functions to respond to the behaviour that is criminalised. The extent to which members of the public will respond to the change is likely to depend on how the behaviour of those authorities changes as a result of the legislation and on how far people are made aware of the new offence otherwise than by its mere passage into law.

This raises the question whether parliamentary scrutiny should be assessed at least partly on the basis of its effectiveness in facilitating the exercise of political leadership. Are its processes those that do all that is necessary and required to achieve the peaceful, cooperative and widespread acceptance of changes in society? The quality of the legislation—the technical and practical effectiveness of the law and of the policy it supports—are obviously relevant to achieving that, but that is not necessarily the whole story.

VII. A PRAGMATIC ROLE FOR PARLIAMENT IN RELATION TO LEGISLATION

These practical factors seem to me to lead to the conclusion that it must be for Parliament, or rather for each House, to define its own role in the scrutiny of legislation. With our unwritten constitution, there are no constitutional restrictions on what that role should be, and there are no constitutionally imposed duties about its legislative function to which Parliament is or can be made subject.

If Parliament is to select its priorities for scrutiny, it can only do so from what is most appropriate in the circumstances. In this process, recognition needs to be given to the Government's role and responsibilities in the preparation of legislation. Legislation is prepared and initiated by the Government. It is the Government that is ultimately directly or indirectly responsible for the form and content of the

---

[15] Discussed above.

legislation, whether through the use of its legislative initiative or through its acquiescence to amendments made to a Bill or to the passing of a Private Members' or Private Peers' Bill. For all practical purposes, the Government has the legislative power, subject to its accountabilities to Parliament. It is inappropriate and unnecessary for Parliament to arrogate the Government's responsibilities to itself. Its job is to scrutinise the Government's work and to hold the Government to account when things go wrong.

Because legislation is ultimately ancillary to the process of implementing government policy, Members of Parliament in the House of Commons are accountable to their constituents for the effects of legislation primarily in their capacity as supporters or opponents of the Government's policy programme. It is as members of the 'electoral college' for government rather than as individual legislators that they need to account to their constituents for the effects of government policy implemented by legislation.

Occasionally an individual MP may be held accountable for how he or she dealt with a particular point of legislative detail of particular interest to his or her constituents, but for most of the criteria on which the quality of legislation is judged, an MP must accept the judgment of those constituents on the Government's handling of those matters, according to whether the MP supported the party in government or was in opposition. In no practical way are MPs really held individually and directly accountable to their constituents for the technical quality of legislation. MPs would be right to see themselves as legitimate critics of proposals for legislation, but they are likely to mistake their function if they see themselves as its authors. They are directly accountable for their influence on the Government so far as legislation is concerned, but only indirectly for the legislation itself.

Similar considerations apply in the House of Lords, even though its members are not, of course, accountable to any electors. The functions of both Houses in relation to legislation should be devised to produce the most beneficial influence on the Government in what it does to formulate legislation. Again, the role needs to be seen to be that of critic rather than author.

Treating Parliament as a critic of legislation (rather than as its author), when taken with the reasons I have given for thinking that the role of critic is more constitutionally appropriate, seems to me to constitute a sound justification for the two Houses to be selective about how they carry out their function of legislative scrutiny. There is no need for them to carry out an exhaustive supervision of every aspect of the production of legislation.

The purpose of scrutiny should be to identify the aspects of the legislation that it is important for Parliament to influence, and to concentrate on those. Necessarily perhaps, this is, to a very large extent, what Parliament already does in practice.

On the other hand, even on the basis that that is the case, it seems to me that the effectiveness of the approach is diminished by the distraction resulting from a belief that it is only second best to trying to perfect the process of collective authorship. Parliament as an institution would be unsuited to carrying on integrated executive government, both because of its size and because of the political diversity of its membership. Its role is necessarily confined to scrutinising the collective decisions of the Government and holding it to account.

For similar reasons, the role of Parliament cannot practically include the collective authorship of legislative instruments. The authorship of legislation, both at the policy level and at the more technical drafting level, always involves the striking of many balances and the making of many compromises.

At the technical drafting level, the needs of different audiences have to be reconciled, the uncertainties in the existing law need to be analysed and avoided or resolved, and methods must be adopted that do not prejudice the construction and effect of existing legislation.

At the policy level, all forms of change involve a compromise between the demands of pace and the need for clarity and effectiveness. Perfection takes time, but it is a commonplace experience of change management of every sort that if it is too slow, it is likely to be more difficult, more painful for those affected by it and ultimately less effective. This is true of legislative change too. Political timetables for changes to different parts of the system may need to be coordinated. Delay can be desirable to produce a better outcome, but in the context of a system that is subject to the pressures of the electoral cycle, it is also a powerful weapon for opposition to change and for bolstering the status quo at the expense of what needs to be done.

The authorship of legislation by Parliament would require it to decide where these balances should be struck and to devise ways of striking them. It seems to me that all that is practicable is that the executive should propose a balance and that Parliament should be able to challenge it. Under our current constitutional arrangements, the Government has sufficient control of the pace of change to ensure that its very highest priorities proceed at the pace the Government chooses for them, particularly on the financial front, but the Government is always accountable to Parliament for its decisions on these matters and has to justify them in that forum.

Giving more emphasis to a critical role for Parliament in relation to legislation, as opposed to an authorship role, has implications both for what Parliament chooses to scrutinise and for the methods it adopts for particular pieces of legislation.

So, once the authorship role is no longer accepted as the premise for parliamentary scrutiny, it becomes legitimate for each House to discharge its role by adopting a sampling process. Sampling is, after all, an accepted and effective form of quality control in other areas.

As a Parliamentary Counsel, I was always conscious of the influence on my work of any risk that a certain sort of provision might attract undue parliamentary attention. It was not necessary, in order for Parliament to influence the way in which legislation is prepared, for it to be inevitable that every instance of such a provision would be challenged or even discussed. It was enough that it was known within the executive that there was a strong risk of challenge if someone's attention happened on the provision during its passage. A provision of that sort would seldom be proceeded with unless it was seen to be essential.

On this premise, parliamentary scrutiny could, perhaps, be made more influential on government by a more systemised selection of samples or by introducing more clarity on what Parliament, or each House, is sampling legislation for. That may be a more practical way of improving legislation than any attempt to make scrutiny more comprehensive, which will always run up against the obstacle of the Government's practical need to be able to manage the pace of the change that represents its highest priority. Of course, government is already influenced by the risk that anything might be sampled for anything remotely relevant, but more focused sampling is likely to be more influential if the focus is known.

Elsewhere in this volume, Jack Simson Caird and Dawn Oliver analyse some of the issues for which the Lords Constitution Committee look in legislation.[16] This seems to me[17] to identify an approach by which a sampling technique can be made more influential on the Government. The approach of the Committee and the analysis of its work are likely, in combination, to enhance the influence of Parliament on the production of legislation by the Government. The analysis is likely to do this by the way it provides a structured account of what sort of provision is likely to attract political attention or criticism in Parliament. It indicates categories of provision for which the Government will need a clear justification.

The purpose of the parliamentary scrutiny of legislation can only really be identified by identifying which aspects of the legislative process Parliament thinks it is most necessary to influence and by asking how that influence is most effectively exercised. Those who assert the inadequacy of parliamentary scrutiny should be seen as just asserting their own priorities for influence over those currently adopted by Parliament, and they need to be able to justify the changes they propose on that basis. Rejecting the myth of parliamentary authorship makes it impossible to argue that any decision to prioritise one matter over another is necessarily a dereliction of a supposed constitutional duty to have regard to every aspect of legislation.

Furthermore, it is both appropriate and inevitable that the allocation of priorities should be a political matter. Parliament exists principally as the political forum of the nation. It is unrealistic to suppose that its priorities could be anything but political. Proposals to add to or change what either House does by way of parliamentary scrutiny will only be accepted and be sustainable if what they are seeking to achieve attracts political support.

The politics will be different in the Commons and in the Lords, but politics will determine the role each House chooses for itself. In the Commons, the factors will be chosen by how the MPs can best use their involvement in the legislative process

---

[16] See ch 4 below.
[17] Subject to what I say below about whether Parliament should concentrate on matters of substance or on process.

to influence the actions of government. They will wish to do so in a way that will best discharge their individual mandates and the political priorities that induced them, individually, to seek election.

The basis on which priorities are likely to be selected in the House of Lords is more complicated but equally political. The Lords choose a role for themselves which gives them influence over legislation in relation to matters on which it is politically acceptable to the country, and therefore to the House of Commons, for them to exercise influence. It seems to be on this basis that one aspect of scrutiny in which the House of Lords has taken a particular interest is adherence to standards that can be said to be standards of constitutional propriety. The House of Lords can also assert a more significant role in the technical 'quality control' of legislation.[18]

Constitutional propriety and technical quality are two aspects of legislation to which Parliament can apply a sampling technique, but there are several other aspects of legislation that could also be looked at in that way. Sometimes they will be politically significant and sometimes they will not be. It is relatively rarely that the technical form and language of legislation will be high up the political priority list. Occasionally, however, there will be something that persuades Parliament to devote particular attention to those matters.

It was my observation, during my career as a legislative drafter, that the technical form and structure of tax legislation did indeed achieve political relevance in the 1990s, when the volume of tax legislation began to grow very rapidly. This resulted in a furore amongst tax professionals about the difficulty of keeping up with and understanding a corpus of law that was undergoing massive annual change. This political factor in turn led to the creation, in 1996, of what subsequently became the Tax Law Rewrite project and, as a result, to a transformation of the way in which tax law changes, and indeed other legislation, are structured and worded.

More often, however, the technical quality of legislation is only indirectly of political relevance to Parliament, giving Parliament only an indirect, but nevertheless real, influence on technical standards. It is rare for someone in Parliament to criticise the drafting of a provision if they are strong supporters of the policy it is implementing. However, the incentive for the drafter to produce technically well-drafted legislation is the risk that a lapse in standards will provide a handle for opposing the substance of the intended policy change or a distraction from the arguments in favour of that change. Neither of these things would be welcome to the drafter's client. This incentive is bolstered by the risk that a technical lapse might result in the Government's intended policy objectives being thwarted in the courts. That is a risk that is more remote in time, but may be more serious in its likely consequences for the Government's intentions.

In the absence of a sufficiently strong political demand for higher technical standards for legislation generally, it is perhaps necessary to recognise that the

---

[18] See the *Report of the Leader's Group on Working Practices* (n 3) ch 3, particularly paras 70–74.

influence of Parliament on technical standards is likely to be confined to matters that are relevant in this indirect way. But it is also important not to underestimate the extent of the influence these incidental factors have.

In my experience, too, different political conditions result in different political priorities at different times when it comes to the parliamentary scrutiny of legislation. My observations are that technical and procedural issues, and other points of detail, are likely to acquire rather more political significance when government dominance of the House of Commons is less firm or relies on alliances between different party groupings. This was the case in the late 1970s and again in the 2010–15 Parliament. Governments that have to build alliances to achieve political majorities for their legislation are more vulnerable than those with large majorities to the argument that 'whatever you think of the substance of this proposal, you cannot like the way it is being implemented'.

This sort of criticism can be applied either to technical drafting issues or, more generally, to the processes adopted by the Government in preparing legislation. Some of the 'constitutional standards' identified by Jack Simson Caird and Dawn Oliver[19] based on reports of the Lords Constitution Committee and the standards proposed by the House of Commons Select Committee on Parliamentary and Constitutional Reform[20] are applied to those processes. Similar standards were also suggested by the Better Government Initiative.[21]

It is my position, of course, that Parliament is constitutionally entitled to choose to call the Government to account on any aspect at all of the way in which it carries out any governmental functions, including the preparation of legislation. However, I am sceptical about the logic of any form of scrutiny that is too reliant on the assumption that the better the process, the better the decision that results from it. This is similar to a point I make in a different context above. In the case of legislation, Parliament is provided with the output of the Government's process of preparation in the form of a Bill. It seems to me that it is an example of obtuseness to assert that, in carrying out the scrutiny of a Bill, the process for its preparation should be a priority for scrutiny ahead of the product that comes out of that process, viz the Bill itself. If you cannot judge the product except by reference to the process by which it was produced, how can you know that bad process produces bad products? And if you have the opportunity to judge the product directly, why would you not make that your priority?

I am sure that there are things for government to learn about how it prepares Bills from a retrospective examination of a period over which a number of pieces of legislation were prepared. It is certainly a function of Parliament to encourage government to learn those lessons, and holding the executive to account is how it

---

[19] See ch 4 below.
[20] See Political and Constitutional Reform Committee, *Ensuring Standards in the Quality of Legislation* (HC 2013–14, 85).
[21] Better Government Initiative, *Good Government: Reforming Parliament and Government* (2010) ch 4, www.bettergovernmentinitiative.co.uk/wp-content/uploads/2013/06/Good-government-17-October.pdf.

does that. What I think is worth questioning is whether preconceived assumptions should be made about what those lessons are and then applied as the basis for the scrutiny of subsequent, individual pieces of legislation. For the reasons given above, the way that, in practice, a government is most often and most effectively influenced to adapt its method of producing legislation is by the way in which Parliament scrutinises both the substance of the legislation itself and the political impact of its enactment. If learning lessons from the past is the objective, a process of post-legislative scrutiny is perhaps the best way to find general lessons for the future. It is difficult to see what other purpose it can serve.

Understandably, it is the policy impact of legislation that is the most frequent preoccupation for the political scrutiny of legislation. It is worth pointing out that there are two levels at which the policy of a piece of legislation is intended to work and that each may be the subject of parliamentary scrutiny. The two levels derive from the two levels of analysis that are required for producing a piece of legislation.

The first stage of policy analysis is to identify the ultimate, practical objective of the policy and to determine exactly what practical changes are needed in the real world to achieve that objective. The assumption is usually that a particular real-world change is needed to produce a desired practical improvement in society. If things are to be made better, it is essential for those who are trying to make them better to know what they think 'better' would be. Parliament may want to scrutinise both the desirability of the proposed practical objective and the assumption that the practical changes that are designed to bring it about would actually do so. There is also then the question whether, even if they did, they would have counterbalancing adverse effects.

The second stage of formulating the policy for a piece of legislation is to identify how (if at all) the existing law is an obstacle to the production of the real-world changes that would, in turn, produce the desired 'better' situation. So the law may be an obstacle to the real-world change either in the sense of imposing legal inhibitions on conduct that is needed to produce that change or in the sense of failing sufficiently to incentivise it. This analysis of the legal 'mischief' is also something that Parliament, in exercising its scrutiny function, may wish to test and challenge. Has the mischief been correctly identified?

However, the second stage of analysis does not end with the identification of the mischief. It is then necessary to work out what change to the legal status quo would be best for removing the mischief. That process produces the legal policy that is to be implemented in legislation. This creates another potential focus for scrutiny. Would the removal of the mischief that has been identified, and the proposed method of removing it, have the desired effect in the outside world and achieve the ultimate policy objective? Would the proposed method of removing the mischief have any adverse or unacceptably risky effects, either in the long term or in the short term?

A discussion of the incidental policy and legal consequences of legislation suggests that there is also perhaps another way in which legislation can be scrutinised, particularly in the context of its long-term effects. An alternative approach would not look so closely at the intended effect, but would look, instead, at the overall effect of the change as a simple system change, and would assess objectively how desirable that is likely to be, and to do so independently of its immediate policy objective. This involves again questioning whether its beneficial effects will outweigh any adverse effects or other risks implicit in its enactment. This approach would be more consistent with what I have described as the myth of legislation as an impartial system change, but it is a method that may still be useful. It is often assumed that the correct way to assess legislation is against the standard of its intended effect. Nevertheless, given the inherent unpredictability of all change, an equally valid test, for post-legislative scrutiny at least, may be a cost-benefit analysis of the overall impact of the legislation, irrespective of its intended effect, as against the likely outcomes had there been no legislation.

It seems to me that, over my career, succeeding Parliaments tended, when scrutinising legislation, to put different emphases on different aspects of the questions to which the analysis of the policy gives rise. My impression was that there was a general trend towards taking more interest in the higher level of practical policy analysis and less in the legal policy. I am tempted to think that this was triggered by what I perceived as a reduction in the number of practising lawyers involved in the parliamentary scrutiny of legislation. However, I suspect that it is probably just as much a question of my own changing perspective as of the changing political context and variations over the years in the composition of either House. It is certainly the case, so far as my perspective is concerned, that I was more often concerned with technical and legal matters as a junior drafter. As a senior drafter, I was more frequently involved in legislation that was more controversial from a political or policy point of view.

Whatever the truth of that, I think, anyone considering the effectiveness of parliamentary scrutiny or how it can be improved needs to be aware of the different aspects of the policy that are always going to be available for analysis. The emphasis will change from Parliament to Parliament, as the political context determines the priorities, but it will also change from Bill to Bill, and it seems to me that Parliament needs to be willing to change its methods of scrutiny according to the factors that politics demands should be given the most attention on a particular occasion.

Parliament adopts various methods for scrutinising legislation. There is the core legislative procedure with the set-piece debates on the whole Bill and other stages at which the Bill may be amended. There are also committees which look at particular aspects of a Bill, such as the Joint Committee on Human Rights, the Delegated Powers and Regulatory Reform Committee and the Lords Constitution Committee,[22] and sometimes the relevant departmental select committee.

---

[22] See, eg, M Hunt, 'The Joint Committee on Human Rights' and A Le Sueur and J Simson Caird, 'The House of Lords Select Committee on the Constitution' in A Horne, G Drewry and D Oliver (eds), *Parliament and the Law* (Oxford, Hart Publishing, 2013).

There are also established procedures for pre-legislative and post-legislative scrutiny.[23]

Some of these seem to be directed at different aspects of what parliamentary scrutiny may be for. Some, perhaps the set-piece debates and the more intensive sampling done by the specialist committees, may be seen as relevant to doing what is necessary to legitimise a political proposal as a rule for everyone. Some, such as pre-legislative scrutiny and the evidence sessions in Public Bill Committee, may be directed at scrutinising different aspects of the policy analysis. Committee and Report stages may concentrate on these and other aspects of the Bill, but they also provide an opportunity for random sampling of the technical detail and of the premises on which the legal policy is built.

It seems to me that no one should seek to determine whether any of these different mechanisms are effective as a means of scrutiny, or whether scrutiny would be improved by modifying them, without considering which of the possible objectives of scrutiny they might best serve.

VIII. CONCLUSIONS

I have discussed various objectives for the parliamentary scrutiny of legislation on the basis that, in practice, it is the Government not Parliament that is legislating. My premise is that it is the Government's responsibility to ensure the quality of legislation and Parliament's function to call it to account for fulfilling that duty.

That function is a political function and can and will be discharged only by the adoption of political priorities. These will be different for different times, for different Bills and as between the two different Houses. The two Houses cannot be expected to be exhaustively responsible for every aspect of legislation. Their role is that of critic, not author. There is a role for sampling. Parliamentary scrutiny is a way for Parliament to influence decision-making in government. It is for the members of both Houses to decide where they wish to exercise influence over that decision-making and how to make that influence most effective. The role of Parliament cannot be decided on any other basis.

Also, it needs to be recognised that the form of parliamentary scrutiny needs to be effective for turning proposals that are politically controversial into rules that are generally acceptable and can be impartially applied. The technical quality of legislation, and the quality of the policy and legal analysis on which legislation is constructed are relevant to this function, but they are not the only things that are relevant to securing that it is effectively carried out.

The processes used for parliamentary scrutiny need to be assessed and, if necessary, reformed according to the different aspects of scrutiny that they need

---

[23] See ch 3 below.

to serve and also according to the political priorities for those different aspects of scrutiny.

If there is a respect in which legislation is seen to fall short of what is best and parliamentary scrutiny is not producing any improvement, then it is likely to be because that aspect of legislation lacks sufficient political importance. It is essential that the political importance of a desired improvement in quality is established before attempts are made to change the process to produce that improvement.

3

Pre-legislative Scrutiny in Parliament

JESSICA MULLEY AND HELEN KINGHORN

I. INTRODUCTION

AS SIR STEPHEN Laws notes in Chapter 2, those examining Parliament's scrutiny of legislation often conclude that there is room for improvement. As far back as 1947, LS Amery described Parliament as 'an overworked legislation factory'.[1] Close on half a century later, the Hansard Commission on the Legislative Process led by Lord Rippon of Hexham (the Rippon Commission) came to a similar conclusion: 'There is undoubtedly widespread concern about the way the legislative process works and about its final product, statute law. For some time many of those who make the law, many of those who have to apply the law and many of those who have to comply with the law have been unhappy about the way legislation is prepared, drafted, passed through Parliament and published.'[2] The Rippon Commission suggested that, where urgency to legislate was not an overriding consideration, Bills might be published in draft as a green paper.

Prominent among the themes explored by such critiques was Parliament's record in amending and improving Bills during formal stages of consideration and its capacity to influence the formation of legislative proposals in Whitehall. The opportunities to do the latter were limited and those which did exist were rarely used even when, in the mid-1990s, John Major's Government began to publish a small number of Bills in draft before their presentation to Parliament. There was a widespread sense that Westminster's culture, which tends to see a minister's ability to steer a Bill through Parliament largely unamended as a mark of political competence, made it too difficult to change a Bill during its formal stages. Pressure for more parliamentary influence over the framing and shaping of laws-in-the-making was made acute by the operation of the Child Support Act 1991. Seen as a weak law with undesirable and unforeseen consequences, the Act's shortcomings were felt by many and were quickly and repeatedly brought to MPs' attention through their constituency work.

---

[1] LS Amery, *Thoughts on the Constitution* (Oxford, Oxford University Press, 1964) 41.
[2] *Making the Law: The Report of the Hansard Society Commission on the Legislative Process* (London, Hansard Society, 1993) 1.

The Modernisation of the House of Commons Committee, first appointed shortly after Labour's General Election victory in 1997, made improving the legislative process its immediate priority. Among a raft of recommendations in its first report, *The Legislative Process*, to amend almost every stage of the House's consideration of legislation, the Committee concluded that 'some, or even all' draft Bills published by the Government should be scrutinised by either an existing or an ad hoc committee.[3] In doing so, it triggered the formalisation of the examination of draft Government Bills by Parliament into a process which has come to be known as pre-legislative scrutiny (PLS). A further series of changes to the House of Commons' law-making processes, again based on a report from the Modernisation Committee, was implemented in 2006. Standing Committees, which examined Bills in line-by-line detail, were overhauled to make the legislative process more informed and more accessible, recast as Public Bill Committees and awarded new powers to receive written submissions and examine witnesses in the course of their scrutiny of a Bill. The Committee also recommended that participation in PLS become one of the criteria considered when appointing MPs to Public Bill Committees. It suggested that 'as a matter of principle', the aim should be 'to include at least four Members who were involved in the pre-legislative scrutiny of the bill (or half the members of the relevant pre-legislative committee, whichever is the fewer)'.[4]

A. Definition

PLS is an occasional, additional stage of parliamentary scrutiny of government proposals for primary legislation. Since the Modernisation Committee's 1997 report, the number of Government Bills or sets of clauses published in draft has risen and almost all of those have been subject to PLS by an existing parliamentary committee or an ad hoc one appointed specifically to consider a draft Bill. Most ad hoc PLS committees have been Joint Committees, with a membership drawn from both Houses, but on occasion a Commons-only ad hoc select committee has examined a draft Bill.[5]

B. General Views over Time

The near-universal consensus of the late 1990s that PLS would be a good thing has been largely unchallenged since and lent some credence by experience. Peter Hain, then Leader of the House, told the Commons' Liaison Committee in 2003 that he

---

[3] Modernisation Committee, *The Legislative Process* (HC 1997–98, 190) para 91.
[4] Modernisation Committee, *The Legislative Process* (HC 2005–06, 1097) para 35.
[5] For instance, the Commons select committee appointed in the 2012–13 session to examine the draft Local Audit Bill.

was 'a very great fan of pre-legislative scrutiny, and the more we can do the better'.[6] Gordon Brown, as Prime Minister, told the House in 2007 that 'we want more draft Bills for scrutiny before they are given a Second Reading … I hope that the practice can become more widespread'.[7] During the debate on the second reading of the Charities Bill, Alan Milburn MP, who had chaired the Joint Committee examining the draft Bill two years earlier, stated:

> I remain a real convert to the pre-legislative process … That process is far less partisan and far more open to analysis and debate, and, as a consequence, makes, where it is possible, for far better law. Indeed, I should like to see it go much further in this House and in the other place.[8]

Speaking in January 2011, Lord McNally, then a Minister in the Ministry of Justice, told the House of Lords that 'the Government are committed to simplifying and improving the quality of legislation. We will improve quality by publishing in draft for pre-legislative scrutiny where possible'.[9]

Commentators also broadly agree, if less unequivocally so, that the PLS experiment has had a positive effect. The Hansard Society reported that: 'The fundamental question is whether pre-legislative scrutiny has improved the quality of legislation. It is impossible to give a definitive answer, as there are no agreed criteria by which to judge. However, all indications would suggest that it has been an extremely positive development.'[10] There are frequent, and well-argued, calls for more Bills to be published in draft to enable more PLS. Professor Robert Hazell has argued for its use to be extended to a broader range of Bills.[11] Richard Heaton, speaking as First Parliamentary Counsel, found it 'on the whole … a good process and it helps to improve the quality of legislation that hits the statute book'.[12]

With one or two notable exceptions, there is little quantitative analysis or independent assessment of the effects of PLS.[13] But now, with close to 20 years of experience against which to test the original proposition, PLS continues broadly to be considered favourably by practitioners and observers, and held as a welcome and valuable addition to Parliament's options for scrutinising legislation.

---

[6] Liaison Committee, Evidence to Committees: oral and written evidence, 19 October 2004, Rt Hon Peter Hain, MP (HC 2003–04, 1180-I) Q 63.
[7] HC Deb 11 July 2007, col 1458.
[8] HC Deb 26 June 2006, col 43.
[9] HL Deb 17 January 2011, cols 2–3.
[10] Hansard Society, *Pre-legislative Scrutiny, Issues in Law Making—Briefing Paper 5*, July 2004.
[11] R Hazell, 'Time for a New Convention: Parliamentary Scrutiny of Constitutional Bills, 1997–2005' [2006] *Public Law* 247.
[12] Political and Constitutional Reform Committee, Session, *Ensuring Standards in the Quality of Legislation* (HC 2013–14, 85) (hereinafter '*Ensuring Standards*') Ev 12, Q 33.
[13] Among the notable exceptions must be counted Jennifer Smookler's case study approach to examining PLS effectiveness: J Smookler, 'Making a Difference? The Effectiveness of Pre-legislative Scrutiny' (2006) 59 *Parliamentary Affairs* 522.

II. THE PURPOSE OF PLS

Drawing on our combined experience in supporting committees examining draft Bills, in this chapter we review how PLS has been done and consider whether it has met the aspirations put upon it and its prospects for the future. The 1997 Modernisation Committee anticipated that PLS would bring benefits to Parliament's consideration of legislation and improve the quality of laws. The potential benefits of PLS, however, do not accrue solely to Parliament or indeed to the cause of better legislation. For majority governments, for whom the cost of enacting legislation is primarily counted in terms of the parliamentary time (Sir George Young, a former Leader of the House, called time 'the oxygen of Parliament')[14] and political goodwill it consumes, PLS offers an economical testing ground, providing a measure of how much time and goodwill may be eaten up by a particular substantive Bill during its passage through Parliament and onto the statute book.

A. Which Bills Get Pre-legislative Scrutiny?

The pattern of Bills selected for PLS often bemuses. In practice, there is rarely a single reason for a particular Bill being published in draft for PLS. Manifesto and other Bills central to a government's agenda are unlikely to be selected for PLS as the executive has little choice but to give these Bills whatever charge they need. Bills which will clearly divide the House along party lines are also unlikely to be promoted for PLS by a government solely to determine the parliamentary cost of the passage of a substantive Bill, as it will already have a good understanding of the relative levels of support and opposition in Parliament. The Modernisation Committee in 2006 noted a propensity not to use PLS for Bills dealing with matters of party political controversy. Similar remarks have been made regarding prima facie constitutional bills.[15] There are also practical difficulties for a government, especially in the first few months after a general election, in producing a significant number of draft Bills. As David Heath MP, then Deputy Leader of the House, explained to the House in 2010:

> It is perfectly clear that it is not possible for Bills to be produced in time to allow full pre-legislative scrutiny in the first 10 weeks of a new Government when those Bills are to be debated in the very near future.[16]

But set aside these types of Bills and what is left is a broad array of legislative proposals for which it is harder to predict the political climate of their passage—Bills which may be controversial, or deeply complex, or less likely to divide Members

---

[14] Sir George Young, Speech to the Hansard Society (March 2010) www.hansardsociety.org.uk/coalition-must-do-better-says-hansard-society-report-card-on-legislative-and-parliamentary-reform.
[15] See, eg, Hazell (n 11).
[16] HC Deb 26 July 2010, cols 711–12.

on purely party lines—where a government has much to gain from learning of Parliament's likely reactions.

Such observations fall short of an overarching rationale governing the selection of Bills for PLS and specific examples suggest that it may be difficult, perhaps even counterproductive, to corral diverse case-by-case judgments in such a way. The draft Enhanced Terrorism Prevention and Investigation Measures (ETPIMs) Bill, examined by a Joint Committee in 2012, was given PLS because, as the Committee recorded:

> [T]he Government's Counter-Terrorism Review noted that 'there may be exceptional circumstances where it could be necessary for the Government to seek parliamentary approval for additional restrictive measures'. To meet this recommendation, the Government has prepared—but not introduced—the ETPIMs Bill. We were established as a Joint Committee of both Houses in order to provide pre-legislative scrutiny of the Bill so that, if in the Government's view 'exceptional circumstances' demanded its urgent introduction, Parliament would have had some opportunity to comment on the legislation and theoretically to allow expedited passage of this 'emergency legislation'.[17]

The Government sought PLS of the 2012 draft Voting Eligibility (Prisoners) Bill because it was right 'that Parliament should be given the opportunity fully to consider the difficult and contentious issue of prisoner voting ... We consider that to be the most appropriate course of action, given the importance of the issue and the strong views that exist across both Houses'.[18] There was also widespread speculation at the time that at least part of the motivation for doing so was to kick the issue into the long grass.[19]

In 2013, the Political and Constitutional Reform Committee argued that governments should be required to publish reasons for not producing a particular Bill in draft for PLS. Although that recommendation was not acted upon, it is perhaps indicative of a desire not just to increase the proportion of Bills available for PLS but also to increase the transparency with which decisions are made on which Bills to publish in draft.

i. How Many Bills Get PLS?

The volume of draft legislation published for PLS by successive governments has been on an upward, if gradual and inconsistent, incline since the early 1990s. Eighteen Bills were published in draft between 1992 and 1997, an average of just over three a year: there were seven in the 2001–02 session, nine in the 2007–08 session, 11 in the long 2010–12 session, 14 in the 2013–14 session and six in the

---

[17] Joint Committee on the Draft Enhanced Terrorism Prevention and Investigation Measures Bill (2012–13, HC 495, HL 70) para 2.
[18] HC Deb 16 April 2013, col 294.
[19] J Landale 'Votes for Prisoners—Opening the Door?' (*BBC News*, 19 November 2012) www.bbc.co.uk/news/uk-politics-2039787; HC Deb 16 April 2013, col 298.

2014–15 session. Such figures, though, can be misleading as to the actual volume of draft legislation as it has increasingly been the practice to publish various sets of draft clauses which, although falling short of being a complete Bill, may also receive PLS.[20] There are also inevitable peaks and troughs with the majority of draft Bills tending to be published during the mid-sessions of a Parliament. It is nevertheless still the case that only a minority of governments' legislative proposals are published in draft and therefore susceptible to PLS.

ii. Which Committee does PLS?

Although the majority of draft Bills published by a government since 1997 have been subject to PLS by Parliament, there is no formal obligation on Parliament to do so. Nor is there a set formula by which it is decided whether PLS will be done by one of the departmental select committees, by another established committee or an ad hoc Committee specifically appointed for the purpose; rather, the allocation of draft Bills to committees is done case by case and on the basis of discussion. The Commons Liaison Committee more than once has criticised government for seeking to determine allocations without adequate consultation stating, for instance, in 2008 that 'it is for the House, not the Executive, to assess the most effective form of scrutiny, and we object strongly to the fact that the Government has sought to preempt the House's consideration of how to scrutinise draft bills … without proper consultation'. Neither the government position that 'scrutiny by a joint committee is likely to be more appropriate … for bills of major constitutional importance' or the Liaison Committee's repeated calls for 'a presumption in favour of draft bills going to departmental select committees for PLS, where they are ready and willing to undertake this', have been formally agreed.[21] A more transparent system for allocation, welcomed by the Liaison Committee, was adopted towards the end of the 2005 Parliament with a commitment on the part of the Government to consult, but it remains true that decisions are made by discussion on a case-by-case basis.[22] The most frequent course is for the relevant departmental select committee in the Commons to conduct PLS.

iii. Different Types of Committee: Pros and Cons

Each type of committee has its own advantages for PLS. A departmental select committee, or another already established specialist committee, is likely to have a wealth of experience and expertise among its members and staff in relevant policy areas and will have established contacts with stakeholders beyond Parliament who

---

[20] The distinction between a draft Bill and a set of draft clauses is not always absolute. Differences in categorisation sometimes result in various sources giving different numbers of draft Bills.
[21] Liaison Committee, *The Work of Committees in 2007* (HC 2007–08, 427) para 25.
[22] Liaison Committee, *The Work of Committees in Session 2008–09* (HC 2009–10, 426) para 32.

can be called upon to inform the committee's work. Such committees can often also conduct PLS more quickly as they do not have to spend time agreeing working practices or experience delay at the outset while the committee's membership, terms of reference and staffing requirements are agreed. They also have more obvious means of following up on their recommendations once they have reported as, unlike ad hoc committees, they continue to exist after reporting. Ad hoc committees, on the other hand, may have members selected specifically for their interest and expertise in the policy area, and can focus exclusively on the draft Bill as they do not have to balance the demands of PLS against those of other ongoing and possibly time-sensitive work. Ad hoc joint committees in particular leverage the expertise from both Houses and are well-placed to test political legitimacy bicamerally. Ad hoc committees also have a publicly specified 'out date', giving stakeholders, Parliament and government a greater degree of certainty about when to expect PLS to conclude.

iv. How does a Committee do PLS?

Each committee either charged with or agreeing to scrutinise draft legislation is largely free, within parameters, to decide for itself how best to do that. This is a valuable freedom, but not one that is unconstrained. We have already noted the articulation of frustration that can occur when the Government is perceived to be trying to determine the PLS path. Convention almost as much as Standing Orders (the rules which govern procedures) impose practices and expectations on all parliamentary committees. And as with other committees, those charged with PLS have to navigate more practical limitations as well, such as members' time, finite resources, deadlines and competing priorities. It is then perhaps unsurprising that the pattern adopted for most PLS is remarkably like that commonly used by select committees engaging in policy and accountability orientated inquiries, but closer examination shows some distinctive features. A PLS committee usually starts its work by agreeing a 'call for evidence', inviting interested parties to submit their views on the draft Bill to the committee. Although there are examples of departmental and other committees doing so, PLS committees frequently issue tight guidance or ask for responses to specific questions in their call for evidence to ensure that the evidence they receive is well targeted to the particular topics they wish to examine in detail. The call for evidence is usually followed by a series of public meetings at which the committee examines experts and interested parties. Departmental select committees often wait to commence their public examination of witnesses until they have received a bulk of written evidence, so that it can be used to inform decisions on the selection of witnesses and priority areas for exploration. Tight deadlines mean that PLS committees can rarely afford to do this, and often they do not need to because, as discussed below, they often inherit a bulk of documentation. As a result, PLS committees tend to gather their written and oral evidence concurrently. In a practice largely exclusive to PLS, a committee may invite one or more officials from the team in charge of the Bill in the relevant government department to attend oral evidence sessions on a 'speak if spoken to' basis, enabling them to respond immediately to straightforward and factual queries about the draft Bill. As well as gathering evidence formally, PLS committees use more informal means to inform their deliberations and frame recommendations, such as visiting relevant organisations, hosting or contributing to other events, or commissioning bespoke research. In the mode of other select committees (and unlike public bill committees), PLS committees usually publish at the end of their PLS a narrative report which typically contains reflections on the adequacy of the draft Bill and aspirations for any subsequent substantive Bill. The latter may include specific recommendations to amend the text of the draft Bill. The Government usually respond to a PLS committee's recommendations by means of a Command Paper, often published at the same time as a substantive Bill.

Ad hoc PLS committees cease to exist at the point at which they report their findings: this is a feature of most ad hoc committees in Parliament, not just those concerned with draft legislation, but it has particular ramifications for PLS committees as it means they have less capacity to pursue or lobby in support of their findings and recommendations after the publication of their report and during the passage of any subsequent substantive Bill through Parliament—an issue to which we return below.

v. Engagement and Evidence

Draft Bills are not published in a vacuum; instead, they are often published and scrutinised alongside other pieces of research or scrutiny work, and may follow or precede other government papers, consultations and reviews. Indeed, the Cabinet Office's *Guide to Making Legislation* goes as far as to consider parliamentary PLS to be 'only one part of pre-legislative scrutiny'.[23] The draft Modern Slavery Bill, published late in 2013 and referred to an ad hoc Joint Committee, provides a good example where prior and concurrent activity within and without the executive shaped every aspect of the Committee's scrutiny.[24]

In addition to many decades of work on the issue by national and international groups, charities and academics, the draft Modern Slavery Bill Committee was also able to draw on many recently published papers, some of which were produced with a Bill or indeed the draft Bill in mind. These included reports by the All-Party Parliamentary Group on Human Trafficking and Modern Day Slavery, the Centre for Social Justice's report *It Happens Here*, a briefing paper from the Anti-Trafficking Monitoring Group and an earlier 'evidence review'.[25] Although it

---

[23] Cabinet Office, *Guide to Making Legislation* (July 2015) 149.
[24] Joint Committee on the Draft Modern Slavery Bill (2013–14, HL 166, HC 1019).
[25] The Centre for Social Justice, Report by the Slavery Working Group, *It Happens Here: Equipping the United Kingdom to Fight Modern Slavery* (London, Centre for Social Justice, 2013); Anti-Trafficking Monitoring Group, written evidence, published 28 February 2014; Modern Slavery Bill Evidence Review, December 2013.

is not unusual for a PLS committee to have a wealth of reports and documentation upon which it may base its work, the modern slavery evidence review was a novel and distinctive element in the mix. Undertaken at the request of the Home Secretary in the weeks preceding the publication of the draft Bill, it was chaired by the Rt Hon Frank Field MP, who was to become chair of the Joint Committee. Two other members of the Joint Committee, Baroness Butler-Sloss and Sir John Randall MP, had also been on the Review Panel. All the evidence gathered by the Review Panel was made available to the Joint Committee. The Joint Committee also invited the Anti-Trafficking Monitoring Group to set out broadly its views at its first public meeting, adding to other expert opinions on the draft Bill.

While the Joint Committee was considering the draft Bill, the Government initiated a review of the National Referral Mechanism (NRM), a key organisation in the identification and provision of assistance to people who have been enslaved, which would not conclude before the deadline set for the Committee to report. As a result, the Committee not only had to consider whether the draft Bill before it would satisfactorily address the criticisms made of the NRM by its witnesses but also had to consider how its findings might affect the Government's operational review. In the light of its evidence and its consideration of the draft Bill, the Committee recommended that the review 'be ambitious and have a wide remit' and that, taking into account its findings, the Secretary of State should take steps beyond the scope of the draft Bill.[26]

Similarly, the announcement by the Home Office that it would run pilot projects for advocates for child victims of slavery informed the Committee's questioning of witnesses, including the Minister in charge of the Bill, as well as its recommendations. The Joint Committee was not, however, prepared to rely solely upon the pilot scheme as an indication of intent and concluded that it was not a substitute for a statutory advocacy scheme—a clear example of a committee refusing a concession by the Government and proceeding to take evidence, investigate and draw its own conclusions.[27] European Union legislation and international policy and action framed the Committee's work: its selection of witnesses included anti-slavery commissioners and rapporteurs from the European Commission, the Netherlands, Finland and the US. The Committee also chose to consider coordination of statute and policy with the devolved Assemblies and Parliament, in particular in relation to child advocacy projects in Scotland and jurisdictional issues arising from the reliance within the draft Bill on the National Crime Agency, which did not have operational powers in Northern Ireland except in the reserved sphere.

Draft Bills may also reflect judgments made in national and European courts. The Joint Committees established respectively in 2012 and 2011 to consider the draft Enhanced Terrorism Prevention and Investigation Measures Bill and the draft Defamation Bill, for instance, were necessarily concerned not only

---

[26] Joint Committee on the Draft Modern Slavery Bill (2013–14, HL 166, HC 1019) para 98.
[27] ibid paras 102–24.

with the Government's legislative proposals but also with case law.[28] The draft Voting Eligibility (Prisoners) Bill reflected the 2004 decision of the European Court of Human Rights in *Hirst v UK (No 2)* and subsequent political and legal developments.[29]

vi. Supporting PLS

Although PLS can look and feel similar to their non-legislative, policy-driven work, committees conducting PLS may need to draw on particular skills and expertise. PLS committees, particularly ad hoc Joint Committees, often include members with distinguished legal careers. The Joint Committee on the draft Protection of Charities Bill was chaired by the Rt Hon Lord Hope of Craighead KT, the former Deputy President of the Supreme Court, and the Rt Hon Lord Phillips of Worth Matravers, the former President of the Supreme Court, was a member of the Joint Committee on the Voting Eligibility (Prisoners) draft Bill. In-house staff include those with relevant specialisms, for example, in financial and legal areas. Staff with these skills make up a large part of the House of Commons Scrutiny Unit, which was established in 2002 with provision of support for PLS as one of its two primary purposes.

It is practice for a legally qualified and experienced member of staff from the Scrutiny Unit to be assigned to support each PLS exercise undertaken by a Commons or Joint Committee.[30] The advice provided by the Legal Specialist is akin to non-litigious legal advice provided to clients in private practice. While the skills needed and tasks undertaken vary according to the draft Bill and the areas of law and policy contained therein, the Legal Specialist's role normally involves: statutory interpretation and legal research on case law, EU and European Convention on Human Rights law, international treaties and academic opinion; fact-checking of legal examples and precedents; analysis of legislative drafting and resolving difficulties and errors; and legislative drafting, perhaps of amendments or exemplar clauses. Legal specialists, working as part of the Committee's secretariat team, also assist in preparing briefing material and providing ad hoc advice throughout the inquiry. If time allows, the Legal Specialist may undertake extensive preparation for a PLS committee, including researching existing statute and case law, and analysing the draft Bill and related documents such as explanatory notes to establish how the draft Bill would affect existing statute law. They may also consider comparable

---

[28] See, eg, discussion in the Report of the Joint Committee on the Draft Enhanced Terrorism Prevention and Investigation Measures Bill (2012–13, HL 70, HC 495) paras 99 ff in relation to *Secretary of State for the Home Department v AF* [2009] UKHL 28, [2010] 2 AC 269. See also in the Report of the Joint Committee on the Draft Defamation Bill (2010–12, HL 203, HC 930-I) paras 42 ff considering the Supreme Court judgment in *Spiller v Joseph* [2010] UKSC 53, [2011] AC 852 in relation to freedom to express opinions.

[29] *Hirst v UK (No 2)* (2005) ECHR 681.

[30] Usually working under the title 'Legal Specialist'. For a full picture of the role of internal and external lawyers in Parliament, see A Kennon, 'Legal Advice to Parliament' in A Horne, G Drewry and D Oliver (eds), *Parliament and the Law* (Oxford, Hart Publishing, 2013).

statutes to work out whether there are any parallels or conflicts between what is proposed and existing legislation. Such preparatory work may then inform the Committee's deliberations and decisions on, for example, approaches to its work, the commissioning of further evidence and the selection of witnesses. They may also be responsible for preparing drafts for those parts of the Committee's report which engage with legal analysis.

A consideration of the work undertaken by Scrutiny Unit lawyers for draft Bill Joint Committees in the last three years shows the breadth of areas of law covered at least at a high level—human rights, crime, delegated legislation, care systems, communications data, modern slavery and trafficking, and charity law. Legal Specialists each have their own areas of expertise, often built up in practice outside of Parliament: current and previous Legal Specialists have practised as barristers and solicitors in private practice and within the Civil Service. For each draft Bill, the Legal Specialist is expected to establish an expertise within that area of law, a task in which they may be greatly assisted by the written submissions received by the Committee from lawyers and legal organisations such as JUSTICE, Liberty, the Bar Council and the Law Society as well as academics. Specialist Advisers appointed may be lawyers practising in the particular area, especially when the area of law under consideration is complex. The breadth of areas of law which the Joint Committee on the draft Modern Slavery Bill wished to consider prompted the appointment of two barristers as Specialist Advisers. That Committee also sought specific advice from academics and other barristers on drafting and particular clauses where existing academic and practitioner comment was slim. The Joint Committee on the draft Protection of Charities Bill was assisted by a solicitor from a City law firm specialising in charity law. Legal Specialists and Specialist Advisers work together to combine expertise and to provide PLS committees with a full spectrum of legal advice.

Legal support undertaken for the Joint Committee examining the draft Modern Slavery Bill included: considering the extent of consolidation of existing offences in Part 1 of the draft Bill; advising on and preparing suggested alternative clauses for the criminal offences in Part 1; evaluating the different statutory basis for existing commissioners (in the UK and internationally) which might be used as models for clauses to establish an Anti-Slavery Commissioner; considering existing case law, particularly in relation to the prosecution of victims of slavery for offences committed while enslaved; and considering the effect of the draft provisions on related areas of statute such as immigration law and legal aid. The Joint Committee decided to produce an alternative draft Bill, based on drafts prepared on its instructions largely by its Legal Specialist, to reinforce its arguments with a practical demonstration of how they could be drafted and translated into statute.

B. When PLS Works ...

Lord Puttnam, the distinguished British film producer and educator, has chaired two PLS Joint Committees: those considering the draft Communications Bill in

2002 and the draft Climate Change Bill in 2007. Drawing on his experience in 2012, he argued that, for PLS to work well, certain preconditions had to be met, including:

> A Government with the humility to acknowledge that it isn't always right; the graciousness to listen to alternative arguments; and a consistent and demonstrable understanding of the sovereignty of Parliament.[31]

In such circumstances, far from simply doing the Civil Service's legwork, PLS can be seen to have had an impact on prospects for legislation or the nature of the laws in question. The following four examples may appear disparate, but in each case, Lord Puttnam's precondition seems to have been in place.

Of the 144 recommendations made by the first pre-legislative committee which Lord Puttnam chaired, 136 were accepted by the then Government. A decade later, the Joint Committee on the draft Communications Data Bill[32] found that although 'there is a case for legislation', the draft Bill was 'too sweeping, and goes further than it need or should'. Its report also indicated that, with fuller consultation, a more proportionate measure could be devised 'which would achieve most of what they really need, would encroach less upon privacy, would be more acceptable ... and would cost the taxpayer less'.[33] The Government decided against pursing a substantive Communications Data Bill at that time (the draft Bill on investigatory powers, anticipated in the Queen's Speech following the 2015 general election and published in autumn 2015 seeks, once again, to address some of the issues contemplated in the draft Data Communications Bill).

The draft Deregulation Bill, examined by a Joint Committee in 2013, contained a clause (known as a Henry VIII clause) enabling a minister to use secondary legislation, which is subject to less or perhaps no parliamentary scrutiny, to repeal or amend primary legislation.[34] As Lord Norton of Louth commented:

> Although many provisions of the Draft Deregulation Bill were not contentious, comprising particular named measures that were no longer required, there was a clause that constituted a massive 'Henry VIII' provision ... The orders made by the Minister required parliamentary approval, but the particular process stipulated was fairly inadequate ... The committee in its report took my view and, in parliamentary terms, pulled no punches in its comments on the offending clause.[35]

---

[31] Lord Puttnam of Queensgate CBE, 'The Role and Importance of Pre-legislative Scrutiny in Parliamentary Life', Parliamentary Outreach Open Lecture (12 December 2012) www.parliament.uk/get-involved/outreach-and-training/resources-for-universities/teaching-resources/open-lecture-series/open-lectures/the-role-and-importance-of-pre-legislative-scrutiny-in-parliamentary-life.

[32] Referred to by some critics as the 'snooper's charter', as it would have required Internet Service Providers to maintain records on users' Internet browsing activities. For more details, see P Ward, House of Commons Library, 'Communications Data: The 2012 Draft Bill and Recent Developments', Commons Briefing Paper 6373, June 2015.

[33] Joint Committee on the Draft Communications Data Bill (2012–13, HL 79, HC 479) para 281.

[34] The name is derived from the 1539 Statute of Proclamations, which gave King Henry VIII power to legislate by proclamation.

[35] Lord Norton of Louth (*The Norton View Blog*, 28 January 2014) https://nortonview.wordpress.com.

The clause was not included in the Government's substantive Deregulation Bill when it was introduced to Parliament.

The Modern Slavery Bill introduced into the House of Commons included several clauses which had not appeared in the draft Bill, but which had been recommended during PLS: for example, a defence for slavery or trafficking victims compelled to commit an offence; special measures for witnesses in criminal proceedings; advocates for trafficked children; and provisions on the age and identification of victims. By the time the Bill moved to the House of Lords, other clauses had been amended in line with the PLS Committee's recommendations, for instance, by providing for transparency in commercial organisations' supply chains and making explicit reference to the Anti-Slavery Commissioner's independence from government. By Report stage in the Lords, the Bill provided for the Commissioner to appoint their own staff, again in line with the PLS Committee's recommendations. As the Bill was ping-ponged between the two Houses, in the final days of the Parliament, an amendment was made to bring the application of immigration rules to overseas domestic workers in line with the Committee's recommendations and is now on the statute book as section 53 of the Modern Slavery Act 2015.[36]

C. And when it doesn't

Equally, some common themes are beginning to emerge where PLS is generally thought to have had less impact. Draft Bills which are too large in scale or are portmanteau Bills create challenges for PLS, especially when conducted to tight and strict deadlines.[37] Despite its success in securing a reversal on Henry VIII powers, the size and range of the draft Deregulation Bill forced the Joint Committee, as it acknowledged in its report, to select specific clauses and themes for detailed scrutiny, while other aspects of the Bill received less attention.[38]

PLS is, by design, intended to enable Parliament to consider legislative proposals which are less than fully formed. There is, however, a risk of a government, perhaps keen to allow as much time as possible for PLS and certain that it can continue to work on the draft Bill during PLS, publishing a draft which may be so far from finished that it does not encapsulate intentions sufficiently. Some committees have felt their capacity to scrutinise compromised by draft Bills which

---

[36] When a Bill has passed third reading in both Houses, it is returned to the House where it started for any amendments made by the second House to be considered. In a process known as 'ping-pong', a Bill may go back and forth between the Houses several times before there is agreement on its exact wording.

[37] Portmanteau Bills are those which cover a number of different topics. They are also sometimes referred to as omnibus Bills or Christmas tree Bills, in reference to the tendency to hang various positions on them, rather like baubles on a Christmas tree.

[38] Joint Committee on the draft Deregulation Bill (2013–14, HC 925, HL 101) paras 3–9.

are fragmentary only or leave much of the detail to yet-to-be-published secondary legislation. The Environment, Food and Rural Affairs Committee, for instance, found that there was a limit to which PLS could influence the shape of legislation when the draft Bill it was considering relied 'too heavily on establishing the broad framework for future reforms whilst leaving the details to be set out in guidance with the likelihood that these will receive less scrutiny'.[39]

By far the most commonly vocalised cause of constrained PLS is insufficient time. The Cabinet Office's *Guide to Making Legislation* says:

> Draft bills should be published in time to give the Committee carrying out scrutiny at least three to four months (excluding parliamentary recess) to carry out its work and still report in time for the department to make any necessary changes to the bill before its planned date of introduction.[40]

Several parliamentary committees have argued for 12 weeks to be accepted as the usual period, or even the minimum period, for PLS.[41]

A specific 'out date', the day by which the committee must report its findings, is usually stipulated in the orders appointing ad hoc and Joint Committees examining draft Bills. For existing committees, an out date may be agreed informally between the committee and the government. For ad hoc and particularly Joint Committees, even a four-month timetable can be punishing, not least because the processes for establishing the committee can take a couple of weeks and must be completed before committee members initiate their work. Even so, in practice, committees are often expected to complete PLS in much shorter periods. In one of the most extreme examples of a curtailed timetable, in 2012–13, the Environment, Food and Rural Affairs Committee was asked to examine and report on the albeit short and tightly focused draft Dangerous Dogs Bill in eight sitting days. As the Committee recorded:

> When asking us to conduct scrutiny of the draft Bill, Defra requested a response within only eight sitting days. We informed the Department that this deadline was an impossible one to meet; it did not provide an adequate opportunity for pre-legislative scrutiny … We are reporting at the very earliest opportunity but Defra must in future allow sufficient time for proper scrutiny of draft legislation.[42]

PLS committees may request an extension to the reporting deadline, but these are not always granted. In deciding out dates and negotiating extensions, both parties have to consider that, if the draft Bill is to be reconsidered and redrafted in the light of the Committee's recommendations, sufficient time to make these amendments

---

[39] Environment, Food and Rural Affairs Committee, *Draft Water Bill* (HC 2012–13, 674) para 7.
[40] Cabinet Office (n 23) 143.
[41] R Kelly, House of Commons Library Standard Note, *Pre-Legislative Scrutiny*, SN/PC/2822, April 2010. See also House of Lords Constitution Committee, *Pre-Legislative Scrutiny in the 2008–09 and 2009–10 Sessions* (HL 2009–10, 78), paras 11–16.
[42] Environment, Food and Rural Affairs Committee, *Draft Dangerous Dogs (Amendment) Bill* (HC 2013–14, 95) para 2.

is also required between the out date and the introduction of any substantive Bill to Parliament. If PLS encroaches too much into this period, it is likely to have less influence. Extensions therefore have the potential to be counterproductive.

The Energy and Climate Change Committee's experience with the draft Energy Bill illustrated the consequences of timing and detail difficulties coming together. The Committee commented scathingly:

> [O]ur efforts to provide robust and effective scrutiny have been hampered by a number of factors. First, the timescale in which we have been asked to conduct and conclude our inquiry—just five sitting weeks—has made examination of what is a very complex set of proposals extremely challenging. This timescale is well below the 12 sitting weeks that a Joint Committee conducting a similar task would, by convention, be granted.
>
> Second, we have been dismayed by the lack of detail provided on key aspects of the proposals ... DECC was still collecting evidence as we carried out our inquiry in many vital areas ... It is very difficult for us to comment constructively on these aspects without having had access to this evidence base.[43]

The Committee also commented on the refusal of Treasury Ministers to give oral evidence on the draft Bill, perhaps an indication that in this instance, Lord Puttnam's precondition was not met, which it felt had 'seriously undermined the pre-legislative scrutiny process'.

These are instances where committees have clearly felt that their PLS efforts have been undermined by weaknesses in the process. But assessing only process presupposes that it is process only which determines the quality of outcome: such is the diversity of approaches towards PLS that it is perhaps more fruitful also to think systematically about the effects of individual PLS exercises, and using that to determine more closely which legislative proposals might benefit from PLS in the future.

D. PLS and Political Legitimacy

The role of PLS in building political legitimacy around a set of legislative proposals should not be underestimated. With the resources of Parliamentary Counsel at its disposal, it is not likely that a government would choose to publish a draft Bill in order to leave the skilled art of legislative drafting to a committee in Parliament; nor is it likely that a government's main purpose is to seek a critique of drafting (although that too can be a useful outcome). Rather, the key benefit for a government is a testing of the political waters, seeing if the draft Bill fits the policy objectives and taking steps towards building, around a set of proposals, the political goodwill and legitimacy required for successful law-making and implementation. At the same time, it may derive the immediate benefits more usually cited as reasons for PLS.

---

[43] Energy and Climate Change Committee, *Draft Energy Bill* (HC 2012–13, 275-I) paras 6–9.

The draft Voting Eligibility (Prisoners) Bill is among the most obvious examples of PLS being used to test the level of political support in Parliament for specific legislative proposals. Published in 2012, it was not so much a draft Bill in the traditional sense as an overt invitation to establish whether sufficient political buy-in could be forged around any one of three options outlined. The Joint Committee charged with considering the draft Bill rejected all three options and recommended yet another alternative approach. This amounted to a strong indication of the extent of difficulty the Government would likely incur in establishing a sufficient consensus in Parliament to support specific legislative changes to prisoners' voting rights. That no substantive Bill has yet been brought forward is, arguably, a demonstration of the effectiveness of PLS in testing political legitimacy and in establishing the soft cost to government of pursuing legislative change. The history of the draft Communications Data Bill is different. Elements of the proposals in that draft Bill have made it to the statute book by means other than a single, coherent Bill, but it again illustrates that a failure to gain political acceptance through PLS not only sends legislative drafters back to the drawing board but can also result in the executive revisiting a decision to use the legislative path to affect its desired rule or behavioural change.

It would be overly bold to assert that PLS has shifted Parliament's role in the law-making process from being exclusively reactive into instigatory waters: it does not challenge the constitutional arrangements which ensure that the executive initiates almost all legislative proposals with a realistic chance of making the statute book. (Bills instigated by private members in the Lords and Commons—those 'fragile vessels' to which Lord Norton refers in Chapter 6 below—are rarely enacted without government support.)[44] But it does offer potential, not always exploited in practice, for parliamentarians to influence the scope, direction and emphasis of legislation far more fundamentally than is usually achievable through Parliament's more long-standing law-making processes. The Joint Committee on the draft Modern Slavery Bill went as far as to produce its own alternative Bill, elements of which made it into the Modern Slavery Act 2015. But the Committee's Bill was still within the scope of the executive's original legislative proposals, and it was only through persuasion, influence and force of argument that parts of the Committee's redrafting reached the statute book.

E. Success or Failure?

In 1997, the Modernisation Committee anticipated several beneficial outcomes from the extension and formalisation of PLS. PLS was to open up Parliament's law-making to those affected by legislation, to provide a means for parliamentarians

---

[44] See Norton, ch 6 below. See also R Rogers and R Walters, *How Parliament Works* 7th edn (London, Routledge, 2015) 205.

to have real input into legislation at a time when ministers would be far more receptive to suggestions for change, to deliver higher quality legislation and to reduce the amount of parliamentary time required for later legislative stages of consideration.

PLS has widened involvement in the formation of legislation through issuing open invitations for comments and submissions, examination of key witnesses and a variety of more informal interactions with interested parties and those potentially affected by the proposed legislation. There are instances of committees conducting PLS without involving those outside Parliament, but these are few and tend to occur because either there is insufficient time or the proposed legislation is very narrow in scope. The majority have adopted a broad, consultative approach. Governments, too, often consult on their legislative proposals, but PLS in Parliament provides a dialogue of a different nature and one which was previously absent from the legislative process. Most obviously, the contact is directly with legislators, and it is usually a public, transparent and recorded exchange of views. At their best, oral evidence sessions provide an effective forum for mutual exploration of areas of interest, filling gaps in knowledge and explaining or illuminating areas which may not be well-understood. PLS offers a structured means of engagement between stakeholders and Parliament. Stakeholders may think a sympathetic hearing more likely from a cross-party committee in Parliament intent on exploring issues than from a government testing or promoting a particular position. A government's dual roles of proposing new laws and enforcing existing ones also lend Parliament an advantage: during PLS of the draft Modern Slavery Bill, for instance, committee members met victims of slavery who may have been less willing to relate their experiences to representatives of the Home Office, the body with oversight of the enforcement of immigration rules.

The range and number of parliamentary and extra-parliamentary individuals and organisations engaged by that committee, which we described earlier, reflected the wide scope of the draft Bill and a recognition of the need for cross-border co-operation in tackling modern slavery. Draft Bills with a narrower scope and policy base may be expected to engage fewer people, but nonetheless public involvement in PLS remains typical. The Irish Government highlighted this point in explaining its extension of PLS to all proposed Bills, as it would 'allow extensive engagement of the public in law-making; allow parliamentary committees to consult civil society and advocacy groups, stakeholders and experts to develop legislation before bills are fully drafted'.[45] In this way, PLS committees pick up, test and lend weight to points which have 'long been pressed by industry, voluntary organisations or think tanks, none of which have the same power to demand a government response'.[46]

---

[45] Oireachtas Library and Research Service, Spotlight, No 8 of 2014, *Pre-legislative Scrutiny (PLS) by Parliament*.
[46] M Russell and M Benton, *Selective Influence: The Policy Impact of House of Commons Select Committees* (London, UCL Constitution Unit, 2011) 86.

PLS committees can, and on occasion do, innovate in terms of the ways in which they engage and communicate with those outside Parliament. The Joint Committee on the draft Communications Bill (2001–02) was one of the first parliamentary committees to have its public evidence-taking meetings webcast and to use an online forum as an additional means of public consultation. The Joint Committee examining the draft Mental Health Bill in 2005 produced a version of its report more readily accessible to those directly affected by the draft Bill's provisions than the usual text-rich committee report, as did the Joint Committee on the draft Care and Support Bill in 2013, although the practice has not been widely adopted.

One measure of the extent to which PLS enables parliamentarians to influence and have input into legislation is to consider how many recommendations made by PLS committees are adopted. The Joint Committee on the draft Communications Bill, as we have already seen, had a success rate of over 90 per cent. Anecdotal observation suggests that this success rate is not unique or unusual, but there is insufficient data on which to base any extrapolation. Moreover, as Kennon argues, a 'simple tally of recommendations accepted or rejected does not give a full impression' of the impact of PLS on legislative proposals.[47] The key, as cited by Russell and Benton, is that the committee's process and report 'creates a climate where it becomes imperative to address issues' and can affect change simply by getting people to explain themselves.[48] Indeed, the regular attendance of Bill Team civil servants at a committee's meetings, and a committee's examination of the minister in charge of the draft Bill are part of creating a constructive dialogue between legislature and executive. Ministers are obliged to 'answer questions in real time, in an interactive setting'.[49] As one former Minister put it, even when government thinks that a PLS committee is 'just wrong, their very existence means you have to address the issues ... think "why do I think this is a bad idea?"'.[50] It is of course the Government's right to disagree with a PLS committee and to persist in pressing its preferred provisions. Yet it is too simplistic to assume simply that when recommendations are rejected, Parliament has had no effect on legislation. As Lord Butler of Brockwell, former head of the Civil Service, put it, criticism from a PLS committee:

> [I]s not undamaging—it may be damaging to the Government; it means that a case can be made against it—but it does sharpen the Government's act in explaining why it is going to insist on its original provision and not accept the advice of the pre-legislative Committee. But the pre-legislative Committee has done a good and necessary job.[51]

Both a committee's report and a government's response can inform debate on the Bill as it passes through its formal legislative stages. Especially in cases when

---

[47] A Kennon, 'Analysis: Pre-legislative Scrutiny of Draft Bills' [2004] *Public Law* 477.
[48] Russell and Benton (n 46) 84–85.
[49] ibid 87.
[50] ibid 86.
[51] *Ensuring Standards* (n 12) Ev 33, Q 134.

recommendations arising out of PLS have not been accepted by the Government, PLS findings can become part of the interplay within the legislative process by providing evidence, considered observations and conclusions, and source material for debate and amendments, its primary audience expanded from government to the entire body of legislators.[52] This phenomenon does not solely result in better informed debate during the legislative stages (although the Modernisation Committee was alive to that benefit too), but can also increase the extent to which PLS recommendations are taken up. As Smookler notes in relation to the Civil Contingencies Act 2004: 'Although the Joint Committee had ceased to exist a couple of months earlier, its recommendations continued to be referenced, and in some cases, resolved throughout the legislative stages.'[53] She concluded that:

> While 32 Joint Committee recommendations were fully or partly accepted by the Government before the Bill was introduced, only a further two of any significance were agreed after its introduction. In the case of this Bill, although pre-legislative scrutiny contributed to changes made in Parliament, it is clear that its greatest opportunity for influence was at the pre-legislative stage.[54]

Regardless of whether and when amendments based upon PLS are accepted, the use of the PLS committee's work in subsequent stages shows how PLS results in 'more rational, considered debate on legislation'.[55]

The impact of PLS on the time taken in Parliament for subsequent legislative stages is less clear. Again, there is little quantitative evidence one way or another. Simple observation seems to suggest that it depends on the nature of the Bill, the sort of conclusions reached by the PLS committee and the extent to which its recommendations are taken up by government before a substantive Bill is introduced. The comments of the then Leader of the House to the Liaison Committee in 2004 typify this ambiguity: he told them that there was 'debate amongst my business manager colleagues and some ministers as to whether it actually does assist with the subsequent passage of a Bill or reveal even more arguments to be had around it'.[56]

Whether PLS promotes better quality in legislation similarly remains a matter of debate, although the case in favour is more compelling. What is 'good law' is a subjective judgment, but coherence, clarity, accessibility to the public, planning, identification of consequential effects and taking into account the views of interested parties are usually accepted as being among its characteristics. Power pointed out that PLS can be particularly effective in improving legislation which has broad

---

[52] Smookler (n 13) 532.
[53] ibid 526.
[54] ibid 527.
[55] M Russell, B Morris and P Larkin, *Fitting the Bill: Bringing Commons Legislation Committees into Line with Best Practice* (London, UCL Constitution Unit, 2013) 28. See also Smookler (n 13) 532.
[56] Liaison Committee, Session 2003–04, *Evidence to Committee: Oral and Written Evidence*, 19 October 2004, the Rt Hon Peter Hain MP, HC 1180-I, Q 63.

cross-party support precisely because it allows potential practical problems to be identified at an early stage.[57]

PLS provides an opportunity for good law characteristics to be met in part because a committee is free to choose to focus its efforts on technical scrutiny of drafting and legal effects. Power reported in very different terms in 2000: his interviewees felt that earlier committees had been unclear about their objectives and had received little guidance. Some had even sought guidance from departmental officials 'and to varying degrees worked with (or against) the civil servants'.[58] Blackburn and Kennon made similar observations in 2003 in *Griffith and Ryle on Parliament*, concluding that PLS was then still experimental and lacking in structure, relying for its development upon government and government's resources in the form of Cabinet, business managers and Parliamentary Counsel.[59] The striking contrast between these earlier analyses and the current situation indicates the extent to which Parliament's capacity to perform PLS effectively has developed since its early days.

Effective technical drafting may be considered another characteristic of good law. The Cabinet Office's *Guide to Making Legislation* says that 'it is generally expected that the committee will not ... become too involved in detailed drafting points'.[60] Few PLS committees considering a suitable draft Bill have fulfilled that expectation. By one measure, as many as 22 per cent of all PLS recommendations made between 2002 and 2012 were for technical changes, with ad hoc committees being slightly more prone to making this sort of recommendation than departmental select committees.[61]

The Modernisation Committee found in 2005 that PLS was 'generally acknowledged to be one of the most successful innovations in the legislative process in recent years'.[62] As the Law Society told the Committee, 'it would probably be difficult to prove scientifically that more pre-legislative scrutiny has improved legislation, but it would seem unarguable in practice that it has'.[63] More recently, the (former) Political and Constitutional Reform Committee considered 'pre-legislative scrutiny to be one of the best ways of improving legislation and ensuring that it meets the quality standards that Parliament and the public are entitled to expect'.[64]

---

[57] G Power, *Parliamentary Scrutiny of Draft Legislation 1997–1999* (London, UCL Constitution Unit, 2000) 16.
[58] ibid 10 and 25.
[59] R Blackburn and A Kennon, *Griffith and Ryle on Parliament: Functions, Practices and Procedures* 2nd edn (London, Sweet & Maxwell, 2003) 727, as quoted in House of Commons Library Standard Note, *Pre-legislative Scrutiny*, R Kelly, April 2010, SN2822, para 5.1.
[60] Cabinet Office (n 23) 148.
[61] T Caygill, 'Ensuring Standards in the Quality of Legislation. Has Pre-legislative Scrutiny Made Progress as a Tool to Improve the Scrutiny and the Quality of Legislation since its Initial Introduction in 1997?' (Dissertation, University of Hull, 2013) 33–35.
[62] Modernisation Committee, *The Legislative Process* (HC 2005–06, 1097) para 12.
[63] ibid para 20.
[64] *Ensuring Standards* (n 12) para 115.

None of this is to suggest that PLS is or has always been welcome. In a House of Lords debate on the Communications Bill in 2003, concerns about PLS being used to delay legislative action, or to filibuster, were mentioned. Lord McNally suggested that the experience had been so bruising that in 'the corridors of Whitehall there will be those who say, "Don't try it again"'.[65] Others too have pointed to weaknesses in parliamentary PLS. Drawing some of these concerns together, Hagelund and Goddard have recently argued that while PLS is a 'lauded innovation ... credited with identifying difficulties in the draft text, forcing redrafting and thus improving the text', valid criticisms remain, such as the proportion of Bills published in draft and the fact that PLS is neither automatic nor obligatory.[66]

PLS is it not a standalone act isolated from Parliament's subsequent formal Bill consideration stages; rather, as the 1997 Modernisation Committee recognised, it is intended to influence and inform subsequent consideration of a substantive Bill. Our examples demonstrate that this has proved to be the case. But some have argued that this very success results in a more opaque and insidious downside: Russell, Morris and Larkin argue that innovations such as PLS are part of a trade-off for setting aside serious reform elsewhere:

> Attempts to sidestep this problem by involving select committees in the consideration of draft bills, or bolting on evidence sessions to committees that remain ad hoc and largely adversarial, can only achieve so much. These changes are, to an extent, simply attempts to paper over the underlying weaknesses in a system of legislative committees which looks increasingly outdated and out of step.[67]

Sir Stephen Laws' 'armchair analysis' in Chapter 2 above questions the commonly held view that Parliament should 'reform itself to match its supposed all-embracing [legislative] function' and allows room for the possibility of Parliament defining its own legislative role based on an understanding of what it is 'best qualified to do, or more capable of doing'.[68] PLS fits comfortably within that second limb—an exercise in allowing Parliament to do what it does best, deciding for itself and on a case-by-case basis, where it can best add value not to the law-making process, but to specific legislative proposals. Nor should concerns regarding other aspects of the legislative process completely obscure the benefits that PLS delivers at present.

III. FUTURE DEVELOPMENTS IN PLS

Most of those commenting on the future of PLS call for its extension to a wider range and higher proportion of Bills. The Select Committee on Reform of the

---

[65] HL Deb 8 July 2003, cols 220–62, eg, col 251 and col 253.
[66] C Hagelund and J Goddard. *How to Run a Country: A Parliament of Lawmakers* (Reform, March 2015) www.reform.uk/wp-content/uploads/2015/03/Parliament-of-lawmakers_AW_WEB.pdf.
[67] Russell, Morris and Larkin (n 55).
[68] See ch 2 above.

House of Commons (more commonly known as the 'Wright Committee' after its chair, Tony Wright MP) in 2009 called for more 'opening up' of the legislative process to give 'a real opportunity to the public to influence the content of draft laws' and contemplated an extension of PLS as one way of doing this; indeed, some of those who gave evidence to that Committee suggested a mandatory period of PLS for forthcoming legislation.[69] The Political and Constitution Reform Committee in 2013 acknowledged PLS as 'an important stage in refining a bill' and, while recognising that it was not appropriate in all circumstances, recommended that it become the default position and that government be obliged to give its reasons for not publishing a Bill in draft.[70] But as Rogers and Walters note, 'draft Bills are not a panacea—at least not for governments. They add to the time before a proposal passes into law … they tie up more resources in the preparation and drafting of Bills … [and] they may make it harder for the government of the day to get its way'.[71] Governments have frequently explained why, although committed to widening PLS in principle (the Cabinet Office *Guide to Making Legislation* says 'the default position should be that Bills will be published in draft prior to formal introduction'), in practice doing so has proved either inappropriate or enormously difficult.[72] The Government did not accept the Political and Constitution Reform Committee's position, but re-iterated a commitment to PLS on a case-by-case basis.[73]

Nor are the practical difficulties in extending the reach of PLS all on the part of government: Parliament too would need to allocate more parliamentary time (inevitably taking time away from other matters) and more staff resources either by redirecting from other priorities or by increasing its overall costs. Most critically, any extension would present a greater draw on that always finite, highly in demand and already fully stretched resource of MPs' and peers' time.

It is worth sounding a note of caution about aspirations for more PLS other than on grounds of impracticality. Implicit in the desire to extend PLS to all Government Bills, barring those in certain categories such as emergency legislation, is an assumption that all Government Bills merit roughly equal treatment, but 'the reality is that each Bill is unique; and any categorisation risks obscuring that fact. The spectrum runs from long, politically controversial and complex Bills to short, wholly uncontentious and simple Bills. It would indeed be remarkable were one single principal route to be appropriate for such a complex array of … Bills'.[74] There are unsurprisingly instances where the absence of opportunity for PLS on particular Bills has been regretted and a government criticised for not publishing

---

[69] Reform of the House of Commons Committee, *Rebuilding the House* (HC 2008–09, 1117) para 276. For further discussion of the Wright reforms, see ch 7 below.
[70] *Ensuring Standards* (n 12) paras 47 and 115.
[71] Rogers and Walters (n 44) 181.
[72] Cabinet Office (n 23) 143.
[73] *Ensuring Standards* (n 12) paras 3, 35–39.
[74] Modernisation Committee, 1997–98 session, *The Legislative Process* (HC 190, para 16).

draft legislation.[75] Overall, however, the absence of sufficient political will within the executive to publish more in draft and sufficient political influence exerted by parliamentarians on the executive for more PLS suggests a tacit acknowledgement that, given the current legislative process, a step change in the number of Bills subject to PLS, albeit generally favoured, is not a top priority on either side.

Committees undertaking PLS are most active while a Bill is still in draft but we have already established that 'pre-legislative scrutiny makes a significant contribution both prior to, and after, the Bill has been introduced'.[76] This puts into sharper relief a persistent limitation on exploiting the benefits of PLS and that conducted by ad hoc committees in particular. Smookler makes the point well: the limited lifespan of an ad hoc committee 'can curtail its ability to provide effective follow-up to government responses that are ambiguous or lacking in detail. While some recommendations are pursued to successful effect at pre-legislative and legislative stages, others become dormant almost by default'.[77] But if the proposition that one of the purposes of PLS is to improve the quality of legislation holds true, it is a weakness that some recommendations are not taken up not because they fail to secure wider political agreement, but because a committee lacks the capacity to press for their proper consideration.

The Parliamentary Commission on Banking Standards (PCBS) was set up in 2012 following the exposure of a series of problems in the financial services sector, culminating with the LIBOR scandal. Its experience, albeit that it was distinctly successful in pressing its recommendations, is pertinent. The PCBS, charged with considering banking standards and culture and making recommendations for legislative action, scrutinised the draft Financial Services (Banking Reform) Bill. Although not established on the same model as a typical PLS Joint Committee, the Commission was nevertheless an ad hoc committee with a limited lifespan, ceasing to exist once it had made its final report and before the substantive Bill had completed its parliamentary stages. Yet MPs and Lords who had served on the Commission continued to draw on the Commission's findings and use their position as former commissioners to lobby the Government to include significant elements of their recommendations into what became the Financial Services (Banking Reform) Act 2013. The Rt Hon Andrew Tyrie MP, who chaired the Commission, discussed the difficulties with 'follow up' in *The Poodle Bites Back: Select Committees and the Revival of Parliament* and in doing so suggests some potentially useful remedies:

> [I]t was a great mistake that the PCBS—and its staff—was dissolved when it made its [final] report ... It should have been kept going longer to do the follow up necessary in order to capitalise on its work and, in particular, to ensure that its recommendations

---

[75] See, eg, the Political and Constitutional Reform Committee's comments on the absence of a draft Bill and pre-legislative scrutiny in its 2013 report, *The Government's Lobbying Bill* (HC 2013–14, 601).
[76] Smookler (n 13) 522–35.
[77] ibid.

were incorporated in legislation ... Commission Members decided that they wanted to continue to operate informally even if the Commission could no longer make formal reports. But the scattering of staff meant an immediate and irrevocable loss of collective memory. This has handicapped follow up work ever since, reducing Parliament's effectiveness.[78]

In a novel development, some parliamentary resources were provided to support follow-up of the PCBS's findings, giving former Commissioners assistance in drafting amendments from House legal advisers 'and one (excellent) person part time from the Scrutiny Unit'. To some extent, it could also draw on the resources of the Treasury Committee which had inherited relevant policy responsibilities from the PCBS and had the same chairman.[79] But as Tyrie explains, it is:

> [A] risk to assume that the relevant departmental or Lords Committees will want, and be able, to do the follow up work. As it happened, the Lords members of the PCBS were assiduous and committed in working with the Chairman to press the Government to move a very long way on a number of key issues. That the legislative follow up was largely successful should not, however, give any false comfort about how parliamentary resources were allocated to this work in the months after reporting.[80]

PLS, as a process, is 'comparatively young, but it supports many of the legitimate and growing expectations for transparent and better informed Government'.[81] Investing more in exploiting its potential benefits, for instance, as Tyrie suggests by fostering greater linkage between pre-legislative and legislative scrutiny, may offer one way of edging PLS into a mature and even more widely effective part of Parliament's law-making.

---

[78] The Rt Hon Andrew Tyrie MP, *The Poodle Bites Back: Select Committees and the Revival of Parliament* (Centre for Policy Studies, June 2015) paras 35–36.
[79] ibid para 37.
[80] ibid para 38.
[81] Lord Puttnam of Queensgate CBE, 'The Role and Importance of Pre-legislative Scrutiny in Parliamentary Life', Parliamentary Outreach Open Lecture (12 December 2012) www.parliament.uk/get-involved/outreach-and-training/resources-for-universities/teaching-resources/open-lecture-series/open-lectures/the-role-and-importance-of-pre-legislative-scrutiny-in-parliamentary-life.

4

Parliament's Constitutional Standards

JACK SIMSON CAIRD AND DAWN OLIVER[1]

I. INTRODUCTION

HOW CAN PARLIAMENTARY scrutiny of Government Bills be improved? Often the first answer to this question is to suggest *procedural* measures that provide parliamentarians with a greater opportunity to engage in parliamentary scrutiny, for example, by increased used of pre-legislative scrutiny[2] or through reform of public Bill committees.[3] The answer put forward in this chapter, the case for substantive parliamentary constitutional standards, is based on a different, albeit complementary logic, which seeks to improve the *substance* of Parliament's engagement with the difficult constitutional questions that frequently arise during the legislative process. The central argument of this chapter is that Parliament's own constitutional standards could and should provide a potentially vital normative focal point for all parliamentarians engaged in the scrutiny of provisions with constitutional implications.

The case for such a normative focal point within Parliament is based upon a conception of constitutionalism that regards politicians' engagement with constitutional values as a desirable feature of a constitutional system.[4] According to such a conception, constitutional values represent a political mechanism for holding the government to account for the substance of its legislative proposals and its use of the legislative process, which in turn can help to facilitate a culture of justification in place of the more traditional culture of authority and mandate.[5]

---

[1] We are grateful to a number of colleagues who have discussed the issues in this chapter with us or given us feedback on previous drafts: Sir Stephen Laws, Jessica Mulley, Steven Mark and Ben Yong.
[2] See discussion in ch 3; House of Lords Select Committee on the Constitution, *Parliament and the Legislative Process* (HL 2003–04, 178).
[3] M Russell, B Morris and P Larkin, *Fitting the Bill: Bringing Commons Legislation Committees in Line with Best Practice* (London, UCL Constitution Unit, 2013); C Hagelund and J Goddard, *How to Run a Country: A Parliament of Lawmakers* (London, Reform, 2015).
[4] D Feldman, '"Which in Your Case You Have Not Got": Constitutionalism at Home and Abroad' (2011) 64 *Current Legal Problems* 1.
[5] For more on the idea of a 'culture of justification', see E Mureinik, 'A Bridge to Where?: Introducing the Interim Bill of Rights' (1994) 10 *South African Journal of Human Rights* 31, 32; see also D Dyzenhaus, 'Law as Justification: Etienne Mureinik's Conception of Legal Culture' (1998) 10 *South African Journal*

In the UK, political accountability is not often associated with substantive constitutional norms, but this is beginning to change. A number of parliamentary committees engage in scrutiny of Bills, with overlapping constitutional remits. They cover the constitution at large (the House of Lords Constitution Committee),[6] the balance between primary and secondary legislation (the Delegated Powers and Regulatory Reform Committee—DPPRC)[7] and human rights (the Joint Committee on Human Rights—JCHR).[8]

Arguably, the impact of the JCHR, the DPPRC and the Constitution Committee on parliamentary scrutiny of Government Bills can in part be attributed to the fact that each has a specific normative focus. These committees, to different extents, articulate constitutional standards to be applied to *particular* Bills and draft Bills in the course of scrutiny. These standards could, and we argue should, form the basis of a set of codified constitutional standards for *general* application: they could be referred to by government, parliamentarians and the population at large to examine and assess the constitutional implications of Government Bills and the ways in which government manipulates the legislative process to minimise scrutiny and promote its proposals. This chapter draws upon our experience of codifying the constitutional standards of the House of Lords Select Committee on the Constitution (the Constitution Committee) for a Constitution Unit Report, the most recent edition of which was published in 2015.[9]

Four main characteristics of parliamentary constitutional standards are worth emphasising at this point. First, they are parliamentary in the sense that they are articulated by a parliamentary actor and not, for example, by judges or government or other outside bodies. Second, they are 'constitutional' because they are based on principles or norms relating to the working of constitutional relationships and procedures.[10] Third, they are not politically partisan. Fourth, they are

---

of Human Rights 11; M Hunt, 'Reshaping Constitutionalism' in J Morison, K McEvoy and G Anthony (eds), *Human Rights, Democracy and Transition: Essays in Honour of Stephen Livingstone* (Oxford, Oxford University Press, 2007); M Hunt, 'Introduction' in M Hunt, H Hooper and P Yowell (eds), *Parliaments and Human Rights* (Oxford, Hart Publishing, 2015).

[6] Its remit is 'to examine the constitutional implications of all public Bills coming before the House; and to keep under review the operation of the constitution'. House of Lords Constitution Committee, *Reviewing the Constitution: Terms of Reference and Method of Working* (HL 2001–02, 11) para 1.

[7] The DPPRC (particularly relevant in its scrutiny of delegated powers) was established in 1992 'to examine Bills before the Lords and report on powers proposed to be delegated to Ministers'.

[8] The JCHR was established in 2001 to examine matters relating to human rights in the UK (but excluding consideration of individual cases), proposals for remedial orders, draft remedial orders and remedial orders made under the Human Rights Act 1998 and, in respect of draft remedial orders and remedial orders, whether the special attention of the House should be drawn to them on any of the grounds specified in HC Standing Order No 151 (Statutory Instruments (Joint Committee)). See M Hunt 'The Joint Committee on Human Rights' in A Horne, D Oliver and G Drewry (eds), *Parliament and the Law* (Oxford, Hart Publishing, 2013).

[9] J Simson Caird, R Hazell and D Oliver, *The Constitutional Standards of the House of Lords Select Committee on the Constitution* 2nd edn (London, UCL Constitution Unit, 2015).

[10] A Kavanagh, *Constitutional Review under the UK Human Rights Act* (Cambridge, Cambridge University Press, 2009) 294.

not legally binding. They alert parliamentarians and others to their existence and the fact that proposals in a Bill or draft Bill appear to be in breach of them and therefore require government's justifications to be provided to Parliament.[11]

These characteristics indicate that parliamentary constitutional standards fit well with defining features of the UK constitution: they are political in origin and do not represent conditions of legal validity. Nonetheless, increasing their prominence within Parliament would represent a shift in the approach to parliamentary scrutiny within Westminster. They represent a move away from a purely reactive approach to scrutiny, which treats each Bill as a freestanding event, towards a more proactive approach, which regards scrutiny as an opportunity to develop and interpret normative principles. They also serve as an acknowledgment of the relevance of the normative content of the constitution to the task of parliamentary scrutiny. Wider and more general use of such standards would mitigate what are often regarded as weaknesses in scrutiny, representing a more principled and systematic approach to legislative scrutiny across Parliament.

The rest of this chapter is divided into three further sections. Section II covers both the nature of the problems that parliamentary constitutional standards are designed to address and the existing debate on the case for a code of standards within Parliament. Section III focuses on the standards developed by the House of Lords Constitution Committee, which are codified in the UCL Constitution Unit Report.[12] In section IV, we conclude with our reflections on these issues.

II. EVALUATING LEGISLATIVE SCRUTINY IN PARLIAMENT

The case for parliamentary constitutional standards rests on the belief that they would remedy some of the defects in the existing approach to legislative scrutiny in Parliament, in particular that the use of constitutional standards would improve the way that parliamentarians engage with the constitutional implications of bills. However, the case for standards must acknowledge that there is significant disagreement over whether there is in fact a problem with the existing approach to legislative scrutiny. Even those who agree that there are major weaknesses, particularly in relation to the current approach to scrutiny in the House of Commons, disagree on the precise nature of the problem and therefore on the solutions.[13] The case for parliamentary constitutional standards seeks to build on existing strengths of parliamentary scrutiny, particular certain features of the Lords' scrutiny of the constitutional implications of Government Bills, and yet there is no consensus that this represents an appropriate template for enhancing scrutiny. Engaging with these arguments against the use of constitutional standards is

---

[11] D Feldman, 'Parliamentary Scrutiny of Legislation and Human Rights' [2002] *Public Law* 323.
[12] Simson Caird, Hazell and Oliver (n 9).
[13] See, eg, M Russell, D Glover and K Wolter, 'Does the Executive Dominate the Westminster Legislative Process?: Six Reasons for Doubt' (2015) 68 *Parliamentary Affairs* 1.

important because it reveals the competing constitutional rationales at the heart of the debate on how to improve the scrutiny of legislation in Parliament.

A legitimate basis for opposing the use of parliamentary constitutional standards might be that they fundamentally conflict with other constitutional norms that underpin the existing role of legislative scrutiny in Parliament, namely that of effective and responsible government,[14] and the connected norm that the elected government must be able to get its legislative business through,[15] both of which are central to the workings of the House of Commons in particular. According to this position, the current arrangements work well and achieve an appropriate balance; moves to increase the autonomy of the House of Commons from government and, for example, to improve the quality and impact of scrutiny in Public Bill Committees is either wrong-headed or at least at odds with the UK's traditions of parliamentary government.

By contrast, there are those who think that the House of Commons in particular should be able to put up a much sterner test of the government's legislative proposals: on that basis, the adoption of constitutional standards could represent a significant improvement. However, as we discuss below, some of those who support reform in principle might object on the basis that the content of such standards would represent an inappropriately politically prejudiced, even if not politically partisan, approach to legislative scrutiny. Thus, the case for parliamentary constitutional standards fits into a wider debate about changes in the nature and interpretations of constitutionalism in the UK.[16]

A. The House of Lords

Part of the argument for the use of constitutional standards in Parliament, including in the House of Commons, is based upon our understanding of the factors that contribute to the effectiveness of the scrutiny in the House of Lords. The Lords' scrutiny of Government Bills is, in the eyes of many, a success story of Parliament in the twenty-first century thus far.[17] As Russell identifies in her extensive analysis of the Lords and as Norton notes in Chapter 6 below, this success can be attributed to a number of political, institutional and procedural factors.[18] The potential for

---

[14] A Birch, *Representative and Responsible Government* (London, Allen & Unwin, 1964).
[15] This norm is most evident in the practice of prioritising government business in the House of Commons. See Standing Order 14(1) of the House of Commons: 'Save as provided in this order, government business shall have precedence at every sitting'.
[16] See, eg, S Gardbaum, *Commonwealth Constitutionalism* (Cambridge, Cambridge University Press, 2013); A Kavanagh, 'The Joint Committee on Human Rights: A Hybrid Breed of Constitutional Watchdog' in Hunt, Hooper and Yowell (n 5).
[17] See ch 6 below.
[18] M Russell, *The Contemporary House of Lords* (Oxford, Oxford University Press, 2013); see also ch 6 below.

defeat in the Lords, where governments do not enjoy a majority, means that the Government often has to win the vote by rational argument rather than rely on party loyalty and discipline.[19] But another important factor is the normative focus on constitutional values in the arguments put forward in the Lords in the scrutiny of bills, both on the floor of the House and in its committees.[20] A significant number of peers have expertise in the constitutional values that should be applied to Government Bills and are able to translate such analysis into workable arguments and amendments. The Lords have institutionalised this normative expertise through their legislative scrutiny committees, which are able to interpret and analyse the constitutional implications of Bills. This focus has had a tangible impact. The greatest 'hits' of the Lords in terms of scrutiny in the 2010–15 Parliament illustrate the point: the Public Bodies Bill,[21] the Fixed-term Parliaments Bill,[22] the Justice and Security Bill,[23] and the Crime and Courts Bill.[24] Each of these Bills had important constitutional implications and was subject to significant changes in the Lords. But the successes of the Lords do not mean that Parliament should rely exclusively on individual peers and committees such as the DPRRC for the scrutiny process; in fact, there are good reasons to suggest that the House of Commons too could and should perform such a role.

B. The House of Commons

In contrast to the Lords, the House of Commons' contribution to parliamentary scrutiny of Bills and draft Bills has not improved to any great degree in the twenty-first century. Members of Parliament (MPs) are more rebellious than they were in the twentieth century, but in terms of scrutinising the detail of Bills, a 'culture of resistance' within government remains.[25] The Government's majority in the House of Commons combined with the institutional rules and conventions that prioritise government business result in a situation where the Government is rarely forced to accept an amendment against its own will.[26] The extent of the Government's

---

[19] D Pannick, '"Respect for Law and Sausages": How Parliament Made Section 31 of the Growth and Infrastructure Act 2013 on the Sale of Employment Rights' (2014) 85 *Political Quarterly* 43, 47.
[20] M Russell, *The Contemporary House of Lords* (Oxford, Oxford University Press, 2013) 187.
[21] J Simson Caird, 'Parliamentary Constitutional Review: Ten Years of the House of Lords Select Committee on the Constitution' [2012] *Public Law* 7.
[22] M Ryan, 'The Fixed-term Parliaments Act 2011' [2012] *Public Law* 213, 215.
[23] T Hickman, 'Turning Out the Lights? The Justice and Security Act 2013' UK Constitutional Law Blog (11 June 2013), http://ukconstitutionallaw.org.
[24] UK Human Rights Blog, 'Three Strikes and Out? Major Defeats for Government Judicial Review Reform Plans in the Lords' (28 October 2014), http://ukhumanrightsblog.com.
[25] L Thompson, 'More of the Same or a Period of Change? The Impact of Bill Committees in the Twenty-First Century House of Commons' (2012) 66 *Parliamentary Affairs* 19; P Cowley, *The Rebels: How Blair Mislaid His Majority* (London, Politico's, 2005).
[26] Thompson (n 25); Russell, Glover and Wolter (n 13).

domination of the legislative process in the Commons is contested, particularly on the grounds that the predominance of government amendments in the Commons should not be taken to mean that MPs have little or no influence.[27] In reality, many government amendments in the Commons can be sourced to points raised by MPs, and proponents of the government domination thesis sometimes understate the influence of MPs and oversimplify the dynamics in the Commons.[28]

The culture of resistance, however, refers to more than just the levels of MPs' influence. It refers to the attitude of successive governments to the legislative process: control of the drafting of a Bill is fiercely guarded by government, and the Government takes a defensive and 'power hoarding' rather than consensual and 'power sharing' approach to the parliamentary process.[29] Rather than see the process as an opportunity to improve a Bill, the Government regards backbench amendments as 'concessions' that are to be managed to minimise changes to a Bill and is often reluctant to respond constructively to proposed amendments. The approach of the Government to Public Bill Committees is where this approach is most evident. This is where careful line-by-line scrutiny takes in place in the Commons. The Government's majority in these committees means that even well-crafted and sensible amendments, designed to enhance rather than weaken a Bill, can be rejected out of hand in the Commons. The identity of the parliamentarian moving an amendment, and the level of support within the relevant chamber for the change, is and should be relevant to the Government's attitude towards the amendment. But amendments moved in the Commons by the Opposition are often given short shrift, only for similar amendments to be accepted in the Lords. Such an approach sends a damaging message to potential scrutineers in the Commons, and serves as a disincentive to invest time and energy in the difficult tasks of crafting amendments that could improve a Bill, and particularly the constitutional implications of a Bill.

This approach to the legislative process and procedures also marginalises many MPs. When Government Bills are scrutinised in the Commons, the Government is often reluctant to reveal its own detailed justifications for certain clauses. The absence of the risk of defeat removes the incentive to reveal the full arguments for the detail of a Bill to its political opponents.[30] Such defensiveness prioritises political point-scoring over effective legislative scrutiny. The Government does now produce memoranda on delegated powers and human rights for the relevant committees, but the failure to reveal in anything resembling frank terms the legal

---

[27] ibid; M Russell and P Cowley, 'The Policy Power of the Westminster Parliament: The "Parliamentary State" and the Empirical Evidence' (2016) 29 (1) *Governance* 121; M Russell, D Gover and K Wollter, 'Does the Executive Dominate the Westminster Legislative Process?: Six Reasons for Doubt' (2015) *Parliamentary Affairs* (forthcoming).
[28] Russell and Cowley (n 27).
[29] A King, *The British Constitution* (Oxford, Oxford University Press, 2009).
[30] See Hagelund and Goddard (n 3).

or constitutional basis of its legislative choices is detrimental to both transparency and the whole enterprise of scrutiny.[31] The dominance of the culture of resistance and the adversarial approach to scrutiny in the Commons do not leave much room for a consensual, principled and detailed approach to scrutiny of legislation to develop. Both discourage questions that relate to the substance and detail of the Bill, and how it could be improved. The sustained resistance by governments to the creation of permanent specialist legislative committees in the Commons should also be seen as partly motivated by the desire of successive governments to preserve this culture of resistance.[32]

This traditional governmental approach encourages the prevailing adversarial approach to scrutiny in the Commons. We are all used to the highly partisan and generally 'at large' and often unstructured scrutiny process that takes place in Public Bill Committees, and on the floor of the House of Commons in second reading debates and at report stage. In turn, this adversarial and partisan approach to scrutiny discourages the Government from changing its approach, because it knows that acceptance of a constructive critique of a Bill is likely to be turned into a broader political point.

To criticise the substance of much of this form of scrutiny is not to say that it is worthless: far from it. It is entirely appropriate that partisan, 'at large' scrutiny should take place in the House of Commons; it is part of the process of the giving or refusing of consent to legislation by our elected representatives. The importance of this role is emphasised to this day in the words of enactment 'by and with the advice and consent' of Parliament.

And despite the many criticisms of the process, scrutiny in the House of Commons is taken very seriously both in the House and in government. In evidence to the Political and Constitutional Reform Committee in 2012, David Cook, Second Parliamentary Counsel, emphasised that the parliamentary scrutiny process is very meaningful and has the advantage that 'the legislation is out there and able to be commented on, not just within Parliament but with groups outside Parliament … before it becomes its final form. That ultimately does produce better legislation'.[33]

There is no principled reason why the 'at large' political form of debate in the House of Commons should not be supplemented by detailed and more consensual line-by-line scrutiny, for example, by select committees, which focuses on the *substance* of the proposed change to the law and its implications for constitutional norms or principles. Indeed, the House of Lords often manages to combine

---

[31] This compares particularly badly with the Swedish Government's approach to the legislative process, where its legal advice on the constitutional basis of a Bill is published for all to read as standard; see T Bull and I Cameron, 'Legislative Rights Review: A View from Sweden' in Hunt, Hooper and Yowell (n 5).
[32] See Russell, Morris and Larkin (n 3) 18–29.
[33] Political and Constitutional Reform Committee, *Ensuring Standards in the Quality of Legislation* (HC 2013–14, 85) Evidence 11.

the two.³⁴ In the Commons, when detailed line-by-line scrutiny takes place in Public Bill Committees, the debates often focus on the merits or demerits of the policy behind a Bill, in part because of the lack of incentives to take a more constructive approach. There are fairly stringent limits on the admissibility of amendments tabled in Public Bill Committees in the Commons:³⁵ amendments should not undermine the central features of a Bill or be outside of the scope of the Bill. The limits on admissibility of amendments during the committee stage are designed to discourage debate on the merits of the policy behind the Bill, which have already been voted on and accepted at second reading. The problem is that in practice, the debates are not always in line with the rationale that underpins the procedure.

It might be said that the limitations of line-by-line scrutiny in the House of Commons are not a problem because of the Lords' role within the legislative process, and that the two chambers should not duplicate each other. This argument has some superficial appeal, but it ignores a number of factors. First and foremost, MPs are elected representatives, and therefore scrutiny within the House of Commons would have strong democratic legitimacy which is lacking in the unelected and appointed Lords. The combination of democratic legitimacy *and* effective legislative scrutiny, particularly scrutiny based on constitutional norms, which only the House of Commons can provide, is worth striving for. If elected representatives can be responsible for effective checks and balances on the legislative power of the government, then this serves to relieve what Tushnet refers to as the tension between self-governance and constitutionalism.³⁶ Elected parliamentarians holding the Government to account using the very principles and procedures that underpin the political process is surely what a system that subscribes to UK-style political constitutionalism should facilitate.³⁷

The issue is not simply of academic concern. The House of Lords' lack of democratic legitimacy means that the Lords' ability to defend constitutional values is limited by their own and others' recognition of the primacy of the House of Commons. The infrequent need for the Government to resort to the Parliament Acts 1911 and 1949 is testament to this. So is the Lords' reluctance to vote down secondary or delegated legislation. Developing standards-based scrutiny of Government Bills in the Commons would not amount to unnecessary duplication of the work of the Lords, but instead would represent a progress towards a system of democratically legitimate constitutional scrutiny in Westminster.

---

³⁴ See M Russell, *The Contemporary House of Lords* (Oxford, Oxford University Press, 2013) ch 5.
³⁵ M Jack and TE May (eds), *Erskine May's Treatise on the Law, Privileges, Proceedings and Usage of Parliament* 24th edn (London, LexisNexis, 2011) ch 27.
³⁶ M Tushnet, 'Interpretation in Legislatures and Courts: Incentives and Institutional Design' in R Bauman and T Kahana (eds), *The Least Examined Branch: The Role of Legislatures in the Constitutional State* (Cambridge, Cambridge University Press, 2006) 355.
³⁷ See M Goldoni, 'Political Constitutionalism and the Value of Constitution Making' (2014) 27 *Ratio Juris* 387, 397; JAG Griffith, 'The Political Constitution' (1979) 42 *Modern Law Review* 1.

C. The Debate about Standards

In response to these and other concerns, interest in the use of standards against which Bills and draft Bills are or should be scrutinised in Parliament has been growing. This is noteworthy because the basic idea of a code or set of generic legislative or specifically constitutional standards conflicts with a range of influential alternative perspectives on how legislative scrutiny should be conducted in Parliament. Central to such perspectives is the idea that parliamentarians' approach to scrutiny should be determined purely and simply by the natural flow of political debate. According to this view, any code of standards applied to Government Bills is likely to be useless for at least two reasons. First, the content of such standards would inescapably be based on particular political agendas, and therefore would not be supported by a consensus in Parliament, and therefore would not be fit for purpose.[38] Second, if the content of the standards were drafted in neutral ways so as to maximise the chances of parliamentary support, they would then be too bland to enhance scrutiny; the only chance of rescuing such bland principles would be through interpretation, which would result in their operation being characterised by interpretive disputes dominated by lawyers, and this would not represent an improvement on the status quo.[39] Despite these arguments, a number of proposals for the use of standards have come from parliamentary committees, voluntary sector organisations, influential think tanks and academics in a relatively short period.

The House of Lords Constitution Committee in its 2003–04 report on *The Legislative Process*[40] recommended the use of a clear and transparent checklist by committees engaged in legislative scrutiny as well as by committees at other stages of the legislative process in order to ensure a more systematic approach to scrutiny.[41] The government response was on the face of it neutral: that this was a matter for the two Houses.[42]

In 2004, Robert Hazell made the important point that the work of three committees—the DPRRC, the Constitution Committee and the JCHR—took the debate on the legal and constitutional values within Bills out of the privacy of internal government negotiations and placed it within the more transparent parliamentary forum.[43] This argument highlights one of the main benefits of applying constitutional standards within Parliament. The standards serve to

---

[38] See Political and Constitutional Reform Committee, *Ensuring Standards in the Quality of Legislation: Government Response to the Committee's First Report of Session 2013–14—Political and Constitutional Reform* (HC 2013–14, 611).
[39] ibid.
[40] House of Lords Constitution Committee, *Parliament and the Legislative Process* (HL 2003–04, 178).
[41] ibid paras 54, 57.
[42] ibid para 21.
[43] R Hazell, 'Who is the Guardian of Legal Values in the Legislative Process: Parliament or the Executive?' [2004] *Public Law* 495.

generate disagreement that can then prompt the Government to reveal the reasons behind the detail within its Bills so that they can be questioned and tested in a public forum—for example, why a Henry VIII power was needed or why a purpose clause was not included. By doing this, Parliament contributes both to the transparency of the legislative process and to the Government's accountability.

In 2006 in *Public Law*, Hazell analysed the parliamentary procedure for passing constitutional legislation between 1997 and 2005, including occasions on which Bills had been considered by a Committee of the Whole House (CWH), as being of 'first class constitutional importance'.[44] He noted 'how difficult it is to deduce any reliable rules' for determining whether a Bill meets the criteria for CWH consideration. He proposed the adoption of a new set of technical conventions to safeguard constitutional change (publication of Green and/or White Papers, cross-party talks, consultation, publication of Bills in draft, public Bill committees empowered to call evidence, the use of checklists to ensure systematic scrutiny etc). Hazell concluded that: 'The committee which is best placed to develop a set of scrutiny standards for constitutional bills is the Lords Constitution Committee.'[45]

As we shall see, this Committee has in effect developed a set of such standards in an incremental way since it was established in 2001.[46] Also in 2006 in *Public Law*, Dawn Oliver made the case for increased use of scrutiny standards through a comparison with how scrutiny standards and checklists are used in other jurisdictions.[47] The article called for a code of parliamentary standards to be developed on the basis of the Constitution Committee's reports. These contributions to *Public Law* formed the foundations of the Constitution Unit and Constitution Society project on constitutional standards discussed in the next section.

In 2010, the Hansard Society recommended the creation of a legislative standards committee and a code of legislative standards in its book *Making Better Law*.[48] In recent evidence to the House of Commons' Political and Constitutional Reform Committee (PCRC), the Hansard Society put the case in the following terms:

> At present, however, there is no means within the legislative process simply to evaluate and confirm the need for fresh legislation and there is no way of imposing a quality standard on the production of a Bill before it is sent to Parliament. A strong case therefore exists for establishing new ground rules to rebalance the legislative relationship between Parliament and government, establishing a consensual approach predicated on mutual acceptance of common standards of legislative consultation, preparation and scrutiny.[49]

The Hansard Society emphasised the need for Parliament, and the House of Commons in particular, to set these standards themselves, and to play an active role

---

[44] R Hazell, 'Time for a New Convention: Parliamentary Scrutiny of Constitutional Bills 1997–2005' [2006] *Public Law* 247.
[45] ibid 297.
[46] These form the basis of discussion in section III, below.
[47] D Oliver, 'Improving the Scrutiny of Bills: The Case for Standards and Checklists' [2006] *Public Law* 219.
[48] R Fox and M Korris, *Making Better Law* (London, Hansard Society, 2010)
[49] Political and Constitutional Reform Committee (n 33) Evidence w18 para 5.

in setting the terms of the checks and balances on the Government. Also in 2010, the Better Government Initiative's publication *Good Government* recommended the use of 11 principles of good legislation, and recommended that Parliament and the House of Commons should use them to improve the rigour and quality of legislative scrutiny.[50]

A significant input to the debate came in the form of the PCRC report *Ensuring Standards in the Quality of Legislation*.[51] This report, published in 2013, recommended the use of a code of legislative standards, which would be enforced by a Joint Legislative Standards Committee. The PCRC argued that a code of good legislative standards should be agreed between Parliament and the Government to ensure that Bills comply with agreed technical and procedural criteria—for instance, purpose or overview clauses, new definitions of legal concepts, index clauses for definitions and formulae.

A Draft Code of Legislative Standards was annexed to the report.[52] The standards focused primarily on procedural matters, but did include some relating to the constitutional content of a Bill, for example, requiring the Government to indicate if there are any Henry VIII powers in the Bill. The standards in the code were not substantive in the sense of expressing constitutional principles, but focused rather on the provision of information (although without justifications) to Parliament (for instance, on whether the Bill has constitutional implications, the policy objectives and desired outcomes, and consultation). The PCRC explained the reasons behind the decision to avoid obligatory language and substantive standards in the following terms: that 'an objective set of quality standards' is necessary 'to compare and judge bills and Acts', but it is important that the standards within the code are 'politically neutral'.[53] The Committee added that the normative standards should 'require policy to be explained by reference to the contents of the Bill, without questioning the substance of the policy'.[54]

The Committee's recommendation for a code was rejected by the Government out of hand: 'The Government does not believe that a Code of Legislative Standards is necessary or would be effective in ensuring quality legislation.'[55] The Government's supporting analysis is worth unpicking. Part of its response essentially argued that the legislative processes that take place before the parliamentary stage are not the business of Parliament.[56] This line of argument is emblematic of a commitment to the culture of resistance that limits the effectiveness of scrutiny in the Commons. The Government added that impact assessments and explanatory notes (which were and still are in the process of being revised) provide sufficient

---

[50] Better Government Initiative, *Good Government* (2010).
[51] Political and Constitutional Reform Committee (n 33).
[52] ibid Annex A.
[53] Political and Constitutional Reform Committee (n 33) paras 55–58.
[54] ibid.
[55] Political and Constitutional Reform Committee (n 38) 2.
[56] ibid 2–3.

information on the content of a Bill.[57] Further, it argued that a code of standards would risk 'encouraging a tick-box mentality'. This criticism is hard to sustain. The PCRC's code was not intended to supplant other forms of scrutiny; rather, the aim was to ensure that the Government was pressurised to provide important information that could form the basis of scrutiny. The PCRC's standards would not diminish or weaken scrutiny in Parliament. Further, if tick-box exercises are undesirable, then why does the Government use them for impact assessments and in other internal guidance in its preparation of bills? Finally, the Government questioned whether the standards were sufficiently objective:

> Nor can a Code, as proposed by then Committee, provide the degree of objectivity it envisages: questions such as 'is it understandable and accessible?' and 'whether the change is politically or legally important' indicate the extent to which the quality of legislation is a subjective judgement. Similarly, whether purpose clauses or sunset clauses are required to meet the expected 'standard' will always be a matter for debate on a case by case basis rather than an objective test. This underlines the difficulty any committee would have in separating the quality of legislation from the policy underlying it.[58]

This strand of the Government's response gets to the heart of the debate on the desirability of constitutional standards: its position is that legislative scrutiny is political activity which should not be constrained by a set of predetermined standards which purport to be neutral, but which are in fact politically prejudiced. The argument also highlights the difficulty of the PCRC's position on the objectivity of its own standards. The Government's response outmanoeuvred the PCRC, but at the same time rather unfairly mischaracterised the PCRC's case for standards. The aim of any set of standards is to extract specific forms of justification for the drafting or handling of a Bill from the Government, so that a political judgment, albeit not necessarily a partisan one, can be formed on what the Government has put forward. The Government was right to point out that whether or not the standards should be followed will be a political judgment determined on a case-by-case basis. But this does not negate the value of standards themselves; on the contrary, providing the opportunity for such a political judgment is the main reason for introducing a set of standards.

The normativity of the UK constitution has long divided constitutional lawyers,[59] but the political reality of today's Parliament is that constitutional norms, in both codified and uncodified form, are increasingly prominent in parliamentary debate and within government itself. These constitutional norms, be they substantive or procedural, are not politically partisan, but neither are they universally regarded as politically 'neutral'. They are the norms that condition the liberal democratic nature of our political system, but they can be interpreted in

---

[57] ibid.
[58] ibid.
[59] See S Lakin, 'Defending and Contesting the Sovereignty of Law: The Public Lawyer as Interpretivist' (2015) 78 *Modern Law Review* 549.

many different ways and are rightly often the subject of political debate. When the Constitution Committee raises the rule of law, or when the JCHR engages Article 8 of the European Convention on Human Rights (ECHR), the Government does not refuse to respond on the basis that the principles are 'subjective'. The existence of disagreement on the meaning and significance of these norms, or of the standards in PCRC's code, should not be taken as evidence that they cannot play a positive role in scrutiny; in fact, the opposite is true. The risk of this focus on neutrality in the Commons is that the Lords and the Government will be left as the dominant actors in the debate on the constitutional implications of bills.

D. The Human Rights Act 1998

A prominent example of the value of codification of principles for parliamentary scrutiny can be found in the form of the Human Rights Act 1998 (HRA). Setting aside the important role of the courts in the HRA for the purpose of this argument, the basic framework of the HRA involves a codified set of constitutional norms; this facilitates a dialogue about the meanings of the rights and their implications for Government Bills between the Government and Parliament, and internal dialogues within both.[60] It has important effects 'upstream' in government before a Bill reaches Parliament. Section 19 HRA requires the Minister in charge of a Bill to make a statement of compatibility. Internal guidance in the *Cabinet Guide to Making Legislation* indicates that the Bill team should develop the Government's reasoning in relation to any possible rights-based issues.[61] Further, this guidance is in part designed to anticipate the rights issues that are likely to be raised in Parliament, particularly by the JCHR.

Thus the JCHR and section 19 HRA together create incentives for government to articulate the rights implications of their legislation and to explain their justifications for any interference with qualified rights. The value of this negotiation process between government and Parliament has been well-documented in the literature on the JCHR.[62] In the early days of the JCHR, the Government took a defensive approach to section 19 and did not provide much in the way of detailed justification for its rights-based evaluations, but following pressure from the JCHR, it began to issue human rights memoranda in order to inform Parliament's and, in particular, the JCHR's scrutiny of the Bill. This practice has significantly

---

[60] See, eg, Hunt, Hooper and Yowell (n 5); M Hunt, H Hooper and P Yowell, *Parliaments and Human Rights: Redressing the democratic deficit* (AHRC, 2012); J Hiebert, 'Governing under the Human Rights Act: The Limitations of Wishful Thinking' [2012] *Public Law* 29. A Sathanapally, *Beyond Disagreement* (Oxford, Oxford University Press, 2012); D Feldman, 'The Impact of Human Rights on the UK Legislative Process' (2004) 25 *Statute Law Review* 91, 104–15; J Hiebert, 'Parliament and the Human Rights Act: Can the JCHR Help Facilitate a Culture of Rights?' (2006) 4 *International Journal of Constitutional Law* 1.
[61] The Cabinet Office, *The Cabinet Guide to Making Legislation* (2014) 11.25.
[62] See n 60 above.

enhanced the Government's accountability for the rights implications of the detail of its legislation. For these purposes, it is important to emphasise that the engagement with and negotiation on the rights-based implications of a Bill are in part facilitated by the codification of the rights within the HRA. The rights serve as a site for negotiation, a point emphasised by Webber, within both government and Parliament, and most critically in the dialogue between them once a Bill is introduced to Parliament.[63] Codified norms enforced politically through Parliament have managed, at least in part, to overcome the culture of resistance within government and to achieve a shift towards a culture of justification.

The HRA demonstrates that clearly articulated normative standards are central to the achievement of influence 'upstream' in government. The Government's ability to anticipate the reasoning within Parliament on a particular point, by reference to the prior parliamentary interpretation of a norm, creates a feedback loop that enhances the scrutiny process. If Parliament takes defined positions on matters relating to the constitutionality of Government Bills, then this creates a clear incentive for the Government to engage with and anticipate the issues likely to be raised during the passage of a Bill.

One of the limitations of the HRA, in terms of its influence in Parliament, is that the primary interpreters of the rights in the ECHR are the courts. In particular, the role of the European Court of Human Rights creates a political issue, which rightly or wrongly hinders MPs' engagement with Convention rights. By contrast, there is a range of constitutional norms rooted in the political process, and particularly the legislative process, which can and should be negotiated between government and Parliament as Convention rights are. There would be good reasons to judge Parliament and government harshly for a failure to give effect to the constitutional norms that underpin the effective operation of the legislative process. It seems odd that successive governments repeatedly promote their commitment to the rule of law and other constitutional principles in a range of contexts, and yet the norms that these principles reflect are not currently systematically articulated or defended within the House of Commons.

III. THE CONSTITUTIONAL STANDARDS OF THE HOUSE OF LORDS CONSTITUTION COMMITTEE

The focus of this section of the chapter is an analysis of the Constitution Unit Report, *The Constitutional Standards of the House of Lords Select Committee on the Constitution* (2015),[64] which sets out a code of constitutional standards based on the reports of the House of Lords' Constitution Committee from 2001 to 2015. First, this section examines the main characteristics of the code. Second, it details

---

[63] G Webber, *The Negotiable Constitution* (Cambridge, Cambridge University Press, 2009).
[64] Simson Caird, Hazell and Oliver (n 9).

two examples of bills from the 2010–15 Parliament that might have benefited from scrutiny based on a code of constitutional standards, particularly in the House of Commons.

A. The Code

The code of constitutional standards is based on the reports of the Constitution Committee since its creation in 2001. We (with Robert Hazell) extracted the standards that are articulated in the Committee's reports and organised them into a code. The code is divided into five sections: the rule of law, delegated powers, the separation of powers, individual rights and parliamentary procedure. Even though the Committee may not have intended to set out constitutional standards for general application, the code demonstrates that many of their recommendations are relevant beyond the specific Bill to which they relate. The Committee frequently refers to its previous reports and builds upon earlier analysis of particular norms. Thought of in these terms, the Committee's output can be understood as a form of 'legisprudence'.[65] This challenges the idea that parliaments are incapable of the sort of normative and interpretive reasoning that is normally associated with courts. The Constitution Committee, like the courts, operates within a normative framework which it has sought to articulate and develop. This code serves as a useful resource for understanding the Constitution Committee's interpretation of the constitution. The code could therefore be used on an informal basis as a tool to analyse legislative proposals, in the absence of formal adoption or endorsement by anyone in Parliament.

Three characteristics of the code stand out. First, the standards demonstrate a focus on justification. Many of the norms articulated by the Committee are not inviolable rules, things that cannot be done, but rather they identify legislative choices that demand specific forms of justification from government. For example, standard 1.1.7 states that 'retrospective legislation should only be used when there is a compelling reason to do so'. In another report, the Committee was specific about the nature of justification required: standard 1.1.8 states that 'a legislative power to make a provision which has retrospective effect should be justified on the basis of necessity and not of desirability'. This use of the language of proportionality, the test used by UK courts in the context of qualified rights protected by the ECHR, is well-suited to the context of the legislative process. The reality of the UK constitution dictates that constitutional principles can be departed from, but best constitutional practice, as identified by the Committee, is that government should specify its reasons for doing so. Too frequently, government relies on the language of authority in defending the decision to depart from constitutional principle. The Committee's approach to justification recognises this

---

[65] Oliver (n 47) 243.

and sets out conditions which have substantive implications for the content of bills. For example, standard 2.4.2 states that 'ministerial assurances as to the purpose of order-making powers are not a substitute for legal safeguards on the face of a Bill'. If Parliament accepted such assurances, this would set a potentially damaging precedent, which would allow the creation of broadly conceived powers that would outlive the authority of the government responsible for their introduction.

Perhaps the most important contribution of the Committee's development of justificatory standards is in the context of Bills that seek to achieve significant constitutional change. Governments can and do rely upon their electoral credentials as sufficient justification of significant changes to the constitution. This is not necessarily problematic, in the sense that few would deny that a majority in the House of Commons is sufficient to effect constitutional change. However, this 'democratic' legitimacy does not defeat the expectation that government's proposals for constitutional change should be accompanied by the very highest standard of justification. Thus, the Committee has set out precise and exacting standards for constitutional change. Standard 5.3.1 demands a written ministerial statement to be presented upon the introduction of a Bill, which explains: the impact of the proposal upon the constitution; the nature of the public consultation performed; the nature of the scrutiny of the proposals within government; and details of any pre-legislative scrutiny.

The recent history of constitutional change is littered with examples of proposals that would have benefited from both greater parliamentary engagement with the potential impact upon existing constitutional arrangements and from pre-legislative scrutiny. There is a clear logic for governments to bring forward constitutional change proposals early in the life of a Parliament: to capitalise on the post-election glow; and to ensure that changes get an opportunity to bed in during the course of a Parliament. The problem is that this logic conflicts with Parliament's duty to ensure that constitutional change is thoroughly scrutinised and, in particular, that it is examined in the context of the overall constitutional framework. The Government has resisted the provision to Parliament of a memorandum on constitutional issues, even though such an analysis is probably produced and circulated within government. Again, this is emblematic of the Government's desire to hold on to a culture of resistance, even in the face of compelling arguments for a different approach based upon justification from within Parliament.

Second, the Committee's standards draw upon and develop the normative foundations of parliamentary government.[66] Constitutional lawyers are naturally inclined to highlight the constitutional principles developed by the courts. On the other hand, parliamentary scholars and political scientists have a tendency to downplay the significance of the normative framework that regulates scrutiny within Parliament. The distinctive *parliamentary* character of the norms

---

[66] See J Griffith, 'The Place of Parliament in the Legislative Process' (1951) 14 *Modern Law Review* 425, 435–36.

articulated by the Committee is a reminder that the parliamentary legislative process is itself underpinned by a normative framework that can and should be harnessed by those engaged in legislative scrutiny. This character is prominent in the standards relating to the boundary between primary and secondary legislation. For example, standard 2.3.8 states that: 'Rules that are central to a Bill of constitutional significance should be to the greatest extent possible on the face of a Bill, so allowing full legislative amendment and debate.' The primary law-making process within Parliament, rather than any secondary law-making procedure, is the proper place for the creation of laws with constitutional implications. The Committee's motivation is clear. The position taken is necessary to safeguard Parliament's role within the constitution and to prevent government from escaping the parliamentary safeguards that are central to the rationale of the primary law-making process.

The Committee's standards that refer to sunset clauses also demonstrate the value of the distinctively parliamentary character of their constitutional analysis. When inserted into a Bill, a sunset clause ensures that the legal validity of a statutory provision will lapse unless it is subject to positive endorsement in the form of a vote from Parliament.[67] Standard 3.2.10 states that 'ministerial assurances are no substitute for a statutory sunset clause' and standard 3.2.11 sets out that 'sunset clauses should be included when provisions are introduced for reasons of expediency in one session ahead of a Bill on the same subject that is forthcoming'. The rationale for both of these standards is to keep law within the reach of parliamentary scrutiny. The parliamentary character of the Committee's analysis is defined by a focus upon setting clear rules to regulate the relationship between Parliament and government. A distinctively parliamentary perspective recognises the competing priorities of each body and seeks to draw boundaries that can be used to highlight when a shift in power between the two is likely to occur. This demonstrates why a distinct and independent parliamentary perspective on constitutional values is so vital to effective legislative scrutiny.

Third, the standards serve to specify the meanings of constitutional principles and procedures as applicable in the context of legislative scrutiny. Many of the standards in the code specify detailed rules that are more easily applied to Bills than broadly framed constitutional principles would be. In the context of the rule of law, standard 1.1.6 states that 'laws should not prevent a court from deciding pending litigation according its merits on the basis of the law in force at the time when the proceedings were commenced'. Whilst some may dispute this rule, the implications for those engaged in scrutiny of a Bill are crystal clear. Clauses with constitutional implications are often buried within bills, and standards such as this make the process of identifying such clauses easier. In the context of delegated

---

[67] A provision in a Bill that gives it an 'expiry date' once it is passed into law. 'Sunset clauses' are included in legislation when it is felt that Parliament should have the chance to decide on its merits again after a fixed period, see Glossary on Parliament's website: www.parliament.uk/site-information/glossary/sunset-clause.

powers, standard 2.2.4 states that: 'Henry VIII powers that relate to constitutionally sensitive subject-matter should use a super-affirmative parliamentary procedure.' The value of this example of specification is that the standard provides a realistic solution to compensate for a departure from constitutional principle. In the legislative process, access to such constructive solutions is a precious commodity for persuading others of the way forward.

B. Advantages of a Code and Examples

A code of soft law parliamentary constitutional norms, such as that in the report, does not attempt to minimise political conflict, as Griffith claimed constitutional 'rights' would do.[68] Many of the norms, partly through their specification and demand for particular levels of justification from government, serve to increase political conflict on the detail of a Bill by drawing attention to issues that otherwise might be overlooked. The code therefore has the potential, through this disagreement, to puncture the culture of resistance that is so damaging to scrutiny.

The Government's reluctance to reveal in frank terms the reasoning that underpins the constitutional implications of Bills is arguably not justifiable either in the context of the legislative process (in the sense of communicating the legal effect of change in the law) or in the constitutional context of the duty to engage in serious deliberation on changes to the constitution. A code of constitutional standards could prompt the Government to produce the sort of memorandum that is offered to the JCHR on the ECHR implications of a Bill and to the DPRRC on delegated powers, and which has been demanded by the Constitution Committee. But even if it did not prompt such memoranda, the systematic use of the sort of code discussed here by committees in both Houses of Parliament would inevitably prompt the Government to consider in advance of introduction whether their legislative proposals would conflict with the relevant standards. Furthermore, the code would provide a resource for all parliamentarians engaged in scrutiny, which would both enable them to identify constitutional issues within a Bill and remind them of the constitutional position taken by the relevant committee in response. The following examples are designed to give a sense of the potential benefits in both Houses of the adoption of a code similar to that in the report.

C. Example 1: The Fixed-term Parliaments Act 2011

Brazier described the passage of the Fixed-term Parliaments Act (FTPA) 2011 as 'constitution-making at its worst'.[69] New governments pushing important

---

[68] Griffith (n 37).
[69] R Brazier, 'A Small Piece of Constitution History' (2012) 128 *Law Quarterly Review* 315, 315.

constitutional changes through Parliament in a hurry is not unusual, but the passage of the FTPA served to highlight many of the shortcomings in the current approach to constitutional change. Many of the problems could be described as procedural: the absence of pre-legislative scrutiny, the lack of public consultation and the speed of the passage through Parliament. But the problems with passage of the FTPA could also be attributed to failings in the substantive constitutional analysis of the provisions within Parliament. Some of these failures were of course a by-product of the procedural failings, but a code of constitutional standards could nonetheless have mitigated some of these problems.

The first problem with the FTPA was the Government's underdeveloped reasoning to justify the specific clauses when they were introduced to the Commons. As is well-known, the FTPA was the product of a hastily drawn-up coalition deal and, as a result, the Government's case for the Bill, when introduced to Parliament, was largely limited to the argument that the Government was giving away the power to decide the date of the election.[70] But beyond that argument, the justification was very thin indeed, partly as a result of the absence of any consultation or research input into the provisions within the Bill. A good example of this was the way in which Nick Clegg MP, then Deputy Prime Minister and the Minister in charge of the Bill, misinterpreted a quotation by Herbert Asquith in a failed attempt to downplay the difference between a five-year fixed term and a five-year maximum term during evidence to the PCRC and during the second reading debate in the Commons.[71] Clegg suggested the provision for five-year fixed terms went 'with the grain' of the foundation texts of the constitution, namely the Septennial Act 1715.[72] To support the point, he quoted the words of Asquith, who during the second reading of the 1911 Act said that the five-year maximum limit would probably amount to a 'working term of four years'.[73] His argument was that Asquith's use of the words 'a working four-year term' referred to the fact that the last year of Parliament is often lost to preparations for the election rather than suggesting that a general election would be called after four years. For Clegg, this meant that the same logic could be applied to a five-year fixed term.[74] Five-year fixed terms are justified because, like a five-year maximum, they too will result in a working term of four years. Asquith's speeches during the passage of the Parliament Act 1911 demonstrate, as Jack Straw MP pointed out during second reading,[75] that Asquith was being misrepresented by Clegg: 'As to the duration of Parliament, if there were quinquennial Parliaments, I have always said that a Parliament would not last more than four out of the five years.'[76] This example was emblematic of

---

[70] See D Laws, *22 Days in May* (London, Biteback, 2010).
[71] Political and Constitutional Reform Committee, *Fixed-term Parliaments Bill* (HC 2010–12, 436) para 10.
[72] ibid.
[73] HC Deb 13 September 2010, col 625.
[74] ibid.
[75] ibid col 626.
[76] HC Deb 1 May 1911, col 85.

the weakness of the Government's constitutional analysis and weakened the case for a five-year, as opposed to a four-year, fixed term.

A more serious failure of the Government's constitutional analysis was the lack of justification for the system of Speaker's certificates, which was in the version of the Bill originally introduced to the Commons.[77] The system of Speaker's certificates gave the Speaker discretion as to when to decide that a motion of no confidence had been moved. The problem, identified in both the Commons and the Lords, was that the system could potentially politicise the role of Speaker of the Commons. The absence of any detailed analysis from the Government to explain the constitutional rationale behind these provisions and, in particular, the impact they would have on existing constitutional arrangements limited the effectiveness of the Commons' scrutiny. The potential difficulties raised by these provisions were identified and debated in the Commons. However, without clear analysis of what the Government sought to achieve, the Commons' scrutiny focused on simply extracting the Government's basic position. A code of standards would not necessarily have changed this, but standard 5.3.1, which requires government to produce a memorandum that explains the impact of the proposals upon existing constitutional arrangements, could have accelerated and focused the scrutiny process in the Commons. These issues were eventually tackled in the Lords, and amendments eventually agreed between the government and critical peers, but fairly late on in the process and without much input from MPs. By revealing more about the justification for particular clauses and, in particular, setting out how the provisions would influence existing constitutional norms, the Government would have placed MPs in a much stronger position to put forward amendments that stuck to the logic of the Bill, but altered its constitutional implications.

Standard 5.3.1 also requires that the Government indicate whether any post-legislative scrutiny is planned. Late on during ping-pong, a provision was added to the Bill which creates a review of the fixed-term arrangements in 2020.[78] Again, such a requirement in a code could have encouraged the Government to offer the sunset clause in the first place or for the Commons to suggest that it do so, and therefore free up more time to discuss other elements of the Bill.

By convention, bills of first-class constitutional importance are introduced to the House of Commons and have their committee stage on the floor of the House. Further, the Lords are limited by the Salisbury Convention in their ability to challenge an Act which has its origins in the governing party's manifesto. Even if it is not in the manifesto, like the FPTA, the Lords will come under pressure not to push amendments far once the Bill has been approved by the House of Commons, particularly in the first session of a new Parliament. This situation, of a new government with a programme for constitutional reform, which at the time of writing is facing the new 2015 Parliament, puts the onus on the Commons to engage in the

---

[77] The Fixed-term Parliaments Bill HC Bill (2010–12) [64] cl 2.
[78] HL Deb 14 September 2011, cols 814–15; Fixed-term Parliaments Act 2011, s 7(4).

effective scrutiny of bills with constitutional implications. There are many reasons why MPs do not always fulfil this responsibility, but if a Commons committee adopted and systematically applied a code of constitutional standards, this would pressurise the Government to provide more justification for specific provisions in the Commons when they are introduced.

D. Example 2: The Jobseekers (Back to Work Schemes) Act 2013

The passage of the Jobseekers (Back to Work Schemes) Act 2013 illustrates why constitutional standards could improve parliamentary scrutiny outside of the context of major constitutional reform bills. Bills such as this one, which are not on their face 'constitutional', sometimes contain provisions of major constitutional significance.[79] Each session, the Constitution Committee identifies issues of major constitutional significance within Bills that have no obvious constitutional subject matter.[80] One of the main benefits of a set of constitutional standards is that in such a scenario, they have the potential to accelerate the identification and scrutiny of the constitutional implications of a Bill.

The Jobseekers (Back to Work Schemes) Act 2013 was enacted in order to reverse the legal impact of a Court of Appeal judgment of *Reilly (No 1)*,[81] released on 12 February 2013, which had ruled that the Government's regulations for its workfare scheme were ultra vires. The Government introduced the Jobseekers (Back to Work Schemes) Bill on 14 March 2013 with the stated intention of avoiding having to repay those who had been issued with benefit sanctions under the then 'illegal' regulations. The Act was passed using the fast-track procedure and so was on the statute book before the Government's appeal to the Supreme Court was heard, even though the legal effect of the original judgment was suspended until the appeal. When the Bill was debated in the Commons, a number of Labour MPs criticised the use of the fast-track procedure, the retrospective effect of its provisions and the consequent contravention of the rule of law.[82] The bulk of the criticism in the Commons focused on the substance of the Government's policy, and yet Labour's official position was not to oppose the Bill: 263 MPs voted for the Bill and only 52 against.[83] The JCHR did not produce a report on the Bill. By the time the Bill had left the Commons, the Government had produced very little in the way of justification for deviating from the rule of law.

---

[79] D Feldman, 'The Nature and Significance of "Constitutional" Legislation' (2013) 129 *Law Quarterly Review* 343, 353.
[80] eg, the Health and Social Care Act 2012; see A Le Sueur and J Simson Caird, 'The House of Lords Select Committee on the Constitution' in Horne, Drewry and Oliver (n 8).
[81] *R (Reilly) v Secretary of State for Work and Pensions* [2012] EWHC 2292 (Admin).
[82] HC Deb 19 March 2013, cols 822–72; see T Bingham, *The Rule of Law* (London, Allen Lane, 2010).
[83] HC Deb 19 March 2013, cols 897–99.

The Constitution Committee produced a report on the Bill on the day of the second reading in the Lords.[84] The Committee criticised the fast-tracking and highlighted the problems with the Government's justification. In particular, the Committee pointed out that this Bill, unlike the previous instance of fast-track retrospective overturning of a court judgment (the Police (Detention and Bail) Act 2011), deprives individuals of their 'right not to have unlawful financial sanctions imposed upon them'.[85] Further, unlike the 2011 Act, the Committee argued, there was no urgency in this case as 'any retrospective effect of the Court of Appeal's judgment in the *Reilly and Wilson* case is suspended pending the government's application for permission to appeal to the Supreme Court'.[86] The strength of the Committee's analysis was in part built on its ability to compare and contrast the Jobseekers Bill with the Committee's 'legisprudence' on previous government attempts to reverse court judgments retrospectively.

In the Lords, where criticism and opposition were stronger than in the Commons, a 'regret motion' criticising the Bill was voted upon and received 104 votes for and 140 against.[87] Many peers made reference to the Constitution Committee's analysis. During the debate in the Lords, Lord Pannick, a member of the Committee, made a powerfully persuasive speech.[88] He informed the House that he had contacted the Supreme Court and was told that the Government could have sought to have the case expedited. He also argued that seeking to punish those who at the time were acting lawfully was a clear violation of the rule of law.[89] In the words of one Lord, he 'destroyed' the Government's case for the Bill.[90] The Government did attempt to respond to these criticisms and offered much more by way of justification than it had in the Commons. But by the time these justifications were put forward, their impact was minimal as the Lords were in a difficult position due to the Government's urgency and the overwhelming majority supporting the Bill in the Commons.

The code in our report contains a large number of standards that would have been relevant to this Act. For example:

1.1.1 Provisions that have retrospective effect should be drafted as narrowly as possible;

1.1.3 Individuals should not be punished or penalised for contravening what was at the time a valid legal requirement;

5.4.9 Fast-track legislation should not be used to retrospectively overturn a court judgment where there is no compelling operational requirement to amend the law retrospectively.

---

[84] House of Lords Select Committee on the Constitution, *The Jobseekers (Back to Work Schemes) Bill* (HL 2012–13, 155).
[85] ibid para 10.
[86] ibid.
[87] HL Deb 21 March 2013, col 757.
[88] HL Deb 21 March 2013, cols 739–43.
[89] ibid.
[90] Lord McKenzie of Luton, HL Deb 21 March 2013, col 757.

If these standards had been in place in a code and applied by the Commons in some form, we could have expected the Government to have produced more by way of justification for departing from a number of standards when the Bill was introduced to Parliament—or to have been deterred from making these proposals. These standards would also have provided a vital reference point for MPs' scrutiny of the Bill. As noted above, while a number of MPs referred to the rule of law, their analysis was not anchored in parliamentary precedent.

The Government's level of justification in Parliament became central during the next stage in this saga: the judgment in *Reilly (No 2)* given by the Administrative Court on 4 July 2014.[91] The claimants sought to challenge the compatibility of the Jobseekers Act 2013 with Article 6 ECHR, which protects the right to a fair trial and the rule of law. Mrs Justice Lang ruled that it did violate Article 6 and issued a declaration of incompatibility.[92] The key test applied was whether the interference with Article 6, legislating in a manner that affects the judicial determination of a dispute involving the state or private parties, was justifiable on compelling grounds of the public interest. The Government's advocate submitted the case the Government had put to Parliament to justify the Bill as evidence of compelling grounds. This did not satisfy Lang J. Lang stated that Lord Freud, the Government Minister responsible for the Bill in the Lords, had misrepresented the legal effect of the Bill. Essentially the Government had failed to justify why the claimants who had already brought a claim did not require special treatment. The Government's appeal to the financial implications did not qualify alone as a sufficient reason. The Government had issued a section 19 HRA statement when it introduced the Bill that said it was compatible. Lang rejected the legal basis of that statement because it did not set out the relevant test and it relied on an ECtHR case which was not comparable, because this case did not relate to a 'technicality or a loophole'.[93] She added:

> I observe that the absence of any consultation with representative organisations, and the lack of scrutiny by the Joint Committee for Human Rights or the Social Security Advisory Committee, may have contributed to some misconceptions about the legal justification for the retrospective legislation.[94]

The application of a code of constitutional standards during the legislative process may not have resolved the issues raised by Lang J, but the judgment nevertheless highlights the difficulties caused by a lack of systematic constitutionally framed legislative scrutiny in the Commons.

The judgment also serves to demonstrate the problems caused by the lack of coordination between Parliament and the courts on constitutional issues.

---

[91] *R (Reilly) v Secretary of State for Work and Pensions (No 2)* [2014] EWHC 2182 (Admin), [2015] 2 WLR 309.
[92] ibid [151].
[93] ibid [116].
[94] ibid [96].

A flexible code of constitutional standards could serve to improve this coordination. The common law principle of legality provides a good example of how this coordination could work. Recently, Kavanagh has highlighted the significance of the principle of legality for the legislative process.[95] Lord Hoffmann's celebrated statement of the principle in *Simms* makes the connection clear:

> The principle of legality means that Parliament must squarely confront what it is doing and accept the political cost. Fundamental rights cannot be overridden by general or ambiguous words. This is because there is too great a risk that the full implications of their unqualified meaning may have passed unnoticed in the democratic process.[96]

Kavanagh argues that the principle of legality should be understood as a 'signalling device to Parliament'.[97] As he notes, a demand that violations of the rule of law or fundamental values may be stated expressly in a provision does not mean that Parliament will actually pay any particular attention to such issues when a provision is debated. But the point is that the principle of legality is designed, at least in part, to encourage consideration of constitutional values in the legislative process. If these are not considered, then decisions or secondary legislation made under the relevant provisions might be struck down. This risk serves as an additional incentive to ensure that the constitutional implications of legislation receive adequate attention.

The problem is in reality that the principle of the rule of law appears to have little impact on the legislative process in Parliament. In part, this is a consequence of the nature of post-enactment judicial review, but to borrow Kavanagh's metaphor, Parliament's ability to receive the courts' signal is currently limited. A code of parliamentary constitutional standards could incorporate and adapt standards developed by the courts, and this could lower the probability that such principles will be overlooked in debate. In turn, the systematic consideration of principles would provide a clearer basis for the courts' evaluation of Parliament's intention.

The passage of the Jobseekers Act is also noteworthy for another reason. As a result of the use of the fast-track procedure, the Government included the justification for fast-tracking the Bill in the explanatory notes.[98] This was a direct result of the Constitution Committee's report on *Fast-Track Legislation*,[99] which recommended that the explanatory notes should respond to eight specific questions designed to extract the Government's reasoning for using the special procedure, which limits the opportunity for scrutiny. These are set out in the code in standard 5.4.6. The explanatory notes provide important insight into the Government's reasoning. For example: 'Fast-tracking the Bill is necessary in order to provide

---

[95] A Kavanagh, 'The Principle of Legality and the Legislative Process', paper presented at the 2014 University of Cambridge Public Law Conference, unpublished, on file with author.
[96] *R v Secretary of State for the Home Department ex p Simms* [2000] 2 AC 115, 131.
[97] Kavanagh (n 95).
[98] Explanatory Notes to the Jobseekers (Back to Work Schemes) HC Bill (2012–13) 149-EN.
[99] House of Lords Select Committee on the Constitution, *Fast-Track Legislation: Constitutional Implications and Safeguards* (HL 2008–09, 116) para 186.

certainty and thus safeguard the government's position.'¹⁰⁰ This shows that when constitutional standards are developed within Parliament, they do stand a realistic prospect of achieving influence within government.

IV. CONCLUSION

Parliamentary reform is very difficult to achieve.[101] As a result, it is safe to predict that in the short to medium term, big procedural changes specifically designed to improve parliamentary scrutiny are unlikely to happen. Nevertheless, the Constitution Committee has shown that even if a parliamentary committee simply articulates constitutional standards in a report, then these may be adopted within government. On one level, the arguments put forward in this chapter can be seen as calling for parliamentary committees, in both the Commons and the Lords, to be bold and to be proactive in their approach to articulating constitutional standards that can be applied to Bills by government and within Parliament. This does not require major parliamentary reform, or even the adoption of a code and the systematic application of a code of standards; instead, a change in attitude in Parliament is necessary.

Each Bill must be judged on its merits, but the constitutional implications of a Bill cannot easily be understood without reference to the constitutional framework within which it exists. The Lords relies upon the expertise of its members and its committees and their advisers to provide that framework. The Commons lacks such a reference point, and this creates an imbalance within Parliament that has important consequences, some of which have been outlined above.

One of the best arguments for the development of parliamentary constitutional standards is that they serve as a form of institutional memory. Articulating such standards enables committees to commit to memory a clear parliamentary position on a constitutional issue in a Bill. The very fact that a parliamentary committee has developed such a position creates a basic incentive for the resulting standards to be applied and developed in subsequent scrutiny. Without that build-up of distinctive institutional reflection on the constitutional values relevant to legislative scrutiny, parliamentary scrutiny will operate in a constitutional vacuum, one that is generally filled by government.

But going even further and developing a parliamentary code of constitutional standards does not require a big systematic change to the way that things work in Westminster. It requires a Commons or Lords or even a joint parliamentary committee to identify and endorse a set of standards. The development of a code

---

[100] Explanatory Notes to the Jobseekers (Back to Work Schemes) HC Bill (n 98) para 13.
[101] M Russell, '"Never Allow a Crisis Go to Waste": The Wright Committee Reforms to Strengthen the House of Commons' (2011) 64 *Parliamentary Affairs* 612; A Kelso, *Parliamentary Reform at Westminster* (Manchester, Manchester University Press, 2009).

could be achieved through partnership between a committee with an academic team, such as the PCRC's relationship with King's College London in the 2010–15 Parliament,[102] or by engaging a legal adviser. The Committee in question could then take on the responsibility for applying the standards systematically. The Government's permission for or agreement to any code is not strictly required.

If a parliamentary committee took on this task, one of the main difficulties it would have to tackle is the problematic division between procedural and substantive constitutional norms. The Government's adoption of the Constitution Committee's standards relating to the use of the fast-track legislative procedure perhaps demonstrates that a procedural focus is more likely to be successful. Despite this, it would be a mistake to focus only on procedure. At the time of writing, big changes to both constitutional procedure and substance, which will have major impacts on the legislative process, are afoot. English votes for English laws (EVEL), further to changes to devolution, increased parliamentary involvement in scrutiny of EU legislation and a British Bill of Rights will all create new challenges for parliamentary scrutiny. The resulting complexity of the constitutional framework means that a distinctive parliamentary constitutional voice is needed now more than ever. An exclusive focus on procedure will not provide that voice. Understanding constitutional procedures requires a grip upon the substantive constitutional principles that underpin them. Parliamentary procedure should be understood in the light of the proper balance of power between the legislature and the executive. Devolution legislation needs to be viewed through the prism of the balance between autonomy and solidarity within the Union.[103] Parliament, and the House of Commons in particular, should develop substantive constitutional standards independently from government to inform scrutiny of the UK's increasingly complex constitutional arrangements. At present, parliamentarians and lawyers within the Government and the House of Lords largely dominate this task. The House of Commons could provide an invaluable and distinctive perspective on the substantive constitutional framework that should inform scrutiny. Parliamentary constitutional standards represent one way of involving a broader range of parliamentarians in the development and interpretation of the normative framework that is becoming increasingly central to legislative scrutiny. Government should not fear such a development, as these norms do not represent red lines that will prevent it from achieving its legislative goals. Instead, their input will serve to enhance the legitimacy of the process of enacting law with constitutional implications by moving away from governmental cultures of resistance and authority towards compliance with parliamentary requirements for justification, legitimacy from which both government and Parliament would benefit.

---

[102] For a document produced by this collaboration, see Political and Constitutional Reform Committee, *A New Magna Carta?* (HC 2014–15, 463) 9.

[103] A Tomkins, 'New Union: New Constitution', Harry Street Lecture University of Manchester (2015) https://notesfromnorthbritain.files.wordpress.com/2015/05/harrystreetlecture.pdf.

5
European Scrutiny

PAUL HARDY*

I. INTRODUCTION

BOTH HOUSES OF Parliament have had committees in place to scrutinise draft European Union (EU) policy and draft EU legislation since 1974, a year after the UK joined what was then the European Economic Community (EEC) and subsequently the European Community (EC) and European Union (EU). Despite the huge evolution of the EEC since then, the essence of the two scrutiny systems—a largely documents-based approach with a scrutiny reserve preventing ministers from agreeing to proposals in the Council (of Ministers)—has remained the same.

This may not last, however. The increasing scope of EU powers, the continuing political controversy over the UK's membership of the EU and the advent of a formal role for national parliaments under the EU Treaties have all led to calls for significant reform of scrutiny procedures, particularly in the House of Commons. Not least among those calling for reform is the European Scrutiny Committee of the House of Commons itself.

This chapter will consider: the purpose of parliamentary scrutiny of the EU; the EU scrutiny procedures of each House; the strengths and weaknesses of each approach; the proposed reforms in the Commons; and the Government's compliance with its scrutiny obligations. It will conclude that the scrutiny system in the Commons needs urgent reform and that the Government should give the current proposals more serious consideration.[1]

---

* The author was Counsel for European Legislation in the House of Commons from 2009 to 2014; since then, he has been the EU Legal Adviser to the House of Lords. He writes in a purely personal capacity: his views do not represent those of either House.

[1] For other studies, see, eg: A Cygan, 'Democracy and Accountability in the European Union—The View from the House of Commons' (2003) 66 *Modern Law Review* 384; A Cyan, 'The Parliamentarisation of EU Decision-Making? The Impact of the Treaty of Lisbon on National Parliaments' (2011) 36 *European Law Review* 480; J-V Louis, 'National Parliaments and the Principle of Subsidiarity—Legal Options and Practical Limits' (2008) 4 *European Constitutional Review* 429; R Bellamy and S Kröger, 'Domesticating the Democratic Deficit? The Role of National Parliaments and Parties in the EU's System of Governance' (2014) 67 *Parliamentary Affairs* 437; Hansard Society, *Measured or Makeshift? Parliamentary Scrutiny of the European Union* (London, Hansard Society, 2013).

II. THE ORIGINAL PURPOSE OF PARLIAMENTARY SCRUTINY

A. Characteristics of EU Law

The particular characteristics of EU law, and the singular way in which it is given legal effect in the UK, significantly limit the scope for national parliamentary oversight.

i. Dualism

The UK is a dualist state; as such, international law has to be incorporated into national law before citizens can rely on it and judges can apply it. On the UK's accession to the EEC, however, this convention was challenged by three principles of EU law: supremacy; direct applicability; and direct effect.

ii. Supremacy

All forms of EU law—the EU Treaties (known as primary EU legislation), EU secondary legislation (Regulations, Directives and Decisions) and judgments of the Court of Justice of the EU (CJEU)—have supremacy over the national law of Member States. This means that, where EU law and national law diverge, EU law must be followed and national law disapplied.[2]

iii. Direct Applicability

EU Regulations are directly applicable or self-executing: as soon as they enter into force, they are legally binding in their entirety on all Member States. No incorporation into national law is required. (A Directive, by contrast, is not self-executing: it legally binds Member States as to the results to be achieved, but leaves the form and method to Member States, through national implementing measures.)

iv. Direct Effect

In addition, some provisions of EU law have been held by the CJEU to have direct effect, even if the EU legislation is not directly applicable. Provisions with direct effect automatically confer rights on individuals, which can be enforced in national courts, without the need for implementing measures.

---

[2] The Merchant Shipping Act 1988 was famously disapplied through inconsistency with EU law in *R v Secretary of State for Transport ex p Factortame (No 1)* [1990] 2 AC 85; *R v Secretary of State for Transport ex p Factortame (No 2)* [1991] 1 AC 603. However, for a more recent example, in which the Court of Appeal disapplied provisions of the State Immunity Act 1978 through inconsistency with EU fundamental rights law, see *Benkharbouche v Embassy of Sudan* [2015] EWCA Civ 33, [2015] 2 CMLR 20.

B. The European Communities Act 1972

These three characteristics of EU law had to be incorporated into national law before they could be given legal effect, given the UK's dualism. This was achieved by the European Communities Act 1972.[3] Under section 2(1) of that Act, provisions of EU law that are directly applicable are deemed to be automatically given effect in national law without the need for further incorporation. Section 2(1) also incorporates the doctrine of direct effect into national law. Section 2(2) of the Act applies to measures of EU law that are not directly applicable. This provision makes it possible to give effect in national law to such measures by delegated legislation, such as statutory instruments. Unusually, such delegated legislation can amend an Act of Parliament. Section 2(4) recognises the doctrine of the supremacy of EU law.

C. The Effect on Parliament's Control of UK Legislation

It follows from the above that the great majority of EU law is not implemented by primary legislation in the UK, and so the detailed scrutiny that accompanies the passage of a Bill through Parliament is absent. Instead, EU law is either directly applicable or effective in national law, or it is implemented through delegated legislation, with the loss of detailed parliamentary scrutiny which that legislative process entails.

The effect of this novel form of law-making on Parliament's role as legislator was a key consideration for the two committees set up to establish scrutiny systems in Parliament: the Select Committee on European Community Secondary Legislation, appointed by the House of Commons on 21 December 1972 (10 days before the UK acceded to the EEC on 1 January 1973); and the Select Committee on Procedures for Scrutiny of Proposals for European Instruments, appointed by the House of Lords one day earlier, on 20 December 1972.

i. The House of Commons Select Committee on European Community Secondary Legislation

In the Second Report[4] of the Select Committee on European Community Secondary Legislation, which was published in October 1973, the Committee asked itself two questions: why it was necessary to consider having any special scrutiny procedure at all; and what the procedure was intended to achieve.[5]

---

[3] The constitutional implications of these characteristics of EU law, and of the European Communities Act, are considered in ch 14.
[4] Select Committee on European Community Secondary Legislation (HC 1972–73, 463-1).
[5] ibid para 32.

In answer to the first of these, the consequences of EU law on Parliament's control over national law-making weighed heavily on the Committee's mind:

> What is under consideration is a part of the making and amending of the law of the United Kingdom no less. As the inevitable consequence of the entry of the UK into the Community substantial and important parts of that law are now and will be made in new and different ways and with new and different consequences, e.g.
>
> (a) by way of Council Regulations which take effect immediately as part of the law of the UK, and prevail over law of the UK which is inconsistent with them; and
> (b) by way of Council Directives which place upon Parliament an obligation to make or change the law of the UK in all such respect as is necessary to give legal effect in the UK to the provision of the Directives.
>
> The outstanding difference between these and the existing processes for making or amending the law are of course that in a) the Executive itself by agreeing with other member Governments to a proposal for legislation makes the law, i.e. *has assumed the constitutional function and power of Parliament*, and that in case b) whilst the semblance of Parliamentary control remains it would in practice be extremely difficult to assert (much more difficult even than in the case of domestic delegated legislation.) (Emphasis added)[6]

The Committee concluded as follows:

> [I]t remains central to the United Kingdom's concept and structure of Parliamentary Democracy that control of the law making processes lies with Parliament—and ultimately with the elected members of it. It follows therefore that new and special procedures are necessary *to make good so far as may be done the inroads made into that concept and structure by these new methods of making law.*[7] (Emphasis added)

In answer to the second question, the Committee considered that the objective of the scrutiny process must be 'to restore to Parliament responsibilities for, and opportunities to exercise its constitutional rights in respect of, the making of these laws'.[8] This would involve acceptance both by the Government that some of its discretion in the Council of Ministers would be curtailed as a consequence, and by Parliament 'that the scope, means and degree of scrutiny and control must be attuned to the fact that it is dealing with a new way of making laws which is very different from that to which it is accustomed'.[9]

ii. Select Committee on Procedures for Scrutiny of Proposals for European Instruments

The Second Report[10] of the Lords Select Committee on Procedures for Scrutiny of Proposals for European Instruments, which was published in July 1973, placed

---

[6] ibid paras 33–34.
[7] ibid para 36.
[8] ibid para 37.
[9] ibid para 37.
[10] Select Committee on Procedures for Scrutiny of Proposals for European Instruments (HL 1972–73, 194).

less emphasis on the loss of parliamentary control over law-making, but listed the following among the implications of joining the EEC for Parliament to consider:

> Parliament should also be concerned with the effect on domestic law of community legislation, which can be directly or indirectly binding on all citizens and which, often, cannot be subject to review or amendment by the national Parliament;
>
> For that reason, and because of the nature of the Community legislative process, the national Parliament has to participate before decisions are taken in Council;
>
> The purpose of Parliamentary scrutiny is to influence UK Ministers prior to discussions in the Council on Community proposals in which they take final form; and to examine ministerial actions in their Community legislative function on decisions reached in the Council on the draft proposal.[11]

III. PROCEDURES COMMON TO THE SCRUTINY COMMITTEES OF BOTH HOUSES

The scrutiny committees for both Houses still largely operate on the basis of the recommendations of the 1973 reports establishing them. The system is premised on two fundamentals: first, the receipt of EU documents and government Explanatory Memorandums (EMs) explaining them; and, second, a 'scrutiny reserve' preventing the Government from giving agreement to an EU document in the Council (with minor exceptions) until it has been cleared by both committees.

The committees do not scrutinise secondary legislation implementing EU law. The Lords Secondary Legislation Scrutiny Committee[12] and the Joint Committee on Statutory Instruments[13] are the principal committees which consider secondary legislation implementing EU law.

A. Documents and EMs

The reports establishing the two scrutiny committees rightly anticipated the importance of receiving timely information from the Government on an EU

---

[11] ibid para 97, points (f)–(g).

[12] The Lords Secondary Legislation Scrutiny Committee (formerly the Merits Committee) considers every negative and affirmative Statutory Instrument (SI), or draft SI, laid before Parliament—about 1,200 per year—with a view to determining whether the special attention of the House should be drawn to it on any of the following grounds: that it is politically or legally important or gives rise to issues of public policy likely to be of interest to the House; that it may be inappropriate in view of the changed circumstances since the passage of the parent Act; that it may inappropriately implement EU legislation; or that it may imperfectly achieve its policy objectives.

[13] The role of the Joint Committee on Statutory Instruments, whose membership is drawn from both Houses, is to assess the technical qualities of each instrument that falls within its remit, but not the merits or the policy behind the instrument, and to decide whether to draw the special attention of each House to any instrument.

proposal. The Commons Select Committee on European Community Secondary Legislation considered 'the fullest supply of the most accurate information to be so vital' that it gave 'much further thought to this requirement'.[14] The Lords Select Committee on Procedures for Scrutiny of Proposals for European Instruments concluded that it was 'important that Parliament should be provided with full information about the European Communities, and that it should be the responsibility of the Government to see that this is done'.[15]

Under present procedures, the Government is required to deposit in each House EU policy and legislative proposals within two working days of their arrival in the Foreign and Commonwealth Office. On average, about 1,000 EU documents are deposited a year.[16]

Within 10 days of the deposit of an EU document, the responsible government department submits an EM on it. An EM sets out the Government's views on the legal, financial and policy implications of the document, and the procedure and timetable for its consideration and adoption. There is Cabinet Office guidance on European scrutiny for civil servants. An EM should contain the following information:

— a summary of the subject matter of the document;
— any previous scrutiny history;
— a statement of where ministerial responsibility lies;
— the interests of devolved administrations;
— notes on legal and procedural issues, including the legal base of the document, the legislative procedure which applies and the voting procedure;
— a statement on any human rights concerns;
— an assessment of whether the proposal complies with the subsidiarity principle;
— an assessment of the factors which will affect the Government's decision whether to opt into a proposal in the field of justice and home affairs;
— the Government's view of the policy implications of the document;
— a statement of the impact on UK law;
— an impact assessment;
— details of financial implications;
— details on what consultation has taken place; and
— the likely timetable for consideration of the document in the EU institutions.

The EM is signed by a minister and serves as the Government's evidence to Parliament. The submission of an EM is the trigger for the scrutiny process to begin.

---

[14] Select Committee on European Community Secondary Legislation (n 4) para 43.
[15] Select Committee on Procedures for Scrutiny of Proposals for European Instruments (n 10) para 136.
[16] See Table 5.1 below.

B. The Scrutiny Reserve Resolution

Scrutiny is underpinned by the understanding that ministers will not normally agree to European proposals ahead of parliamentary scrutiny clearance. Originally resting on the undertakings of successive governments,[17] this understanding was formalised by a Resolution of the House of Commons on 30 October 1980. The Resolution related only to proposals recommended by the Scrutiny Committee for debate. In 1984, the Government agreed that its spirit should apply to all proposals, and this was enshrined in a new Resolution in 1990. A revised Resolution was agreed on 17 November 1998 (this pre-dates changes made to the EU legislative process by the 2009 Treaty of Lisbon and is now out of date).

Similarly, the scrutiny system in the House of Lords originally rested on an undertaking given by the Government that it would not, except in special circumstances, agree to any proposal in the Council until it had been cleared by the Committee. This was formalised in a Resolution of the House of Lords on 6 December 1999 and was updated on 30 March 2010.

According to these Resolutions, UK Ministers may not agree to any proposal in the Council until the committees have finished their scrutiny. Ministers may override this scrutiny reserve if there are 'special reasons', but in such cases must explain their reasons to the Committee at the first opportunity. Scrutiny overrides are meant to be unusual and the Government is required to explain them immediately, following which the Committee writes back, indicating whether it considers the override to be acceptable (acting in the national interest, for example) or not (administrative error, for example). Most overrides occur in the case of fast-moving policy areas, such as decisions to impose sanctions or take other emergency measures in the field of foreign policy. All overrides are reported to the Committee and full data on overrides are published online.

IV. THE EUROPEAN SCRUTINY COMMITTEE OF THE HOUSE OF COMMONS

A. Terms of Reference

The primary purpose of scrutiny in the Commons is to hold the UK Government to account for what it does at the EU level, particularly in the Council of Ministers, and to scrutinise proposed EU legislation. The functions of the European Scrutiny

---

[17] Questions were raised about the legal and constitutional effects of such a resolution at the time that the Commons scrutiny committee was being established. The Second Report from the Select Committee on European Community Secondary Legislation considered that (at para 52) 'it inconceivable that any Government would act contrary to such a resolution even if, which is doubted, it were legally and constitutionally entitled to do so'.

96 Paul Hardy

Committee (ESC) are formally laid down in Standing Order No 143 of the House of Commons:

(a) to report its opinion on the legal and political importance[18] of each such document and, where it considers appropriate, to also report on the reasons for its opinion and on any matters of principle, policy or law which may be affected;
(b) to make recommendations for the further consideration of any such document pursuant to Standing Order No 119 (European Committees); and
(c) to consider any issue arising upon any such document or group of documents, or related matters.[19]

B. Activity Levels of the ESC Between 2006 and 2014

Of the 1,000 or so documents that the ESC considers each year, it finds approximately half to be of political or legal importance and reports substantively on them. Documents of insufficient political or legal importance are reported to the Committee, but are not published in more detail for the House as a whole. The table below shows annual figures for the number of documents considered legally and politically important, and the number of those recommended for debate, between 2006 and 2014.

C. Membership and Staff

The ESC consists of 16 MPs. MPs are nominated to serve on the ESC by the Committee of Selection (which acts on the recommendations of the party business managers—the whips) for the duration of each new Parliament. Unlike the chairs of departmental select committees, who since 2010 have been elected by the House, the chair of the ESC is still appointed. The quorum is five MPs. The balance of MPs from each political party on the ESC reflects the balance of political parties in the whole House. The ESC has a staff of 16, headed by a clerk. This is substantially more than any other House of Commons select committee. In addition to the normal complement—clerk, second clerk, administrative secretariat—the ESC is served by two legal advisers and four 'clerk advisers' who assist in the

---

[18] The criteria of political and legal importance derive from the recommendation in Select Committee on European Community Secondary Legislation (n 4) para 69: 'The object of the Committee will be to inform the House as to any proposals of legal or political importance and to make recommendations as to their further consideration. Its task would not be to debate the reasons for or against a proposal but to give the House the fullest information as to why it considered the particular proposal of importance and to point out the matter of principle or policy which it affects and the changes in UK law involved.'
[19] Standing Order No 143.

Table 5.1

Financial year	2006–07	2007–08	2008–09	2009–10	2010–11	2011–12	2012–13	2013–14
EU documents scrutinised	1,045	1,044	941	915	1,013	1,138	980	1,136
Reported as legally/politically important	484	472	443	416	454	643	506	608
Debates in European Committee	42	34	32	33	40	35	38	39
Debates on the floor of the House	6	3	5	1	6	10	12	12

scrutiny of the very large volume of documents it examines. In September 2015, two more clerk advisers were appointed to enable the ESC's staff to provide advice to departmental select committees.

D. Powers

The ESC has the usual powers of a select committee. It has the power to recommend documents for debate. Debates recommended by the Committee take place either in a European Committee[20] or (more rarely) on the floor of the House. European Committees are ad hoc committees with no permanent membership. They are set up to debate a specific proposal which has been referred to them by the ESC. The table above shows that the ESC recommends about 40 documents for debate in European Committee each year, and a handful for debate on the floor, although the number of floor debates has increased in recent years.

E. Proceedings in European Committee

There are three ad hoc European Committees ('A', 'B' and 'C'), covering separate fields of EU policy.[21] Each Committee has 13 members. A specific membership

---

[20] See Standing Order No 119: Standing Order on European Committees.
[21] ibid.

is nominated by the Committee of Selection for each debate according to the document or documents referred. The nominations should include at least two members of the ESC and at least two members from the relevant Departmental Select Committee. Sittings are chaired by members of the Chairmen's Panel. Any Member of the House may attend and speak at a European Committee, but may not move a motion, vote or be counted in the quorum. Any Member of the House may also table an amendment and move it if the amendment is selected by the Chair.

At the beginning of the sitting, a member of the ESC makes a brief statement explaining the ESC's decision to refer the document(s) to a European Committee. Proceedings then begin with up to an hour of questions to the responsible Minister or Ministers (who may open with a short introductory statement). The Chairman may allow up to an additional half an hour for questions if necessary. The Committee then debates the document or documents on the basis of a motion moved by the Minister. The Chair puts the questions necessary to dispose of the business not later than two-and-a-half hours after the start of proceedings.

Where a proposal has been debated in European Committee, the motion must then be put to the House the following day, when it is agreed to without debate. A proposal is cleared from scrutiny when the motion is agreed to by the House.

F. Proceedings on the Floor of the House

Debates can take place on the floor of the House only if the Government is willing to provide time. Standing Order No 16 provides that debates can last for an hour and a half, but the Government has sometimes agreed to the ESC's requests for a longer period. As in a European Committee, it is up to the Government to table the motion on which the document is to be considered by the House.

G. Inquiries

The Committee can conduct inquiries into legal, procedural or institutional developments relating to the EU,[22] but, unlike the Lords, the volume of weekly scrutiny prevents it from conducting inquiries regularly.

---

[22] In the last Parliament, the ESC published the following inquiry reports: *The EU Bill and Parliamentary Sovereignty* (HC 2010–12, 633-I); *The Treaty on Stability, Co-ordination and Governance: Impact on the Eurozone and the Rule of Law* (HC 2010–12, 1817-I); and *The Application of the EU Charter of Fundamental Rights in the UK: A State of Confusion* (HC 2013–14, 979-I); and *Reforming the European Scrutiny System in the House of Commons* (HC 2013–14, 109-I).

V. THE SELECT COMMITTEE ON THE EUROPEAN UNION OF THE HOUSE OF LORDS

The House of Lords' system of EU scrutiny is conducted by the House of Lords Select Committee on the European Union (hereinafter the Select Committee) and its six sub-committees.

A. Terms of Reference

The Select Committee and sub-committees seek 'to inform the House of Lords, to influence and hold to account the Government, to influence the European institutions, and to engage with stakeholders'.[23] The formal terms of reference are:

1. To consider European Union documents and other matters relating to the European Union.
2. To assist the House in relation to the procedure for the submission of Reasoned Opinions under Article 5 of the Treaty on European Union and the Protocol on the application of the principles of subsidiarity and proportionality;
3. To represent the House as appropriate in interparliamentary cooperation within the European Union.[24]

B. Membership and Staff

A total of 73 members are involved in the work of the EU Select Committee and its sub-committees. They are supported by a staff of 24, including two legal advisers.

C. The Select Committee

The Select Committee is responsible for scrutinising cross-cutting issues not falling within the ambit of one of the sub-committees and may conduct inquiries on these topics. Recent reports have examined the role of national parliaments in the EU[25] and the previous Government's Balance of Competences Review.[26] It has recently begun holding hearings with the Minister for Europe before each European Council. It also holds informal meetings with the ambassador of each incoming presidency. All reports are issued by the Select Committee, so a key task is to consider draft reports from the sub-committees.

---

[23] *Report on 2014–15* (HL 2015–16, 11) para 5.
[24] See www.parliament.uk/documents/lords-committees/eu-select/terms-of-reference.pdf.
[25] *The Role of National Parliaments in the European Union* (HL 2013–14, 151).
[26] *The Review of the Balance of Competences between the UK and the EU* (HL 2014–15, 140).

The Chairman of the EU Select Committee, who is also Principal Deputy Chairman of Committees,[27] is non-aligned. The EU Select Committee has 18 members (excluding the chairman), each of whom serves on one of the six sub-committees, through which most of inquiries are conducted.

D. Sub-committees

The sub-committees, which each have 12 members, undertake the bulk of scrutiny work. They decide their own programme of work to a large extent, although the EU Select Committee may occasionally request that a sub-committee look at a particular subject or contribute to a joint exercise, such as the review of the European Commission's annual work programme for the following year. The six sub-committees are as follows:

— the Energy and Environment Sub-Committee (also covering agriculture and fisheries);
— the External Affairs Sub-Committee;
— the Financial Affairs Sub-Committee;
— the Home Affairs Sub-Committee (also covering health and education);
— the Internal Market Sub-Committee (also covering infrastructure and employment); and
— the Justice Sub-Committee (also covering institutions and consumer protection).

E. The Scrutiny Process

Whilst the ESC must consider all deposited EU documents, the Chairman of the EU Select Committee conducts a selection procedure known as a 'sift'. On the basis of the EMs, the EU documents and advice from staff, he clears the less important documents from scrutiny himself; the more important (around 30–40 per cent) are sifted to be examined by the sub-committee with responsibility for the relevant policy area, or occasionally by the Select Committee itself.

It is for the sub-committee then to decide how to scrutinise the document. There are two main aspects to the sub-committees' work: scrutiny of documents; and inquiries into EU proposals and policies. In the course of scrutinising EU proposals, the sub-committees may engage in detailed correspondence with ministers, hold evidence sessions and conduct seminars with stakeholders. The main objectives are to identify issues of legal or political significance and to ensure

---

[27] The post is one of only three full-time salaried posts for members of the House, the others being the Chairman of Committees and the Lord Speaker.

that the Government's position is clearly and transparently put on the record. All correspondence is published on the committees' webpages. The committees also undertake inquiries into particularly important issues.

F. Inquiries

Inquiries vary in length, but all rely on evidence presented by witnesses. Short inquiries may focus on a specific proposal, involving one or two public meetings at which invited witnesses appear in person. Longer inquiries involve the preparation of a public call for evidence, setting out a list of questions to which the committee seeks responses. In such cases, committees are likely to receive a large amount of written evidence and to hold public meetings with witnesses, over a period of months, before preparing a report. At the end of an inquiry, the Select Committee normally publishes a report, containing wide-ranging conclusions and recommendations for action. Recommendations may be directed either to the Government or to other bodies, including the EU institutions. The Government has undertaken to respond to recommendations within two months of any report being published; all responses are published online.

VI. THE ENHANCED ROLE OF NATIONAL PARLIAMENTS: MONITORING COMPLIANCE WITH SUBSIDIARITY AND OPT-IN DECISIONS

A. Monitoring Compliance with Subsidiarity

i. Reviewing Legislation

A Protocol on the Application of the Principles of Subsidiarity and Proportionality was added by the Treaty of Lisbon.[28] Subsidiarity is the principle that action should only be taken at the EU level if effective action cannot be taken at the national, regional or local level. It is intended to ensure that decisions are taken as close to the citizen as possible. The Protocol gives national parliaments the power to submit a 'reasoned opinion' within eight weeks of publication in all EU languages to the institution proposing the draft legislative act, outlining why the proposal does not comply with the principle of subsidiarity. If a third or more of EU national parliaments submit reasoned opinions (the threshold drops to a quarter for legislation in the field of cooperation in criminal matters), the originating institution, usually the Commission, is bound to review its proposal with a view to maintaining, amending or withdrawing it.[29] This has become known as the 'yellow card'. If more than a half submit reasoned opinions and the originating

---

[28] Protocol No 2.
[29] The full details of the thresholds and their consequences are set out in art 7 of the Protocol.

institution decides to maintain the proposal, it in turn must submit a reasoned opinion in support of this decision to the Council and the European Parliament, each of which can strike down the proposal if it is in agreement with national parliaments. This has become known as the 'orange card'.

To date, the orange card has not been reached; the yellow card has been reached on only two proposals:

(i) In an attempt to address concerns that, in the single market, economic freedoms would prevail over fundamental freedoms such as the right to strike, the Commission proposed to clarify the relationship between them (the Monti II proposal).[30] It set out provisions on resolution mechanisms in the case of employment disputes in circumstances with a cross-border character. Several national parliaments were unconvinced either that the proposal was justified or that it would help to clarify the relationship between the freedoms. Reasoned opinions amounting over a third of national parliaments were issued, triggering the first yellow card in May 2012. The Commission withdrew the Monti II proposal, but asserted that it was being withdrawn because of political disagreement in the Council and not because of the yellow card.

(ii) The proposal on the European Public Prosecutor's Office (EPPO)[31] will establish an EU level body with the exclusive power to investigate and prosecute criminal offences affecting the financial interests of the EU and closely related offences. Many national parliaments considered that the Commission had failed to demonstrate the desirability of the proposed EU level action and that the proposal would undermine national prosecuting systems. Reasoned opinions amounting to a third of national parliaments were issued, triggering the second yellow card in October 2013. Nonetheless, the Commission quickly decided to maintain the EPPO proposal, and its fate now lies in the hands of the Council and the European Parliament.

There is a widespread perception that the thresholds for a yellow and orange card are too high to confer meaningful powers on national parliaments to ensure that the principle of subsidiarity is respected. In its report on *The Role of National Parliaments in the European Union*, the EU Select Committee of the House of Lords concluded that ways should be found to make the reasoned opinion procedure more effective and recommended that 'the Commission should make an undertaking that, when a Yellow Card is issued, it will either drop the proposal in question, or substantially amend it in order to meet the concerns expressed'.[32]

---

[30] COM(2012) 130 final: Proposal for a Council Regulation on the exercise of the right to take collective action within the context of the freedom of establishment and the freedom to provide services.

[31] COM(2013) 534 final: Proposal for a Council Regulation on the establishment of the European Public Prosecutor's Office.

[32] EU Select Committee of the House of Lords, *The Role of National Parliaments in the European Union* (HL 2013–14, 151) para 95.

ii. Legal Challenges to Legislation

Under the same Protocol, national parliaments or their individual chambers can now apply to the Court of Justice (acting through their Member States) for judicial review of an EU legislative act within two months and 10 days of its adoption, on the grounds of infringement of the principle of subsidiarity.[33] This is the most significant change to the role of national parliaments introduced by the Treaty of Lisbon: it gives each parliament, or chamber thereof, the right to challenge EU legislation unilaterally. The Lords Select Committee has threatened to use this power in relation to a proposal on occupational pension schemes.[34]

iii. Parliamentary Procedure

Where the ESC or the Select Committee considers that a particular proposal breaches the principle of subsidiarity, it invites the House to agree a reasoned opinion after a debate on the basis of a report. The reasoned opinion is then forwarded to the president of the EU institution proposing the legislation. The Commons issued 15 reasoned opinions in the last (2010–15) Parliament, and the Lords seven. The Commons or the Lords can only ask the Government to bring a legal challenge once a motion has been agreed to; in so doing, they act separately, and either House can bring a challenge. Both Houses have agreed a Memorandum of Understanding[35] with the Government on how such challenges would be brought.

B. Opt-in Decisions

The Lisbon Treaty extended the list of measures subject to the UK opt-in, which is to say the areas where EU legislation will apply to the UK only if the Government notifies the Council that it wishes to participate.[36] The list of measures covered by the opt-in fall under Title V of the Treaty on the Functioning of the European Union, 'Freedom, Security and Justice', and now includes judicial cooperation in civil and criminal matters, police cooperation, asylum and immigration.

Protocol No 21 to the EU Treaties governs the opt-in process. The UK is able to opt into a proposal within three months of its being forwarded to the Council, or any time after the measure has been adopted by the Council. The ESC and EU Select Committees' scrutiny of measures to which the opt-in applies is governed by a separate scrutiny procedure. This was agreed by Baroness Ashton of Upholland, then Leader of the House, prior to the Lisbon Treaty entering into

---

[33] Article 8 of Protocol No 2.
[34] COM(2014) 265: Proposal for a Regulation laying down a prohibition on driftnet fisheries. See *Report on 2014–15* (n 24) paras 27–29.
[35] See www.parliament.uk/documents/commons-committees/european-scrutiny/Final-MoU-text.pdf.
[36] See Title V of the Treaty on the Functioning of the European Union.

force, and was supplemented by an agreement with the Minister for Europe, David Lidington, in January 2011. These agreements are now known as the Ashton-Lidington undertakings.

The Ashton undertakings require government departments to produce an EM within 10 working days of the publication of a proposal and to indicate the Government's preliminary views on whether it will opt in. The Government will not reach a final view on the matter for eight weeks and will take account of any views expressed in that time by the ESC or Select Committee. A Resolution formalising the eight-week scrutiny reserve was adopted on 30 March 2010 in the Lords. Where the Select Committee makes a report to the House that it recommends for debate, the Government undertakes to arrange a debate as soon as possible, on an amendable motion. The procedure for handling such reports was agreed by the House on 16 March 2010.

On 20 January 2011, the Minister for Europe made a Written Statement undertaking that the Government would continue to honour the Ashton undertakings and would also extend them. He committed to making 'a written statement to Parliament on each opt-in decision, and the reasons for it', and undertook to make an oral statement 'where appropriate and necessary'. He urged the Houses' EU Committees to 'take full advantage of their existing right to call a debate on an amendable motion on any opt-in decision'. He also undertook to set aside government time for a debate where there was a 'particularly strong Parliamentary interest'. In addition, the Minister's statement included opting-out of Schengen-building measures under Article 5(2) of Protocol 19, which had not been specifically mentioned in the Ashton undertakings.

VII. STRENGTHS AND WEAKNESSES OF THE COMMONS SCRUTINY SYSTEM

A. Strengths

i. Breadth of Scope

The breadth of the Commons system is one of its strengths. The ESC considers all EU documents other than the most mundane. Table 5.1 above shows the number of documents scrutinised by the ESC from 2006 to 2014. For each one, the Committee would have received either a short report from its advisers recommending that the report was not of sufficient legal or political importance, or a full report because of its legal or political importance, which would then form a chapter of the ESC's published weekly report. This is a good thing in terms of democratic accountability. It means that members of the ESC receive a report on every proposal of other formal document emanating from Brussels—so they are fully apprised. It also means that, in considering whether to approve the staff's recommendation on a document, particularly whether to clear it or keep it under scrutiny, they have to exercise their political judgment as elected representatives. The ESC made the importance of this clear in its report, *Reforming the European Scrutiny System in the House of Commons* (hereinafter 'the Scrutiny Reform Report'): 'we provide a crucially-important mechanism for the House to focus on the most important proposals on the basis of a judgement made by elected politicians, with expert support'.[37]

ii. Debates on the Floor of the House

In the last Parliament, the number of debates on the floor of the House on European documents increased considerably, as Table 5.1 shows. This is a consequence of two factors. First, the Committee, under the chairmanship of Sir William Cash MP, was more active in recommending documents for debate on the floor of the House, particularly on contentious issues with backbench interest. Second, the new procedures for debates on reasoned opinions and opt-in decisions meant that more documents were debated on the floor of the House, despite the Government's refusal to list all of them for debate.[38] The profile of the ESC, within and beyond the House, increased as a result.

iii. Influence

It is hard to assess the influence of the ESC because the Government does not often acknowledge the fact that the views of the ESC, or of the Lords Select Committee, have changed its policy. But the ESC's influence can be traced, for example, in the draft Directive on animal cloning.[39] On a larger scale, it may also not be coincidental that two areas of focus of the Scrutiny Reform Report—a red card, or veto, for national parliaments over new EU legislation, and criticism of the BBC—have found themselves reflected to a certain extent in the new Government's policy.

B. Weaknesses

i. Lack of Detailed Scrutiny

Whilst being a strength, the volume of documents which are considered by the ESC is a weakness: fewer can be scrutinised in depth. The number of staff is very limited compared to the House of Lords; yet, without a chairman's sift, the ESC

---

[37] ESC, *Reforming the European Scrutiny System in the House of Commons* (n 23) para 44.
[38] Discussed below.
[39] COM(13) 892: Draft Directive on the cloning of animals of the bovine, porcine, ovine, caprine and equine species kept and reproduced for farming purposes. See the evidence session with George Eustice MP, the then Parliamentary Under-Secretary of State for Farming, Food and Marine Environment, Department for Environment, Food and Rural Affairs, on 9 April 2014.

scrutinises more documents. This in turn affects the extent to which the ESC can have an impact on government policy. It will only have a chance of influencing policy on those documents it considers in detail, often over a length of time, or on the issues on which it conducts occasional inquiries. For some policy areas, however, the ESC has a habit of holding a document under scrutiny because it is important and the Government has concerns about it, and then clearing it when the Government reports that its concerns have been met in the course of negotiations. Whilst this may be informative for anyone who reads the weekly ESC reports, it is largely a reactive approach to scrutiny.

ii. Department Select Committees: Mainstreaming

It is clear that one select committee alone cannot effectively scrutinise all EU proposals on behalf of the Commons. Much thought has been given to how to involve the departmental select committees in the scrutiny process. The answer has, unfortunately, been elusive, as the ESC concluded in its Scrutiny Reform Report:

> We recognise that much of the strength of Departmental Select Committees comes from their autonomy and the independence they have to set their agenda. We are aware that our colleagues on Departmental Select Committees already have busy work programmes and it is also right to acknowledge that for some Committees EU matters may prove divisive. For all these reasons there appears to be no appetite for full mainstreaming of EU legislative scrutiny to Departmental Select Committees, but in our view the current situation is not sustainable. It is 15 years since our predecessor Committee wrote to the Modernisation Committee concluding that 'There has been wide agreement that DSCs "should do more about Europe", but in practice nothing much has happened.' The fact that the debate still has a similar tone, given all that has happened in the EU over those 15 years, is disappointing.[40]

iii. European Committee Debates

Until the early 1990s, referred documents were automatically debated on the floor of the House unless the Government tabled a motion to refer them to a Standing Committee. The default was then changed to referral to European Standing Committees. These committees had permanent memberships of 13, appointed sessionally until 1998 and thereafter for the length of the Parliament. The then European Legislation Committee was still able to recommend that a document be debated on the floor of the House, but the decision on whether or not that floor debate took place was in the Government's hands, as remains the case today.

But the situation changed, 'much for the worse' according to the ESC,[41] following the 2005 General Election. Sessional Orders were made to set aside the requirement of Standing Order No 119 for a permanent membership and to replace this

---

[40] ESC, *Reforming the European Scrutiny System in the House of Commons* (n 23) para 204.
[41] ibid para 225.

with a provision for the Committee of Selection to nominate new and different members to the 'European Committees' for each debate. The reforms have not been successful in bringing important EU proposals to wider attention within and beyond the Commons. The ESC summed up the evidence it had received on European Committees in its Scrutiny Reform Report:

> We were also told that the Committees were 'off the radar' of the broadcasters; and there was further, broad, consensus that the current system has significant problems, with some going so far as to describe it as 'dysfunctional'. The FCO commented that some debates 'have been sparsely attended or have been concluded very quickly'. The Liberal Democrat PPC on International Affairs recommended scrapping the Committees altogether, citing a lack of engagement and poor timetabling. Chris Bryant MP spoke about the problem of long delays in scheduling debates which rendered them pointless when they took place, likening the eventual debates to 'when somebody writes to the MP about the planning decision that was taken last night by the council'. In September 2013 there was a striking example of this when European Committee B debated a set of documents, relating to measures to reduce financial fraud against the EU, which had been adopted by the Council in February.
>
> Others spoke of further practical problems—short notice of meetings and too many papers. 66% of the Members who responded to our survey agreed that one of the weaknesses of the current system was that 'Members do not know enough about the subjects covered'.[42]

The author's experience reinforces these views. European Committees are composed of MPs who rarely participate because they have little or no expertise in the subject matter to be able scrutinise the Government's policy and are unfamiliar with the procedures. The Scrutiny Reform Report put the significance of this in context: 'It must be remembered that many of the documents we refer for debate are legislative proposals which will have direct effect on the citizens of the United Kingdom, and would—if enacted through domestic legislation—be the subject of an Act of Parliament.'[43]

C. Proposals for Reform: The Scrutiny Reform Report

The ESC Scrutiny Reform Report made the following recommendations.

i. Revision of Standing Order No 143

The ESC proposed changes to Standing Order No 143, building on a set of proposed standing orders and a scrutiny reserve resolution originally published in 2010 by its predecessor committee. Overall, however, it concluded that it should continue to review all EU documents for legal and political importance.

---

[42] ibid paras 229 and 230.
[43] ibid para 156.

ii. Earlier Engagement

The ESC decided to recommend documents for debate at an earlier stage of the legislative process, if possible before the Council reaches political agreement.

iii. The Scrutiny Reserve

The ESC concluded that the scrutiny reserve 'must remain the centre of gravity of the House Commons scrutiny system'.[44] It therefore proposed two major changes to reflect the reality of EU decision-making: first, that an override should be regarded as having occurred when the Government abstained on a vote on a document held under scrutiny, not just when it voted in favour; and, second, that agreement in COREPER[45] on a document held under scrutiny, when the Government does not intend to object to the matter being agreed by a minister in the Council, should also trigger an override.

iv. Oral Questions

The ESC concluded that a session of oral questions (including a session of topical questions) on EU matters should be introduced and that this should take place on the floor of the House, timed to coincide with the run-up to a European Council meeting.

v. Departmental Select Committees: Mainstreaming

The ESC concluded that 'without broader analysis conducted across the departmental select committee system the scrutiny process is incomplete'.[46] It recommended that departmental select committees should appoint an 'EU Reporter' to ensure that EU issues made their way onto these committees' agendas in the face of the many other demands on their time. The Liaison Committee recognised the potential advantages of an EU Reporter system, but decided the decision should lie with the individual committees. Two committees (the Justice Committee and the Business, Innovation and Skills Committee) appointed EU Reporters in the 2010–15 Parliament. In the 2015–20 Parliament, at the time of writing the following committees have appointed EU Reporters to date: Energy and Climate Change; International Development; Health; Justice; and Work and Pensions.

In addition, the ESC recommended that departmental select committees should be obliged to consider which of the proposals in the Commission's Annual Work

---

[44] ibid para 26.
[45] The most senior Council working group, attended by the Permanent Representatives of the Member States.
[46] ESC, *Reforming the European Scrutiny System in the House of Commons* (n 23) para 205.

Programme (which sets out the Commission's agenda for the forthcoming year) they would aim to scrutinise, following the model used in the Dutch *Twede Kamer*.

vi. European Committees

The ESC concluded:

> We remain of the opinion that the best solution would be to revert to the previous system of permanent membership. Moreover, giving European Committees a permanent membership, with a permanent Chair, would enable them to make decisions about their business and timetabling, as well as developing expertise among their members and potentially making them more independent from the Whips. It would also give interest groups the opportunity to make their views known in advance to members of the relevant Committee. Given the impact of EU legislation on the voter, and the fact that many matters which come before European Committees would be the equivalent of an Act of Parliament—and have not necessarily originated for Government policy—we recommend that European Committees should not be whipped.[47]

VIII. STRENGTHS AND WEAKNESSES OF THE LORDS SCRUTINY SYSTEM

A. Strengths

i. Size

There greatest strength of the EU scrutiny system in the House of Lords is the number of committees dedicated to the role. The Lords does not have departmental select committees, unlike the Commons, so much scrutiny of government policy is conducted through the EU Select and Sub-Committees. Each of the sub-committees operates within a defined scope and so is able to build up expertise. Each is supported by a clerk, a policy analyst with a background in the policy areas covered, and a committee assistant who administers the operation of the sub-committee. Each can call on the services of one of the two legal advisers. In addition, sub-committees are able to appoint specialist advisers to help with an inquiry.

The Select Committee is equally well-staffed, with a principal clerk, clerk, committee assistant and legal adviser.

ii. Wider Engagement

The size of the scrutiny system allows it to engage much more often with a wider community of stakeholders.

---

[47] ibid para 234.

iii. Experience

Peers bring considerable experience to the business of scrutiny, which is reflected in the quality of the committees' output. Many are experts in fields of relevance to the committees, but many too are highly experienced politicians. The number of former Members of the European Parliament (MEPs) in the Lords brings an insider's knowledge of how that vital institution works, which is lacking in the Commons. Chris Bryant MP, a former Minister for Europe, told the ESC inquiry that appearing before a Lords EU committee was far more nerve-racking than appearing in the Commons:

> However, if I am very honest, no Commons Committee got anywhere near as nerve-wracking as the Lords Committee. I was only Minister for 10 minutes; in that time, I do not know how many various European debates and so on I did, but the House of Lords Committee was by far more rigorous, embarrassing, nerve-racking and detailed.[48]

iv. The Sift

The Lords Committee established in 1972 to consider scrutiny procedures recommended a sifting process to manage the volume of documents:

> The Committee were at first dismayed by the number of Community proposals, and by the mass of papers which it was feared would overwhelm those members called upon to consider them. Evidence suggests, however, that this problem can without difficulty be overcome by a sifting mechanism to distinguish between the majority of instruments which deal … with matters of technical detail or are of short duration, with which it is unnecessary for Parliament to be concerned, and the minority, to which attention should be drawn.[49]

The committee's concerns were prescient: the sifting process safeguards the Lords Select and sub-committees from having to report on the 1,000 or so documents that are deposited.

v. Inquiries

The sifting process frees up time for the sub-committees to conduct inquiries in addition to the weekly scrutiny of documents. Reports are evidence-based, balanced and widely read—they are the committees' main product. Their credibility comes from the quality of the evidence taken, the detail with which it is analysed and the impartial manner in which it is reported. The last point is an important one: the Lords has, historically, been more pro-European than the Commons, which gives its reports additional influence in Brussels and other European

---

[48] ibid Q 287.
[49] Select Committee on Procedures for Scrutiny of Proposals for European Instruments (n 10) para 117.

capitals. Publication of reports is now accompanied by sophisticated media campaigns, including the use of Twitter. Reports are also regularly followed up in order to press the Government to implement recommendations.

vi. Pre-European Council Evidence Sessions

The Select Committee has successfully introduced a system of pre-European Council evidence sessions with the Minister for Europe, giving the Committee an opportunity to examine publicly the Government's negotiating position on key issues.

vii. Influence

As mentioned above, it is difficult to measure the influence of the scrutiny committees on the Government without clear acknowledgement. Nonetheless, the Home Affairs Sub-Committee's report[50] on the right to be forgotten (under EU data protection rules) is an example. It was part of the scrutiny of the draft Data Protection Regulation and was not something in which the Government was particularly interested until a judgment of the Court of Justice of the EU against Google last May.[51] At that point, the Government was invited to give evidence to the Sub-Committee. Since the publication of the report, it has followed the Sub-Committee's principal recommendation.

The influence of the House of Lords is most visible in the reaction and responses to its reports, however. In the year 2014–15, its reports were featured in nearly 400 regional, national and international broadcast features and print articles.[52]

The House of Lords has taken forward its proposals for enhancing the role of national parliaments in the EU by promoting the establishment of a 'Green Card' to help national parliaments to play a role in setting priorities for EU action. It issued the first Green Card on food waste,[53] with the support of 16 other chambers. The fact that so many supported the initiative is a reflection of the high regard in which the Select Committee is viewed by other national parliaments.

B. Weaknesses

i. Publishing Correspondence

Whilst sub-committee reports are well-publicised and easily accessible, the weekly scrutiny of documents is less so. Once a document has been sifted to a

---

[50] *EU Data Protection Law: A 'Right to Be Forgotten'?* (HL 2014–15, 40).
[51] Case C-131/12 *Google Spain SL, Google Inc v Agencia Española de Protección de Datos, Mario Costeja González* [2014] WLR(D) 202.
[52] *Report on 2014–15* (n 24) 5.
[53] By letter dated 12 June 2015.

sub-committee for examination, the sub-committee clerk or policy analyst will write a scrutiny note with a detailed analysis of it and recommendations for further action. The sub-committee's views will be expressed in correspondence to the Government, to which the Government responds. The correspondence can last less than a month or more than two years, depending on the document. This correspondence reflects the policy of the sub-committee on the document and is also the means by which it seeks to influence the Government's policy. For technical reasons, it is difficult to publish the correspondence online contemporaneously; instead, it is published every six months in a single chronological list. This makes it very difficult to trace the progress of a sub-committee's scrutiny of a document, an aspect of the sub-committee's work which, in the author's view, can be as important as an inquiry.

IX. GOVERNMENT COMPLIANCE WITH SCRUTINY OBLIGATIONS

A. Parliament Has its Say; Government Gets its Way

A reality of the scrutiny systems of both Houses is that, on issues where the Government and the committees have opposing views, those of the committees can, ultimately, be ignored. This is a feature of all non-mandating systems of scrutiny—without a veto right, they rely on persuasion rather than power. Persuasion takes many forms: reports, correspondence, evidence sessions with ministers, debates on the floor of the House or in Grand Committee, and press campaigns. But in the final reckoning, if the Government persists with a policy to which the ESC or the Select Committee objects, there is little that the committees can do.

i. Opt-in Policy

This point is well-illustrated in the following example. The Lords EU Justice Sub-Committee inquired last year into the Government's interpretation of its opt-in rights in relation to EU justice and home affairs (JHA) proposals. These rights are set out in a Protocol to the EU Treaties.[54] The Government asserted that it could opt out of any proposal which it alone considered had justice or home affairs content; the Protocol, on the other hand, appeared to make the UK's opt-in rights dependent upon the relevant JHA treaty base being cited. None of the evidence taken in the course of the inquiry supported the Government's interpretation: all of it concluded that the Government's policy undermined the principle of legal certainty in EU law. The Justice Sub-Committee's conclusions reflected this evidence, strongly recommending that the Government abandon its policy. The Government's written response to the Committee's report is outstanding at the time of writing, although it was due by June 2015. The Committee's report was

---

[54] Protocol No 21.

debated in July 2015 in Grand Committee, in the unusual circumstances of the absence of a government response.[55] In reply to the debate, the Government said that it stood by its interpretation of the opt-in Protocol.

ii. The Scrutiny Reform Report

The Government's response to the Scrutiny Reform Report was not only very late, but also rejected nearly all of the reforms proposed, as the ESC commented in its follow-up report:

> When we published the Scrutiny Reform Report 18 months ago we asked the Government 'to ensure that it responds to our Report within the customary two-month deadline … so that this matter is brought to the floor of the House no later than Easter 2014'. This did not happen. The Government response was received on the day the House rose for the summer recess, 22 July 2014, eight months after the Report's publication. Moreover, the tone of the Government's response to the key recommendations was overwhelmingly negative and did not sufficiently address our proposals.[56]

B. Hindrance

There are other examples where the Government has hindered scrutiny by failing to comply with procedural obligations.

i. Scheduling Debates in the House of Commons

There is an understanding that the Government will make time available for a floor debate if the ESC recommends one. However, there were problems with long delays towards the end of the last Parliament, and what the ESC described as 'a war of attrition'[57] with HM Treasury in particular, which at one point had a series of floor debates outstanding. One debate on the Commission's *Blueprint for a Deep and Genuine EMU* and the European Council's report *Towards a Genuine Economic and Monetary Union*, both of which set out important reforms to the eurozone, took five months to schedule and only took place on the floor of the House following direct representations by the ESC to the Prime Minister. Even then, it was combined with a significant debate on the unrelated subject of the Financial Transaction Tax.[58]

The ESC reported that the situation got worse, rather than better, after the publication of its Scrutiny Reform Report. From 2014–15, there were only three

---

[55] HL Deb 15 July 2015, cols GC 41–56.
[56] *Scrutiny Reform Follow-up and Legacy Report* (HC 2014–15, 918) para 5.
[57] ESC, *Reforming the European Scrutiny System in the House of Commons* (n 23) para 152.
[58] ibid.

debates on the floor of the House, compared with 12 in the year 2013–14, and there were 20 European Committee debates, compared with 39 in 2013–14. There were no floor debates at all between 9 June 2014 and 9 March 2015.[59]

ii. Parliamentary Scrutiny of the UK's Block Opt-out

The date of 1 December 2014 was the fifth anniversary of the entry into force of the Treaty of Lisbon and was also the date on which, under Article 10 of Protocol (No 36) to the EU Treaties, the Government's block opt-out from all JHA measures adopted before 1 December 2009 took effect, as did its application to re-join some of those measures. These were matters of political and legal significance.

In October 2012, the Home Secretary had informed the House of Commons of the 'Government's full commitment to holding a vote on the 2014 decision in this House and the other place, [and] the importance that we will accord to Parliament in the process leading up to that vote'.[60] In May 2014, Lord Faulks QC, Minister of State for Justice, repeated this undertaking to the House of Lords: 'The Government have been clear throughout this process that Parliament will be given a vote on the final list of measures that the Government apply to re-join.'[61] In the six months between June and the end of November 2014, it was therefore incumbent on the Government to keep both Houses fully informed of the progress of negotiations on opting back into 35 of the measures, and to ensure that the negotiations were completed, and the draft legislation (both in the UK and the EU) prepared in good time to be considered by committees, and debated on the floor of both Houses, before 1 December 2014. The Government did not meet these obligations:

> The Government signally failed on every count. It was not until 30 October 2014 that Ministers were able to resolve discrepancies between their list of 35 measures and that of the Commission, and finally to confirm which 35 measures they were seeking to opt back into. The UK Regulations to transpose some of these measures into UK law, which were required before the Commission would implement the opt-in, were laid before Parliament only on 3 November. A debate on 17 November on a motion to approve those Regulations (which did not include controversial measures such as the European Arrest Warrant) was the only opportunity given to the House to debate the Government's policy on opting back in, notwithstanding the undertakings already referred to.
>
> Moreover, although the Commission and Council Decisions implementing the opt-in were adopted and came into force on 1 December, the Committee did not receive the text of the Decisions, and Explanatory Memoranda, until some days later. The Government's handling of the whole Protocol (No. 36) exercise reflects poorly on Ministers and was an entirely avoidable own-goal.[62]

---

[59] *Scrutiny Reform Follow-up and Legacy Report* (n 57) paras 20–22.
[60] *Report on 2014–15* (n 24) para 54.
[61] ibid.
[62] ibid paras 55–56.

X. CONCLUSIONS

In the author's view, it is invidious to compare the strengths and weaknesses of the Commons and Lords systems of scrutiny, because they are of such different design: the former is one select committee which scrutinises all EU documents; the latter a total of seven select committees which scrutinises only sifted documents.

The received wisdom is that the systems of scrutiny in either House complement each other well: the Commons does breadth, while the Lords does depth. Dr Julie Smith of the University of Cambridge,[63] in evidence to the ESC's inquiry into reforming European scrutiny, summed up this view:

> The advantage of the UK system is precisely that you have the depth of the Lords scrutiny and the breadth of the House of Commons system. The work that is done [in the UK] is very effective and efficient.[64]

This is only true to an extent. The scrutiny role of the ESC could be more effective by making time for enhanced scrutiny, including evidence sessions with stakeholders and the Government, on a selected number of proposals that it has identified in advance as particularly important in the Commission's Annual Work Programme. Further key reforms are the involvement of the departmental select committees in EU scrutiny and the creation of permanent European Committees.

A last word on the original purpose of Parliament scrutiny of the EU. The architects of the original Commons and Lords committees were right: the manner in which EU law is negotiated in Brussels and directly applied in Member States undermines parliamentary control of national law-making. It is even more important now, with the exponential increase in EU legislation since 1973, that the scrutiny systems of both Houses are able to hold the Government to account on the negotiation of the most significant EU proposals.

---

[63] Senior Lecturer in International Relations, University of Cambridge (now Baroness Smith of Newnham).

[64] *Reforming the European Scrutiny System in the House of Commons* (n 23) Q 136.

6

Legislative Scrutiny in the House of Lords

PHILIP NORTON (LORD NORTON OF LOUTH)

I. INTRODUCTION

HOW THE HOUSE of Lords deals with legislation is shaped by the fact that it is a chamber of appointed members. This has two dimensions. The first derives from its relationship to the elected chamber. By virtue of not being elected, the House of Lords accepts that the elected chamber is entitled to get its way and therefore sees its role as complementary to, rather than competing with, that of the Commons. The Commons is able to determine the ends of legislation. The Lords focuses on the means. Its role is one of detailed scrutiny of the content of measures brought before the House. This is facilitated by procedures that are distinctive to the House.

The other dimension is the membership. In the mid-twentieth century, the House of Lords, comprising primarily hereditary peers, was almost a moribund institution, poorly attended and not contributing much to the legislative process.[1] It was largely overlooked, Parliament being taken as synonymous with the House of Commons. When the Hansard Society published a symposium, *Papers on Parliament*, in 1949, there was one notable omission: the House of Lords.[2] The creation of life peers under the Life Peerages Act 1958 created a new stream of active members.[3] The removal of most hereditary peers from membership under the House of Lords Act 1999 completed a process of transformation. Over the half-century after the Life Peerages Act, the House essentially reinvented itself as a chamber of legislative scrutiny.

That reinvention has enabled peers to utilise procedures that distinguish it from the Commons. Writing in 1948, Strathearn Gordon observed:

> The procedure has developed on much the same lines in both Houses, but since the Lords have never had to cope either with the sustained pressure of business or the systematic

---

[1] P Norton, *Parliament in British Politics* 2nd edn (Basingstoke, Palgrave Macmillan, 2013) 38.
[2] Hansard Society, *Papers on Parliament* (London, Hansard Society, 1949). The only mention of the Lords, or rather some Lords, was in reference to the Statutory Instruments Reference Committee at 102.
[3] See NDJ Baldwin, 'The House of Lords: Behavioural Changes' in P Norton (ed), *Parliament in the 1980s* (London, Basil Blackwell, 1985) 96–113.

obstruction which have afflicted the Commons, there has been no necessity for the same number of restrictive rules, and the practice approximates much more to the leisured ways of the Commons 100 years ago.[4]

The changes in the composition in the House have not so much resulted in major changes to the procedures and rules of the House (though there have been some), but rather in the exploitation of the existing procedures. The House differs from the House of Commons in that it is a self-regulating chamber and employs procedures that facilitate detailed legislative scrutiny, giving peers a more extensive capacity than that enjoyed by MPs to pursue amendments to Bills. The nature of membership protects the procedures. In recent years, the House has extended its capacity for legislative scrutiny through the use of committees. This has encompassed the use of Grand Committee for taking the Committee stage of some Bills, the creation of sessional committees for reporting on particular aspects of Bills and the appointment of ad hoc committees for undertaking post-legislative scrutiny.

We address the process, and how it has developed in recent years, before we consider the composition of the House and the impact that it has on legislation. The procedures may be seen as necessary but not sufficient for the House to affect significantly the content of legislation. The dual aspects of composition (the political and the individual) provide the sufficient conditions.

II. PROCESS

A. Scrutinising Government Bills

Although Bills go through analogous stages in the two Houses, there are notable differences in the processes each House employs. Because the Commons is responsible for granting supply, 'bills of aid and supply'—primarily the Finance Bill in respect of taxation and the Consolidated Fund Bill in respect of expenditure—receive different treatment in the Lords to other measures. Although formally the Lords may reject such Bills, it cannot amend them. Also, if a Bill is certified as a Money Bill, dealing exclusively with raising money, it will be presented for Royal Assent within one month of being sent to the Lords, regardless of whether it has received the assent or not of the Lords. Money Bills are not coterminous with Supply Bills.[5] The Lords may amend Money Bills, but the Commons is not obliged to consider such amendments. Supply Bills may not be amended and so Committee stage is negatived. In practice, the House has generally avoided also going into Committee on Money Bills. The result is that little time is given over to such Bills, the content of which may not be amended or which, even if amendable, may invite conflict with the Commons. Instead, the House focuses on the other measures

---

[4] S Gordon, *Our Parliament* 3rd edn (London, Hansard Society, 1948) 141.
[5] See M Jack (ed), *Erskine May's Treatise on The Law, Privileges, Proceedings and Usage of Parliament* 24th edn (London, LexisNexis Butterworths, 2011) 797–98.

brought forward by government. Our concern here is with how the House deals with these other Bills—the bulk of the legislative programme each session—and, in particular, how it is distinguishable from the House of Commons in doing so.

The Lords differs from the Commons in that at Second Reading, the practice is to debate, but not to divide on a Bill. It is possible for peers to oppose a Bill by moving an amendment to the motion for Second Reading and even to negative the motion. However, the Salisbury-Addison Convention, enunciated by Lord Cranborne (later the Marquess of Salisbury) in 1945, prescribes that the House does not deny a Second Reading, or agree wrecking amendments, to a Bill embodied in the election manifesto of the governing party. By extension, this has usually applied to any measure brought forward by the Government.[6] The House debates the Bill, with members signalling areas that may prove problematic, but accepts that the House of Commons as the elected House is entitled to determine the ends of legislation.

The other principal difference occurs after Second Reading in terms of what the House does not do. It does not consider a programme motion, formally limiting consideration to a specified timetable. The House utilises neither allocation of time (guillotine) nor programme motions. There will usually be agreement between the usual channels[7] as to the number of days that should be allocated to the Committee and Report stages of a Bill, but this is no more than an estimate as to the time required. If the House fails to complete a stage within the number of days allocated, more time has to be found. On occasion, this may be achieved by sitting later than the target rising time (10.00 pm on Mondays to Wednesdays, the principal days for taking legislation), where the remaining amendments are not numerous, and by allocating additional days or part-days where they are.

The absence of a formal timetable applies to the different stages of a Bill as it goes through the House and also applies in the event of amendments made by the House of Commons. Consideration of Commons amendments may take little time, but, if contested, may attract contributions from several members.

The difficulty of estimating the time required to complete each stage is compounded by another feature distinctive to the House. As *Erskine May* succinctly puts it: 'There is no selection of amendments in the Lords.'[8] All amendments tabled by peers are published and put before the House. Where amendments address the same provision or seek to achieve essentially the same goal, they may be grouped together for consideration. (Only the lead amendment is moved, but debate takes place on all the amendments in a group, with the minister replying to all of them.) The Government Whips' Office, which serves the whole

---

[6] Joint Committee on Conventions, *Conventions of the UK Parliament* Vol 1 (2005–06, HL 265-I, HC 1212-I) ch 3.

[7] In the Lords, the usual channels usually comprise the chief whips of the three main parties and the private secretary to the Government Chief Whip and Leader of the House, plus on occasion the convenor of the cross-bench peers and party leaders. M Rush and C Ettinghausen, *Opening up the Usual Channels* (London, Hansard Society, 2002) 16.

[8] *Erskine May* (n 5) 607.

House, makes a preliminary grouping: this is then circulated in advance to those who have tabled amendments for comment. Members may insist that their amendment be 'de-grouped' and considered separately or recommend that they be put in another group. Agreement is usually reached before a list of groupings is published.

Even where discussed with others, an amendment is still called at its appropriate place in the marshalled list (where the amendments are listed sequentially). If amendment 44 is discussed, say, with amendment 20, the Speaker or Deputy Speaker (or Chairman or Deputy Chairman if in committee) will still call amendment 44 after amendment 43. At that point, it is then up to the peer in whose name the amendment stands to decide whether to press the amendment or not. If the latter, the peer will say 'not moved'. (This does not preclude returning to the issue at Report stage.) If the former, the peer may say 'moved formally' (usually where it is clear there is not expected to be a vote) or indicate that he or she wishes to test the opinion of the House. Some amendments are pressed to a division, though most votes take place at Report stage.[9] As we shall see, if in Grand Committee, the amendment can only be put if there is no opposition.

There is also another major difference with the House of Commons at Committee stage. It used to be standard practice for the Committee stage of each Bill to be taken on the floor of the House. Given the growth in the volume of public legislation[10] and the complexity of some measures, the House now variously resorts to the use of Grand Committee. Bills which are technical and not contentious (at least between the parties) may be committed to Grand Committee rather than a Committee of the whole House. The rule is not invariable: one politically contentious Bill in the 2010–15 Parliament was sent to Grand Committee by vote of the House, despite the objections of the Opposition.

The Grand Committee is particular to the House of Lords. It is not the same as a Public Bill Committee in the Commons, not least because there is no selection of members to serve on the committee. The membership of Grand Committee is the membership of the House. As such, it is analogous to debates in Westminster Hall in that it constitutes a parallel chamber. Any member can attend and participate. This also means that any member can table amendments for consideration in committee. As with Bills taken in the chamber, the number of amendments may be substantial.

The nature of the Bills selected for Grand Committee tends to mean that attendance is not high, but rather confined to members with a particular expertise or interest in the Bill or parts of it. It also enables a flexible attendance, peers attending for their particular amendments or to consider the sections or clauses in which they take a particular interest. As in the chamber, there will be a continuous

---

[9] M Russell, *The Contemporary House of Lords* (Oxford, Oxford University Press, 2013) 136–37.

[10] See Hansard Society, *Making the Law: The Report of the Hansard Society Commission on the Legislative Process* (London, Hansard Society, 1992) 10–13. Occasionally, a Bill has been so substantial that it has been published in two volumes.

presence by the Opposition, with the largest number of amendments tabled being usually from the Opposition, complemented by a variety of amendments put by peers with a particular knowledge of the subject.

Grand Committee meetings are held usually in the Moses Room of the House of Lords. This is a large committee room just off the Peers' Lobby, and as such only a few yards from the chamber. Exceptionally, they make take place in a standard committee room on the main committee corridor in the Palace.

The fact that there is no designated membership, coupled with meeting in a committee room, dictates that no votes are held in Grand Committee. Given that all peers are entitled to attend, and hence to vote if divisions were permitted, one would need the facility for division lobbies to accommodate a vote. The House met after 1941 in the Robing Room of the Palace to allow the Commons, having lost its chamber to enemy bombing, to sit in the chamber of the Lords. Wooden screens were erected either side of the Robing Room to enable peers to vote by trooping behind one or other of the screens. However, similar arrangements for divisions in Grand Committee are not feasible: the Moses Room is considerably smaller than the Robing Room and the active membership of the House is considerably larger than in the 1940s. Several hundred peers suddenly crowding into the Moses Room for a vote would not be physically possible. As a result, amendments can only be made in Grand Committee when there is no opposition. Any peer with an amendment to which opposition has been expressed has the option of withdrawing it and returning to it on Report.[11]

The House also has provision for other types of committee to be appointed to consider Bills, but these are rarely employed. The House does have provision for appointing a Public Bill Committee, which is a select committee with a membership of between 12 and 16 designated peers. (Any peer can attend and move amendments, but not vote.) It is designed to deal with technical and non-controversial Government Bills. In practice, the use of such committees has essentially been superseded by the use of Grand Committee.

The House also has the facility to employ two other forms of committee in circumstances where it is felt appropriate to take evidence. The House may refer a Bill to a select committee, enabling evidence to be taken and a report made to the House, recommending whether the Bill proceed or not, before it considers the Bill in Committee.[12] This has occasionally been employed, but primarily for Private Members' Bills. One notable exception in respect of a Government Bill was the referral in 2004 of the Constitutional Reform Bill. The House may also use a Special Public Bill Committee, which is similar to the Public Bill Committee in the Commons. It differs from a select committee in that the same committee

---

[11] As any change to a Bill can only be made in Grand Committee by unanimity, it means that a single voice in support of the question that a clause or schedule stand part of the Bill is sufficient for it to be agreed.

[12] Formally, a motion may be moved at any point before Third Reading to refer a Bill to a select committee, but the usual practice is to move such a motion following Second Reading.

takes evidence prior to considering amendments to the Bill. The procedure is used primarily, nowadays more or less exclusively, for Bills originating from the Law Commission.

Report stage, as in the Commons, is more formal than Committee stage. Peers may only speak once on an amendment and a backbencher may not speak, unless the sponsor of the amendment, after the minister has replied to the debate. Amendments are taken where they cover matters not resolved in Committee. (If an amendment has been defeated in Committee, it cannot be pursued at Report stage.) They are thus less numerous than in Committee. Coupled with the limitation on peers intervening on an amendment, the time taken is less than in Committee. A Bill allocated five or six days in Committee, for example, may only be allocated two on Report. As with Committee, though, if the amendments are not completed within the days allocated, more time has to be found. Also, as in Committee, there is no selection of amendments. All amendments that are tabled are considered.

Third Reading is the final stage where there is a major difference to practice in the Commons. Standing Orders prevent two stages of a Bill from being taken on the same day. Third Reading cannot therefore follow immediately Report stage (unless the Standing Order is suspended). There is a practical reason for this. Unlike in the Commons, amendments can be taken on Third Reading. There thus needs to be a gap between Report and Third Reading for members to table amendments. When Third Reading is taken, the motion for Third Reading is put formally and carried. The House then moves on to any amendments. The scope is limited in that they should seek to clarify any remaining uncertainties, improve the drafting or enable government to give effect to commitments made at Report stage.[13] However, it is not unusual for the number on occasion to run into double figures. Once the amendments have been dealt with, the motion 'That the Bill do now pass' is put. This, rather than the Third Reading motion, signals the completion of proceedings on a Bill.

There are three other differences compared to the Commons in the passage of a Bill. One is that, as with all proceedings in the Lords, peers wishing to contribute do not have to catch anyone's eye to speak. As the House is a self-regulating chamber, there is no presiding officer with authority over the chamber: the authority rests with the chamber itself. On Second Reading (classed as a set-piece debate), peers sign up in advance to speak. Having put their names down to speak, they then appear on the speakers' list for the debate: no one can deny them the opportunity to speak. There is a meeting of the usual channels on the day of a debate to agree the order in which peers will speak, but that is the only involvement of any authority of the House. When putting their names down in advance, peers may signal if they wish to speak early or late in the debate.

---

[13] *Companion to the Standing Orders and Guide to the Proceedings of the House of Lords* (London, The Stationery Office, 2013) 156.

The usual channels seek to ensure that there is some alternation between the sides in the debate, and may list someone obviously eminent on the subject to speak early, but in that respect may be spoilt for choice. There is rarely any complaint about the ordering of names on the speakers' list. Each backbench peer taking part has up to 15 minutes in which to speak.[14] The number of speakers may be relatively short on a non-contentious measure. On major contested measures, it may reach in excess of 50. On the Second Reading of the Marriage (Same Sex Couples) Bill in 2013, for example, almost 100 peers signed up to speak, necessitating the Government Chief Whip having to allow the debate to run over two days rather than the originally scheduled one.

In the remaining stages of a Bill, where there is no set-piece debate, peers simply get to their feet to speak. If another peer or peers stand at the same time, one or more give way. Given that everyone who wishes to speak will have the opportunity to do so, there is usually no particular pressure for two peers to compete to be heard first.

The second principal difference with the Commons is the insistence on gaps between each stage. There should normally be two weekends between First and Second Reading, 14 days between the Second Reading and start of the Committee stage, 14 days between Committee and Report stage for Bills of considerable length and complexity, and three days between Report stage and Third Reading. There is no formal requirement for the gaps to be maintained, but the House tends to be reluctant to see the usual period between each stage reduced. Exceptionally, the period is reduced, usually by agreement between the usual channels. Where this happens, notice is given. Where it occurs as part of an expedited process (fast-tracking) for a Bill, the reasons are published in the Explanatory Notes to the Bill.

These constitute differences that are manifest whenever a Bill goes through. The third difference is in respect of a practice that is virtually never employed. A peer can insist on an amendment being put before the House, even if the Public Bill Office has advised that it is inadmissible. The normal practice is for peers take the advice of the clerks in the Public Bill Office. However, if a peer persists, it is ultimately a matter for the House. Where the Public Bill Office has advised that an amendment is inadmissible, the Leader of the House draws the attention of the House to the advice when the amendment is called and asks the House to endorse the opinion of the Public Bill Office. The only case in recent history, of notable political significance, took place in January 2013 when the Labour peer Lord Hart of Chilton moved an amendment to the Electoral Registration and Administration Bill to delay implementation of the orders on constituency boundaries, made under the Parliamentary Voting System and Constituencies Act 2011. He insisted

---

[14] Where there are a great many speakers, an advisory time limit may be issued, indicating that if each speaker keeps to x minutes, the House will be able to rise by the target time of 10 pm. Such guidance is purely advisory, though speakers tend to abide by it.

on the amendment, despite being advised that it was outside the scope of the Bill. The Leader of the House advised the House to endorse the opinion of the Public Bill Office.[15] The House nonetheless approved the amendment by 300 votes to 231.[16] The fact that it was outside the scope of the Bill was in effect acknowledged when subsequently the long title of the Bill was amended to encompass the changes made by the amendment.

B. Committee Assessment

This, though, does not exhaust consideration of how the House of Lords deals with legislation. Scrutiny by committees with dedicated memberships is involved, but not in the form of a committee taking the Committee stage of a Bill. It comes in the form of reports from permanent (known as sessional) select committees.[17] Like the House of Commons, the Lords has become more specialised in recent decades through the appointment of dedicated select committees. Two are especially relevant in the context of legislative scrutiny.

The Delegated Powers and Regulatory Reform Committee (DPRRC), first appointed in 1992, is empowered 'to report whether the provisions of any bill inappropriately delegate legislative power, or whether they subject the exercise of legislative power to an inappropriate degree of parliamentary scrutiny'. The DPRRC considers each Bill when it is introduced into the House and seeks to report before Committee stage. The DPRRC does not address the merits, but confines itself to the consideration of the delegation in question. It may, for example, recommend that an order-making power subject to the negative resolution procedure be subject to the affirmative procedure. Its recommendations are reported to the House and the Government normally accepts them.[18]

The Constitution Committee was created in 2001 with the remit of examining the constitutional implications of all public bills coming before the House and of keeping under review the operation of the constitution.[19] It has been active in undertaking substantial inquiries as well as examining Bills introduced into the House to determine whether they have constitutional implications. It applies what is known as to 'two P's test' (whether the Bill affects a principal part of the constitution and raises an issue of principle); if it meets the test, the Committee reports to the House.[20] The Committee has been especially influential in

---

[15] HL Deb 14 January 2013, cols 491–92.

[16] HL Deb 14 January 2013, cols 523–26.

[17] Select committees are appointed on a sessional basis, their order for appointment remaining in force from one session to the next unless the House orders otherwise. 'Sessional committees are for the most practical purposes thus in permanent existence.' *Erskine May* (n 5) 891.

[18] Russell (n 9) 219–20.

[19] See House of Lords Constitution Committee, *Reviewing the Constitution: Terms of Reference and Method of Working* (2001–02, HL 11). See also J Simson Caird, 'Parliamentary Constitutional Review: Ten Years of the House of Lords Select Committee on the Constitution' [2012] *Public Law* 4.

[20] I declare an interest. As the first Chairman of the Committee, I was responsible for devising the test.

shaping debate in the House, not least in the long 2010–12 session of Parliament on measures such as the Health and Social Care Bill, the Public Bodies Bill, the Fixed-term Parliaments Bill, and the Parliamentary Voting System and Constituencies Bill. It has become, according to Andrew Le Sueur and Jack Simson Caird, 'a well-respected part of the House of Lords' arsenal against misguided and badly prepared legislation'.[21]

C. Promoting Legislation: Private Members' Bills

The House, like the Commons, is essentially a reactive body in relation to the executive. There is scope for MPs to promote legislation through Private Members' Bills, but such Bills are, as Rogers and Walters put it, 'fragile vessels'.[22] Relatively few Bills make it to the statute book.[23] The same applies to the Lords,[24] though there are two principal differences. The first is that the scope for introducing a Bill has been greater, at least until 2015, for a peer than an MP. The second is that it is even more difficult for a peer to get a Bill on the statute book than an MP. As a means for raising an issue, a Private Member's Bill in the Lords is very good; as a means for achieving a change in the law, at least directly, it is very poor.

Until 2015, peers could introduce Private Members' Bills on a first-come, first-served basis. Those introducing Bills at the start of the session were usually assured of time to consider their Bills. However, the number of Bills became so large that there was insufficient time to consider most of them. At the close of the 2014–15 session, there were 26 Bills that had not been scheduled for debate and four that had been committed to committee, but no time for such consideration. It was agreed that in future, Private Members' Bills submitted at the start of a session would be subject to ballot (not altogether dissimilar to the practice in the Commons),[25] with Bills submitted later in the session joining the queue as in the past.

Unlike in the Commons, Standing Orders make no distinction between Government Bills and Private Members' Bills. The House is formally able to take each when it so chooses. Deliberation on Private Members' Bills is not confined to Friday sittings. Although the practice is to give priority to Government Bills on most days other than Fridays, the stages of Private Members' Bills may be scheduled for debate on any day. Where no amendments have been tabled, it is not unusual for Committee and Report stages to be taken after Question Time and before government business on a normal weekday.

---

[21] A Le Sueur and J Simson Caird, 'The House of Lords Select Committee on the Constitution' in A Horne, G Drewry and D Oliver (eds), *Parliament and the Law* (Oxford, Hart Publishing, 2013) 281.
[22] R Rogers and R Walters, *How Parliament Works* 7th edn (Abingdon, Routledge, 2015) 205.
[23] Norton (n 1) 80–81.
[24] Russell (n 9) 193–95.
[25] Though different in that peers do not simply submit their names for the ballot, but must have ready the Bills they wish to introduce.

Although occasionally a Private Member's Bill makes it to the statute book—four originating in the House of Lords were enacted in the 2005–10 Parliament[26]—the principal value of promoting a Bill is to ensure that it is debated. It is a way of testing opinion and soliciting a government response. A good example would be the Assisted Dying Bill, promoted initially in 2003 by Lord Joffe and pursued in the 2014–15 session by the former Lord Chancellor, Lord Falconer. The end goal is to stimulate action by MPs or the Government.[27]

Opponents may occasionally seek to divide the House on Second Reading, or on amendments at Committee or Report stages, but the normal practice is to allow a Bill through. It is a convention that the Government does not oppose Private Members' Bills in the Lords. They thus normally pass. They then usually get no further as, having been sent to the Commons, they join the queue of Private Members' Bills waiting consideration at 2.30 pm on Fridays. There are exceptions, notably when the Government supports or at least does not oppose a Bill. A recent example is the House of Lords (Expulsion and Suspension) Bill in the 2014–15 session introduced by Baroness Hayman. Most, though, will languish in the Commons and never make it to the statute book.

D. Secondary Legislation

The House also employs procedures for dealing with secondary legislation that distinguish it from the Commons. As we have seen, the House engages in the input side of legislation in the form of the Delegated Powers and Regulatory Reform Committee. The House also considers the output side, examining Statutory Instruments when promulgated by government departments. The House in 2003 approved the creation of a committee, the Merits of Statutory Instruments Committee, to consider all Statutory Instruments subject to the affirmative or negative resolution procedure. The Committee is empowered to draw to the attention of the House any Instruments that have important political or legal obligations or which give rise to issues of public policy likely to be of interest to the House; are inappropriate because of changes since the parent Act was passed; implement EU legislation inappropriately; or achieve their policy objectives imperfectly. In 2012, the remit of the Committee was extended to cover orders made under the Public Bodies Act 2011 to abolish or transfer functions of public bodies. As a consequence, it was renamed the Secondary Legislation Scrutiny Committee.

The Committee engages in detailed scrutiny of Instruments and reports to the House any that it deems to fall within the categories listed. It is assisted by two legal advisers as well as by the fact that the House follows its usual practice

---

[26] Norton (n 1) 80.
[27] See D Shell, *The House of Lords* 2nd edn (Manchester, Manchester University Press, 2007) 93–94.

of appointing members with particular experience or expertise in the field. The Committee will usually include leading lawyers and peers with knowledge of government. For much of the 2010–15 Parliament, it included a former law lord renowned for detailed scrutiny of every order laid before the Committee. Other members had served in government as ministers or officials.

Another difference with the Commons is that when a motion is made to annul an Instrument subject to the negative resolution procedure, or one regretting the introduction of an order, time is usually found to debate the motion. Motions to approve orders subject to the affirmative order procedure are normally taken on the floor of the House, during the evening dinner break,[28] or are referred to Grand Committee; motions tabled to annul or regret an order are usually taken on the floor of the House during the dinner break.

The process employed by the House ensures that all Instruments subject to parliamentary approval are considered. The work of the Secondary Legislation Scrutiny Committee has value in engaging with Departments to address ambiguities or improve drafting. On occasion, its work has resulted in orders being withdrawn and re-laid. It can have a deterrent effect in that no Department wants a reputation for producing poorly drafted secondary legislation. (The Committee has criticised Departments for badly drafted orders, on occasion commending others for good practice.) The use of motions to annul or regret enables the Opposition, and on occasion backbench peers, to generate debate on orders that they believe are flawed or require justification.

The House has a veto over secondary legislation—the provisions of the Parliament Act do not apply—and has asserted 'its unfettered freedom to vote on any subordinate legislation submitted for its consideration'.[29] However, successive governments have claimed that it is a convention that the House does not vote down an order. The justification for this is that the Government has no way of overturning such a rejection by the unelected House. Though on occasion peers have forced divisions, and most accept that they should if necessary reject secondary legislation,[30] the House in practice has proved reluctant to use its power to reject secondary legislation. The only occasion it has done so in recent years was in 2007 on an order to allow for the creation of a super-casino in Manchester.[31] The tendency is to rely more on the persuasive capacity of the House, members drawing on reports of the Secondary Legislation Scrutiny Committee as the basis for moving non-fatal motions of regret.

---

[28] When the House is engaged in scrutiny of Bills at Committee or Report stage, there is normally a break, at a convenient point around or shortly after 7.30 pm, to take a Question for Short Debate or a motion on a Statutory Instrument. A Question for Short Debate is limited to a maximum of one hour. There is no time limit on a debate on secondary legislation, though the expectation, or hope, is that it will not last much beyond an hour.

[29] *Lords Journal* 1993–94, 683; *Companion to the Standing Orders and Guide to Proceedings of the House of Lords* (n 13) 200.

[30] See Russell (n 9) 140–41.

[31] See ibid 141.

E. Scrutinising Acts: Post-legislative Scrutiny

The other recent development in the Lords has been the use of ad hoc committees to undertake post-legislative scrutiny. Each session, the House normally appoints at least one ad hoc committee to investigate a particular subject. The committee has a confined life span (the session) and once it has reported, it ceases to exist, though within the time available, it is sometimes possible to produce more than one report. In 2012, the use of such committees was expanded and at least one committee appointed each session to review particular Acts or legislation in a particular field. During the Parliament, committees were appointed to consider adoption legislation,[32] the Inquiries Act 2005,[33] the Mental Capacity Act 2005[34] and the Extradition Act 2003.[35] At the end of the 2014–15 session, the House agreed that in the first session of the new Parliament, a committee should be appointed to consider the disability provisions of the Equality Act 2010. In addition, the Delegated Powers and Regulatory Reform Committee in 2015 reviewed the Legislative and Regulatory Reform Act 2006, following the assessment of it by the Department of Business, Innovation and Skills.[36]

The use of ad hoc committees has enabled the House to fill a gap, following the recommendation of the Constitution Committee of the House in 2004 that post-legislative scrutiny should be a routine feature of parliamentary scrutiny.[37] Although the Government in 2008 accepted the case for post-legislative review by Government Departments, with the reviews being published and sent to Departmental Select Committees, the Committees have not had time to pursue post-legislative scrutiny on any regular basis. The work of ad hoc committees in the Lords has enabled the House to engage in targeted scrutiny, based on recommendations from peers and approved by the House. The reports elicit a government response and are debated in the House. Given that they tend to cover topics that are important but not contentious in partisan terms, the committees have been able to engage in what has tended to be a constructive dialogue with government.[38]

The House has also addressed the problems deriving from the temporary nature of the committees. Once ad hoc committees have reported, they lose the

---

[32] House of Lords Select Committee on Adoption Legislation, *Adoption: Pre-Legislative Scrutiny* (HL 2012–13, 94); *Adoption: Post-Legislative Scrutiny* (HL 2012–13, 127).

[33] House of Lords Select Committee on the Inquiries Act 2005, *The Inquiries Act 2005: Post-Legislative Scrutiny* (HL 2013–14, 143). On post-legislative scrutiny generally, see also ch 3 above.

[34] House of Lords Select Committee on the Mental Capacity Act 2005, *Mental Capacity Act 2005: Post-Legislative Scrutiny* (HL 2013–14, 139).

[35] House of Lords Select Committee on Extradition Law, *The European Arrest Warrant Opt-in* (HL 2014–15, 63); *Extradition: UK Law and Practice* (HL 2014–15, 136).

[36] House of Lords Delegated Powers and Regulatory Reform Committee, *Post-Legislative Assessment of the Legislative and Regulatory Reform Act 2006* (HL 2014–15, 132).

[37] House of Lords Constitution Committee, *Parliament and the Legislative Process* (HL 2003–04, 173-I).

[38] See, eg, the Government's response to the Select Committee on the Mental Capacity Act. HM Government, *Valuing Every Voice, Respecting Every Right: Making the Case for the Mental Capacity Act*, June 2014, Cm 8884.

protection of parliamentary privilege as well as the opportunity to engage in any follow-up to their reports. As a result, the Liaison Committee of the House decided in 2013 to invite the committees to identify issues they thought likely to merit a follow-up a year after they had reported. The Committee can then pursue the issues with government.[39]

The way in which the House deals with legislation thus differs substantially from the manner in which it is considered in the House of Commons. There are greater opportunities for members to participate, primarily in Committee, yet it is not just the process that is particular to the House, but also those who participate. The nature of the membership is central to the House making a difference to the outcome of legislative scrutiny.

III. PEERS

The composition of the House is crucial to explaining how the procedures are exploited and affect legislative outcomes. It enables the House to exercise, in Blondel's terms, a notable degree of legislative viscosity.[40] There are two dimensions to the composition: the political and the individual.

The political composition refers to the collective groupings in the House. When Gordon was writing about the House of Lords, he was able to refer to a 'permanent Conservative majority'.[41] The Life Peerages Act led to an increase in peers from the Labour Parry and the Liberal Democrats. The House of Lords Act 1999 resulted in over 500 hereditary peers being excluded from membership. This effectively transformed the House into a House predominantly of life peers and one in which no one party held a majority. The effect since has been that, whichever party is in office, it cannot carry a vote relying solely on its own party members in the House. The House is notable for having three large groupings: the Conservative Party, the Labour Party and the cross-bench peers (see Table 1). The Liberal Democrats constitute the fourth-largest grouping.

The consequence of this for legislative scrutiny is that the Government has to carry at least some other part of the House with it if its legislation is contested. It consequently has to engage in the politics of justification rather than, as is possible in the Commons, the politics of assertion. The absence of an absolute majority, the presence of a sizeable body of peers with no party political affiliations and the appointed nature of the House (members not seeing one another as electoral threats) have resulted in a less adversarial approach and fewer divisions than in the Commons. Government ministers will work on persuading the House rather than adopting a confrontational stance.

---

[39] House of Lords Liaison Committee, *Review of Select Committee Activity and Proposals for New Committee Activity* (HL 2013–14, 145) paras 20-24.
[40] See J Blondel et al, 'Legislative Behaviour: Some Steps Towards a Cross-national Measurement' (1970) 5 *Government and Opposition* 67.
[41] Gordon (n 4) 142.

Table 6.1: Membership of the House of Lords

As of 3 April 2015	
Conservative	224
Labour	215
Cross-bench	179
Liberal Democrats	103
Other parties	15
Non-affiliated	21
Bishops	26
TOTAL	783

(Excludes ineligible peers)

The other dimension is the individual—the collection of individual peers who form the membership. They sit in particular groupings, but are able to express their own views on measures. Formally, the writ of summons is personal—other than frontbenchers, no peer speaks in a representative capacity—and the whips have few if any powers to ensure compliance with the party line.[42] In the case of the cross-bench peers, there is no party line.

Equally important, the House can be characterised as a full-time House of part-time members. Like the House of Commons, the House of Lords is one of the busiest legislative chambers in the world. However, unlike in the Commons, membership is not seen as a full-time occupation, which is reflected in the fact that members are not salaried. Peers can claim an attendance allowance for those days that they attend. Any salary comes from posts they hold outside the House (except for the Leader of the Opposition, the Opposition Chief Whip and three office holders). The House thus draws on members who have or have had outside responsibilities. Indeed, another way of describing the House is one of experience and expertise.

Peers may be appointed because of positions they hold or have held or because they are recognised as experts in their particular fields.[43] The experience and expertise of peers inform debates. That may be sufficient to influence a response from government. A junior Justice minister at the despatch box may be responding to an amendment supported by peers who are among the nation's leading lawyers. These can include former Justices of the Supreme Court who have been

---

[42] P Norton, 'Cohesion without Discipline: Party Voting in the House of Lords' (2003) 9(4) *Journal of Legislative Studies* 57.
[43] See M Russell and M Benton, *Analysis of Existing Data on the Breadth of Expertise and Experience in the House of Lords*, Report to the House of Lords Appointments Commission(London, UCL Constitution Unit, 2010).

Law Lords,[44] as well as those who have held office as Lord Chancellor, Lord Chief Justice, Attorney General or Director of Public Prosecutions. It may also include former Commissioners of the Metropolitan Police and heads and members of the intelligence services. A junior minister responding to an amendment affecting higher education may face an array of heads of university colleges, professors, university chancellors, those who have served as vice-chancellors, and experts on education, as well as former Education Secretaries and Ministers for Higher Education.

The collective and individual composition of the House creates an environment conducive to constructive engagement and consensus. Most amendments, as we shall see, are agreed without a division. Ministers are keen to reach agreement without risking a division. This influences not only the approach taken at the despatch box, but also between stages. In effect, there is an additional stage—that of informal discussion. If a minister comes under pressure at Committee stage, it is not unusual to resist accepting an amendment as it stands, though not ruling out looking at the issue, and then meeting the peer between Committee and Report stage to see if an amendment (usually drafted by the Government) can be agreed. It is thus not unusual for Report and Third Reading to be used for government amendments to be moved to give effect to commitments made at an earlier stage or between stages. Occasionally, the Government will accept the amendment as tabled by a peer.

IV. IMPACT

It is generally accepted that the House of Lords makes a notable difference to the detail of legislation. 'Almost all observers agree that the quality of peers' work is usually high and the outcomes useful', wrote Emma Crewe. 'They give more time to scrutiny than MPs and make a huge number of improvements to Bills: 2,557 amendments in 2001–02 and 2,996 in 2002–03.'[45] The activity has increased as a consequence of the revitalization of the House and the growth in the volume of legislation.[46]

However, most amendments agreed are government amendments—generally more than 90 per cent of all amendments agreed are moved by ministers[47]—and the House has been characterised by Donald Shell as being 'diligent but on the whole docile'.[48] In terms of legislative revision, the House is, he claims, a 'convenience to the government'.[49] The House, as both Shell and Crewe have observed, can be

---

[44] Law Lords who were translated to the Supreme Court upon its creation in 2009 resume membership of the House upon their retirement.
[45] E Crewe, *Lords of Parliament* (Manchester, Manchester University Press, 2005) 195.
[46] Shell (n 27) 98–99.
[47] ibid 100.
[48] ibid 126.
[49] ibid 126.

too self-congratulatory about its work and hence resistant to change, but what this masks is the impact that it does have, which is not confined to carrying backbench amendments against the wishes of government.

The House of Lords, by its actions, is playing to its strengths. As Lord Gould mentioned in his maiden speech, drawing on his role as a pollster, the House was respected by the public because 'it can achieve balance, transcend politics and play a crucial revising role'.[50] The nature of its work adds value. In terms of legislation, providing the Government with a convenient means of making amendments to its own Bills is not necessarily a bad thing if a consequence is to improve the wording of legislation. However, the impact of the House extends beyond being a convenience.

The House is important both in terms of its unseen and its seen impact. The most significant unseen impact in respect of legislation is acting as a deterrent. Ministers and officials anticipate reaction in the House and shape their behaviour accordingly. When ministers fail to anticipate accurately, they can encounter serious difficulties in the House. They bring forward provisions that they think they can justify to the satisfaction of the House. If they miscalculate, they can find themselves in trouble at the despatch box and having to make concessions in order to avoid defeat. Anticipating reaction is thus crucial, but it is most effective when government elects not to bring forward a measure. In other words, non-decision-making is an important dimension of the Lords' power in the legislative process.

The most pervasive impact of seen activity is arguably in ensuring that ministers and officials are able to justify the provisions of Bills. The key difference between the two Houses is that already identified, between the politics of assertion and the politics of justification. The nature of the House of Lords means that ministers have to listen—the time and procedures of the House mean that they cannot avoid it—and that they have frequently to engage with peers who are recognised as having considerable experience or expertise in the field.

In terms of influencing the specific content of government measures, peers may be both proactive and reactive. They may employ the opportunities available to them, through Private Members' Bills and motions, to fulfil an agenda-setting role and get ministers thinking about concerns that may merit action. However, the most extensive impact occurs in reacting to measures brought forward by government.

Once government has decided to pursue a measure, peers may contribute when a draft Bill is sent to a joint committee of the two Houses for pre-legislative scrutiny. Bills published in draft are usually referred for scrutiny by select committees in the Commons. However, some Bills, not least if they are of constitutional significance or are complex, may be referred to joint committees. Peers often tend to take a more active role than MPs in such committees, partly a consequence of

---

[50] Quoted in ibid 114.

their expertise in the area and also because MPs tend to have more competing demands on their time. Some peers will play a particular leading role, including on occasion chairing the committee.[51]

When legislation is being considered, Meg Russell has advanced six modes of legislative debate in the Lords: the probing, quasi-academic (expert), interest group, constitutional propriety, second thought and adversarial modes.[52] These are not mutually exclusive and may be in danger of confusing the purpose with the source. The purpose of tabling amendments is normally to probe, to challenge or to object. These may originate from the experience, expertise, ideology (or partisanship) or general interest of peers.

Amendments to Bills are often moved in Committee as probing amendments, seeking to elicit the purpose of a particular provision. An informed response may be sufficient to satisfy the peer moving the amendment and the House. Others may be moved by peers who understand the purpose of a provision, but wish to challenge government, perhaps offering alternatives designed to strengthen, limit or clarify. Others may be designed to remove a particular provision based on clear objections to it. Here the debate becomes one between contending parties, with the amendment often, but by no means always, moved from the Opposition frontbench.

The House is at its most effective in utilising its persuasive rather than its coercive capacity to achieve outcomes.[53] The persuasive capacity derives from ministers listening to peers during the passage of a Bill and conceding that there is a case for some action. The result is an agreed amendment, achieved without a division. The coercive capacity derives from groupings in the House combining against the Government. In the period from 1999 to 2010, the Liberal Democrats were essentially the swing group in the House. If they joined with the Conservative Opposition, the Government was likely to be defeated.[54] In the 2010–15 Parliament, with the Liberal Democrats being in coalition with the Conservatives, the swing voters were the cross-benchers.[55] They were prone to turn out in greater numbers than in preceding Parliaments and if they did so and divided disproportionately against the Government in conjunction with the Labour Opposition, the Government lost. In the 2015 Parliament, the Liberal Democrats resumed their role as the swing group, a combination of Labour and Liberal Democrat peers usually being sufficient to defeat the Government.

The number of times the Government is defeated in the House of Lords is significant, not least relative to the number of defeats in the House of Commons.

---

[51] Thus, for example, former film director Lord Puttnam chaired the Joint Committee on the Draft Communications Bill in 2002 and the former Leader of the House, Lord Richard, chaired the Joint Committee on the Draft House of Lords Reform Bill in 2012.
[52] Russell (n 9) 181–93.
[53] See Shell (n 27) 101.
[54] M Russell and M Sciara, 'Why Does the Government Get Defeated in the House of Lords? The Lords, the Party System and British Politics' (2007) 2 *British Politics* 299; Russell (n 9) 117–18.
[55] Russell (n 9) 120–22.

In the 2010–15 Parliament, the Coalition Government was defeated 99 times in the division lobbies. The combination of the two coalition partners resulted in the average number per session being fewer than in previous sessions under a Labour Government (see Table 2)—an average of 49 per session in the 2001–05 Parliament, 35 per session in the five-session 2005–10 Parliament and 25 per session in the 2010–15 Parliament—but it remained a large number. Following the return of the new Parliament in May 2015, the Government suffered 10 defeats within the first two months.

Table 6.2: Government defeats in the House of Lords

Parliament	Number of defeats
1997–2001	108
2001–05	245
2005–10	175
2010–15	99

Sources: House of Commons Library, *Government Defeats in the House of Lords*, PIL, SN/PC/03252, 2010; UCL Constitution Unit, *Government Defeats in the House of Lords*, www.ucl.ac.uk/silva/constitution-unit/research/parliament/house-of-lords/lords-defeats

However, in terms of amendments achieved in the House, those carried by a vote constituted a small minority. More than 9 out of every 10 amendments agreed in the House are carried without a vote. Where the Government is defeated, Meg Russell and Maria Sciara found that more than 40 per cent of the amendments carried by the House were accepted by the Government; somewhat counter-intuitively, it tended to be the more important defeats which elicited concessions by the Government.[56]

It is the changes brought forward by government in response to amendments moved by peers, or points raised by peers on Second Reading or in discussions with ministers, which are most significant in terms of achieving substantive changes to Bills. Meg Russell's study of 12 Government Bills in the period from 2005 to 2012 found that a majority of substantive government amendments (55 per cent) could be traced to amendments moved earlier by peers, with others attributable to reports from committees or pressure from MPs.[57] The proportion is significant, but it is some of the individual changes achieved to Bills that can be the most important aspect of the impact of the House of Lords. The House is especially vigilant on constitutional issues, not least through the Constitution Committee. A good example of it achieving excision of a major

---

[56] M Russell and M Sciara, 'The Policy Impact of Defeats in the House of Lords' (2008) 10 *British Journal of Politics and International Relations* 571.

[57] Russell (n 9) 173.

'Henry VIII' power (enabling ministers by order to amend primary legislation) occurred with the Public Bodies Bill in 2012. The Bill allowed ministers to make orders at later dates to abolish or transfer functions of a long list of public bodies. Pressure from the House resulted in the Minister agreeing to its removal.[58] There was substantial discussion with ministers between stages, the Government accepting the arguments advanced without the House having to divide on the provision.

It is possible to identify the conditions in which concessions by government are most likely to be conceded. They are most likely in situations where the House is pursuing an issue in which it has recognised strength, such as human rights or criminal justice. This is especially so where amendments are moved by leading experts who are widely respected in the House and critical reports are published by committees such as the Constitution Committee. The likelihood of concessions is reinforced where the stance taken by the House has some resonance among government backbenchers in the Commons, the Government being unable to draw on a unified party in the Commons in the event of a dispute between the two Houses ('ping-pong'). The House may also occasionally have leverage because legislation needs to be enacted by a particular date (as, for example, with anti-terrorism legislation in 2005).[59] Prior to the introduction of fixed-term Parliaments, there was also a time constraint in the period of the 'wash-up' at the end of the Parliament. Where such conditions come together, the prudent reaction of the Government is to concede. Such occasions may be infrequent, but they can be extremely important in terms of the content of a Bill.

Thus, for example, the Coalition Government of 2010–15 achieved the passage of the Fixed-term Parliaments Bill, but only after accepting a backbench amendment that replaced the key section of the Bill providing conditions for an early general election and bringing forward its own amendment to provide for a review of the Act in 2020. The Bill had encountered criticism in both Houses, was the subject of a critical report by the Constitution Committee (as well as one by the Political and Constitutional Reform Committee in the Commons) and was subject to criticism by constitutional experts in different parts of the House. The Bill that made it to the statute book was notably different from the Bill as introduced.[60]

---

[58] See ibid 188–89.
[59] During the passage of the Prevention of Terrorism Bill in 2005, the Government working to a tight deadline to ensure enactment before the extant legislation expired, there was a dispute between the two Houses, resulting in amendments going back and forth during the longest recorded sitting of the House. The Lords sat, from 11 am on the morning of Thursday 10 March to 7.31 pm on the Friday evening, variously adjourning while the Commons considered the amendments sent back by the House. HL Deb 10 March 2005, cols 999–1066.
[60] See P Norton, 'From Flexible to Semi-fixed: The Fixed-term Parliaments Act' (2014) 1 *Journal of International and Comparative Law* 203.

In short, the impact of the House of Lords cannot be seen, let alone measured, purely in discrete and observable actions. It has to be viewed holistically, both in terms of process and effect.

V. BUILDING ON STRENGTH?

Peers, as we have noted, have been described as notably self-congratulatory and resistant to change, regarding their procedures as good and superior to those of the Commons. In practice, the House has been willing to reform and to adapt. There has clearly been something of a dynamic, not least in terms of utilising permanent committees for undertaking scrutiny of particular aspects of Bills, and ad hoc committees for undertaking post-legislative scrutiny. Such changes may be seen as playing to the strengths of the House, through filling gaps in the parliamentary scrutiny of legislation and drawing on the particular skills of members.

It is also possible to identify pressure to strengthen further the means of scrutiny. There have been calls by some peers to enhance the House in dealing with secondary legislation. Some peers have challenged the convention that the House does not reject Statutory Instruments, arguing that if an order is rejected, the Government can bring forward a new order and do so quickly. If the Instrument is adapted to meet the concerns of the House, there is no reason why it should not then be accepted. Such critics see it as illogical not to utilise the power, or at least be willing to, if the House wants to ensure that the work of the Secondary Legislation Scrutiny Committee is effective.

The Constitution Committee in its 2004 Report on *Parliament and the Legislative Process* did recommend that each Government Bill should, at some stage during its passage, be subject to examination by an evidence-taking committee. Where a Bill comes from the Commons and has been to a Public Bill Committee, it will normally have been subject to such examination. Bills starting life in the Lords are not considered by such a committee. Some peers favour making greater use of the facility to send Bills to an evidence-taking committee, either a Public Bill Committee or a select committee. Utilising such a procedure would add some time to the Bill's progress through the House, but peers would not necessarily see that as a particular impediment, preferring time to improve the measure rather than be seen to rush it through.

In practice, much will depend on broader political pressure in respect of the House, but proposals for Lords reform focus on composition rather than structures and procedures. There is a general acceptance that what the House does it does well. For some, the functions should be fulfilled by a different membership. For members within the House, the pressure is to do better what it already does well.

Part 2

Accountability

7

Parliamentary Reform and the Accountability of Government to the House of Commons

RICHARD KELLY AND LUCINDA MAER

I. INTRODUCTION

IN MAY 2009, the House of Commons was rocked by the expenses scandal. The Government responded with legislation that established the Independent Parliamentary Standards Authority to devise and police a new scheme for MPs' expenses. Long-standing proponents of parliamentary reform—particularly reform that would wrest some control of the House of Commons away from government and back to Parliament—saw that the expenses crisis, which raised concerns about public confidence in the House of Commons, provided an opportunity to implement reform.[1]

Parliamentary procedure had not stood still in the preceding years. There had been significant changes to sitting times, to programming and scrutinising legislation, and the establishment of Westminster Hall for debates initiated by backbenchers and select committees. However, as Alexandra Kelso observed in her survey of parliamentary reform in the twentieth century, the structured institutional context, 'geared towards facilitating strong government', meant that reform had tended to improve the ability of the Commons to expedite government business rather than increase the effectiveness of the Commons as a check upon the executive and its actions.[2] This could be ascribed to the fact that much reform was instigated and taken forward by or under the control of government. As Rogers and Walters commented in the 2004 edition of *How Parliament Works*, 'reform' or 'modernisation' to the person speaking:

> [R]eally mean no more than 'change of which I approve'. After all, the 'Balfour' reforms of a century ago, which entrenched the government's control over business and time of

---

[1] M Russell, '"Never Allow a Crisis to Go to Waste": The Wright Committee Reforms to Strengthen the House of Commons' (2011) 64 *Parliamentary Affairs* 612.

[2] A Kelso, *Parliamentary Reform at Westminster* (Manchester, Manchester University Press, 2009) 185–86.

the House of Commons, were hardly a milestone in the democratic accountability of the executive. And in the present debate over the role of Parliament, 'modernisation' and 'reform' mean different things to different people.[3]

The expenses crisis offered an opening for a different approach. A committee of backbenchers—the Select Committee on Reform of the House of Commons (commonly referred to as the Wright Committee, after its chairman, Tony Wright)—was appointed to consider ways in which backbenchers could be empowered to better hold the Government to account—through select committee reform, and by giving backbenchers and the public easier access to the agenda of the House. It reported in late 2009 and many of its recommendations were implemented by either the Labour Government shortly before the 2010 General Election or the Conservative–Liberal Democrat Coalition shortly after May 2010.

This chapter considers whether the reforms have contributed to increasing the accountability of the Government to the House of Commons. It briefly reviews the process of reform under the Labour Governments from 1997 onwards in order to outline the context in which the Wright Committee was established. It then describes the Committee's recommendations and their acceptance by the House of Commons. Three key aspects—the democratisation of select committees, backbench control of the agenda and public access to the House—are then examined to assess whether the reforms have resulted in the Government being more accountable to the House of Commons.

II. FROM MODERNISATION TO REFORM

Since 1997, parliamentary reform has been initiated in some cases as part of a programme of reform and in some instances in response to a particular event or series of events. For example, there were a series of reforms made in the early years of the Blair administration which were trailed as part of a change in the way politics would be conducted. In 2007, the new Brown administration launched a programme of reform, including parliamentary reform, under the banner of the 'Governance of Britain'. Others, such as the creation of the Select Committee on Reform of the House of Commons and its proposals for select committee reform and the consequent creation of a backbench business committee, were in part a response to the expenses crisis of 2009.

The Select Committee on Modernisation of the House of Commons was set up in June 1997 with a remit to 'consider how the practices and procedures of the House should be modernised'. The establishment of the Committee had been one of the proposals of the Joint Consultative Committee on Constitutional Reform agreed by the Labour Party and the Liberal Democrats before the 1997 General Election, and its creation was a Labour Party manifesto commitment.

---

[3] R Rogers and R Walters, *How Parliament Works* 5th edn (Harlow, Longman, 2004) 368.

The Committee was chaired by the Leader of the House of Commons, a Cabinet Minister. On occasion, this made the Committee subject to some criticism as it was considered unlikely that the Committee would propose reform that would be to the detriment of the Government. Others have pointed to this as a strength, as the Committee's recommendations were likely to receive government backing. Changes initiated by the Committee included reforms to the sitting hours and the introduction of an evidence stage during the legislative process for some Bills. It became moribund in 2008 after its proposals for Regional Select Committees split the Committee along party lines.[4]

Although the Government, through the Modernisation Committee, largely drove the reform of the Commons during this period, options for change were presented by a number of different actors. The Liaison Committee (a committee of select committee chairs), a Conservative Party Commission on Strengthening Parliament, groups of backbench MPs, independent Hansard Society Commissions, academics and special advisers all put forward proposals. Often the same individuals were members of more than one of these groups; consequently, the ideas were cross-fertilised and frequently enjoyed cross-party support.

It was not always easy to frame proposals that would win the House's support. The Liaison Committee's call to change the way in which select committee members were appointed was initially ignored by the Government. It had suggested that a group of independent senior MPs, rather than party whips, should be responsible for appointing chairs and members to select committees. In 2002, similar proposals, introduced by Robin Cook, the Leader of the House of Commons and Chairman of the Modernisation Committee, were rejected by the House.

Despite this, a number of backbenchers continued to call for changes that would increase accountability and scrutiny of government. Groups such as Parliament First argued that party whips should not determine who sat on committees responsible for scrutinising government departments.[5] Concerns were also expressed about the limited time that backbenchers had, in the Chamber, either to debate issues they wanted to consider or to discuss rafts of government amendments, often tabled with very little notice, at Report stage.[6] There was also growing pressure for making the House more relevant to the public who elected its Members.

III. SELECT COMMITTEE ON REFORM OF THE HOUSE OF COMMONS

Tony Wright, who was Chairman of the Public Administration Select Committee from 1999 until his retirement in 2010, wrote to Gordon Brown in the wake of the

---

[4] House of Commons Library Standard Note, *Regional Accountability at Westminster*, SN/PC/4411, November 2008.
[5] Parliament First, *Parliament's Last Chance* (London, Parliament First, 2003) para 4.7.
[6] Russell (n 1).

2009 expenses scandal and suggested that 'we should do something serious about House of Commons reform to show that we could reform ourselves in the wake of the expenses scandal'.[7]

Brown accepted the idea and on 10 June 2009, in a statement made in the House of Commons on constitutional renewal, announced that:

> We must also take forward urgent modernisation of the procedures of the House of Commons, so I am happy to give the Government's support to a proposal from my hon. Friend the Chairman of the Public Administration Committee that we will work with a special parliamentary commission comprising Members from both sides of this House, convened for a defined period to advise on necessary reforms, including making Select Committee processes more democratic, scheduling more and better time for non-Government business in the House, and enabling the public to initiate directly some issues for debate.[8]

The Select Committee on Reform of the House of Commons was established and its membership agreed on 20 July 2009, with Tony Wright as its Chairman.[9] There had been some wrangling over the terms of reference and how to appoint members to it. The Committee was required to consider and make recommendations on all the issues that Brown announced, and to report in November 2009. Its main recommendations were as follows:

— Chairs of departmental and similar committees should be directly elected by secret ballot of the House. Members of select committees would be elected within party groups.
— Backbench business should be organised by a Backbench Business Committee, responsible for all business which was not strictly ministerial. This Committee would then join with the representatives of the Government and Opposition in a House Business Committee, which would be obliged to come up with a draft agenda for the week ahead. This agenda would then be put to the House for its agreement.
— The Procedure Committee should become for a trial period a 'Procedure and Petitions' Committee dealing with petitions under the current rules. At the same time, there should also be a number of changes designed to give petitions a higher profile in Parliament, including taking forward urgently further discussions on the introduction of e-petitions.
— This would, the Committee believed, help change the House of Commons' emphasis on public engagement from providing the public with information to achieving a greater degree of public participation.

---

[7] Wright's evidence to the Constitution Committee, *Constitutional Reform Process* (HL 2010–12, 177) Q 79.
[8] HC Deb 10 June 2009, col 797.
[9] See House of Commons Library Standard Note, *Establishment of the Select Committee on Reform of the House of Commons*, SN/PC/5140, 25 January 2010.

In February and March 2010, two debates were held on the Committee's reform proposals. The motions to implement the changes were tabled by the Government. However, the motions and the Labour Government's approach to the debates suggested a certain amount of reluctance towards implementing the recommendations. On 4 March 2010, the House of Commons agreed that a Backbench Business Committee should be established to schedule non-ministerial business in time for the new Parliament. The House also approved the establishment of a House Business Committee during the course of the next Parliament, but no Standing Orders were made to give effect to these agreements in principle. The House agreed to new Standing Orders so that, at the beginning of the next Parliament, select committee chairs were to be elected by the whole House—chairs would be allocated to parties following discussions between the parties who qualified for chairs. The House also endorsed the principle that parties 'should elect members of select committees in a secret ballot by whichever transparent and democratic method they choose'.[10] On 11 March, members of the Wright Committee tabled motions in order to give effect to the resolution of the House on the Backbench Business Committee and to set a timetable for the establishment of the House Business Committee. On 15 March, the Committee published a report, *Rebuilding the House: Implementation*,[11] which set out the explanation for the proposed Standing Order changes. The Labour Government published its proposed Standing Order changes on 25 March. The Standing Order changes were not brought to the House for a decision before the dissolution of Parliament in April 2010.

A. The 2010 Parliament

The Conservative–Liberal Democrat Coalition Government took office after the 2010 General Election. Both the governing party manifestos had committed the parties to implementing some of the Wright Committee proposals. The Conservatives announced that they would establish a Backbench Business Committee, allow MPs time to scrutinise legislation, allow petitions to be debated, give the public the opportunity to comment on Bills online and provide means for the public to table a bill to be voted on in Parliament.[12]

The Liberal Democrats committed themselves to 'give Parliament control over its own agenda so that all Bills leaving the Commons have been fully debated'.[13]

---

[10] HC Deb 4 March 2010, cols 1062–100.
[11] Select Committee on Reform of the House of Commons, *Rebuilding the House: Implementation* (HC 2009–10, 372).
[12] Conservative Party, *Invitation to Join the Government of Britain—Conservative Manifesto 2010* (2010) 66–67.
[13] Liberal Democrats, *Liberal Democrat Manifesto 2010* (2010) 88.

The Coalition Agreement included the following commitment:

> We will bring forward the proposals of the Wright Committee for reform to the House of Commons in full—starting with the proposed committee for management of backbench business. A House Business Committee, to consider government business, will be established by the third year of the Parliament.[14]

IV. THE BACKBENCH BUSINESS COMMITTEE

The Coalition Government's motions to establish the Backbench Business Committee (BBCom) were published on 10 June 2010 and were debated on 15 June 2010. There were some differences between the Government's motions and the Reform Committee's proposals:

— the motion established the BBCom, but its chair and members were appointed for one session only rather than for the whole Parliament; and
— the motion stipulated that the BBCom would have control of the business for 35 days, split between the Chamber and Westminster Hall, whereas the Reform Committee had recommended that it should control 35 days in the Chamber.

The Reform Committee had identified 15 days spent on set-piece debates and 12 days spent on general debates in the 2008–09 session. In addition, it noted that the Leader of the House had selected topical debates. It concluded that this equated to 35 days of debate in the chamber in each normal-length session.[15] It proposed that ministers should no longer schedule such business. The Coalition Government's motions also provided that the BBCom should be reviewed at the beginning of the next session of Parliament.[16]

During Business Questions on 10 June 2010, the Leader of the House of Commons, Sir George Young, was asked about the difference in terms of the number of days in the Chamber the Business Committee would have control over in the Government motion compared to the Reform Committee's proposal. Sir George explained that if the Wright Report stated that the proposals needed to be implemented 'in stages'. He continued:

> There is a real issue with moving straight to having 35 days in the Chamber: there would be implications regarding the amount of time for which the House sits and, more seriously, it would run the real risk of squeezing out time for the Report stage of Bills— an issue that concerns hon. Members on both sides of the House. I hope that we can debate the matter more extensively on Tuesday, but I can say that at least 27 of those

---

[14] HM Government, *The Coalition: Our Programme for Government* (May 2010) 27.
[15] Select Committee on Reform of the House of Commons, *Rebuilding the House* (HC 2008–09, 1117) paras 145–47, 211–18.
[16] HC Deb 15 June 2010, col 846.

35 days will be on the Floor of the House. That is an improvement on the 12 days for set-piece debates that we have at the moment.[17]

When he introduced the motions for debate on 15 June, Sir George addressed criticism that the Committee would only be elected for a single session:

> The committee will have power to schedule business in the House and Westminster Hall. Given the significance of this, we believe that members of the committee should be accountable to their peers for the decisions they take in scheduling debates. This will not affect the eligibility of the chair and members, who will still be able to offer themselves for re-election. This will be by secret ballot, so there is no question of members coming under the malign influence of the usual channels in making their choices. As well as providing accountability, it will, I hope, also provide a way of bringing new blood on to the committee from time to time, keeping its thinking fresh.[18]

On the matter of the review to be held after the first session of this Parliament, he said that the object of the review would be to move the House forwards, not to wind back:

> There is absolutely no intention to shut down the Back-Bench committee after the first Session. We are committed to establishing a House business committee, dealing with both Government and Back-Bench business, by the end of the third year of this Parliament, so a review of the Back-Bench business committee any later than that would make no sense.[19]

At the end of the debate, the motions were agreed and new Standing Orders provided for the establishment of the BBCom, and the election of its chair and members by the whole House. The first Chair, Natascha Engel, was elected on 22 June and the remaining members were elected on 29 June.[20]

After its appointment, the BBCom issued a report setting out its provisional approach in July 2010. It stated that:

> In making decisions on the scheduling of business we will take into account the numerical support for a topic amongst backbench members, but also the diversity of backbench interests; and will aim to balance the merits of a particular proposal with a fair distribution of days amongst different individuals, groups and interests. The Committee will wish to ensure that a proportion of backbench time is reserved for the debate of topical issues. We will also take into account the existence of other opportunities for the debate of proposed subjects which may be or have been provided either in Government time or through Urgent Questions, adjournment debates and other opportunities.[21]

The first session (2010–12) of the 2010 Parliament was unusually long, following the decision, in the wake of the Fixed-term Parliaments Act 2011, to move to

---

[17] HC Deb 10 June 2010, cols 469–70.
[18] HC Deb 15 June 2010, cols 780–81.
[19] HC Deb 15 June 2010, col 782.
[20] HC Deb 22 June 2010, col 165; and HC Deb 29 June 2010, col 717.
[21] Backbench Business Committee, *Provisional Approach: Session 2010–11* (HC 2010–12, 334) para 3.

annual sessions running from spring to spring. In total, the BBCom determined the business to be considered in the Chamber on the equivalent of 41 days,[22] selecting four select committee report launches, 22 general debates and 38 debates on substantive motions. The number of days it determined the business in the Chamber and the number of debates it scheduled in the 2010 Parliament are set out in Table 7.1 below.

Table 7.1: Types of business scheduled in the Chamber by the Backbench Business Committee in the 2010 Parliament

Session	Days allocated to BBCom		Debates scheduled		
	Days	Hours	General	Substantive	Sel Com
2010–12	41	201.06	22	38	9*
2012–13	29	127.42	21	22	11**
2013–14	35+	174.38	41	22	18***
2014–15	25++	132.26	32	27	7****

Source: House of Commons, *Sessional Diaries*, 2010–12 to 2014–15

Notes:
+ 10 short debates on other days were determined by the BBCom (these debates are included in later columns)
++ six short debates on other days were determined by the BBCom (these debates are included in later columns)
* four select committee report launches; and five debates on substantive motions, two of which implemented recommendations, from the Procedure and Standards and Privileges Committees
** seven select committee report launches; debates on reports from Liaison, Finance and Services, Procedure, and Public Administration Committees
*** 12 select committee report launches (7 under the new Standing Order); three debates on substantive motions from the Procedure, Finance and Services, and Standards Committees; and three general debates on select committee reports
**** six select committee report launches and 1 debate on a substantive motion from the Finance and Services Committee

David Foster reviewed the effectiveness of the BBCom in its first session. He concluded that the BBCom had 'had to battle against the values of an executive dominated Parliament. This included pressing to be allocated sufficient days, and to be provided with adequate notice of them, as the government resisted the attack on the norm that it determines the business of the House'. Despite this, however, he said that 'the Committee made a significant impact during its inaugural session' and reported Richard Ottaway's evidence to the Procedure Committee that it had been 'perhaps "remarkably effective"'. It had 'demonstrated a willingness to innovate': Foster cited changes it made to the format of pre-recess adjournment debates; the Committee's public representation sessions, in which MPs made

---

[22] Comprising 39 full days, that is, the 27 allocated days, in accordance with the Standing Order (some full days and some separate half-days), and 12 unallocated days, three unallocated half days and one unallocated part-day.

their case to the BBCom for time for debates; and the introduction of committee mini-statements. He also concluded that the Committee had shown 'considerable effectiveness in meeting the hopes [of] increasing the transparency of scheduling non-Government business and improving the topicality of, and public interest in, parliamentary debates'. He also reported John Baron's comment that the BBCom had proved to be '"an excellent method of holding the executive to account", scheduling debates that would not have come to light under the former system and influencing government policy in a number of areas'.[23]

At the end of the first session, ahead of the review of the BBCom, the Government proposed changes to the way in which the chair and members of the BBCom were elected. From the beginning of the 2012–13 session, the chair had to come from a party that was not in the Government, and members were elected from their party groups, not by the whole House.[24] Foster wondered whether these changes would undermine its potential to alter the institutional context of Parliament. Although there was a considerable change in BBCom members between 2010–12 and 2012–13, Natascha Engel was re-elected as chair at the beginning of each subsequent session in the 2010 Parliament. She told the Political and Constitutional Reform Committee (PCRC) that there were benefits to the BBCom being elected at the beginning of each session. She said that although it would be 'easier' if the Committee were elected for a whole Parliament, 'it is quite important, since we are a Committee that is supposed to represent Back Benchers, that Back Benchers have a regular opportunity to replace us if they want to'. She considered that it was 'much more for the benefit of Back Benchers than it is for the benefit of the Executive'.[25]

The Committee continued to operate in a similar way throughout the Parliament. Although there was a reduction in the proportion of debates that took place on substantive motions, the debates it scheduled contributed to holding the Government to account in ways that debates chosen by the Government could not.

Adam Afriyie effectively used the BBCom's procedures to criticise the Independent Parliamentary Standards Authority (IPSA), then to initiate a select committee inquiry by the Committee on Members' Expenses to review the Parliamentary Standards Act 2009, and subsequently to debate the Committee's report on a motion that the House approved the report (an amendment was agreed referring the report to the IPSA).[26] A similar approach led to the establishment of the House of Commons Governance Committee.[27] Clearly, it is a potential vehicle

---

[23] D Foster, 'Going "Where Angels Fear to Tread": How Effective was the Backbench Business Committee in the 2010–2012 Parliamentary Session?' (2015) 68 *Parliamentary Affairs* 116.
[24] HC Deb 12 March 2010, cols 35–68.
[25] Political and Constitutional Reform Committee, *Revisiting Rebuilding the House: The Impact of the Wright Reforms* (HC 2013–14, 82) para 44.
[26] HC Deb 2 December 2010, cols 1018–74; HC Deb 12 May 2011, cols 1386–404; HC Deb 15 December 2011, cols 944–78.
[27] HC Deb 10 September 2014, cols 1014–48.

for a cross-party group of Members to press for an issue to be examined in detail. It has been used to debate contentious subjects such as calling on the Government to hold a referendum on European Union membership and on prisoner voting (for more on this, see chapter 12); in addition, the Government responded positively to a debate on releasing documents relating to the Hillsborough disaster. Members also used a debate on mental health to reflect on their own experiences.

However, there is no mechanism that the BBCom can use to force the Government to take action. Debates on substantive motions might express the will of the House, but do not bind the Government. Debates in BBCom time called for the pilot badger cull to be halted[28] and that circuses should be banned from using wild animals.[29] However, the badger culling trial has continued and been extended, and although the Government published the draft Wild Animals in Circuses Bill, a subsequent Private Member's Bill did not make any progress.

V. THE HOUSE BUSINESS COMMITTEE

Despite the commitment in the Coalition Agreement to establish a House Business Committee, this was never done. When he gave oral evidence to the PCRC's review of the impact of the Wright reforms in May 2013, the then Leader of the House, Andrew Lansley, told the Committee that:

> Such is the diversity of views on the composition and role of a House Business Committee, I do not at the moment see the possibility of establishing the level of consensus necessary for a proposal to have a realistic chance of success. I wanted to tell you upfront that I do not have any proposals to give you today—ones that would meet the tests that I believe are required to be met before a House Business Committee can be established.[30]

The PCRC also reported the Shadow Leader of the House, Angela Eagle, as having 'doubts about the feasibility, and indeed the purpose, of a House Business Committee'.[31]

The Committee illustrated these difficulties in identifying six different approaches that could be taken to move towards establishing a House Business Committee. Evidence to the Committee also highlighted fears, among some, that the establishment of a House Business Committee would put at risk the success of the BBCom:

> A number of witnesses said that there was a risk that a House Business Committee would undermine the progress already achieved by the Backbench Business Committee. For others, the success of the Backbench Business Committee inspired confidence that a House Business Committee was a realistic and feasible further reform.[32]

---

[28] HC Deb 13 March 2014, cols 456–520.
[29] HC Deb 23 June 2011, cols 548–85.
[30] Political and Constitutional Reform Committee (n 25) para 83.
[31] ibid para 85.
[32] ibid para 69.

In some way, the difficulties in establishing a House Business Committee can be seen as a measure of the success of the BBCom. Proponents of the BBCom did not want to see its decisions subject to questions by the House Business Committee, whilst, perhaps, the Government and Opposition frontbench, having seen the way in which the BBCom provided time for debate on issues they would have preferred to avoid, fought shy of ceding any further control over or influence on the agenda-setting of the House.

The Conservative Government elected in 2015 has ruled out establishing a House Business Committee in the 2015 Parliament. On 9 July 2015, Dr Thérèse Coffey, the Deputy Leader of the House, told the House that: 'There was an absence of consensus on this issue at the end of the previous Parliament, and there is still no consensus at the beginning of this Parliament. The Government therefore have no intention of bringing forward proposals.'[33]

VI. SELECT COMMITTEES

It is widely considered that elections have enhanced the credibility of select committees. In its review of the impact of the Reform Committee's proposals, the PCRC reported that: 'Many witnesses considered that the introduction of election for committee members and chairs had been particularly important in reinforcing their credibility and authority.' The Committee cited Tony Wright, who commented that: 'There are key Committees that are being led in a different way now because of the fact of election.' Sir Alan Beith, then chair of the Liaison Committee, told the PCRC that the election of chairs and members of select committees 'strengthened the position of Select Committees' with 'indirect as well as direct effects on the self-confidence of Committees'.[34]

The Committee reported analysis from Democratic Audit that showed that 'these more self-confident select committees have increased their media impact in recent years, and especially since the changes implemented as a result of Wright'. Professor Patrick Dunleavy, co-director of Democratic Audit, told the PCRC that there had been 'a substantial growth in the overall [press] mentions of Commons committees across the five years [from 2008]'. Although 'four exceptionally prominent committees: Culture, Media and Sport, Home Affairs, Public Accounts and Treasury' accounted for much of the increase, the PCRC observed that 'the trend was broadbased, with press coverage of a further seven committees increasing significantly'.[35]

Lucy Fisher has argued that: 'The most significant reform recommended by Tony Wright was the election of committee chairs, which has strengthened the

---

[33] HC Deb 9 July 2015, col 448.
[34] Political and Constitutional Reform Committee (n 25) para 12.
[35] ibid para 13.

power, credibility and independence of select committees.' Fisher drew on interviews with select committee chairs and members. She was told that elections had made chairs more independent and confident, and members of select committees were more independent and assertive because they had wanted to be elected to committees. She contended that 'The election of chairs has also strengthened the legislature, both in terms of perception and process', reporting that: 'A number of MPs surveyed for this article noted that as select committees achieved greater independence and autonomy throughout the 2010 to 2015 Parliament, departments responded more diligently to recommendations and took inquiries increasingly seriously.'[36]

In March 2015, *The Independent* columnist Ian Birrell identified a number of recent select committee evidence sessions and commented that they 'highlighted the high-profile role now played by Commons' select committees'. He also considered that, during the Parliament, 'many of the most dramatic moments in Westminster have come in select committees rather than in the chamber'. He thought that working together in a non-partisan way, as committees did, was what the public wanted. Despite 'some showboating when there are high-profile witnesses and intense media interest', he concluded that: 'The result is that select committees are displaying increasing authority, courage and independence, especially when they have a strong chair.'[37]

The PCRC heard similar evidence. It was told that select committees had taken on 'major investigative tasks' and had persisted with areas of inquiry. Andrew Tyrie, chair of the Parliamentary Commission on Banking Standards and the Treasury Committee, said that select committees were 'increasing the effectiveness of Parliament in its core tasks. They are requiring the Government to explain its proposals and justify its actions in unprecedented detail' and were the only way that Parliament could 'hope to hold the wider "quango state" to account'.[38]

The PCRC also reported that as the profile and confidence of committees grew, their chairs were being invited to participate in more meetings and events outside the House.[39] Indeed, in its own review of select committee resources, the Liaison Committee identified the need for 'greater support for committee chairs'. The Liaison Committee noted that committee chairs were being invited 'to attend events, make speeches and respond to media inquiries above and beyond what used to be expected of a committee chairs'.[40] In its 'Legacy Report' published at the end of the 2010 Parliament, the Liaison Committee noted that it was pleased that the House had agreed to its modest request for an increase in scrutiny resources to

---

[36] L Fisher, 'The Growing Power and Autonomy of House of Commons Select Committees: Causes and Effects' (2015) 86 *Political Quarterly* 419.

[37] I Birrell, 'All Hail Our Select Committees: Asking the Questions that Public Wants Answers to', *The Independent* (1 March 2015), www.independent.co.uk/voices/comment/all-hail-our-select-committees-asking-the-questions-that-public-wants-answers-to-10078772.html.

[38] Political and Constitutional Reform Committee (n 25) para 16.

[39] ibid para 14.

[40] Liaison Committee, *Select Committee Effectiveness, Resources and Powers* (HC 2012–13, 697) paras 117–20.

enable committee staff to provide additional support for chairs in their wider role in the next Parliament.[41]

The Wright Report called for select committees to be given 'greater access to the agenda' of the Chamber.[42] Initially, the BBCom provided time for 'statements' for select committee chairs to launch new reports in the Chamber.[43] In December 2013, the House agreed a new Standing Order to formalise this process and allow the BBCom to provide time for statements from select committee chairs within a week of the publication of a report.[44] However, committees have been reluctant to ask for Backbench Business time for debates on substantive motions on their reports or particular recommendations from their reports. The BBCom provided time for recommendations of the Procedure and Standards and Privileges Committees to be implemented and to accept the Finance and Services Committee's recommendations for the House's budget, but few scrutiny committees have sought debates on their recommendations. In the 2010–12 session, there were debates on substantive motions on:

— the Foreign Affairs Committee's report on the BBC World Service;
— motor insurance; and
— the operation of the Parliamentary Standards Act 2009.

In 2012–13, there was a debate on a Public Administration Select Committee report on the Prime Minister's Adviser on Minister's Interests and, in 2013–14, on student finance. Also in 2013–14, the BBCom provided time for general debates on three select committee reports on aviation strategy, rural communities and civil service reform.

While the PCRC welcomed many post-Wright achievements of select committees, it cautioned that there was 'no room for complacency'. It heard, in evidence, that elections had not increased the diversity of committee membership—elections did not favour MPs who challenged the mainstream view.[45] Paul Flynn MP has commented that the: 'Election of chairs by MPs in place of selection by the whips produced some fine chairs that were unselectable by the whips. [However, the] new system failed to give a reasonable choice of candidates for some committees.'[46] However, there is some evidence that the election of chairs has affected who becomes a select committee chair. In the 2010 Parliament, by-elections were held after the chairs of the Health and Defence Committees resigned during the course of the Parliament. Both elections were won by Mem-

---

[41] Liaison Committee, *Legacy Report* (HC 2014–15, 594) para 22.
[42] Select Committee on Reform of the House (n 15) para 191.
[43] The process was not formalised when it first began. The BBCom allocated approximately 20 minutes for a committee chair to make a speech. In order for it to be similar to a ministerial statement, the chair allowed other MPs to intervene on his or her speech.
[44] HC Deb 2 December 2013, cols 730–48; Standing Order No 22D.
[45] Political and Constitutional Reform Committee (n 25) para 21.
[46] P Flynn, 'The Most Successful Select Committee in the Last Parliament is Now the Most Degraded' (*LSE British Politics and Policy Blog*, 16 May 2014) http://blogs.lse.ac.uk/politicsandpolicy/the-most-successful-select-committee-in-the-last-parliament-is-now-the-most-degraded.

bers who were first elected in 2010, Dr Sarah Wollaston and Rory Stewart, respectively. In 2011, Dr Wollaston had expressed objections to attempts to prevent her tabling amendments to the Health and Social Care Bill.[47] In the past, whips would have put forward long-standing members to serve as select committee chairs. There was a much higher incidence of MPs who had completed only one or two full terms being elected as select committee chairs in the 2015 Parliament, compared to the 2010 Parliament, when chairs were elected by the whole House for the first time, and in 2005, when chairs were not elected by the whole House. When select committee chairs were elected in 2015, 11 of the 26 chairs first sat in the House of Commons in the 2005 (six) or 2010 (five) Parliaments (including Dr Wollaston, who was re-elected); in 2010, two of the 24 first sat in the 2001 and 2005 (two) Parliaments. In 2005, when chairs were not elected by the whole House of 22 chairs of committees, corresponding to those elected in 2010, four sat in the House for the first time in either 1997 (three) or 2001 (one).

As in previous Parliaments,[48] some committees also reported that they struggled to find sufficient members and sometimes even those with full complements struggled with quorums.[49]

The election of chairs has strengthened their standing inside and outside the House, and has raised the profile of select committees. At the end of the Parliament, the Liaison Committee concluded that any attempt to end the election of chairs would be a 'retrograde step' that would 'harm the standing of select committees in their role of holding to account the Government of the day'.[50]

The election of chairs has not addressed other important aspects of the constraints placed on the way in which select committees work. In a *Spectator* blog post, Steve Barclay MP argued that much wider change was needed: powers needed to be clarified; external experience utilised, alongside a more thematic approach to work; and the House as a whole needed to demonstrate that it could change.[51]

Some of these issues were echoed in the Institute for Government's review of the impact of committee inquiries on government, which reviewed the whole of the 2010 Parliament, using case studies and more general analysis. Tony Wright's foreword to the report began by welcoming the confidence and authority select committees had displayed in the course of the Parliament, but accepted the report's conclusions about how committees could be more effective:

> The last parliament has been described as the 'parliament of the select committee'. It is not difficult to see why. With their chairs and members now elected, the committees have

---

[47] T Helm, '"New Politics" Claim a Sham, Senior Conservative MP Warns David Cameron' *The Observer* (13 February 2011); S Wollaston, 'Creeping Patronage, New Politics and the Payroll Vote' *The Guardian* (11 February 2011).
[48] See, eg, Modernisation Committee, *Select Committees* (HC 2001–02, 224) para 50.
[49] Political and Constitutional Reform Committee (n 25) paras 21–23.
[50] Liaison Committee, *Legacy Report* (HC 2014–15, 954) para 21.
[51] S Barclay, 'Are Parliament's Select Committees Working?—I Say No' (*Spectator Blog*, 5 November 2013) http://blogs.spectator.co.uk/coffeehouse/2013/11/are-parliaments-select-committees-working-i-say-no.

displayed a new confidence and authority. Their profile rose sharply, as they put themselves at the centre of the big issues of the day. Their activities helped to restore the reputation of the Commons, so damaged by the expenses scandal, and Members themselves began to see work on the committees as a parliamentary career path in its own right. All this represented a major advance for the scrutiny role of parliament.

So why not simply celebrate what has been achieved and leave it there? This report provides the answer. What has been achieved so far is really only a glimpse of what might be achieved if the select committee system set about the task of making itself as effective as it might be. Committees are not good at evaluating what they do and working out how they might do things better. They are often unclear about the outcomes they want to achieve and the sort of impact they want to make. There is a difference between making a headline and making an impact. An individual committee may not work collectively enough to maximise its effectiveness; and committees may be more concerned with protecting their own territory than exploring how they might work together.[52]

Previous parliamentary and academic reviews on the effectiveness of select committees have made similar points.[53]

VII. PUBLIC INVOLVEMENT

In 2004, the Modernisation Committee (under Peter Hain as Leader of the House) called for the House of Commons to 'make itself more accessible to those outside, both as interested visitors and as citizens wishing to be more involved in proceedings, it can do more to make it easier for people to understand the work of Parliament, and it can do more to communicate its activity to the world outside'.[54] Then, in 2005, the Hansard Society's Puttnam Commission, *Members Only? Parliament in the Public Eye*, was established to consider how Parliament communicated with the public.[55]

The Wright Committee recommended that: 'The primary focus of the House's overall agenda for engagement with the public must now be shifted beyond the giving of information towards actively assisting the achievement of a greater degree of public participation.' The Committee advocated: 'Opening up the process of legislation and giving a real opportunity to the public to influence the content of draft laws.'[56] It called for urgent discussions on introducing an e-petitions system

---

[52] H White, *Select Committees under Scrutiny—The Impact of Parliamentary Committee Inquiries on Government* (London, Institute for Government, 2015) Foreword.
[53] Liaison Committee (n 40); M Benton and M Russell, *Selective Influence: The Policy Impact of House of Commons Select Committees* (London, Constitution Unit, June 2011).
[54] Modernisation Committee, *Connecting Parliament with the Public* (HC 2003–04, 368) para 9.
[55] Hansard Society Commission (Lord Puttnam), *Members Only? Parliament in the Public Eye* (London, Hansard Society, 2005).
[56] Select Committee on Reform of the House (n 15) paras 232 and 276.

and suggested that the Procedure Committee became for a trial period a Procedure and Petitions Committee, dealing with petitions submitted under existing rules. The Procedure Committee had been considering the question of petitioning Parliament. It had brought forward proposals for an e-petitioning system in April 2008.[57] The following May, it called for government action on its proposals. However, the Labour Government had suggested that the proposed system should be redesigned in light of the need to contain costs.[58]

A. Public Involvement in Legislation

In relation to 'agenda initiative' which might enable the public to ensure that a given issue is debated in the House, the Wright Committee called for the House to commission an investigation of the practicalities of such a procedure at the national level. It concluded that opening up the process of legislation and giving the public a real opportunity to influence the content of draft laws should be a priority in the new Parliament.[59]

Plans for a public reading stage of Bills were announced at the 2009 Conservative Party Conference.[60] In its 2010 General Election manifesto, the Conservative Party outlined plans for giving the general public opportunities to initiate parliamentary proceedings. It announced that:

> [A]ny petition that secures 100,000 signatures will be eligible for formal debate in Parliament. The petition with the most signatures will enable members of the public to table a Bill eligible to be voted on in Parliament. And we will introduce a new Public Reading Stage for Bills to give the public an opportunity to comment on proposed legislation online.[61]

The Coalition Agreement set out commitments on ensuring that petitions securing 100,000 signatures would be eligible for debate in the House of Commons, allowing members of the public to table a Bill linked to the petition with most signatures, and introducing a public reading stage for Government Bills, which would allow the public to comment on proposed legislation online whilst Parliament was considering legislation.[62]

Although an e-petitions system was introduced by the Government (see below), no mechanism was devised to ensure that the petition with the most signatures was turned into a Bill in the 2010 Parliament.

---

[57] Procedure Committee, *e-Petitions* (HC 2007–08, 136).
[58] Procedure Committee, *e-Petitions: Call for Government action* (HC 2008–09, 493).
[59] Select Committee on Reform of the House of Commons (n 15) Summary.
[60] N Watt, 'Parliament: public offered chance to alter bills', *Guardian*, 5 October 2009; William Hague, speech to Conservative Conference, 5 October 2009, reported on Epolitix at www.epolitix.com/latestnews/article-detail/newsarticle/william-hague-bringing-change-to-britain/.
[61] Conservative Party, *Invitation to join the Government of Britain—Conservative Manifesto 2010* (2010), 66.
[62] HM Government, *The Coalition: Our Programme for Government* (May 2010) 27.

Pilot public readings were held for three Government Bills in the 2010 Parliament:

— the Protection of Freedoms Bill 2010–12;
— the Small Charitable Donations Bill 2012–13;
— the Children and Families Bill 2012–13.

In addition, the draft Care and Support Bill was subject to an online consultation, whilst it was undergoing pre-legislative scrutiny. Public reading stage pilots for the Protection of Freedoms Bill 2010–12, the Small Charitable Donations Bill 2012–13 and the draft Care and Support Bill were administered by the Government. The House of Commons administered the public reading pilot of the Children and Families Bill 2012–13. Information gathered from the public was prepared by the Government or the House and was given to the public Bill committee considering each Bill (for more details of these pilots, see chapter three).

In January 2013, the Leader of the House issued a written statement, in which he outlined public engagement with the Government-administered pilots. He stated that: 'The Government remain committed to promoting public engagement in Parliament and specifically in the legislative process. The pilot results indicate that approaches to consultation should be carefully tailored to the Bill.'[63]

Mr Lansley reiterated the 'mixed economy' approach to scrutinising legislation in response to an oral question on the same day, saying that 'public reading stages will form part of a tool kit to consider legislation on a case-by-case basis'.[64]

B. e-petitions

In line with the Coalition Agreement, the Government took the lead in developing an e-petitions system in the early part of the 2010 Parliament. It indicated that in line with commitments, e-petitions that secured 100,000 signatures would be eligible for debate in the Commons, but that it would be for the BBCom to determine whether debates were held.[65]

On Friday 29 July 2011, the Leader of the House of Commons announced that 'public petitions which secure the backing of 100,000 signatures will be eligible for debate in Parliament through a newly launched website'.[66] The website went live on 4 August 2011.

The Procedure Committee reported on e-petitions in January 2012. The Committee observed that while the initiative was welcome in principle, there had been some practical problems with its operation. The Committee drew attention

---

[63] HC Deb 17 January 2013, cols 44WS–45WS.
[64] HC Deb 17 January 2013, col 1022.
[65] HC Deb 20 January 2011, cols 1005–06, 1021.
[66] Office of the Leader of the House, *Announcements* (29 July 2011).

to two issues—time for debating e-petitions and public understanding of the process. It was concerned that the BBCom controlled a finite amount of debating time which was put under additional pressure as the Government did not provide any extra time for debates on e-petitions. It proposed that extra time should be found for debating e-petitions and suggested that it would be possible for Westminster Hall to sit on Mondays, with the BBCom determining whether e-petitions were debated. It recommended a one-year trial.[67]

The Government welcomed the Procedure Committee's review of e-petitions. However, it did not accept that the system was poorly explained. It argued that the Committee overstated the effect of e-petitions on the BBCom. Nevertheless, it supported proposals for debating e-petitions on Mondays on a pilot basis.[68]

On 17 July 2012, the House agreed a proposal to allow e-petitions to be debated in an additional time slot in Westminster Hall. The motion, moved by the Chair of the Procedure Committee, Greg Knight, provided that an experiment would last until the end of the next session of Parliament (ie, the end of the 2013–14 session). However, an amendment, which was accepted by the House, shortened the length of the experiment until the end of the 2012–13 session of Parliament. The House agreed the amended motion without a division.[69]

On 17 September 2012, the first e-petition to be debated in Westminster Hall in time specifically allowed for debating e-petitions related to the West Coast Mainline franchise decision.[70]

On 4 July 2013, the House agreed to the change to the temporary Standing Orders to alter the motion on which e-petitions were debated and agreed that they should operate until the end of the 2010 Parliament.[71]

In addition to approving the extension of the trial period for debating e-petitions in Westminster Hall, the Government also suggested that it would like to work with the Procedure and Backbench Business Committees to improve the system.

The Procedure Committee undertook this work and published its report, *E-petitions: A Collaborative System* in December 2014.[72] The report recommended a joint system of e-petitions to be owned by both the Government and the House of Commons via a Petitions Committee, which would also oversee the paper petitions system.

The House approved the Procedure Committee's report on 24 February 2015 and agreed Standing Orders to establish a permanent Petitions Committee from the beginning of the 2015 Parliament to oversee the e-petitions website on behalf of the House of Commons; to make permanent the arrangements for debating

---

[67] Procedure Committee, *Debates on Government e-petitions* (HC 2010–12, 1706).
[68] Procedure Committee, *Debates on Government e-petitions: Government Response to the Committee's Seventh Report of 2010–12* (HC 2010–12, 1902).
[69] HC Deb 17 July 2012, cols 955–56.
[70] HC Deb 17 September 2012, cols 191WH–236WH.
[71] HC Deb 4 July 2013, col 1159.
[72] Procedure Committee, *E-petitions: A Collaborative System* (HC 2014–15, 235).

petitions in Westminster Hall on Mondays; and giving responsibility for determining which petitions should be debated in Westminster Hall to the Petitions Committee. Responsibility for providing time to debate petitions in the Chamber (on a substantive motion) would remain with the BBCom.[73]

The e-petitions website was relaunched over the summer of 2015, with the Petitions Committee staff determining whether the subjects of e-petitions fall within the responsibility of government and therefore being eligible to appear on the website. The Committee met on 21 July 2015, outlined its provisional approach and asked for views on that approach. At its meeting on 8 September, it announced that two petitions that had attracted 100,000 signatures would be debated. The e-petition 'To debate a vote of no confidence in Health Secretary the Rt Hon Jeremy Hunt' would be debated on 14 September, on the motion 'That this House has considered the e-petition relating to contracts and conditions in the NHS', and the e-petition 'Make the production, sale and use of cannabis legal' would be debated on 12 October, on the motion 'That this House has considered the e-petition relating to making the production, sale and use of cannabis legal'.[74]

The implementation of recommendations that allowed the public to be more directly involved in the House's business have proved much longer in gestation than those affecting select committees and establishing the BBCom. Indeed, public reading stages have not been formalised, but may be used on an ad hoc basis. However, the Petitions Committee is now established and has already demonstrated that issues securing public support can be debated in the House of Commons.

VIII. REFLECTIONS ON ACCOUNTABILITY POST-WRIGHT REFORMS

The Wright Committee had hoped that the establishment of a Backbench Business Committee would 'create new opportunities for all Members, giving them a greater sense of ownership and responsibility for what goes on in their own House'. Rather than suggesting that the reform would increase accountability directly, the Committee reform's aimed to do so by making 'debates more responsive to public concerns' and 'strengthen[ing] the position of the widely-respected select committees'.[75]

Both frontbenches told the PCRC that the Committee had been successful. Andrew Lansley, whilst Leader of the House, told the Committee that the BBCom had 'exceeded expectations', and his shadow, Angela Eagle, considered that the BBCom had been a 'refreshing addition' to the structures of the House.[76]

---

[73] HC Deb 24 February 2015, cols 248–56.
[74] Petitions Committee, *Committee Schedules its First Debates on e-petitions* (8 September 2015) www.parliament.uk/business/committees/committees-a-z/commons-select/petitions-committee/news-parliament-2015/8-sept-committee-decisions.
[75] Select Committee on Reform of the House of Commons (n 15) para 181.
[76] Political and Constitutional Reform Committee (n 25) Q 278, Q 256.

The BBCom has clearly provided time for backbenchers to debate subjects that they have requested. The support throughout the Parliament for the same chair can be seen as indicative that the House has broadly supported the decisions of the Committee in relation to the choice of subjects it has made. The original chair's subsequent election as deputy speaker following the 2015 General Election is also perhaps evidence of her, and the Committee's, success.

Select committees have undoubtedly become increasingly confident and commanding of media coverage. But are they now more effective at holding the Government to account? Their greater willingness to use existing powers to call for persons, papers and records, and to require witnesses to take the oath can be seen as a parliamentary flexing of muscles. However, the limits of these powers and processes have also been brought into relief.[77] The Liaison Committee in 2012 noted that the Murdochs were summoned to appear before the Culture Media and Sport Committee, and there had been considerable discussion of what would have occurred if they had refused to attend. The Public Accounts Committee's use of the oath to question an HM Revenue & Customs civil servant led to questions about the effectiveness of this process, given the inability of the courts to question proceedings in Parliament under Article 9 of the Bill of Rights. The episode also drew criticism from a former Cabinet Secretary, Lord O'Donnell, who expressed concerns about civil servants being made answerable to Parliament (beyond their role of accounting officers or heads of department).[78] Meanwhile, the Parliamentary Commission on Banking Standards showed a new and different approach to a parliamentary inquiry, with use of counsel and rapporteurs to conduct in-depth scrutiny in the wake of the financial crisis.

The Petitions Committee and the new e-petitions process for the House of Commons is still too new to assess. At the time of writing, only one petition had been debated having received over 100,000 signatories. As noted above, this change has been a long time in coming. However, individual select committees have meanwhile innovated using social media and a 'campaigning' style. The Education Committee used Twitter to source questions for Ministers (using #askGove to harvest over 5,000 suggestions online) and the PCRC ran public engagement events for its 'new Magna Carta' inquiry.[79]

This chapter has set out the changes made as a result of the Wright reforms and has attempted to consider their relationship with the effectiveness of Parliament to call the executive to account.

---

[77] See discussion in the Liaison Committee (n 40) 46–47; A Horne, 'Evidence under Oath, Perjury and Parliamentary Privilege' (*UK Constitutional Law Blog*, 29 January 2015) http://ukconstitutionallaw.org.

[78] 'Gus O'Donnell's Anger Reflects a Growing Rift between Mandarins and MPs' *Daily Telegraph* (1 February 2012).

[79] Education Committee, 'Michael Gove Answers #AskGove Twitter Questions' (31 January 2012) www.parliament.uk/education-committee-askgove-twitter-questions; Political and Constitutional Reform Committee, *Consultation on a New Magna Carta?* (HC 2014–15, 599).

The Wright Report stated (in the context of the BBCom) that 'gains will not be realised unless individual backbenchers are committed to parliamentary activity and avail themselves of these opportunities'.[80] It can be argued that the Wright reforms provided more opportunities for effective scrutiny by empowering backbenchers. Where parliamentarians have sought to use these new processes and structures, there have been some successes. Others have used the powers and processes already available to them (for example, the Speaker's willingness to grant urgent questions compared to his predecessor and most recently Jeremy Corbyn's crowdsourcing of questions to the Prime Minister).[81] The Wright reforms themselves may not have *directly* increased accountability, but they empowered backbenchers to better hold the Government to account and provided a new framework for parliamentarians and the public to have access to the parliamentary agenda.

---

[80] Select Committee on Reform of the House of Commons (n 15) para 181.
[81] See Commons Briefing Paper 04148, *Parliamentary Questions: Recent Issues*, appendix; J Stone, 'Jeremy Corbyn is crowdsouring questions to ask David Cameron at PMQs' *The Independent* (13 September 2015), http://www.independent.co.uk/news/uk/politics/jeremy-corbyn-is-crowdsourcing-questions-to-ask-david-cameron-at-pmqs-10498633.html; HC Deb 16 September 2015, col 1037.

8

The Regulation of Lobbyists

OONAGH GAY

I. INTRODUCTION

LOBBYING IS AN organic part of politics, but from time to time, a scandal erupts and the question of appropriate access to decision-makers becomes topical. This chapter focuses on lobbying in relation to UK parliamentarians and is not a more general examination of the history and growth of lobbying in national government and international institutions. There is recent legislation affecting Parliament, the implications of which will take time to appreciate.

Receiving payment for lobbying and being lobbied has been the subject of regulation for 30 years in Parliament. As the lobbied, MPs have a responsibility to listen to representations, whether from constituents or business interests, and so any regulation has to take account of this legitimate activity. MPs and peers may also be ministers, who have executive as well as legislative roles. So the rules on lobbying ministers are also relevant and may overlap with those affecting Members. Controls over MPs and peers acting as lobbyists have been gradually tightened, but the ability to undertake external work is in contrast to the ban on second jobs in the US Congress. Finally, lobbying by MPs' staff and All-Party Parliamentary Groups raises new difficulties in regulating such short-term operators in the parliamentary arena.

The initial policy reaction to dealing with concerns about privileged access to law-makers has tended to be the introduction of transparency. This was the motivation behind the adoption of a system of declaration and registration of interests by the Commons in the 1970s. As scandals have recurred, calls for regulation, both of those being lobbied and those lobbying for reward, have grown louder. The non-statutory Committee on Standards in Public Life initially played a pivotal role in developing non-legislative methods of regulating lobbying both in Parliament and in government, but legislation was finally implemented in 2015.

Prime Minister David Cameron said just before the 2010 General Election that lobbying was the next great scandal waiting to happen, when a set of ex-Labour ministers were the subject of a media sting. The Coalition Government set out lobbying reform in its Programme for Government in 2010. Once in government, action was delayed until another scandal occurred, involving a Conservative MP, Patrick Mercer.

New legislation designed to regulate the activity of multi-client lobbying firms came into force in April 2015. Part 1 of the Transparency of Lobbying, Non-Party Campaigning and Trade Union Administration Act 2014 provides for a statutory register of consultant lobbyists. Organisations and individuals that engage in consultant lobbying, as defined by the Act, are required to register, disclose the names of the clients, declare whether they subscribe to a code of conduct and comply with other relevant provisions of the Act. The register is maintained and updated by the independent Registrar of Consultant Lobbyists, a part-time post held by Alison White, a former accountant, who led operations and commercial business for the Royal Mail Group.

At the end of the 2010–15 Parliament, a media sting caught out former ministers Sir Malcolm Rifkind MP and Jack Straw MP. They were filmed undercover discussing the possibility of working for a fictitious Chinese company and indicating previous consultancy activity.[1] Both referred themselves to the Parliamentary Commissioner for Standards, who exonerated them in a report published in September 2015,[2] but this came too late to save the immediate damage to their reputations. Both argued that they had not broken parliamentary rules (and this was later confirmed by the Parliamentary Commissioner for Standards), but this did not prevent fallout. Straw had already indicated that he would be retiring in 2015, but after a couple of days' resistance, Rifkind was forced to stand down as a candidate in the forthcoming General Election and to resign as Chair of the Intelligence and Security Committee. The question of appropriate behaviour for ex-ministers and ex-MPs is likely to come under scrutiny in the new 2015 Parliament as a result. Former Members are not allowed to use the parliamentary estate for lobbying, and security passes can be forfeited if misused, but otherwise censures by the Standards Committee have no effect.

II. BACKGROUND: PARLIAMENTARY REGULATION OF LOBBYING

Lobbying can be defined broadly as seeking to influence decisions made by public office holders or officials; it can therefore involve a wide variety of activities and motivations, and it can be targeted at a range of persons. Many organisations lobby on their own behalf, while others employ multi-client lobbying firms to seek to influence on their behalf. Such firms may also offer other services under the banner of 'public affairs', such as media monitoring or media strategies. Bodies which lobby or employ lobbyists can include companies, charities, public bodies, trade associations and professional membership organisations, as well as individuals who may 'lobby' their MP.

---

[1] C Newell, E Malnick, L Heighton and L Telford, 'Jack Straw and Sir Malcolm Rifkind in Latest "Cash for Access" Scandal' *Daily Telegraph* (22 February 2015).

[2] House of Commons Committee on Standards, *Sir Malcolm Rifkind and Mr Jack Straw* (HC 2015–16, 472) 6.

The concern is that parliamentarians who act as lobbyists offer some form of privileged access to governmental or legislative processes. The process of parliamentary scrutiny of legislation has long been susceptible to external pressure, and parliamentary corruption has a long history. Speaker John Trevor was expelled in 1697 following evidence of his corruption, and bribery of MPs was declared to be a high crime and misdemeanour. The principle of parliamentary privilege was already in existence, so such crimes could not be prosecuted in an ordinary court.

Privilege has two components: freedom of speech, set out in Article 9 of the Bill of Rights 1688; and exclusive cognisance, or self-regulation. The principle is important in ensuring the independence of Parliament from the executive and from the courts. It is the latter which ensures that paid advocacy by MPs is dealt with by parliamentary self-regulation, but the inability to use parliamentary proceedings as evidence in court also inhibits prosecutions of MPs for corruption. At the European level, opportunities for challenge are limited. In December 2014, the European Court of Human Rights rejected the former minister Geoff Hoon's assertion that a Commons Standards Committee report following a media sting against him would affect his right to a fair trial. The Court found the application inadmissible because the parliamentary proceedings did not determine or give rise to a dispute as to the applicant's civil rights.[3]

The devolved parliaments did not inherit parliamentary privilege and breaches of the rules relating paid advocacy were treated as a criminal offence. There has been debate in Parliament about the continuing inherent nature of parliamentary privilege, but no changes appear likely. A government consultation paper on privilege issued in 2012 appears to have sunk without trace, with no parliamentary appetite for reform.[4] The consultation paper proposed removing the protection of Article 9 from Members accused of various criminal offences, such as bribery. The Government was concerned that the Bribery Act 2010 had not altogether answered concerns about prosecutions. However, the Joint Committee on Parliamentary Privilege 2013–14 considered that there was no need to disapply the Article in order for bribery prosecutions against Members to be successful. The Government accepted this approach in its response to the Committee, and dropped any plans for reform.[5] In the event, determined opposition from senior Commons and Lords officials to comprehensive parliamentary privilege legislation appears to have won the day.[6] However, the position could change if another scandal occurs similar to the Members' expenses crisis.

---

[3] *Hoon v UK* App No 14832/11 (2015) 60 EHRR.

[4] Issues around parliamentary privilege, free speech and the criminal law are covered extensively in the chapters by O Gay and H Tomlinson and S Lipscombe and A Horne in A Horne, G Drewry and D Oliver (eds), *Parliament and the Law* (Oxford, Hart Publishing, 2013).

[5] Joint Committee on Parliamentary Privilege report HL Paper 30 HC 100 July 2013 and Government response to the Joint Committee on Parliamentary Privilege Cm 8771 December 2013 p4. See also Richard Gordon QC and Sir Malcolm Jack KCB, PhD, FSA, Parliamentary Privilege: Evolution or codification? The Constitution Society (London, 2013).

[6] Joint Committee on Parliamentary Privilege, *Parliamentary Privilege* (2013–14, HL 30, HC 100).

A. The Ban on Paid Advocacy

The modern era of regulating ethical conduct began in 1947 when a parliamentary resolution was passed to make clear that MPs should not be bound by external interests. The resolution banned paid advocacy by prohibiting contractual arrangements with an outside body which controlled or limited an MP's independence. The resolution was prompted by an MP, WJ Brown, who complained that the Civil Service Clerical Association, with whom he had a contractual arrangement, was pressurising him to act in a certain way. The principle applied to all external interests, but was frequently breached. In the post-war UK, with its tripartite model of unions, businesses and government, lobbying of government existed, but lobbying of Parliament was seen as less useful. MPs were generally whipped tightly and were slow to break ranks.

Public relations firms began to grow in the 1960s and pressure built for the regulation of the targets of lobbying, particularly after Gordon Bagier MP was found to be in the pay of a PR firm working for the Greek Colonels.[7] The Poulson scandal of the early 1970s propelled the incoming Labour Government of February 1974 to table motions for the creation of a register of financial interests and a system of declaration of those interests before speaking in debate. Both were to apply to the Commons only and were overseen by a select committee. Very few accusations were brought against MPs and some, including Enoch Powell, flouted the register openly. Powell was concerned that the regulation should be by statute, if at all. The House took its first step towards regulating non-Members engaged in lobbying in 1985 when it agreed to registers of interests for journalists, MPs' staff and All-Party Parliamentary Groups. These too were not enforced with any degree of severity.

The lobbying industry grew apace in the 1980s and 1990s, with privatisation set off under Margaret Thatcher, and opportunities to influence the resulting legislation. The Commons Select Committee on Members' Interests undertook an inquiry in 1990, finding that the industry was growing annually at a pace of 25 per cent a year. A Study of Parliament (SPG) study illustrated the growth in parliamentary consultancy among MPs. A total of 13.5 per cent of all MPs were acting as parliamentary consultants according to an analysis of the 1975 register; by 1985, this proportion had risen to 24.1 per cent.[8]

The Alan B'Stard model of parliamentary work was a caricature,[9] but was rooted in reality. An analysis undertaken by the Nolan Committee of the 1995 register found 30 per cent (168) of MPs (excluding ministers and the Speaker) held consultancy arrangements with PR firms or the equivalent. Most of these were in

---

[7] There was a coup in Greece in 1967 led by a group of colonels, who overthrew a left-wing government due to concerns about a potential communist takeover. The junta employed PR professionals to gain support in Europe.

[8] O Gay and M Rush, 'Introduction' in O Gay and P Leopold (eds), *Conduct Unbecoming* (London, SPG/Politicos, 2004) 15.

[9] *The New Statesman*, TV series, 1987–92.

relation to causes espoused by the relevant MP, but the growth of multi-client lobbying firms were of particular concern. The level of MPs' pay and the belief in the importance of retaining a foot in employment external to the Commons lay behind this growth.

The failure of self-regulation became all too apparent during the 'cash for questions' scandals of the 1990s.[10] The Prime Minister, John Major, had little alternative but to establish a committee of 'the great and the good' to sort out the mess. He set up the Committee of Standards in Public Life (CSPL), but unusually made it a standing committee to examine ethical behaviour in public life. This was in contrast to the Royal Commission model used after the Poulson corruption scandal in the early 1970s, whose recommendations remained largely unimplemented.

Major deserves some recognition for this achievement as the Committee has completed 15 reports of varying quality, which have brought much soft law-style regulation to public life. The austere and influential chairman, Lord Nolan, carried through a package of changes in his first report affirming the right of MPs to have interests outside of Parliament and dismissing the need for a register of lobbyists, but requiring stricter regulation of the behaviour of individual MPs and records of gifts received by ministers and civil servants.

By 1996, the Commons, humbled by media and popular outrage, had largely implemented Nolan's recommendations. A semi-independent Parliamentary Commissioner for Standards (PCS) would uphold and enforce a toughened register of interests. There would be full disclosure of consultancy fees and arrangements and of trade union sponsorship. A new code of conduct for MPs was explicit in banning paid advocacy.

B. The Current Rules for MPs and Peers on Lobbying

The new rules were subject to some adjustment in the following decade or so, but in the main, the Nolan arrangements have proved robust. Crucially, the 1997 General Election produced a large turnover of MPs due to the scale of the Labour victory and this contributed to a culture change within the Commons, whereby consultancy arrangements with PR firms were no longer normal. The implementation of the Nolan recommendations were reviewed by the CSPL in 2002: this aimed at strengthening the impartiality of the PCS and the Select Committee on Standards and Privileges. The report did not consider the lobbying industry in any depth. A CSPL report on lobbying as an ethical challenge was not published until 2013, by which point there were an estimated 4,000 lobbyists operating in the UK, with a total spend of £2 billion.[11]

---

[10] In the 1990s, Conservative junior ministers and backbenchers were alleged to have tabled parliamentary questions in return for payment. For details of the cash for questions episode, see G Lock, 'The Hamilton Affair' in Gay and Leopold (n 7).

[11] 'Data from Action for Transparency on Lobbying', cited in Transparency International UK, *Lifting the Lid on Lobbying* (March 2015).

So, at the beginning of the twenty-first century, both Houses had introduced detailed regulation for cases where Members were being paid by lobbyists to advance particular causes. The major scandals in the 2005 Parliament did not involve lobbying, but instead related to inappropriate use of parliamentary allowances, not only in the Commons but also in the Lords.[12] However, problems with lobbying did occur in the 2005–10 Parliament. In its dying months, a number of former ministers, Stephen Byers, Geoff Hoon and Patricia Hewitt, were characterised as 'available for hire' in a *Sunday Times* sting. An investigation by the Commons Standards and Privileges Committee found Mr Byers and Mr Hoon guilty of a 'serious' breach of parliamentary rules, while Ms Hewitt was cleared.

C. The Position of the House of Lords

From 1990, the Lords had followed the Commons in introducing a register and requiring transparency in lobbying. The House had changed in nature since 1998 with the abolition of hereditary peers and there is evidence that lobbying had increased, as peers from much wider range of backgrounds joined the House, and as rebelliousness grew. The Lords was investigated by the CSPL in 2000 and, in 2002, the Lords made registration compulsory, including peers with financial interests in lobbying companies. Only a handful of complaints were investigated until 2009. Once again, the House developed new procedures in reactive mode.

A non-statutory Commissioner of Standards for the Lords was created in 2010, following scandals on the claiming of allowances and allegations that four peers were being paid by lobbyists. For the first time since the seventeenth century, the House of Lords exercised its power to suspend peers, suspending Lord Truscott and Lord Taylor of Blackburn from the summer of 2009 until the end of the Parliament, following a *Sunday Times* sting.[13]

In June 2014, a strengthened House of Lords Code of Conduct prohibited peers from offering paid parliamentary advice including to lobbyists, lowered the threshold for registering gifts and hospitality from £500 to £140 and introduced a Code of Conduct for Members' Staff with requirements to register interests in parliamentary lobbying and abstain from lobbying or using access to Parliament to further outside interests in return for a payment or other reward.[14] This was in response to a critical report on lobbying from the CSPL and a more general review by the Council of Europe Group of States against Corruption (GRECO).[15]

---

[12] See discussion in Horne, Drewry and Oliver (n 4).

[13] The *Sunday Times* secretly filmed the peers apparently willing to table amendments to a Bill in return for payment. This was a breach of the Lords Code of Conduct. The Committee for Privileges recommended suspension.

[14] These recommendations were contained in the House of Lords Committee for Privileges and Conduct, 13th Report (HL 2013–14, 123) and 15th Report (HL 2013–14, 128) in March and May 2014.

[15] Council of Europe Group of States against Corruption, *First Report from the Committee for Privileges and Conduct* (July 2015).

In contrast, the Commons Standards Committee's attempt to update the overall Guide to the Rules by debate and approval had to wait until the very end of the 2010–15 Parliament. Whips on all sides were reluctant to allow an opportunity for individual cases to be debated on the floor of the House and there were concerns about a related proposal to amend the Code of Conduct so that the private life of an MP might be subject to investigation. Following another report by the Standards Committee in November 2014, making some modifications, the new Code and Rules were approved on 17 March 2015.[16]

The new Guide harmonised the rules on registration and reduces the number of registration categories, with just one, rather than the current three, for outside employment. It also brings in a lower threshold for the registration of gifts or visits at £300. But there is no requirement for MPs to register contact with lobbyists or record meetings. The lobbying rules do not prevent a Member holding a paid outside interest as a director, consultant or adviser, or in any other capacity, whether or not such interests are related to membership of the House. The Code simply warns former MPs to abide by the rules on lobbying for six months after their departure, with the sanction of losing their parliamentary pass. One new paragraph does acknowledge the damage of inappropriate lobbying:

22. The Committee on Standards and Privileges has indicated it would expect the Committee on Standards to regard it as a serious matter if a sitting Member were influenced in his or her actions by the prospect of becoming a paid lobbyist, or entered into improper agreements relating to future lobbying activities.[17]

There continued to be problems with particular positions of influence, such as chairs of select committees. When pay for the chairs of select committees was introduced in 2003, the then Committee on Standards and Privileges considered whether changes to the rules were necessary, concluding that transparency was the answer.

In 2013, Tim Yeo, chair of the Commons Energy and Climate Change Committee, was secretly filmed by *Sunday Times* journalists who were posing as representatives of a fictional energy company seeking to hire his services.[18] He stood aside while his conduct was examined. The Parliamentary Standards Commissioner exonerated him, but called for a wider review into whether committee chairmen's outside interests should be restricted, saying that while these positions could help their work on specialist committees, 'there is equally a reasonable concern that that a Member is then placed in a privileged position which he or she may be able to exploit for their own interests with few checks and balances'.[19]

---

[16] House of Commons Library, 'The Code of Conduct for Members: Recent Changes', Standard Note 5127 (16 March 2015) http://researchbriefings.parliament.uk/ResearchBriefing/Summary/SN05127.

[17] House of Commons Code of Conduct for MPs together with the Guide to the Rules relating to the conduct of Members (March 2015).

[18] 'Tim Yeo Stands Aside in Probe into Committee Coaching Claim' (*BBC News*, 13 June 2013) www.bbc.co.uk/news/uk-politics-22844988.

[19] House of Commons Committee on Standards, *Mr Tim Yeo* (HC 2013–14, 849) para 58.

168 *Oonagh Gay*

The Rules prohibit Members who receive an outside reward or consideration from a third party from initiating proceedings which would have the effect of conferring any financial or material benefit on such a third party. Initiating proceedings would include proposing a draft report in a select committee. Committee members are expected to stand aside from an inquiry in which their interests are closely involved. Within Parliament, there was a lack of appetite for tighter regulation following the Yeo case, despite pressure from the Speaker. The Committee on Standards subsequently issued a consultation paper in January 2014, which elicited only five responses.

Yeo was deselected by his constituency party in February 2014 by a narrow majority. His moderate Conservative views made him a target. But he was also criticised for earning more than £400,000 from business interests since 2009. There is growing evidence that candidates who are seen as earning well above the average are not popular in constituencies, which want to see local people elected who are familiar with local concerns.[20] Pressure grew markedly for MPs to be banned from holding second jobs following the Members' expenses scandal in 2009, and Labour promised to bring in statutory regulation. This is discussed further in the concluding section of the chapter.

D. All-Party Parliamentary Groups

All-Party Parliamentary Groups (APPGs) are a particular focus at the heart of debate on the ethics of lobbying MPs. These are essentially informal groupings, established by individual Members, which appear to be formal parliamentary bodies and therefore attract influence in a particular policy area. The number of APPGs has expanded rapidly in the last few decades. By the time they began to be noticed as a source of lobbying in the 1980s, there were around 150; by the 2010 General Election, this had grown to nearly 600. As of August 2014, there were 614.[21] The first APPG Register of the new 2015–20 Parliament was published in August 2015, with 385 entities appearing, but many more can be expected to be registered over the course of the Parliament.[22]

Often funded by particular interests, whether charitable, business or foreign, APPGs offer a way into Westminster. There have been a series of reports into their regulation and transparency, and the extent to which they are manipulated by lobbyists and interest groups. Corporate funding of APPGs gives widespread access to parliamentarians with very little in the way of transparency. The APPG on health received more than £100,000 in 'membership fees' from 12 companies

---

[20] Rosie Campbell and Philip Cowley, 'Politicians—We Warn You Not to Be Wealthy' (*YouGov*, 20 April 2012) https://yougov.co.uk/news/2012/04/20/politicians-we-warn-you-not-be-wealthy.
[21] Transparency International UK (n 10).
[22] Register of All-Party Groups as at 30 July 2015: www.publications.parliament.uk/pa/cm/cmallparty/memi01.htm.

in the past year, including Pfizer and Alliance Boots Ltd. The APPG on beer, which has about 300 MPs as members, was given more than £50,000 in funding from some of the UK's biggest drinks companies over the past year. Staff paid by APPGs understand their role in promoting their funders.[23] Yet they are often equated in the media as equivalent to select committees.

Professional lobbyists complain that a lack of transparency in APPG funding is the result of their use by think tanks and charities. A survey by *PR Week* in 2013 found that of the 388 APPGs that use secretariats to assist with the administration and facilitation of their activities, just 15 per cent engage professional consultancies. Charities and not-for-profit organisations account for 56 per cent of secretariats.[24]

As usual, scandals lead to action. An expose by *The Times* in 2006 led to an inquiry by the Standards and Privileges Committee reporting in 2009, which noted that it was important that outside interests should not control an APPG.[25] Both Houses established the Speakers' Working Group on All-Party Groups, which reported in June 2012. The Commons Standards Committee examined them again in 2013, but halfway through, the scandal of the Conservative backbencher Patrick Mercer broke, in which he was alleged to have set up an APPG at the request of a political consultancy. The Standards Committee subsequently found that it was 'not aware of a case relating to a sitting MP which has involved such a sustained and pervasive breach of the House's rules on registration, declaration and paid advocacy'.[26] Its recommendation of an unprecedented six-month suspension was not enforced as Mr Mercer resigned his seat. However, he was not subject to a subsequent criminal process, simply of breaching parliamentary rules. Lord Laird was investigated and punished by the Lords standards machinery in 2013 for same type of offence—offering to establish an APPG for money. He was suspended for four months.[27] Following the Mercer case, the Commons Commission agreed to withdraw the category of APPG staff passes at Westminster.

In each investigation into APPGs, the solution was greater regulation and transparency, an approach which relies on individual MPs associated with a group having the time to make sure that the appropriate paperwork is filed. The dangers are clear. This is one area where tighter regulation would be repaid by prevention of scandals. Removing passes is a start, but more serious risk-based investigation by the Commons authorities of APPG governance would be a more proactive stance in an area where there is a clear likelihood of abuse.

---

[23] 'Corporate Funding of All-Party Groups Next Big Scandal after Huge Rise under the Coalition' *The Independent* (18 May 2015).

[24] 'Parliament's Power Players Hide in Shadows' *PR Week* (13 June 2013) www.prweek.com/article/1185925/parliaments-power-players-hide-shadows.

[25] *The Times* ran a series of articles in 2006 alleging that selected APPGs were being manipulated by outside interests. The allegations were investigated by the then Commissioner for Standards, Sir Philip Mawer: House of Commons Committee on Standards and Privileges, *All-Party Groups* (HC 2008–09, 920).

[26] House of Commons Committee on Standards, *Patrick Mercer* (HC 2013–14, 1225).

[27] House of Lords Committee for Privileges and Conduct, *The Conduct of Lord Laird* (HL 2013–14, 96).

Almost one in five staff members employed by MPs and peers also has outside interests, according to a survey undertaken by *The Guardian* in March 2015. Iain Anderson, the chair of the Association of Professional Political Consultants, was quoted as saying that it was 'wholly unethical' to allow anyone who undertakes lobbying to hold a parliamentary pass. But each House is relying on transparency as the main form of regulation.[28]

III. REGULATION OF LOBBYING: MINISTERS AND SENIOR CIVIL SERVANTS

At the same time as the regulation of MPs came under consideration, attention began to focus on lobbying and central government, with the same dilemma—whether to regulate the lobbied or the lobbying, or both. The practice of transferring employment from the public sector to the private sector developed in terms of scale for senior civil servants in the 1980s. Privatisation, generous remuneration and a pro-business rhetoric fuelled the increase. Senior civil servants as well as ministers brought impressive contact books with them.

After Nolan, the practice of recording ministerial interests began in 1995. This remains a private arrangement, notified to the permanent secretary, but the Coalition Government required transparency on gifts, which have to be registered if over £140. The gift may only be kept if the minister or special adviser pays for it. However, there is a large degree of discretion on how to handle conflicts of interests and, unlike in Scotland, UK ministers may choose to register gifts either in the Register of Members' Financial Interests or in the ministerial register. Private interests of civil servants must be disclosed to the permanent secretary, but are not published.

Nolan turned his attention to the revolving door syndrome, strengthening the Business Appointment Rules which had first been formulated in 1975 by Prime Minister Harold Wilson with the independent Advisory Committee on Business Appointments (ACOBA). Long-standing non-statutory rules required permanent secretaries and deputy secretaries to submit any employment plans in the private sector for approval by the Committee. Nolan recommended that a similar advisory system be applied to former ministers. Eventually these requirements found their way into the Ministerial Code. He also recommended that special advisers be subject to ACOBA.

In the next decade, there was persistent criticism from the Commons Public Administration Select Committee (PASC) that the rules were not enforced strictly and that the membership of ACOBA itself was part of the problem. It appeared to be a cosy club of former ministers and senior civil servants who could empathise with those being regulated. There were examples of ex-ministers refusing to obey ACOBA recommendations, including David Blunkett in 2005, who took a post without consulting the Committee.

---

[28] R Syal and C Barr, '300 Staff Working for Peers and MPs Have Lobbying Interests' *The Guardian* (5 March 2015).

For Opposition politicians, ACOBA and its flimsy rules are a clear target. David Cameron promised in February 2010 that under a Conservative government, any former minister who did not follow the guidelines should lose his or her ministerial pension and promised to increase the cooling-off period to two years, during which time an ex-minister would be bound by ACOBA advice and would not be able to lobby government directly. These changes were implemented by the Coalition Government. For those senior civil servants at SCS1 level and above (and equivalents), the rules apply for two years after leaving the Civil Service. For those below SCS1 level (and equivalents), they normally apply for one year after leaving the Civil Service. The Ministerial Code requires ministers not to lobby government for two years on leaving office, but does not prevent them from taking up other work, subject to ACOBA advice.

However, ACOBA itself is a purely advisory body and cannot enforce compliance with its advice: compliance tends to be a matter of goodwill and acceptance by the individual and new employer of the benefits of being seen to be behave with propriety. There is a distinct lack of data compiled by the Cabinet Office on the extent to which the Rules are complied with. PASC recently undertook another inquiry into ACOBA in 2012, finding that a board made up of party nominees and ex-politicians did not inspire public confidence, and that legislation on lobbying should take the opportunity to make the Rules statutory and binding. The Government's response took over 20 months to appear and was defensive in tone. The subsequent legislation did not extend to the Rules.[29]

The CSPL report on lobbying in November 2013 recommended that Commons Code of Conduct should penalise MPs who do not abide by ACOBA recommendations and recommended that the Cabinet Office undertake a best practice post-implementation review of the Rules, including consideration of the extent to which public employment restrictions should be applied to all public office holders and whether a riskbased approach can and should be adopted to the implementation of the Rules. It argued that it was a mistake to confine regulation to senior civil servants only.

Again, the Government took no action. Yet without a risk-based form of regular auditing of transfers in and out of the private sector, there is no hope of ACOBA offering effective regulation. Civil servants at and below the rank of permanent secretary should be investigated by an external body, which would ask pertinent questions. The contrast with the US Office of Government Ethics is instructive here, with the latter conducting extensive statutory regulation of civil servant behaviour.[30]

---

[29] House of Commons Public Administration Select Committee (PASC), *Business Appointment Rules* (HC 2012–13, 404); PASC, *The Failure of the Cabinet Office to Respond to Our Report on the Business Appointment Rules* (HC 2013–14, 1156); PASC, *Business Appointment Rules: Government Response to the Committee's Third Report of 2012–13* (HC 2014–15, 563).

[30] US Office of Government Ethics, 'Understanding the Revolving Door: How Ethics Rules Apply to Your Job Seeking and Post-Government Employment Activities', www.oge.gov/uploadedFiles/Education/Education_Resources_for_Ethics_Officials/Resources/phrevdoor_07.pdf.

In December 2014, Angela Browning, a former Conservative minister, was appointed chair of ACOBA for a single five-year term, signalling that there were no plans for any substantial reform. PASC approved her as suitable in the pre-appointment hearing in terms of the existing role of the organisation.[31] The change of government in 2015 may put further pressure on the non-statutory nature of the Rules, as a new set of ex-ministers take up posts in the private sector.

IV. THE TRANSPARENCY OF LOBBYING, NON-PARTY CAMPAIGNING AND TRADE UNION ADMINISTRATION ACT 2015

The Coalition Agreement of 2010 contained a commitment to introduce a statutory register of lobbyists. Pressure for reform did not come entirely from the scandals, but also from a PASC report of 2009 which examined the growth in the lobbying industry, international trends of regulation and argued strongly for regulation. More transparency in lobbying was in alignment with a Coalition emphasis on government transparency, with the publication of datasets and internal targets by departments and agencies. Departments were committed to publishing quarterly lists of external meetings by ministers and permanent secretaries, in which the interests represented in a meeting would be generally apparent. The exception was a multi-client lobbying company where the identity of the client would not necessarily be evident. The Government issued a consultation paper on lobbying, *Introducing a Statutory Register of Lobbyists*,[32] the responses to which were published in July 2012. It proposed to regulate only those companies whose main business was lobbying rather than lobbyists within law or other professional firms.

The proposals met with a generally critical reception. The Political and Constitutional Reform Select Committee (PCRC) concluded that the proposals were minimalist, catching only a minority of actions undertaken by multi-client or third party lobbyists. It recommended a wider register of anybody lobbying professionally in a paid role, thus including in-house lobbyists, and favoured a code of conduct for lobbyists.[33]

In an exchange in the House of Lords in December 2012 on the next steps to be taken, Lord Wallace for the Government remarked on the dilemma:

> The Government's summary of replies to the consultation document remarks at one point, in effect, that a lot of those consulted regard themselves as a legitimate part of the political process but regard everyone else as lobbyists. That is part of the problem. The paid lobbyists are a small part of those with whom we are talking, and they wish charities, think tanks, trade unionists and others also to be included on any register of lobbyists.[34]

---

[31] House of Commons Public Administration Select Committee, *Appointment of the Chair of the Advisory Committee on Business Appointments* (HC 2014–15, 759).
[32] Cm 8412, 16 July 2012.
[33] House of Commons Political and Constitutional Reform Select Committee, *Introducing a Statutory Register of Lobbyists* (HC 2012–13, 153).
[34] HC Deb 12 December 2012, col 1056.

Thereafter lobbying plans appeared to languish, until the Patrick Mercer scandal in early June 2013 prompted action. The Transparency of Lobbying etc Bill, as it became generally known, was published in July 2013, just as the House was rising for the summer recess, without any opportunity for further pre-legislative scrutiny. There were immediate protests about the lack of consultation and the absence of a draft Bill. The PCRC rushed out a report in time for second reading on 3 September 2013, which repeated many of its earlier criticisms of the consultation paper.

The Bill defined lobbying as direct communication, orally or in writing, on behalf of someone else with UK government ministers or permanent secretaries in return for payment. Requirements to register only apply to those who lobby the UK Government, not officials of the Scottish Government, the Welsh Government or the Northern Ireland Executive, or local government officers or councillors. Only those working for lobbying firms whose main business was lobbying were required to register. During the passage of the Bill in the Commons, an amendment excluding smaller, non-VAT-registered lobbyists was passed. Businesses registered for VAT are in general those with an annual turnover exceeding £79,000.

The Government argued that the legislation would 'address the problem of information asymmetry' by requiring openness by lobbying firms over the clients they represent in similar meetings. It rejected calls for a code of conduct, arguing that this should be established within the lobbying industry itself. An independent registrar, financed by registration fees, would have the power to levy fines. It took the opportunity to include within the Bill further regulation of the campaigning activities of charities and other third party campaigners in the run-up to a general election and stricter requirements for trade unions to reveal their membership lists. Most of the controversy surrounding the passage of the Bill focused on the implications for charities in Part 2, and this tended to overshadow criticisms of the lobbying provisions in Part 1.

The scope of the register was criticised within the lobbying industry. Some argued that the requirement for lobbying as defined by the Bill to be the 'main business' of the person concerned would mean many public affairs firms would not be required to register, as they also carried out a range of communications work. The Chief Executive of MHP Communications, Gavin Devine, suggested that his company would not have to register as it would fall into the category of those whose main business is not lobbying. He stated that the lobbying of ministers and permanent secretaries 'is not a substantial part of our business'. Peter Bingle, formerly of Bell Pottinger, said on the publication of the legislation: 'I will not be covered by the bill as it is drafted and nor will most of the major players in the public affairs consultancy world.' Aidan O'Neill QC, commissioned by lobbying trade bodies, argued that the Bill could be discriminatory and therefore could fall foul of EU law, since it imposes obligations on only one type of lobbyist. In fact, Bell Pottinger and MHP have both registered subsequently. *The Guardian* found in March 2015 that of the 300 peers' and MPs' staff that it identified as holding outside interests, only a maximum of 11 were likely to be required to register and only if they met a minister or a senior civil servant in the course of their activities.[35]

Despite a chorus of criticism in both Houses as to its limited impact on lobbying, Part 1 of the Bill passed substantially unchanged. Amendments made by the Lords required those registering to indicate whether they belonged to one of the lobbying association codes of conduct,[36] and brought the activity of lobbying special advisers within the framework of regulation. There were more government concessions on Part 2 in response to the formidable charity lobby in the Lords. The type of activities which qualified as election campaigning were restricted from the original drafting, the regulated period was shortened and the thresholds for registration as a third party campaigner in an election were raised. It was an irony that the legislation, which had been designed to address lobbying, was itself subject to a mass lobbying campaign by the charity umbrella body, the Commission on Civil Society and Democratic Engagement, chaired by the former Bishop of Oxford, Lord Harries of Pentregarth. Section 39 contains a requirement for an external reviewer of the Act, but only in respect of election expenditure and not lobbying provisions.[37]

A. The Act in Detail

Section 1 prohibits consultant lobbying unless registered. Section 2 defines a 'consultant lobbyist' as a person who, in the course of a business and in return for payment, personally makes communications on behalf of someone else to a minister or a permanent secretary (or equivalent position) in the UK Government; organisations that only lobby officials of devolved administrations are not required to register. There is provision for special advisers to be an equivalent position through regulations under section 3(3). This follows an amendment tabled by Lord Tyler at Report stage in the Lords. These regulations have not yet been made. The communications fall within the legislation if they are about government policy, legislation, the award of contracts, grants, licences or similar benefits, or the exercise of any other government function. This applies to communications made abroad as well as in the UK, so that offences under the Act are extra-territorial.

The consultant lobbying does not have to be on behalf of the person making the payment, nor does payment have to be linked to a particular communication. It appears to follow that if payment is received to engage in lobbying on behalf of a person, the person receiving the payment will need to register, whoever is

---

[35] Syal and Barr (n 27).
[36] The three main lobbying associations—the Chartered Institute of Public Relations, the Public Relations Consultants Association and the Association of Professional Political Consultants–all have separate codes of conduct.
[37] The reviewer is Lord Hodgson of Astley Abbotts. See PQ 8576, 10 September 2015.

paying (so long as the other conditions, such as lobbying being the main business, apply). The guidance issued by the new Registrar in February 2015 warns that law or accountancy firms with a government relations team, a lead partner or any other employee whose job it is to communicate with ministers and permanent secretaries on behalf of the firm's clients may be required to register. The fact that the firm considers this service incidental to its business does not mean that it is not lobbying: it is the making of relevant communications that is significant.

The Guidance sets out when registration is required.

'Organisations and individuals are considered to be carrying out the business of consultant lobbying if they fulfil the following criteria. They have made direct oral, written or electronic communications personally to:

— a Minister of the Crown, Permanent Secretary (or equivalents) currently in post, referred to as "Government Representatives" relating to:
— The development, adoption or modification of any proposal of the Government to make or amend primary or subordinate legislation;
— The development, adoption or modification of any other policy of the Government;
— The taking of any steps by the Government in relation to any contract, grant, financial assistance, licence or authorisation; or
— The exercise of any other function of Government.

This communication is made in the course of a business and in return for payment on behalf of a client, or payment is received with the expectation that the communication will be made at a later date.

They are registered under the Value Added Tax Act 1994.'[38]

Practical issues as to how the legislation's definition of communications will operate in practice were dealt with as follows:

'Making communications personally means communicating directly with a Government Representative by name or by title, using oral, written or electronic communication. An example would be writing an email to a Minister of the Crown in which the email is addressed to the Minister specifically

— Communications made to a government department, special adviser, administrator or a private secretary are not made to a Government Representative personally. However communications addressed to a Minister, but sent to a private office would have to be registered.
— It does not matter from where the communication is made: it could be a face-to-face meeting within a government office, at a restaurant, at a party-political conference or made from overseas: if the criteria for consultant lobbying are met, then this will trigger the requirement to join the Register.

---

[38] Office of the Registrar for Consultant Lobbying, *Guidance on the Requirement to join the Register of Consultant Lobbyists* (30 January 2015) para 4.1 www.gov.uk/government/uploads/system/uploads/attachment_data/file/399991/Guidance_on_the_requirement_to_join_the_Register_of_Consultant_Lobbyists_v.1.0.pdf.

— In the case of electronic communications, emails that are sent directly to a minister's address will trigger registration. If using social media where a message directed to a minister's (official or personal) account is made which fits the criteria for consultant lobbying, this will require registration. However, if an organisation were to refer to a minister's account indirectly, such as by mentioning that the minister is speaking at an event and tagging the minister's account, then this would not require registration.'[39]

FAQs subsequently issued by the Registrar at the request of the lobbying industry make clear that drafting communications for a client to send would not be an act that requires registration as no direct communication with a government minister has taken place:

> Inviting a Minister or Permanent Secretary (or equivalents) to a meeting or event will not trigger the requirement to register in of itself unless it involves the subjects above and is made of behalf of a paying client. An example might be issuing an invitation to a Minister for a meeting which also contains text that relates to Government policy or legislation—this would require registration.[40]

Where a person's business mostly consists of activities other than the lobbying of government, and communications with government are incidental to non-lobbying activities, they are exempt under Schedule 1. People who act generally as representative of people of a particular class or description and whose communications with government are also incidental to their main business are also exempt. But trade or membership organisations are exempt only when lobbying on behalf of a class or body of people and when their income is derived wholly from that class or body of people and their communications are incidental to their general activity. Charities are exempt from registering as long as they do not receive payment for making communications from the person upon whose behalf they are made.

Following concerns from Members, Schedule 1(5) makes clear that payment for consultant lobbying does not include salaries or allowances paid to MPs and peers. This does not mean that these representatives cannot be consultant lobbyists, simply that the mere fact of receiving these payments is not enough on its own to qualify them. The Registrar attempted clarification in February 2015, stating to *The Guardian* that 'although the Lobbying Act is not specific on this point, my view is that serving MPs and members of the House of Lords in the context of their normal duties would not be required to register'.[41] But if they

---

[39] Ibid para 4.3. The guidance has been superseded by a new version *Guidance on the Requirements for Registration* (15 November 2015) registrarofconsultantlobbyists.org.uk/wp-content/uploads/2015/12/20151111Guidance-on-the-requirement-for-registration1.pdf.

[40] Questions on the requirement to join the Register of Consultant Lobbyists (25 March 2015) www.gov.uk/government/uploads/system/uploads/attachment_data/file/416316/Questions_on_the_requirement_to_Join_the_Register.pdf.

[41] R Syal, 'New Whitehall Lobbyists Register to Be Launched within Weeks' *The Guardian* (25 February 2015).

undertook activities outside their normal duties which might be defined by the Act as consultant lobbying, and where other exemptions such as VAT registration did not apply, they would be required to register. She would expect MPs to register meetings with ministers under the Act when they knew they were lobbying on behalf of a paid client and were not otherwise exempt.

Section 3 establishes a registrar of consultant lobbyists and Schedule 2 sets out the details of the appointment and the powers of the new official. The Registrar is an independent statutory office holder, not an Officer of Parliament such as the parliamentary ombudsman or Comptroller and Auditor General. The maximum term of office is four years, and the Registrar can be dismissed if her or she is found to be unfit to fulfil the functions of the office. There is no parliamentary involvement in appointment or dismissal. Former ministers or permanent secretaries, or consultant lobbyists are ineligible until five years have elapsed since they left office or employment. There can be up to two re-appointments, for a maximum of three years each. Civil servants are to be seconded to the Registrar, who is made subject to the parliamentary ombudsman, and public records and freedom of information legislation.

Section 4 provides for the register and its contents. The entry for each person on the register must include:

— companies;
— the name, registered number and registered address;
— the names of directors, company secretaries and shadow directors;
— partnerships;
— the names of partners and address of the main office;
— individuals;
— the name and address of main office (or home if no office);

for all persons, the entry must include any other names under which they do business as a consultant lobbyist and their 'client information'. The latter, which is to be submitted in a quarterly 'information return', is defined in section 5 as the names of anyone on whose behalf they lobbied in that quarter in return for payment (regardless of whether the payment was actually received) and anybody who paid them to lobby during the quarter (regardless of whether the lobbying took place). Lobbyists must also include the names of anyone on whose behalf they were paid to lobby in the three months preceding registration.

When joining the register, registrants have to declare whether they subscribe to a relevant code of conduct (from a lobbying association) and, if so, where that code can be found. A hyperlink to a code which is hosted online can be provided, or the address of the individual or organisation that holds the code.

The Registrar has a duty to keep the register up to date in section 6 and publish it on a website and in another form in section 7. She must monitor compliance with the register and has powers under section 9 to serve 'information notices', requiring recipients to reveal certain information. These may be served on registered lobbyists and on those whom she has reasonable grounds to believe are consultant lobbyists. Appeals against a notice are provided for in section 11. Section 21 gives the Registrar power to issue guidance on the operation of the registration scheme.

The Act creates both civil and criminal liability for falling foul of the registration requirements. Section 12 criminalises the following activity:

— carrying on the business of consultant lobbying whilst unregistered (section 12(1));
— carrying on the business of consultant lobbying without an accurate and up-to-date entry on the register (section 12(2));
— failing to supply information required in an information return (section 12(3)(a));
— providing inaccurate or incomplete information in an information return (section 12(3)(b));
— failing to supply information in response to an information notice (section 12(4)(a)); and
— providing inaccurate or incomplete information in response to an information notice (section 12(4)(b)).

When section 85 of the Legal Aid, Sentencing and Punishment of Offenders Act 2012 comes into force, the fine on summary conviction in England and Wales will be unlimited. Section 14 provides the Registrar with the power to impose civil penalties on a person if she is satisfied that their conduct amounts to one of the four offences specified in section 12(1)–(4). It is envisaged that civil sanctions would be used where there are less serious cases of non-compliance, such as administrative oversight. Under section 18, it is not possible for an individual to be prosecuted and subject to civil sanctions for the same conduct. A defence against failure to register or failure to supply required information to deadline is the exercise of all due diligence to avoid committing the offence. Both the decision to impose a penalty and the amount of that penalty may be appealed to the Tribunal, as may any decision to vary a penalty notice. The maximum civil penalty which can be levied is £7,000.

Section 22 allows the Registrar to impose charges in accordance with regulations, which are to be paid into the consolidated fund. The registration scheme is meant to be self- financing. According to paragraph 173 of the Explanatory Notes to the Bill, the fees were likely to be £200–450 per year. The Impact Assessment for the Bill estimated that the annual impact on lobbyists required to register would be £350,000, assuming 1,000 consultant lobbyists would register.[42] In fact, the 2015 fee was set at £750, suggesting running costs were increasing over estimates.

---

[42] Cabinet Office, *Statutory Register of Lobbyists: Impact Assessment* (July 2013) www.parliament.uk/documents/impact-assessments/IA13-22A.pdf.

B. Implementation

The post of Registrar was first advertised in May 2014 and was re-advertised in August 2014 at an increased daily rate of £420 on the expectation that the post would warrant 30–50 days a year and then the time commitment would decline. The PCRC held a pre-appointment hearing in September 2014 which expressed some disappointment with the preferred candidate Alison White, an ex-commercial director of the Royal Mail Group who lacked detailed knowledge of the lobbying industry, the potential deficiencies in the Act, as well as knowledge of Parliament. The Committee expressed annoyance that the Government had given it just one day's notice of the pre-appointment hearing.[43]

Draft regulations on the statutory register of lobbyists were issued by the Cabinet Office in September and consultation closed on 17 October 2014, with just 13 responses. The consultation covered the form of application and form of information return, limitations on the duty to supply information, charges and supply of information regarding VAT registration. These were detailed points of implementation, which did not involve substantial policy issues. In response to concerns about the burden of regulation, the Cabinet Office sought to minimise the charge by providing certain services, namely accommodation, IT and secretariat staff to the Registrar.[44] The regulations were laid on 26 February 2015.[45]

Implementation followed swiftly, when Alison White published the first register on 25 March 2015.[46] A total of 53 organisations registered in the first tranche. By the end of July, there were 85, including some firms whose main business was not multi-client lobbying. The accountants Ernst & Young is one example. Law firms have been noticeably reluctant to register. There are many familiar names of lobbying firms and lists of clients, but the full impact of the legislation will not be felt for some time. No MPs or peers have registered. Most commentators expect further regulation as soon as another scandal indicates its ineffectiveness.

The Act is likely to be the opening part of a larger drama leading to more widespread regulation. Effective regulation requires detailed rules, extensive training and prompt enforcement when rules are breached. Appropriate resources and a culture change are essential to achieve this outcome. Yet the UK has not yet come to a conclusion as to whether a heavily regulated system is the right outcome, since there would be further reputational damage to its legislature when wrongdoing is exposed.

---

[43] House of Commons Political and Constitutional Reform Committee, *Pre-appointment Hearing: Registrar of Consultant Lobbyists* (HC 2014–15, 223).
[44] Cabinet Office, *Government Response to Consultation on Statutory Register of Lobbyists: Draft Regulations* (February 2015) http://qna.files.parliament.uk/ws-attachments/223801/original/Government%20response%20to%20Consultation%20Final.pdf.
[45] The Registration of Consultant Lobbyists Regulations 2015 (SI 2015/379).
[46] Register of Consultant Lobbyists (25 March 2015).

V. WIDER CONSIDERATIONS

The allegations against Sir Malcolm Rifkind and Jack Straw in February 2015 reignited the question of outside earnings by MPs.[47] In data gleaned by *The Guardian* from official parliamentary registers, more than 50 MPs had directorships of at least one company, while 295 declared at least some kind of minimal earnings from outside work. All major parties were affected. The then Leader of the Opposition, Ed Miliband, drew up proposals to cap outside earnings at £10,000, with an eventual ban on outside jobs. Under his proposals, no MP would have been able to hold paid directorships or consultancies from the beginning of the 2015 Parliament.[48] The new Labour leader Jeremy Corbyn can be expected to confirm this direction of travel. Nolan's original comments in 1995 that Parliament benefited from the external perspective of outside interests look very old-fashioned, as new MPs expect to work 80-hour weeks at Westminster and in their constituency. Some may retain traditional professions, but overall the trend is clear.

The House may be poorer as a result, as it loses expertise from the Bar and small businesses, but the public will always find sleazy paid consultancies acquired as a result of parliamentary knowledge. The Standards Committee pointed out on the publication of its findings on Rifkind and Straw that: 'Members of Parliament should be aware that even if their behaviour is within the rules, they may not escape criticism ... Although no rules were broken both men acknowledged to the Commissioner that they had made errors of judgment.'[49]

These were not new Labour proposals. The party has been re-positioning itself as the party of full-time MPs for some years. Harriet Harman, as Leader of the House in 2009, introduced much more rigorous rules both on the declaration of outside income and on time spent on such interests, in response to the Members' expenses scandal. There were similar proposals in an Opposition Day debate on 17 July 2013.

During the debate on the new Code of Conduct for MPs in March 2015, the Shadow Leader of the House, Angela Eagle, promised:

> If Labour wins the election we will introduce tough new limits on lobbying and an effective register of all professional lobbyists, backed up by a code of conduct and enforced with sanctions. We will also review whether lobbyists should be allowed to provide the secretariats for all-party parliamentary groups, and continue to support the ban on parliamentary passes for any APPG staff.[50]

The Conservative and Liberal Democrat General Election manifestos did not mention lobbying, but the Scottish National Party (SNP) promised support for

---

[47] See n 1.

[48] B Worthy, 'Cash for Access Scandal: What Impact Will Miliband's Proposals Have on MPs and the Public?' (*LSE British Politics and Policy Blog*, 24 February 2015) http://blogs.lse.ac.uk/politicsandpolicy/cash-for-access-scandal-what-impact-will-milibands-proposals-have-on-mps-and-the-public. See also Opposition Day Commons Debate, HC Deb 25 February 2015, col 381.

[49] House of Commons Committee on Standards (n 2) para 55.

[50] HC Deb 17 March 2015, col 703.

any plans to abolish restrictions on campaigning by charities introduced in Part 2 of the Transparency of Lobbying Etc Act.[51]

Under the membership requirements of the Parliamentary Labour Party, no Labour MP may currently hold remunerated directorships or consultancies. It remains to be seen whether in practice this will refer to new posts, since existing directors of companies would then be forced to divest themselves of businesses. As retiring Labour MP Frank Dobson put it: 'The public's real concern is not about people with a continuing interest; it is about people who become Members of then obtain directorships and consultancies, who are perceived as being in something like a system of outdoor relief for grasping MPs.'[52]

Independent bodies are also considering the next steps to be taken. The CSPL produced a report on lobbying in November 2013, but this was not designed to be a commentary on the Transparency of Lobbying Bill. Its recommendations to Parliament included a series of changes to the Code of Conduct for MPs designed to tighten the rules for ex-Members; to prevent approaches to ministers for two years after leaving Parliament; and increase the restrictions on chairs of select committees. It recommended the refusal of all but insignificant gifts from lobbyists. It made similar recommendations for the House of Lords to review the Code of Conduct and guidance to peers on registering employment payments, gifts, benefits and hospitality, and in relation to lobbying which were accepted. A blog from CSPL chair Lord Bew in February 2015 lamented lack of action in the Commons, which contrasted with a tightening of rules in the Lords.[53] As noted above, a requirement for ex-Members not to lobby was added to the new Code of Conduct in the Commons in March 2015.[54]

The CSPL also recommended more timely, detailed disclosure about all significant meetings and hospitality involving external attempts to influence policy decisions, arguing that the problems around lobbying were not confined to central government and Parliament. It advocated that these disclosure arrangements should be widened to cover special advisers and senior civil servants as well as ministers, permanent secretaries and departmental boards. Public office holders outside the scope of the Freedom of Information Act (including MPs, peers and councillors) should be encouraged to disclose the same information.

One big area of focus was tackling the revolving door syndrome. The CSPL considered that departments (and other bodies) should be required, regularly, to publish consistent summary information on cases they consider under the Business Appointment Rules and the number of secondments and interchanges in

---

[51] SNP Manifesto, *Stronger for Scotland* (2015) 22.
[52] HC Deb 25 February 2015, col 397.
[53] Lord Bew, 'Lobbying: Current Arrangements are Not Enough' (*Blog of the Committee on Standards in Public Life*, 11 February 2015) https://cspl.blog.gov.uk/2015/02/11/lobbying-current-arrangements-are-not-enough.
[54] The Code of Conduct for MPs together with the Guide to the Rules Relating to the Conduct of Members, March 2015, para 20.

and out of their organisations. These concerns were picked up by Labour, which promised a tougher regulatory framework in 2015. The CSPL also attempted to make senior civil servants accountable for ethical standards. Accounting officers personally should certify annually that they have satisfied themselves about the adequacy of their organisation's arrangements for safeguarding high ethical standards and this should include ensuring that officials are vigilant about contact by lobbyists and, in the case of permanent secretaries, that their ministers and special advisers are reporting relevant contacts. Tricky issues are involved. The Adam Werritty and Liam Fox affair, where the Secretary of State for Defence was found to have breached the Ministerial Code, was investigated by the Cabinet Secretary, not the Independent Adviser on Ministerial Interests, as an apparent damage limitation exercise.[55]

More generally, a Transparency International UK (TI) report *Lifting the Lid on Lobbying* published in February 2015 found that the Commons was amongst the weakest of the public bodies in regulating lobbying.[56] This is even in contrast with the Lords. A blog by the CSPL chair Paul Bew in early 2015 made similar points— a worrying warning for the future. Inevitably, MPs are slow to regulate themselves. A recommendation from the Parliamentary Standards Commissioner in 2012 to require former Members to register any approach they make to ministers, MPs or public officials for two years was reduced to six months by the Standards Committee.[57] The Register of Members' Interests is not easily searchable and does not meet open data standards, unlike the Lords Register. As the TI report makes clear, devolved bodies have been more proactive in introducing transparency into meetings where lobbying is taking place. MPs are lagging behind, and this may cost them dear in the future.

---

[55] Mr Werritty visited Mr Fox in the Ministry of Defence on a number of occasions, was allowed to accompany him on foreign trips where he met diplomats, defence staff and defence contractors, and had handed out business cards suggesting he was Mr Fox's adviser, despite having no official role in government.

[56] Transparency International UK (n 10).

[57] House of Commons Standards and Privileges Committee, *Proposed Revisions to the Guide to the Rules Relating to the Conduct of Members* (HC 2012–13, 636) para 27.

9

Robot Government: Automated Decision-Making and its Implications for Parliament

ANDREW LE SUEUR

I. GOVERNMENT BY COMPUTERS

D IGITAL TECHNOLOGIES ARE seeping into almost every aspect of private and public life, from leisure to business, from cyber warfare to government administration. This chapter focuses on one particular aspect of this digital revolution: automated decision-making by government. It aims to start a debate about its constitutional implications in the UK, concentrating on how Parliament should respond to this development.[1] It is a change in government working methods that has, to date, received little attention from parliamentarians and that has hardly been noticed by British academics working in the fields of constitutional and administrative law.[2]

One reason for this lack of interest could be that the rise of automated decision-making is not particularly noteworthy: it might be thought that there is little difference between a human official deciding individual cases in accordance with legislation and a computer system doing the same task. In both scenarios, Parliament confers executive power and decisions are made. The lack of openly available information about the scale and deployment of automated decision-making is probably also a contributing factor in its low profile. To take this complacent view is, however, the equivalent of thinking that the use of electronic

---

[1] I am grateful to colleagues who commented on previous iterations of this chapter, including Maurice Sunkin and participants at a UK Constitutional Law Association seminar held at UCL on 15 April 2015. All errors, omissions and any muddle are of course my responsibility alone.

[2] Some academics in the field of cyberlaw have engaged with rule of law issues but have not set their work in the contexts of administrative decision-making and automated decision-making; see, eg, A Murray, 'Looking Back at the Law of the Horse: Why Cyberlaw and the Rule of Law are Important', keynote address to the 2013 BILETA Conference, http://theitlawyer.blogspot.co.uk/2013/04/my-keynote-address-to-bileta.html; and C Reed, 'How to Make Bad Law: Lessons from Cyberspace' (2010) 73 *Modern Law Review* 903.

surveillance is unremarkable because it is no different from being seen by police officers as you go about your daily business.³

This chapter explores the implications of automated decision-making, arguing that we need to consider how its use fits with conventional legal frameworks of executive power and parliamentary control. Like digital technologies in other contexts, the rise of automated decision-making challenges orthodox thinking and long-established practices. This is not necessarily a bad thing, but we should be aware of its capacity to disrupt how we do and think about things so that the benefits of automation can be maximised and unintended consequences avoided.

The chapter starts by defining automated decision-making using a couple of examples (section II), before examining more closely one of the few provisions on the statute book for automation—in the Social Security Act 1998 (section III). Section IV explores how automation provides some fresh impetus to long-running debates in constitutional and administrative law—about achieving compliance with the rule of law, about the relative benefit of 'rules versus discretion', about the legal basis for executive action and about the permissible limits of delegation— and questions why we can opt out of private sector automated decision-making (under section 12 of the Data Protection Act 1998), but not in relation to such decision-making by government. Section V calls for a select committee inquiry on automated decision-making and suggests ways—some of them radical—in which Parliament could redesign legislative scrutiny and accountability practices to harness the broad transformative effects of automation.

II. WHAT IS AUTOMATED DECISION-MAKING?

The first applications of digital technologies in government were directed at improving the efficiency of back-office operations, then at improving the quality and quantity of information available to citizens online.⁴ There was also a start on automation of some kinds of decisions.

Automated decision-making involves breaking down a decision to a set of 'if then' rules and criteria: a decision is understood as an algorithm (a sequence of reasoning) that selects from predetermined alternatives. An 'inference engine' can systematically check whether the condition of a rule is met; if so, it can 'conclude' that the consequent of that rule applies.⁵ Automated decision-making systems draw on

---

³ Parliament has shown significant interest in this development, with select committee inquires in both Houses: House of Lords Constitution Committee, *Surveillance: Citizens and the State* (HL 2008–09, 18-I) and House of Commons Home Affairs Committee, *A Surveillance Society?* (HC 2007–08, 58-I).
⁴ See generally H Margetts, 'E-Government in Britain—A Decade on' (2006) 59 *Parliamentary Affairs* 250.
⁵ See J Svensson, 'The Use of Legal Expert Systems in Administrative Decision Making' in Å Grönlund (ed), *Electronic Government: Design, Applications and Management: Design, Applications and Management* (Hersey, PA, Idea Group Inc, 2001) 156. This chapter is the work of a humble lawyer; it does not set out to explain in any detail the various technologies that facilitate automated decision-making.

technologies from sub-fields of artificial intelligence and 'decision-support tools'. In private and public sector organisations, automated decision-making is often based on a collection of software products called Oracle Policy Automation (OPA) that enable 'executable business rules' to be modelled and used.[6]

Human involvement in the process of reaching a conclusion is minimised or eliminated. A decision may be fully automated, or 'zero touch', where a citizen initiates the decision-making process through a self-service online tool, submits all relevant information, and the outcome is reached and communicated by the computer without any human involvement. Alternatively, decision-making processes may involve a mix of work by human and computer. Human participation may occur at different points, eg, near the outset in collecting information by interview or towards the end if a human checks an automated decision or if the automated decision is in the form of a recommendation requiring human judgement to finalise and approve it.

UK government policy on the digital transformation, of which automated decision-making is one aspect, has since 2011 been led by the Government Digital Service (GDS), a unit in the Cabinet Office with a staff of 500.[7] The overarching goal is 'making public services digital by default, and simpler, clearer and faster to use'. The GDS is working with departments to redesign services, based on its 'number one design principle: "User needs, not government needs"'.[8] This involves 'dismantling silos' and focusing on transactions from the citizen's perspective (so 'buying a house' rather than 'HM Land Registry'). There is a vision of 'Government as a Platform',[9] enabling different parts of government to share 'digital systems, technology and processes'.

The accuracy of automated decision-making depends on citizens being truthful when they provide information to the system (as with decision-making by human officials). Automation, however, facilitates the retrieval or verification of information from data and knowledge bases shared between different government bodies. (For example, if I tell the system that I live in Wivenhoe, this could be verified by checking that my name appears on the electoral register or that I pay council tax to the relevant local authority.)[10] A broad range of benefits of automated decision-making has been identified. It enables efficient handling (in terms of cost and

---

A succinct starting point for novices is J Harris and T Davenport, *Automated Decision Making Comes of Age* (London, Accenture Institute for High Performance Business, 2005); and Australian Government, *Automated Assistance in Administrative Decision-Making: Better Practice Guide* (2007) www.ombudsman.gov.au/docs/better-practice-guides/aaadm_guide.pdf.

[6] Owned by the Oracle Corporation, the second-largest software maker by revenue after Microsoft. See www.oracle.com/technetwork/apps-tech/policy-automation/overview/index.html.
[7] See https://gds.blog.gov.uk and Twitter @gdsteam.
[8] See www.gov.uk/transformation.
[9] See https://gds.blog.gov.uk/2015/09/08/building-a-platform-to-host-digital-services.
[10] Data sharing between different parts of government has given rise to concerns about privacy and data security. This is a large subject that cannot be explored here; for further discussion, see http://datasharing.org.uk.

186 *Andrew Le Sueur*

speed) of large numbers of decisions based on complex rules: many types of social security payments and calculating tax liability are paradigm examples.[11]

A good way to understand automated decision-making is to look at a couple of practical examples. The first is already in use by HM Revenue & Customs (HMRC). The second imagines how local authorities may in the future use automated decision-making in relation to their homelessness functions.

A. Example: The ESI Tool

A small business is considering expanding its workforce. It needs to know whether the new worker will be an employee or a self-employed contractor. The distinction is important for income tax, National Insurance, VAT and other reasons. The HMRC website provides an 'Employment Status Indicator' (ESI) tool:

> When you have answered all the questions, the ESI tool will provide it's [sic] indication of the worker's employment status. You can rely on the ESI outcome as evidence of a worker's status for tax/NICs/VAT purposes if both of the following apply:
>
> — your answers to the ESI questions accurately reflect the terms and conditions under which the worker provides their services
> — the ESI has been completed by an engager or their authorised representative (if the tool has been completed by or on behalf of a worker the result is only indicative)
>
> However, you should download and print or save the PDF bearing the 14 digit ESI reference number from the summary of outcome screen. If the worker's employment status is questioned in the future, HMRC will only be bound by the ESI outcome if this document can be produced.[12]

The questions asked include 'Under the terms of their contract, if the worker is unable or unwilling to carry out the work personally, are they obliged to send someone else to do it?', 'If the worker is unwilling to carry out the work personally, do they have any right to send someone else to do it?', 'Is the worker a skilled person or expert in their field?' and 'Which statement best describes when the work has to be done?' (there are four options). Over 10 pages, there are 15 questions, some of which require a selection to be made from different options. The questions seem to be based on a mix of statutory rules and case law on the distinction between

---

[11] It may also have a role to play in relation to infrequently made decisions that must be made with great speed (for example, shutting down a power station in an emergency or air traffic control), but these are not the focus for present purposes.

[12] See http://tools.hmrc.gov.uk/esi/screen/ESI/en-GB/summary?user=guest. Elsewhere in this chapter, the term 'app' (application software) is used in a non-technical way to refer to a set of computer programs designed to permit the user to perform a task.

different kinds of employment. At the end of the process, a PDF is generated—saying (for example):

> Thank you for using the Employment Status Indicator. The answers you gave to the questions asked indicate that this worker is self-employed in respect of this engagement (*a contract for services*).
>
> This outcome is based on the following grounds:
>
> — There is a low indication of substitution.
> — There is a low indication of control over the worker.

Thus, without any human intervention by an HMRC official, a definitive decision is made.

B. Example: Suitability of Accommodation Decisions

A second and this time hypothetical illustration imagines how in the future automated decision-making could be deployed by English local authorities in making decisions under the Homelessness (Suitability of Accommodation) (England) Order 2012 (SI 2012/2601), which sets out the criteria that determine whether private sector rented accommodation is suitable to be offered to the applicant under the Housing Act 1996. Article 2 provides:

> In determining whether accommodation is suitable for a person, the local housing authority must take into account the location of the accommodation, including—
>
> (a) where the accommodation is situated outside the district of the local housing authority, the distance of the accommodation from the district of the authority;
> (b) the significance of any disruption which would be caused by the location of the accommodation to the employment, caring responsibilities or education of the person or members of the person's household;
> (c) the proximity and accessibility of the accommodation to medical facilities and other support which—
>   (i) are currently used by or provided to the person or members of the person's household; and
>   (ii) are essential to the well-being of the person or members of the person's household; and
> (d) the proximity and accessibility of the accommodation to local services, amenities and transport.

How might a hypothetical automated decision-making app approach this task? In relation to 2(a), Ordinance Survey data could be used to measure the distance of the flat from the boundary of the local authority. Perhaps it would be relevant to draw on centrally held data about distances that have in the past been regarded as acceptable by other local authorities across England to determine the reasonableness of the proposed accommodation. Decisions about 2(b) would require information from the applicant and is the most difficult element to envisage as true/false rules. Moving on to 2(c)(i), parts of the NHS records of the applicant and applicant's family could be interrogated by the app to determine the location of their GP's surgery and any hospital where they are outpatients, as well as the frequency of their visits. For 2(d), across large parts of the country, online journey planner apps provide information about travel door-to-door. Applicants could select from pull-down menus a basket of 'local services' and 'amenities' that they regularly use and the computer could, as part of its decision-making process, rank the ease or difficulty of reaching them by public transport or on foot. For sure, this type of multi-factor decision, embodying significant elements of professional judgement on the part of housing officers, would seem to present significant hurdles for automation. But as the government moves to be 'digital by default', it is possible to speculate that it will become a candidate for automation.

III. AUTOMATED DECISION-MAKING ON THE STATUTE BOOK

Section 2 of the Social Security Act 1998 on 'Use of computers' was the first statutory provision to make provision for computer-based decision-making. It provides that any decision falling to be made by the Secretary of State 'may be made or issued not only by an officer of his acting under his authority' but also '(a) by a computer for whose operation such an officer is responsible'. This acknowledged that computers had moved from being merely tools used by officials to being 'the decision-maker'. Section 2 seems to have been prompted by unease about how, precisely, the rise of automated decision-making fitted into the traditional model described above. As the minister in charge of the Bill in 1998 said in the House of Lords: 'Making provision in the Bill for automated decision-making will legitimise what happens at present. They [sic] will be able to calculate and award benefit in … straightforward cases without the need for human intervention.'[13] But during the Committee stage of the 1998 Bill, a Conservative peer and a Liberal Democrat peer argued (as Lord Goodhart put it) 'that computers should be treated as a tool of decision-making and not as the decision-maker itself'.[14] Responding for the Government, Baroness Hollis of Heigham said:

> Clearly, there are some kinds of decisions which are not suitable to be made by a computer process. I can assure the Committee that decisions which require the exercise of discretion or judgment will continue to be made by the department's trained staff.

She gave as examples 'where there is a question whether for benefit purposes the couple are living together as husband and wife, or whether a claimant has deprived himself of capital, or whether a 16 or 17 year-old would suffer hardship if refused benefit'.[15] The exchange ended rather inclusively.

---

[13] HL Deb 30 March 1998, col 54 (Baroness Hollis of Heigham).
[14] ibid col 53.
[15] ibid col 54.

In the House of Commons, the minister handling the Bill said:

> There are significant benefits to be had from greater automation. Computers—if they are programmed correctly—are not subject to human error, and can be relied upon to produce consistent decisions. This will lead to improvements in quality and will allow staff in agencies to refocus their efforts on making improvements in overall customer service ... [We] believe that using computers effectively will allow staff to be much more customer-oriented, giving them more time to explain decisions and help customers to understand the whole social security system ... [W]e believe that sensible use of new technology will help us to refocus the whole nature of the social security system on the customer rather than on the complexities of the current system.[16]

A few parliamentarians were unconvinced. Opposition backbencher Oliver Letwin, then a new MP, expressed his concerns, apologising to other members of the standing committee considering the Bill for taking time on 'a subject which may appear to be an eccentric worry'. He continued:

> What is important here is ... the fact that the complainant feels even more strongly that he is not dealing with a group of human beings who in any sense understand the human problems that he may be experiencing. He will feel that he is dealing with a monolith that will take on the appearance of a large network of computers producing pieces of paper—sometimes correctly, sometimes not—with never a human hand behind them.
>
> The long-term effects of this increasing depersonalisation of the Department of Social Security are, and will become, even greater than many imagine. Many individuals receiving or seeking benefit undoubtedly find that this impersonal approach, which contrasts strikingly with the way that they are dealt with by other Departments, including the national health service, or by commercial entities, makes them continue to feel that they are pawns. The ethic of all of us ... should be to re-integrate as fully as possible into the wider community individuals who receive benefit, by making them feel that they are not pawns in the hands of a monolith. Clause 2 moves significantly in the opposite direction, and runs counter to our perception of the proper way to proceed, as well as to Government policy.[17]

The world has moved on in several ways since 1998. By 2014, Mr Letwin was the minister in charge of the Cabinet Office, which has overall responsibility for e-government and the 'digital revolution'.[18] The appetite of government for the transformative impacts of digital technologies has continued to grow, fuelled by the twin aspirations of reducing administrative costs and providing better services to citizens (goals that are probably not always compatible). The software that drives automated decision-making has become gradually more sophisticated and

---

[16] Standing Committee B, 28 October 1997 (Morning), Keith Bradley MP, Parliamentary Under-Secretary of State for Social Security.

[17] ibid.

[18] On the use of the revolutionary terminology, see the letter from Martha Lane Fox to Francis Maude, published as *DirectGov 2010 and Beyond: Revolution Not Evolution* (2010) www.gov.uk/government/uploads/system/uploads/attachment_data/file/60993/Martha_20Lane_20Fox_s_20letter_20to_20Francis_20Maude_2014th_20Oct_202010.pdf.

'agile'. Increasingly, automated decision-making takes place by citizens directly inputting information online without the need to complete a paper application form, speak to a human civil servant on the telephone or visit government offices. Moreover, as online transactions and automated decision-making increase across the private sector (eg, for insurance and mortgage underwriting and bank credit applications), feelings about what decisions can appropriately be made by government without human involvement are probably changing.

IV. CONSTITUTIONAL QUESTIONS

An important principle of the rule of law is that government action must be authorised by law ('rule by law'). Parliament, through the enactment of legislation, has a major role in producing this legal basis for decision-making by public bodies. Commonly used words are 'the Secretary of State may' (or 'shall') and—referring to local authorities and other public bodies—'the authority may' (or 'shall').

The assumption made until comparatively recently is that the decision-maker using the executive power conferred by Parliament is a human being or an institution composed of humans and that here is a human who will be accountable and responsible for the decision. In the case of central government, it was acknowledged in 1943 that Secretaries of State could not possibly make all decisions personally and civil servants in a Secretary of State's department can lawfully make decisions without falling foul of the legal principle that a person to whom Parliament has given executive power cannot delegate it to a third party.[19] The Secretary of State nonetheless remains answerable to Parliament for officials' decision-making.[20] The constitutional model is thus seen as a virtuous circle: Parliament confers legal power; Secretaries of State (or, more often than not, their officials) and other public authorities exercise power by applying the rules to individual cases;[21] the legality of the decision may be tested in the courts through judicial review; and Parliament retains the power to call the Secretary of State or other decision-maker to account politically for their actions (though select committee enquiries, written questions etc). At the heart of this model are humans.

For British constitutional and administrative lawyers, automated decision-making adds fresh stimulus to some long-running debates—about achieving compliance with the rule of law, about the relative benefit of 'rules versus discretion', about the legal basis for executive action and about the permissible limits of delegation.

---

[19] *Carltona Ltd v Commissioners of Works* [1943] 2 All ER 560.
[20] For a recent discussion, see House of Lords Constitution Committee, *The Accountability of Civil Servants* (HL 2012–13, 61).
[21] This is a rather naïve view of the implementation of legal rules. In real day-to-day administrative practice, non-legal or extra-legal considerations may often come into play in street-level bureaucracy.

A. Can Automation Enhance Compliance with the Rule of Law?

Empirical socio-legal studies show that human officials may fail to operate in complete conformity with rules laid down in legislation when making decisions about individuals. There are various possible reasons for this, including lack of awareness of relevant rules or misunderstanding what they require, professional administrative cultures in which legal rules are only one of a number of competing pressures, and uncertainties built into the particular legal rules being applied.[22]

Automated decision-making may achieve more consistent implementation of the formal rules approved by Parliament than can be offered by human officials. Automation based on the application of objective criteria holds out the promise of legal certainty (similar cases are treated identically), the elimination of bias, ensuring that no irrelevant considerations are taken into account and that all relevant factors are included. To this extent, automation can be regarded as enhancing the rule of law. Moreover, it can be contended that the outcome will always be right. Discussing automated decision-making in 1997, De Mulder and van Noortwijk suggest:

> If a computer program that has been designed by the legislative power has come up with a decision, and given that the input has been correct, such a decision would be exactly according to the law and it would arguably not need to be subject to any form of appeal.[23]

The proposition that automated decision-making guarantees error-free conclusions is, however, open to doubt. Some early and small-scale empirical studies have identified mistakes in computer-generated decisions—though they also show examples where automation led to fewer errors.[24] It would be constitutionally dangerous to assume that 'the computer is always right'; even more worrying is the idea (no doubt attractive to government) that automation may require less provision to be made for citizens to challenge decisions.

An element of the rule of law is that processes must be provided for citizens to resolve disputes with government without undue delay or cost. Grounds for challenging a decision can often only be identified if reasons are given by the decision-making. English law has a complicated relationship with the idea of reason giving: there is no general common law requirement for reasons, but the common law is recognising a growing number of exceptions to this rule, where

---

[22] See S Halliday, *Judicial Review and Compliance with Administrative Law* (Oxford, Hart Publishing, 2004) especially ch 9; and see further M Hertogh and S Halliday (eds), *Judicial Review and Bureaucratic Impact: International and Interdisciplinary Perspectives* (Cambridge, Cambridge University Press, 2004).

[23] R De Mulder and K van Noortwijk, 'More Science than Art: Law in the 21st Century', 12th BILETA Conference, The Future of Legal Education and Practice, 24–25 March 1997, www.bileta.ac.uk/content/files/conference%20papers/1997/More%20Science%20Than%20Art%20-%20Law%20n%20the%2021st%20century.pdf.

[24] Discussed in Svensson (n 5).

reasons are required; legislation often requires reasons in particular situations.[25] One reason for the patchy enthusiasm for a right to reasons in English administrative law is concern about the costs of providing explanations. Here, automation may provide a solution. As the ESI tool (discussed above) and the automatically generated liability calculations produced by the Self-Assessment tax system show, different automated systems can produce different types of explanation that are suitable to the particular context. Requiring automated decision-making systems to provide explanations for their outcomes would be a positive contribution to the rule of law.

B. Will Automation Lead to a Shift from Administrative Discretion and Judgement to Rule-Bound Decision-Making?

The 'rules versus discretion' debate is a long-running conversation among administrative lawyers and policy-makers. Most fields of administration have, over the years, included a mix of hard-edged rules leading to legal entitlements (eg, no licence may be issued to a person who has an unspent criminal conviction) and issues on which professional judgement or discretion needs to be brought to bear because the power conferred on the administrator is flexible or open-textured (eg, licensees must be a 'fit and proper person'). At different times, the political preferences for one or other approach have waxed and waned. The reality has usually been nuanced. As Titmuss explains:

> Law and discretion are not separated by a sharp line but by overlapping zones. Exercising discretion may be a part of finding facts and applying law, and finding facts may be a part of exercising discretion.[26]

One hypothesis about automated decision-making is that it will provide an incentive for decision-making systems to be designed that emphasise hard-edged rules and reduce or eliminate the capacity of officials to provide personalised solutions. Computers have to work within the straitjacket of the algorithms with which they are programmed. This challenges the model described in 1980 (before the rise of automation) by Lipsky in his classic account, where he argued that: 'The essence of street-level bureaucracies is that they require people to make decisions about other people. Street-level bureaucrats have discretion because the nature of service provision calls for human judgment that cannot be programmed and for which machines cannot substitute.'[27]

---

[25] See A Le Sueur, 'Legal Duties to Give Reasons' (1999) 52 *Current Legal Problems* 150; H Woolf, J Jowell, A Le Sueur et al, *De Smith's Judicial Review* 7th edn (London, Sweet & Maxwell, 2013) para 7-085.

[26] R Titmuss, 'Welfare "Rights", Law and Discretion' (1971) 42 *Political Quarterly* 113, 119; and see generally J Jowell, 'The Legal Control of Administrative Discretion' [1973] *Public Law* 178.

[27] M Lipsky, *Street-Level Bureaucracy: Dilemmas of the Individual in Public Services* (New York, Russell Sage Foundation, 1980).

More broadly, Roman echoes concerns voiced by Oliver Letwin MP in 1998 during the debate on section 2 of the Social Security Bill:

> Limited discretion, while theoretically desirable in a principal-agent model, might lead to disinterested and morally detached agents. For instance, as frontline public servants take upon less decision-making responsibility they could minimize or even stop their typical challenges of interpretations that come from 'the top'. Furthermore, failure to ethically connect with administrative decision making might lead to a moral collapse, an inability to diagnose or understand the real implications of one's actions. Ethical deliberation is a dynamic process that demands personal involvement; yet, human judgment is often found to be normatively objectionable under the design of e-government infrastructures as it is believed to muddle the process.[28]

Whether, and if so how and where, automation may shift the style of decision-making towards specific rules and away from professional judgement and discretion is a matter on which empirical research is needed.[29] It should also be recognised that a trend towards using precisely specified rules may be occurring for reasons other than automated decision-making.[30]

C. What is the Legal Basis for Automated Decision-Making?

Apart from section 2 of the Social Security Act 1998, and provisions along similar lines in section 50A of the Child Support Act 1991 and in Northern Ireland secondary legislation relating to social security, the statute book appears to be silent on automated decision-making by government. The fact that these provisions were enacted can be seen as recognition that, at least in some situations, there is a legal and constitutional need for an express legal basis for automation. In Australia, a distinction has been drawn between different forms of automation:

> The use of an expert system to make a decision—as opposed to helping a decision-maker to make a decision—should be legislatively sanctioned to ensure that it is compatible with the legal principles of automated decision-making.[31]

The Australian guidance provides that: 'The authority for making [fully automated] decisions will only be beyond doubt if specifically enabled by legislation. The construction of such an authorisation should nominate a position or title of a person with ultimate responsibility for the decision, such as the Secretary of the relevant department.'[32]

---

[28] A Roman, 'Framing the Questions of E-Government Ethics: An Organisational Perspective' (2013) XX(X) *American Review of Public Administration* 1, 12.
[29] See further A Buffat, 'Street-Level Bureaucracy and E-government' (2015) 17 *Public Management Review* 149, which calls for further research on the topic.
[30] See Reed (n 2).
[31] Australian Government (n 5).
[32] ibid 4.

Comparisons with approaches adopted by other constitutional systems can, however, be misleading. In the UK, a remarkably relaxed approach is taken on the need for specific legislative authority for executive action. The so-called Ram doctrine permits government departments to have at their disposal the common law powers or freedom of action enjoyed by a natural person, provided the department is not forbidden from doing the thing it wants to do.[33] HMRC might seek to rely on this to explain the legal basis on which it makes available the ESI tool discussed above: Fred Bloggs could set up a website with an app to help people work out their employment status and nothing on the statute book prohibits HMRC from doing the same. The difference between Fred and HMRC, of course, is that the HMRC ESI tool is determinative and definitive of the user's rights, in the sense that the conclusion generated by the tool is legally binding on HMRC (because it has said it is). Regrettably, the courts in recent years have taken a generous approach to the Ram doctrine, permitting departments to act on the basis of common law powers even beyond the doctrine's original purpose of achieving incidental powers.[34]

The Ram doctrine does not apply to local authorities and other public bodies established by Act of Parliament, but such bodies may have statutory power to take action incidental to their statutory functions (such as that conferred by section 111 of the Local Government Act 1972). Moreover, Part 1 of the Localism Act 2011 gives local authorities a general power of competence 'to do anything that individuals generally may do'. So, while the matter is not entirely free from doubt, there is a plausible case for saying that the use of automated decision-making may be lawful without express statutory authorisation in each situation. Whether this is desirable is, however, a different question.

D. Does Automation Involve the Delegation of Executive Power to a Computer?

A further complexity that needs to be considered is the rule against delegation of statutory functions to somebody other than the person specified in the legislation. When English lawyers used Latin, this was rendered in the maxim *delegata potestas non potest delegari*. The legal presumption is that 'when a power has been conferred to a person in circumstances indicating that trust is being placed in his individual judgment and discretion, he must exercise that power personally unless

---

[33] See discussion in Woolf et al (n 25) para 5-022.
[34] See eg *R (on the Application of Shrewsbury and Atcham BC) v Secretary of State for Communities and Local Government* [2008] EWCA Civ 148, [2008] 3 All ER 548 (permitting consultation on local government reorganisation beyond the statutory framework).

he has been expressly empowered to delegate it to another'.[35] The thinking behind section 2 of the Social Security Act 1998, discussed above, suggests that a distinction should be drawn between situations: (a) where there is complete automation, so the computer has to be regarded as the decision-maker; and (b) where there is automation of only part of the decision-making process and the person named in the Act (the Secretary of State, officer, local authority etc) retains control over the outcome. In (b), the presumption against delegation does not apply because there *is* no delegation: the automated process is merely a tool to aid the human decision-maker. While this dichotomy looks attractive at first sight, applying it to real-life scenarios may not be so straightforward as the concept of 'control' is open to debate. For example, if an official body always or usually treats a computer-generated risk assessment as determinative of a decision, this could be regarded as an impermissible abdication of legal authority.

The prudent conclusion to be drawn from this discussion is that express legislative authorisation is needed where a computer actually makes a decision. In the absence of an explicit statement on the statute book along the lines of section 2 of the Social Security Act 1998—authorising computer-based decisions and pinning responsibility on the Secretary of State or an official—there is a risk that decisions will be unlawful.

E. A Right to Object to Decisions Being Taken by Automated Means?

Another issue that has received little or no attention is the desirability of a right to be told that a government decision has been automated and a right to opt out from that process. In relation to private sector decision-making, section 12 of the Data Protection Act 1998 creates a special regime in respect of wholly automated decisions using personal data, where the decision will have a significant effect on the individual concerned.[36] A person has three rights: (a) to give notice to an organisation not to make a wholly automated decision; (b) if no notice is given, the organisation must inform the individual that automated decision-making has taken place; and (c) a right to ask, within 21 days of a wholly automated decision, for the decision to be taken on a different basis. An example would be an individual who in reality has an exemplary history of managing his or her financial affairs responsibly, but who is denied a loan because his or her circumstances do not fit an automated credit-scoring system.

This regime does not, however, apply to most government decision-making because decisions 'authorised or required by or under any enactment' are exempt

---

[35] See discussion in Woolf et al (n 25) para 5-014; and *R v Secretary of State for the Home Department ex p Oladehinde* [1991] AC 254.
[36] This gives effect to EU Data Protection Directive 95/46/EC, art 15. An earlier version of the Data Protection Bill sought in effect to ban automated decision-making, but during the passage of the Bill, it was accepted that this was unnecessary gold plating of the Directive.

under section 12(6)(b). Explaining the purpose of section 12, the Information Commissioner's Office states in relation to private sector decision-making that: 'These rights can be seen as safeguards against the risk that a potentially damaging decision is taken without human intervention.'[37] If it is accepted, as surely it must be, that public bodies are capable of making such decisions, there seems no clear justification for such different regimes applying in private and public sector decision-making.

F. Should there be No-Go Areas for Automation?

A final constitutional issue is whether there should be no-go areas, where government is forbidden from operating fully automated decision-making and decisive human involvement is preserved. Bouvens and Zouridis conjure the image of 'a more true-to-life vision of the term "bureaucracy"' these days as 'a room filled with softly humming servers, dotted here and there by a system manager behind a screen'.[38] A future (still distant in 2015) in which *all* government decisions affecting citizens are taken by computers feels like a dehumanised dystopia. But some automation seems uncontroversial. We do not, for example, expect officials in HMRC to work out each taxpayer's liability using pen and paper to make mathematical calculations. Are we equally sanguine about a computer making or significantly contributing to a decision as to whether the Parole Board should release a murderer? In the US, at least 15 states use risk assessment computer programs to determine whether a prisoner should be released, a decision-making process that is reported to be changing outcomes.[39]

Various criteria could be used to demarcate computer-reduced or computer-free zones. One approach might be to focus on the impact of decisions: for example, decisions that impinge on the most fundamental rights, such as liberty of the person. This may, however, be a blunderbuss method if computers can help the state make better decisions, which may be advantageous to the individual (as in the case of parole boards). A different approach would be to focus on the dividing lines between what is appropriately rule-based and what requires professional human

---

[37] https://ico.org.uk/for-organisations/guide-to-data-protection/principle-6-rights/automated-decision-taking.

[38] M Bouvens and S Zouridis, 'From Street-Level to System-Level Bureaucracies: How Information and Communication Technology is Transforming Administrative Discretion and Constitutional Control' (2002) 62 *Public Administration Review* 174, 175.

[39] J Walker, 'State Parole Boards Use Software to Decide Which Inmates to Release', *Wall Street Journal* (11 October 2013) ('Such methods can contradict the instincts of corrections officials, by classifying violent offenders as a lower recidivism risk than someone convicted of a nonviolent robbery or drugs offence', in part 'because people convicted of crimes like murder are often older when considered for release').

judgement. Three principles have been adopted in Australia that would provide a basis for developing a framework in the UK:[40]

— Automated systems that make a decision—as opposed to helping a decision-maker make a decision—would generally be suitable only for decisions involving non-discretionary elements.
— Automated systems should not automate the exercise of discretion.
— Automated systems can be used as an administrative tool to assist an officer in exercising his or her discretion. In these cases, the systems should be designed so that they do not fetter the decision-maker in the exercise of his or her power by recommending or guiding the decision-maker to a particular outcome.

V. HOW SHOULD PARLIAMENT RESPOND TO AUTOMATION?

A. The Need for a Select Committee Thematic Inquiry

The issues discussed in this chapter call out for a select committee inquiry, either by the House of Commons Public Administration and Constitutional Affairs Committee or the House of Lords Constitution Committee. An inquiry could bring into public view the scale of automation and the Government's strategy for its future development. We know that we are heading for an era of 'digital by default', but what that means in the specific context of automated decision-making is not yet clear. Computer experts could describe what is possible now and the direction of travel for decision-making technologies. Legal experts would be able to shed more light on the particular administrative law issues raised above. Oliver Letwin MP, now the minister with oversight for digitalisation, will be able to discuss how the concerns he expressed as a backbencher in 1998 about the 'increasing depersonalisation' of administration by computer have been allayed (if that is the case). The public sector ombudsmen could reflect on the implications of automation for their work as complaint handlers and champions of good administration; it seems that the Australian Ombudsman is further advanced in standard setting about automation than those in the UK.[41]

A useful outcome of an inquiry along these lines could be political impetus for the development of standards, either in the form of a good practice guide (for designers and operators of automated systems) or a statutory framework, or both.

---

[40] Australian Government (n 5) Appendix B: ARC Best-Practice Principles.
[41] Australian Government (n 5). There may also be scope for lesson learning from the Financial Services Ombudsman.

B. Better Scrutiny of Automated Decision-Making

Whether or not an overarching legal framework is created for automated decision-making or good practice standards are adopted, Parliament should also consider automation issues when Bills and draft statutory instruments are scrutinised during the legislative process. The following questions could usefully be asked—perhaps by a new specialist committee in the House of Lords—of any executive power-granting provision:

(a) Does the Secretary of State (or other decision-maker) intend to automate some or all of the decision-making process?

(b) Is there express legal authority to do so if the decision is *in effect* going to be made by a computer rather than a human? (See the example of section 2 of the Social Security Act 1998 discussed above.)

(c) The automated process will rely on rules rather than discretion or professional judgement: is this appropriate in the particular circumstances? Is it preferable to preserve discretion and scope for professional judgement or other human intervention? If so, how could this best be achieved? Is there a method for identifying 'hard cases' in which the application of clear rules may lead to unfairness in individual circumstances?

(d) What data will the automated decision-maker draw from across government? Is data sharing acceptable in the particular circumstances? (For instance, it will almost never be appropriate to draw on an individual's NHS personal medical records on issues about health, but would it be acceptable to draw on data about the frequency of a person's visits to a GP or hospital for the purposes of verifying a need to have accommodation conveniently situated for such visits, as discussed above?).

(e) Can the committee preview the app? How many questions does it ask? Is this an acceptable number or does it put an undue burden on the citizen? How closely are the questions based on the legislation creating the executive power? Do they properly implement the intention of Parliament? Will the questions be intelligible to self-service users? What is the source of each question—primary legislation, secondary legislation, case law, departmental policy etc? In relation to policy, what mechanisms will prevent the computer from fettering its discretion by the overly rigid application of policy?[42]

(f) Will the system generate a reasoned explanation of the decision? Is the type of reasons given appropriate to the specific context?

(g) What steps are being taken by the Secretary of State to ensure digital equality? An automated decision-making app for elderly people, people with learning difficulties or people who do not read English proficiently will pose a range of challenges.

---

[42] See Woolf et al (n 25) para 9-002 ('A decision-making body exercising public functions which is entrusted with discretion must not disable itself from exercising its discretion in individual cases. It may not "fetter" its discretion').

(h) Does the citizen have a right to opt out of the automated decision-making process to discuss his or her case with a human official? If so, at what point does that occur?
(i) How can the citizen appeal against the decision of the automated decision-maker?

C. The Catalyst to Organisational Change in Parliament

The rise of automated decision-making and other aspects of e-government is intended to have a broad and deep effect on the way public bodies work beyond the development of particular apps. For quite a while, it has been recognised that automated decision-making 'is not simply about making procedures more effective, but can in many cases be about changing values and premises upon which the system was once based'.[43] In the UK, this transformative aspiration is documented on the GDS blog. The GDS uses ideas and language that stand in stark contrast to the formalities of the legislative process in Parliament (it is like comparing Google HQ with the Athenaeum). This challenges traditional thinking and practices around Parliament's role in the legislative process. Three of the GDS's interconnected exhortations merit closer attention: 'service patterns', 'user focus' and 'breaking down silos'.

Current parliamentary scrutiny during the legislative process focuses on text, not the experience of end-users of the legislation. This stands in stark contrast to the thinking of the GDS. Louise Downe, Head of Service Design, says that one of the important things that the GDS is focusing on is:

> Creating standards for 'what good looks like' for certain types of services e.g. getting permission to do something, exchanging the ownership of a thing, or delegating responsibility to someone etc. We're calling these 'service patterns'—consistent (but not uniform) standards for the way that a repeated activity (like getting permission) should work both for users and government.[44]

In the GDS, traditional organisational structures are pejoratively labelled 'silos', which need to be 'broken'. In an exercise to develop a graphic representation of the criminal justice 'landscape', specific organisations disappear:

> [Y]ou might notice that the map doesn't name any organisations or government departments. That's because that's not how users see the system. They talk about going to court, rather than dealing with 'HM Courts and Tribunals Service'; they talk about going to prison, rather than being part of a 'National Offender Management Service' process.

---

[43] Grönlund (n 5) 4.
[44] L Downe, 'Better Services with Patterns and Standards' (*GDS Blog*) https://gds.blog.gov.uk/2015/08/06/better-services-with-patterns-and-standards.

Also, this is a living map, something that can be maintained and updated as the team learns more'.[45]

A world of 'service patterns' and 'landscapes' sits uneasily with the experience of parliamentarians scrutinising primary and secondary legislation.[46] (The distinction between primary and secondary legislation is a 'silo' par excellence.) MPs and peers have before them mere fragments of decision-making design ripped out of context and set out as legal text. The use of framework Bills, where all detail is left to be developed in secondary legislation, makes their task of making real sense of the design of the decision-making system still more difficult. 'Christmas tree Bills', where proposals for unconnected policy areas are hung on the same Bill for political convenience, can further muddy the waters. Often a Bill or draft statutory instrument is amending an existing and usually already complex decision-making process. Parliamentarians are normally told little or nothing about how the rules they are asked to approve will be implemented. Nor are they usually told about relevant case law that may impinge on the decision-makers. Even the most assiduous parliamentarian is likely to struggle to get any real understanding of how officials (or computers) will implement the legislative words or how this will impact on citizens.

Parliament needs to bridge the gap between the established procedures for legislative scrutiny and the new ways of thinking about government decision-making brought in by the digital revolution. One step forward would be a House of Lords Committee on Government Service Standards Design. This cross-cutting committee would complement the work of the other specialist committee such as the Constitution Committee, the Committee on Delegated Powers and Regulatory Reform, the Joint Committee on Statutory Instruments and the Joint Committee on Human Rights. The new committee would break down the silos between primary and secondary legislation with a remit of reviewing Bills *and* draft statutory instruments against a template of 'what good looks like'. A programme of work for the committee would include sampling the experience of citizens as they navigate their way through interactions with government (claiming benefits, starting a small business, buying a house and so on). They would carry out post-legislative scrutiny of all relevant legislation (and pre-legislative scrutiny on any proposed changes), consider judicial engagements with the legislation, and hear from academic experts, representative groups, users and the department(s) concerned with the service pattern under scrutiny.

---

[45] https://gds.blog.gov.uk/2015/08/18/mapping-new-ideas-for-the-digital-justice-system-2.
[46] The author was the legal adviser to the House of Lords Constitution Committee for three-and-a-half years, a role requiring all Government Bills to be read from start to finish.

D. Fourth-Generation Law

A final, and most fundamental, proposal is that automated decision-making requires us to reconsider what we regard as 'the law'. In conventional thinking, the whole legislative process in Parliament is seen as focusing on the text of the Bill or draft statutory instrument. Without a text, there is nothing to process. Once enacted, the text is 'the law'. Automated decision-making challenges this orthodox model.

Taking a long historical view of forms of law, De Mulder and van Noortwijk postulate four generations of law.[47] The most ancient form was spoken law: law declared orally by judges. Then came writing, which enabled law to be recorded and systematised. Then came the printing press, through which 'the law became an instrument of bureaucracy'. The fourth generation, digital law, 'provides essentially new options as well'.

The notion of digital law calls into question the role of parliamentarians in the current legislative process. Writing in 2002 about the Netherlands, Svensson forecast 'a development towards legislation that is directly formulated to fit into decision-making systems' and a trend 'to make legislation as unified, straightforward and cheap to execute as possible'.[48] When an MP or peer scrutinises a decision-making power in a Bill, or considers a similar power in a piece of delegated legislation, he or she is looking at text that may or will be used by the code writers to an automated decision-making app—the series of machine-readable questions or selection of variables that will determine the outcome of individual cases. Across the UK statute book, there are tell-tale signs of 'legislation for automation' (for example, in rules relating to Universal Credit).[49] Parliamentarians are therefore left scrutinising something (the Bill or draft statutory instrument) that sits between the policy design and the rules that will *really* apply to individuals.

So here is a radical proposal: we should treat 'the app' (the computer programs that will produce individual decisions) as 'the law'. It is this app, not the text of legislation, that will regulate the legal relationship between citizen and state in automated decision-making. Apps should, like other forms of legislation, be brought under democratic control. They should in principle be subject to parliamentary oversight, perhaps like secondary legislation on an affirmative (it requires the express approval of Parliament to become valid) and negative procedure (it becomes valid unless annulled by Parliament within a set time).

---

[47] De Mulder and van Noortwijk (n 23); and R De Mulder, 'The Digital Revolution: From Trias to Tetras Politica' in I Snellen and W van de Donk (eds), *Public Administration in an Information Age: A Handbook* (Amsterdam, IOS Press, 1998).
[48] See Svensson (n 5).
[49] See generally www.gov.uk/government/publications/2010-to-2015-government-policy-welfare-reform/2010-to-2015-government-policy-welfare-reform.

VI. CONCLUSIONS

In the *Little Britain* television comedy sketch show, a rude woman called Carol Beer (played by David Walliams) sits behind a computer screen responding to reasonable requests with the bored retort 'the computer says no' and coughs—leaving the bemused client powerless. This neatly encapsulates many of our fears about a dystopian future in which computers rule our lives. Against this, as discussed above, the digital revolution is having a transformative effect on government administration, bringing fresh thinking about how decisions are made with users centre stage. This chapter has sought to contribute to a debate that needs to take place about the use and control of automated decision-making, focusing in particular on the role of Parliament. In the 1920s, Lord Hewart warned in *The New Despotism* about the rise of unfettered executive power rolling out through delegated legislation and subordinating Parliament.[50] Most of us now see those warnings as too shrill, taking a more balanced view of the costs and benefits of executive law-making. But automated decision-making presents challenges to Parliament of the same scale. Creative thinking and action by parliamentarians can help strike a balance between its benefits and risks.

---

[50] Lord Hewart, *The New Despotism* (London, Ernest Benn, 1929).

10

Parliament and National Security

ALEXANDER HORNE AND CLIVE WALKER[*]

I. INTRODUCTION

THIS CHAPTER SEEKS to address a number of issues relating to Parliament's responsibility for holding the Government to account on national security matters. As will be clear to readers who take an interest in this topic, Parliament's accountability oversight is diffuse.[1] In addition to debates on the floor of both Houses, a number of committees are responsible for holding the Government to account on national security. These include: the Foreign Affairs Committee; the Defence Committee; the Joint Committee on the National Security Strategy; the Committees on Arms Export Controls;[2] and the Intelligence and Security Committee (not to mention the parliamentary committees that are focused on human rights and the constitution—which frequently consider the human rights compatibility, constitutionality and proportionality of the Government's policy).[3]

---

[*] The authors would like to thank Paul Evans, Andrew Kennon and Claire Mills for their assistance. Any errors or omissions remain our own.

[1] For other studies, see L Lustgarten, and I Leigh, *In from the Cold: National Security and Parliamentary Democracy* (Oxford, Clarendon Press, 1994); H Born and H Hänggi (eds), *Double Democratic Deficit: International Security Cooperation and the Problem of Parliamentary Accountability* (Aldershot, Ashgate, 2004); H Born et al, *Who's Watching the Spies: Establishing Intelligence Service Accountability* (Dulles, Potomac Books, 2005); H Born and M Caparini, *Democratic Control of Intelligence Services: Containing Rogue Elephants* (Aldershot, Ashgate, 2007); H Born et al (eds), *International Intelligence Cooperation and Accountability* (Abingdon, Routledge, 2012); H Bochel, A Defty and J Kirkpatrick, *Watching the Watchers* (London, Palgrave Macmillan, 2014). Note also the European Commission for Democracy through Law (Venice Commission), *Report on the Democratic Oversight of the Security Services* (CDL-AD(2007) 016, Strasbourg, 2007) and *Update of the 2007 Report on the Democratic Oversight of the Security Services and Report on the Democratic Oversight of Signals Intelligence Agencies* (CDL-AD(2015) 006, Strasbourg, 2015).

[2] The Committees on Arms Export Controls consist of four select committees meeting and working together to examine the Government's expenditure, administration and policy on strategic exports (that is, the licensing of arms exports and other controlled goods). The four Committees are: the Business, Innovation and Skills Committee; the Defence Committee; the Foreign Affairs Committee; and the International Development Committee. Each Committee nominates four members, though any member of the four committees can attend.

[3] See, eg, M Hunt, 'The Joint Committee on Human Rights' and A Le Sueur and J Simson Caird, 'The House of Lords Select Committee on the Constitution', both in A Horne, G Drewry and D Oliver (eds), *Parliament and the Law* (Oxford, Hart Publishing, 2013).

This chapter focuses on Parliament's experiences of scrutinising national security by identifying and exploring three case studies from the 2010–15 Parliament. Following a brief consideration of the historical background (section II), the first case study (section III) will consider whether a new convention has been established that Parliament needs to be consulted when the Government wishes to deploy the armed forces. The second case study (section IV) analyses the work of Parliament's Intelligence and Security Committee, as re-established under the Justice and Security Act 2013 (comparing it with the previous version that had been set up under the Intelligence Services Act 1994). The final case study (section V) assesses how effectively Parliament has scrutinised counter-terrorism legislation. Each of these studies will note the shared challenges that face the parliamentarians who conduct this work. These include access to information, and questions of secrecy and the problem of 'urgency' (be it fast-track counter-terrorism legislation or the need to respond quickly to world events). By contrast, and in favour of accountability, national security remains a core responsibility of government: 'Providing security for the nation and for its citizens remains the most important responsibility of government.'[4] Consequently, there is less divestment or dilution of accountability because of transfers to agencies or the private sector than in many other activities of the late modern government.[5]

We must also define the meaning of holding the government to account. At one level, 'accountability involves the idea that a person or body should give an account, or an explanation and justification for its acts'.[6] There is also the recognised convention of individual ministerial accountability (the doctrine by which ministers alone are accountable to Parliament for the conduct of their department).[7] But the concept can be used in a wide variety of contexts, including: simple audit requirements; performance accountability' (eg, focus on delivery and outcomes, including targets); and 'process accountability' (where public authorities are called upon 'to explain and justify the decision making processes they adopt in carrying out their task').[8] This chapter will take a wide view of the term, considering the effectiveness of existing parliamentary processes and relevant proposals for reform. It will be assumed, without further argument, that accountability is desirable as an

---

[4] Cabinet Office, *The National Security Strategy of the United Kingdom Security in an Interdependent World* (Cm 7291, 2008) para.1.1.

[5] See M Bevir et al, 'Traditions of Governance: Interpreting the Changing Role of the Public Sector' (2003) 81 *Public Administration* 1; GA Hodge and K Coghill, 'Accountability in the Privatized State' (2007) 20 *Governance* 675.

[6] D Oliver and G Drewry, 'The Law and Parliament' in D Oliver and G Drewry (eds), *The Law and Parliament* (London, Butterworths, 1998) 10. For a comprehensive description of accountability, see N Bamforth and P Leyland (eds), *Accountability in the Contemporary Constitution* (Oxford, Oxford University Press, 2013).

[7] See, eg, O Gay, *Individual Ministerial Accountability*, House of Commons Library Standard Note SN6467, http://researchbriefings.parliament.uk/ResearchBriefing/Summary/SN06467.

[8] See, eg, A Le Sueur, 'Developing Mechanisms for Judicial Accountability in the UK' (2004) 24 *Legal Studies* 73, 81–88. See also D Woodhouse, *Ministers and Parliament* (Oxford, Clarendon Press, 1994).

instrumental support to fundamental societal values such as democracy, human rights and the rule of law.

II. HISTORICAL BACKGROUND

Unsurprisingly, there has been a long history of Parliament and its select committees taking an interest in both national security and military matters.

In relation to the armed forces, the conflicts between Parliament and the sovereign in the seventeenth century led to Article 6 of the Bill of Rights 1688. This curtailed that part of the royal prerogative relating to the raising and keeping of a standing army.[9] The Article provided that the keeping of a standing army in time of peace would be against the law unless it was with the consent of Parliament. This historical provision still has some impact today (through the mechanisms of the five yearly renewals of the Armed Forces Acts (most recently in 2011) along with the annual publication of Ministry of Defence Votes A, which specify the maximum number of personnel that may be maintained in the Army, the Air Force and Navy in the forthcoming year).[10]

Furthermore, although the departmental select committee system dates back only as far as 1979, committees were appointed by the House to examine various matters as early as the reign of Charles I. By 1667, a committee of the House of Commons had taken the perhaps audacious step of launching an inquiry into the conduct of the Second Anglo-Dutch War.

The Dutch raid on the English fleet in the Medway in June 1667 (a successful attack on the largest English naval ships, which were laid up in the dockyards of their main naval base in Chatham) was a political and military disaster: a number of capital ships were destroyed and (amongst others) the flagship of the English fleet, the *Royal Charles*, was captured and taken to Amsterdam. The English sued for peace under the Treaty of Breda in July 1667. Thereafter, a Committee 'to inquire into the Miscarriage of Affairs in the late War' was set up by the Commons.[11] It had the power to send for persons, papers and records—and it

---

[9] See, eg, P Rowe, 'The Crown and Accountability for the Armed Forces' in S Payne and M Sunkin (eds), *The Nature of the Crown: A Legal and Political Analysis* (Oxford, Oxford University Press, 1999) 267–68.

[10] See P Evans, *Dods Handbook of House of Commons Procedure* 8th edn (London, Dods, 2011), which states at para 10.5.7 (in respect of the estimates, supply and appropriation Bills) that: 'In February, the Ministry of Defence Votes A are published. In accordance with the provision of the Bill of Rights of 1688 that the Crown may not maintain a standing army in peacetime (and a war has not been formally declared since 1939) without the authorisation of Parliament. The Defence Votes specify the maximum number of personnel that may be maintained in the Army, Air Force and Navy in the forthcoming year and in certain specified categories of reserve forces. Under S.O. No. 55(3) the House is required to approve the Supplementary Estimates, Excess Votes and Defence Votes A by 18 March.' At the time of writing, the most recent publication was for the year ending 31 March 2016 (Ministry of Defence Votes A, February 2015, HC 1054).

[11] Journal of the House of Commons 17 October 1667, Journal of the House of Commons: Vol 9, 1667–1687.

wanted answers, some of them from the famous diarist Samuel Pepys (who was then the Clerk of the Acts of the Navy Board). It is clear from an entry in Pepys' diary for February 1668 that the Committee, reaching the end of its investigations, had called him back once too often to answer questions on matters which had not been his responsibility. He recorded:

> At the office all the morning, where comes a damned summons to attend the Committee of Miscarriages to-day, which makes me mad, that I should by my place become the hackney of this Office, in perpetual trouble and vexation, that need it least.

Present-day civil servants may well empathise with his discomfort. In evidence given in 2012 to the Liaison Committee,[12] the then Clerk of the House of Commons, Sir Robert Rogers (as he then was), suggested that what might be thought of as the first 'modern' select committee inquiry was held by the Select Committee on the Army before Sebastopol (1854–55), which considered the conduct of the Crimean War. Rogers noted that the inquiry 'put reputations on the rack'.[13] The establishment of the Committee of Enquiry to look into the conduct of the Crimean War led to the resignation of the then Prime Minister, Lord Aberdeen. He was subsequently summoned before the 'Sebastopol Committee', which reported in June 1855 'with a moderate report' that refrained from censure of individuals despite its criticism of government policy.[14]

Criticism has also been voiced on the floor of the House. It has been argued that 'in the eighteenth and nineteenth centuries particularly, debates in the House of Commons on issues of foreign policy and war were frequent and in depth'.[15] During the Second World War, there is evidence of debates (particularly following defeats or setbacks), most notably the 'Norway Debate' on 7 and 8 May 1940 (and vote of 281 to 200), which prompted the resignation of Prime Minister Neville Chamberlain on 10 May and the formation of a coalition government led by Winston Churchill.[16] There was a debate on a substantive motion on 5 July 1950, approximately a week after the announcement to deploy British forces in the Korean War.[17] A debate was held during the Suez Crisis on 2 August 1956 (but was not followed by a vote). Subsequently, a vote took place on a motion endorsing the Government's approach to the crisis. More recently, debates were held during the

---

[12] The House of Commons Liaison Committee is made up of the Chairs of each of the Commons select committees.

[13] Liaison Committee, *Select Committee Effectiveness, Resources and Powers* (HC 2012–13, 697) Ev W80.

[14] D Englefield, J Seaton and I White, *Facts about the British Prime Ministers* (London, Mansell Publishing, 1995) 174.

[15] R Joseph, *The War Prerogative: History, Reform and Constitutional Design* (Oxford, Oxford University Press, 2013) 62.

[16] HC Deb 8 May 1940, cols 1251–366. By contrast, following the fall of Greece (in spite of British efforts), the ensuing debate was said to have been designed to 'demonstrate confidence in the Government's war strategy'. See C Mills, *Parliamentary Approval for Military Action*, House of Commons Library Research Paper CBP-7166, 13 May 2015, 4.

[17] HC Deb 5 July 1950, col 485.

course of the Falklands conflict (1982), the Gulf War (1991) and Kosovo conflict in 1999.[18]

Despite these examples, it is important to note at the outset that in constitutional terms, Parliament has no legally established role in the deployment of the armed forces: the Government has no legal duty to either consult Parliament or abide by any simple resolution which Parliament has agreed.[19] As the then Attorney General, Lord Goldsmith, explained in 2003:

> [I]t is well established that the conduct of foreign affairs and defence policy are matters that fall within the Royal prerogative. It would, therefore, be lawful and constitutional for the Government, in exercising the Royal prerogative, to make a declaration of war or to engage United Kingdom forces in military action without the prior approval of Parliament.[20]

Essentially, the pressure that Parliament can bring to bear is entirely political. Following the Iraq War of 2003, a number of parliamentary select committees conducted inquiries looking into the decision to commit the armed forces to war and other related matters.[21] It is likely that it was the messy aftermath of this action (and the failure to find the alleged 'weapons of mass destruction' that had been used by the Government as a justification for the conflict) which prompted soul searching on the part of parliamentarians (and the eventual moves towards consolidating a new convention on parliamentary approval of the deployment of the armed forces).

The history of parliamentary scrutiny of counter-terrorism legislation and policy is just as long and convoluted. Its importance in shaping the very procedures of Parliament is also remarkable. Three examples will illustrate these features.

The first example relates to the Irish Parliamentary Party policy of parliamentary 'obstructionism'.[22] Thus, from around 1874 onwards, Irish Nationalist MPs, such as Joseph Gillis Biggar, adopted obstructive tactics, including long filibustering speeches in the House of Commons, to delay the passage of counter-terrorism legislation. The legislation in that period, known generally as the Irish 'Coercion Acts', included the Peace Preservation (Ireland) Act 1875, the Protection of Person and Property (Ireland) Act 1881 and the Prevention of Crime

---

[18] See Mills (n 16) for further background. There are a number of examples of debates where Members have been critical of the Government's conduct of conflicts. See, eg, R Joseph, *The War Prerogative: History, Reform and Constitutional Design* (Oxford, Oxford University Press, 2013) 62–63.

[19] Mills (n 16).

[20] HL Deb 19 February 2003, col 1138.

[21] See, eg, Foreign Affairs Committee, *The Decision to Go to War in Iraq* (HC 2002–03, 813); Defence Committee, *Lessons of Iraq* (HC 2003–04, 57-I); Public Administration Committee, *Taming the Prerogative: Strengthening Ministerial Accountability to Parliament* (HC 2003–04, 422); Public Administration Select Committee, *Iraq Inquiry* (HC 2008–09, 721).

[22] See G Jellinek, 'Parliamentary Obstruction' (1904) 19 *Political Science Quarterly* 579; GW Rutherford, 'Some Aspects of Parliamentary Obstruction' (1914) 22 *Sewanee Review* 166; D Thornley, 'The Irish Home Rule Party and Parliamentary Obstruction' (1960) 12 *Irish Historical Studies* 38; A Jackson, *Home Rule: An Irish History 1800–2000* (Oxford University Press, Oxford, 2004) 39–42.

(Ireland) Act 1882.²³ Charles Stewart Parnell, who in 1880 became leader of the Irish Parliamentary Party, was another leading exponent of this tactic, which was deployed to obstruct the business of the House and force the British political parties to address the Irish Home Rule question. The Nationalist party bloc held considerable sway in the House of Commons and was courted by both the Conservatives and the Liberals; the concession of Home Rule Bills was extracted in 1886 and 1893.²⁴ The tactics of 'obstructionism' also resulted in major modifications to parliamentary process, including the advent of closure and timetable (guillotine) motions, though these also reflected wider changes in the assumption of governmental responsibilities as part of modernity.²⁵

The second example related to the Irish prisoner hunger strikes of 1981. The candidature of Irish prisoners in parliamentary elections was by no means a novel tactic in Ireland, but the election of hunger-striker, Bobby Sands, for the Fermanagh and South Tyrone constituency in 1981 provoked state reaction.²⁶ The Representation of the People Act 1981 disqualifies from nomination for, and membership of, the House of Commons any person convicted of an offence and sentenced to more than 12 months' imprisonment either in the UK or in the Republic of Ireland.

The third example relates to the passage of the first counter-terrorism legislation in Britain of the contemporary era, the Prevention of Terrorism (Temporary Provisions) Act 1974. This Act had 'a swift but painful public birth'.²⁷ On 21 November 1974, bombs planted by the Provisional IRA caused explosions in two public houses in Birmingham—21 people were killed and 184 injured. The conception of the Bill was announced on 25 November, when the Home Secretary, Roy Jenkins, warned that: 'The powers ... are Draconian. In combination they are unprecedented in peacetime. I believe these are fully justified to meet the clear and present danger.'²⁸ However, Parliament was fanatically enthusiastic and had passed the Bill by 29 November, virtually without amendment or dissent. This appearance of a Bill being conjured out of thin air does not conform to reality, as preparations were well in hand for such legislation following earlier attacks. However, shortcomings in terms of accountability and especially the disproportionate infringements of human rights soon came to be recognised. As a result, two features have developed as props to parliamentary accountability.

---

²³ See G Hogan and CP Walker, *Political Violence and the Law in Ireland* (Manchester, Manchester University Press, 1989) 12–14.
²⁴ See Government of Ireland Bills 1886 and 1893; E Biagini, *British Democracy and Irish Nationalism 1876–1906* (Cambridge, Cambridge University Press, 2010).
²⁵ See J Redlich, *The Procedure of the House of Commons* (London, Archibald Constable, 1908) Vol 1, 210.
²⁶ See C Walker, 'Prisoners in Parliament—Another View' [1982] *Public Law* 389; J Finn, 'Electoral Regimes and the Proscription of Anti-democratic Parties' (2000) 12 *Terrorism & Political Violence* 51; T Hennessy, *Hunger Strike: Margaret Thatcher's Battle with the IRA* (Dublin, Irish Academic Press, 2014).
²⁷ CP Walker, *The Prevention of Terrorism in British Law* 2nd edn (Manchester, Manchester University Press, 1992) 31.
²⁸ HC Deb 25 November 1974, col 35.

One is that sunset clauses[29] were inserted into the Prevention of Terrorism Acts of 1974, 1976 and 1984 in order to allow more sober and leisurely review. The sunset clause was dropped as such in 1989, though an annual renewal by statutory order, subject to the affirmative procedure, still remained under section 27 of the 1989 Act. These annual debates continued until the Terrorism Act 2000. By that time, it was argued that the persistence of terrorism (international as well as Irish) demanded permanent legislation, and this development was allied to the recognition that there had been a general lack of parliamentary interest in review, with the result that the debates tended to be short, poorly attended and conducted late at night. In addition, the passage of time hardened official support for the legislation. More recently, the Government has even argued against sunset clauses on the basis of the disquieting interpretation that they would 'send the message to terrorists ... that we are uncertain'.[30]

The more persistent prop has been the appointment of independent reviewers. After renewal of the 1974 Act in 1976, it was clear that counter-terrorism legislation was set to continue for some time. Therefore, in December 1977, the Home Secretary announced that Lord Shackleton was to carry out a: 'Review into the operation of the Prevention of Terrorism (Temporary Provisions) Acts 1974 and 1975.'[31] Other periodic reviews of this kind have ensued, the latest by Lord Macdonald in 2011.[32] In addition to these isolated reviews, a more continuous system of scrutiny was set in place in 1984, when the Home Secretary decided that a single commissioner should be appointed to review the legislation in a concentrated period just before each annual renewal.[33] Reviewers have continued in one shape or another since then, the core appointment becoming statutory only recently, under section 36 of the Terrorism Act 2006, which requires review of the operation of both the Terrorism Act 2000 and Part 1 of the Terrorism Act 2006.[34] There are also requirements under section 20 of the Terrorism Prevention and Investigation Measures Act 2011 and section 31 of the Terrorist Asset-Freezing etc Act 2010 to appoint a reviewer for those Acts. A single person is currently

---

[29] See J Finn, 'Sunset Clauses and Democratic Deliberation: Assessing the Significance of Sunset Provisions in Antiterrorism Legislation' (2010) 48 *Columbia Journal of Transnational Law* 442; A Lynch, 'The Impact of Post-enactment Review on Anti-terrorism Laws: Four Jurisdictions Compared' (2012) 18 *Journal of Legislative Studies* 64; J Ip, 'Sunset Clauses and Counter-terrorism Legislation' [2013] *Public Law* 74.

[30] HC Deb 9 March 2005, col 1626 (Hazel Blears MP).

[31] See Cmnd 7324, 1978.

[32] Lord Macdonald, *Review of Counter-Terrorism and Security Powers* (Cm 8003, 2011). See also *Report of the Operation of the Prevention of Terrorism (Temporary Provisions) Act 1976* (Cmnd 8803, 1983); *Review of the Operation of the Prevention of Terrorism (Temporary Provisions) Act 1984* (Cm 264, 1987); *Inquiry into Legislation against Terrorism* (Cm 3420, 1996); *Privy Counsellor Review Committee, Anti-Terrorism, Crime and Security Act 2001 Review Report* (HC 2003–04, 100). The equivalents in Northern Ireland will not be covered here, but see CP Walker, *The Anti-terrorism Legislation* 3rd edn (Oxford, Oxford University Press, 2014) ch 10.

[33] HL Deb 23 February 1984, col 945 and HL Deb 18 March 1984, col 405, Lord Elton.

[34] There was a requirement for a report under s 126 of the Terrorism Act 2000, but no details were specified as to its provenance. See further Counter Terrorism and Security Act 2015, ss 44–46, discussed below.

appointed for all. The appointment is not by, or to, Parliament, but the output is highly influential in debates and reports, especially for those reviewers who are also parliamentarians and are thereby enabled to take part directly in debates.[35] This attribute applied especially to Lord Carlile of Berriew QC (who held office from 2001 to 2011), though the current Independent Reviewer of Terrorism Legislation, David Anderson QC, is no less prominent or influential.[36]

III. CASE STUDY 1: WAR-MAKING POWERS AND A NEW CONVENTION?

A. Introduction

Foreign relations, including the declaration of war, the deployment of the armed forces and the conclusion of treaties[37] are conducted under the royal prerogative. While there may have been historical precedent for Parliament to inquire into the conduct of these activities, the idea of Parliament seeking to control the executive's ability to go to war is a fairly new innovation. The basic position has been usefully summarised by Gavin Phillipson as follows: the Queen holds the legal power to command the armed forces, through the royal prerogative; by well-established convention, this power is exercised on her behalf by the Prime Minister and/or the Cabinet. By a second, emerging convention, it now seems to be the case that the House of Commons must be consulted before action is taken (unless urgent action is required).[38] This case study will seek to trace the development of this second convention and assess its impact.

In 1982, almost a month after the Argentinian invasion of the Falkland Islands,[39] Michael Foot (the then Leader of the Opposition) raised the issue of negotiations being conducted by the then Secretary-General of the United Nations. He argued that the House of Commons had 'the right to make a judgement on this matter before any decision is taken by the Government that would enlarge the conflict'. In reply, Margaret Thatcher argued that it was an 'inherent jurisdiction of the Government to negotiate and to reach decisions. Afterwards, the House of Commons can pass judgment on the Government.'[40]

---

[35] See further Walker (n 32) ch 10. A more critical view is taken by J Blackbourn, 'Evaluating the Independent Reviewer of Terrorism Legislation' (2014) 67 *Parliamentary Affairs* 955.

[36] See https://terrorismlegislationreviewer.independent.gov.uk; D Anderson, 'The Independent Review of Terrorism Laws' [2014] *Public Law* 403 and 'The Independent Review of UK Terrorism Law' (2014) 5 *New Journal of European Criminal Law* 432.

[37] For more on this, see ch 12 below.

[38] See G Phillipson, '"Historic" Commons' Syria Vote: The Constitutional Significance (Part I)' (*UK Constitutional Law Association Blog*, 19 September 2013) http://ukconstitutionallaw.org; A Blick, 'Emergency Powers and the Withering of the Royal Prerogative' in C Walker (ed), *Contingencies, Resilience and Legal Constitutionalism* (Abingdon, Routledge, 2015).

[39] Following the deployment of the British task force and the sinking of the *Belgrano*, but prior to the commencement of land operations.

[40] HC Deb 11 May 1982, cols 596–602.

The Government did not seek parliamentary approval for military operations in Yugoslavia in 1999 or in Afghanistan in 2001.[41] Yet, before commencing the second Iraq war, the Government obtained the support of the House of Commons on a vote on a substantive motion that 'the United Kingdom should use all means necessary to ensure the disarmament of Iraq's weapons of mass destruction'.[42] At the conclusion of the debate, the then Foreign Secretary, Jack Straw, recognised the novelty of the procedure, stating:

> I have been present when military action by British troops has been debated. However, never before, prior to military action, has the House been asked on a substantive motion for its explicit support for the use of our armed forces. The House sought that, but, more important, it is constitutionally proper in a modern democracy.[43]

Commentators have questioned the normative value of the Iraq precedent, however, since the attitude of the Blair Government seemed to be that 'while it was permitting a vote (and would respect its outcome, as a matter of political necessity) it did not normatively admit to the existence of a convention that it was bound to do so'.[44]

B. The Aftermath of the Iraq Conflict

If the controversy before the second Iraq War might be seen as the genesis of a new convention, its development was fairly rapid. In July 2006, the House of Lords Constitution Committee observed in its report, *Waging War: Parliament's Role and Responsibility*, that the: 'Prime Minister himself has said, there are unlikely to be any circumstances in which a government could go to war without the support of Parliament.' However, it went on to note that:

> The precise meaning of 'support' is, of course, elusive: it could be implicit, as the Lord Chancellor would have it, in the sense that in the absence of disapproval, the support can be assumed; or it could be explicit, through a more formal parliamentary process.[45]

The Committee noted 'concerns about the legality of deployment decisions' and suggested that the 'character' of any legal advice given to the Government should be 'provided in as much detail as possible'.[46] It concluded that it was not

---

[41] There has never been a parliamentary vote on a government-sponsored motion on the deployment of troops in Afghanistan between 2001–14. There was, however, a debate and vote on a substantive motion tabled by the Backbench Business Committee on 9 September 2010. That motion (which was agreed by 310 votes to 14) stated that: 'This House supports the continued deployment of UK Armed Forces in Afghanistan.'
[42] HC Deb 18 March 2003, col 760.
[43] ibid col 900.
[44] Phillipson (n 38).
[45] House of Lords Constitution Committee, *Waging War: Parliament's Role and Responsibility* (HL 2005–06, 236-I) para 98.
[46] ibid para 99.

persuaded by a statutory solution (particularly since this could lead to the creation of a legislative architecture which could lead to 'the possibility of judicial review of Government decisions over matters of democratic executive responsibility'). It nonetheless considered that:

> [T]he exercise of the Royal prerogative by the Government to deploy armed force overseas is outdated and should not be allowed to continue as the basis for legitimate war-making in our 21st century democracy.[47]

Accordingly, it recommended that there should be a parliamentary convention determining the role that Parliament should play in making decisions to deploy force or forces outside the UK to war, intervention in an existing conflict or to environments where there is a risk that the forces will be engaged in conflict.[48] It suggested that the Government should seek parliamentary approval (for example, by the laying of a resolution in the House of Commons) if it proposed the deployment of forces outside the UK into actual or potential armed conflict. Such a resolution would indicate the deployment's objectives, its legal basis, likely duration and, in general terms, an estimate of its size. If, for reasons of emergency and security, such prior application was impossible, the Committee argued that the Government should provide information within seven days of commencement or as soon as it was feasible (after which the suggested process should be followed). Finally, it said that the Government should keep Parliament informed of the progress of deployments (and, if their nature or objectives altered significantly, should seek a renewal of the approval).

The Government's response was published some months later as an Appendix to a supplementary report from the Committee.[49] The Government indicated that it was not persuaded of the case for establishing a new convention, arguing that 'it must be the Government which takes the decision' because 'that is one of the key responsibilities for which it has been elected'. The Constitution Committee criticised the 'brevity and paucity' of the Government's response, describing it as 'inadequate'.[50] It noted that 'the executive draws its strength and legitimacy from a democratic Parliament' and argued that the response did not address its conclusion that 'Parliament's ability to challenge the executive must be protected and strengthened'.[51] The Committee concluded that:

> We consider that a cross-party political consensus appears to be emerging that the current arrangements are unsustainable. Accordingly, we are optimistic that our recommendations will be revisited in the very near future.[52]

---

[47] ibid para 103.
[48] ibid para 108.
[49] House of Lords Constitution Committee, *Waging War: Parliament's Role and Responsibility Follow-up* (HL 2006–07, 51) and *Government Response to the House of Lords Constitution Committee's Report. Fifteenth Report of Session 2005–06—'Waging War: Parliament's Role and Responsibility'* (Cm 6923, 2006).
[50] ibid paras 5–6.
[51] ibid para 6.
[52] ibid para 9.

The Committee was soon proved correct. The Government sought to re-address the issue as part of the *Governance of Britain* review which took place during the premiership of Gordon Brown.[53] The (then) Prime Minister gave a statement in the House of Commons on 3 July 2007 in which he said, inter alia, that:

> [T]he Prime Minister and the Executive should surrender or limit their powers [including] the power of the Executive to declare war ... to make for a more open 21st-century British democracy which better serves the British people.[54]

An extensive consultation paper entitled *The Governance of Britain—War Powers and Treaties: Limiting Executive Powers* was published shortly thereafter. The Government acknowledged that 'it has been rare in the past for Parliament to have a substantive vote on a proposed deployment before the troops are committed'.[55] However, it also acknowledged that there was 'significant scope for giving Parliament the opportunity to have a much greater say'.

The review paper posed a variety of options for reform, questioning whether any mechanism for obtaining approval should take the form of a parliamentary convention or if it should be made statutory. It included four options (a detailed House of Commons' resolution, legislation, a general resolution and a 'hybrid option').[56] The consultation noted the potential tensions which could arise, indicating that:

> In seeking to give Parliament the final say in decisions to commit UK troops to armed conflict overseas, it is nevertheless essential that we do not undermine the ability of the executive to carry out its proper functions. The responsibility to execute such operations with minimum loss of British lives has to remain with the executive.

It also suggested that there were a number of hurdles that would need to be overcome, including the fact that any reforms could not 'undermine the operational flexibility and freedom of the commanders in the field' or 'impact on the morale of the armed forces'. Moreover, the paper stated that the mechanism 'must provide sufficient flexibility for deployments which need to be made without prior Parliamentary approval for reasons of urgency or secrecy'.

The House of Lords held a debate on the consultation document on 31 January 2008.[57] During the course of the debate, issues were raised such as the need for flexibility, security and surprise, as well as the fact that during a single deployment,

---

[53] See, eg, HM Government, *The Governance of Britain—War Powers and Treaties: Limiting Executive Powers*, Consultation Paper CP26/07 (October 2007) and *The Governance of Britain—Constitutional Renewal* (Cm 7342, 2008).

[54] HC Deb 3 July 2007, cols 815–16.

[55] HM Government, *The Governance of Britain—War Powers and Treaties* (n 53) para 6.

[56] The 'hybrid option' contained elements of both the legislative and resolution options. It provided that the House of Commons must approve any decision to engage armed forces in armed conflict abroad. It set out the definition of armed forces and armed conflict, and it provided for the House to allow for retrospective approval, but did not mandate it. Otherwise, it left all the detailed arrangements to be determined by the House itself.

[57] HL Deb 31 January 2008, cols 747–96.

there might be a need to change swiftly from peacekeeping to defensive action and back again.

In 2008, the Government published a further document indicating its view on the way forward. It argued that 'while not ruling out legislation in the future, the Government believes that a detailed resolution is the best way forward'. It said:

> [T]his will take the form of a House of Commons resolution which sets out in detail the processes Parliament should follow in order to approve any commitment of Armed Forces into armed conflict. The resolution could be underpinned by a specific standing order, but that is ultimately a matter for each House and not the Government.[58]

No such resolution was brought forward before the end of the 2010 Parliament. However, it could be argued that the existence and the tone of the review, combined with the acceptance of the Government that 'in practice, no government these days would seek to commit troops to a substantial overseas deployment without giving Parliament the opportunity to debate it', to some extent underpinned the development of a new convention.[59] While the *Governance of Britain* review did lead to some constitutional changes in other spheres, nothing more was done in relation to the question of war powers and, by 2011, Turpin and Tomkins were still of the view that the idea that parliamentary authority was required before the use of military force was undertaken by the Government was a 'doubtful convention'.[60]

C. The War Prerogative in the 2010–15 Parliament

The issue of war powers was to receive considerably more attention in the 2010–15 Parliament. There were three separate events that brought the convention to the fore: the conflict in Libya in 2011, the proposed intervention in Syria in 2013 and the subsequent military action in respect of ISIS/ISIL/Islamic State in Iraq in 2014.

i. Libya

The conflict in Libya was the first occasion that the Coalition Government had to consider the deployment of troops overseas. Perhaps due to the perceived urgency of the crisis, there was no debate before the announcement of the operation on 18 March 2011. Nonetheless, the Prime Minister promised that a substantive motion seeking retrospective approval would be tabled for debate. This duly took place on 21 March 2011. The motion, a substantive one, approving the use of UK armed forces to enforce UN Security Council Resolution 1973 by protecting civilians and enforce the No-Fly Zone, was approved by a vote of 557 to 13.

---

[58] HM Government, *The Governance of Britain—Constitutional Renewal* (Cm 7342, 2008) para 215.
[59] HM Government, *The Governance of Britain—War Powers and Treaties* (n 53).
[60] C Turpin and A Tomkins, *British Government and the Constitution* 7th edn (Cambridge, Cambridge University Press, 2011) 192.

ii. Syria

In August 2013, there was an event of great significance for this convention, when the House of Commons considered a motion which included the possibility of taking military action in Syria. The House was recalled on 29 August to debate and vote on the principle of taking action in Syria following the alleged use of chemical weapons by the Assad regime. The Government's motion was that the House deplored the use of chemical weapons in Syria by the Assad regime, 'which caused hundreds of deaths and thousands of injuries of Syrian civilians', adding that 'a strong humanitarian response is required from the international community and this may, if necessary, require military action that is legal, proportionate and focused on saving lives by preventing and deterring further use of Syria's chemical weapons'.

The motion was defeated by 272 to 285, and the Prime Minister told the House that the Government would act accordingly.[61] The House of Commons Library noted that this was the first defeat of the Government in relation to military action 'reportedly since the late 18th century', when Lord North had lost a vote over whether to continue fighting the US War of Independence.[62]

iii. ISIS/ISIL/Islamic State

On 26 September 2014, the House was recalled to consider a motion which included support for the use of air strikes, but not the deployment of ground troops, to support efforts against IS in Iraq alone.[63] The House of Commons supported the motion by a vote of 524 to 43.

On both of the most recent occasions, the convention to consult the House was followed, but the decision as to whether or not military action was taken was ultimately made by the Prime Minister.

At the time of writing, it appeared that the Government might return to the House of Commons with a new motion for an extension of air strikes against IS into Syria in the autumn of 2015. There was also some controversy when it emerged in July 2015 that some UK pilots had been embedded with coalition forces (including the US) which had taken part in air strikes in Syria against IS, in spite of the vote against military action in Syria.[64] The Secretary of State for Defence, Michael Fallon, made a statement in Parliament on 20 July 2015.[65]

---

[61] HC Deb 29 August 2013, col 1555.
[62] C Mills, *Parliamentary Approval for Military Action*, House of Commons Library Briefing Paper 7166 (12 May 2015).
[63] HC Deb 26 September 2014, col 1255.
[64] J Halliday, E MacAskill and F Perraudin, 'British Pilots Took Part in Anti-Isis Bombing Campaign in Syria' *The Guardian* (17 July 2015).
[65] He said: 'Embedded UK personnel operate as if they were the host nation's personnel, under that nation's chain of command, but they remain subject to UK domestic, international and host nation law. Ministerial approval is required for UK embeds to deploy with allied forces on operations. Over

The Government was the subject of some criticism (with concerns expressed about the fact that Parliament had not been informed about the embedded pilots and about the potential for 'mission creep').[66]

iv. Mali

In addition to the above-mentioned incidents, there was also a rather more low-key deployment of forces in Mali, which was announced in 2013. This commenced as 'logistical assistance' and was expanded to include 'the deployment of a surveillance aircraft' and 'up to 40 military personnel to the EU Training Mission in Mali'.[67] The Government reiterated that no British personnel would be deployed in combat (and the deployment was regarded as a response to an emergency request from France and Mali, and in support of a UN Security Council Resolution). On that basis, no government-led debate and no parliamentary vote was held.[68]

v. Parliamentary Reports

In addition to these debates, there were also a series of reports from parliamentary committees. The first foray was a report from the Political and Constitutional Reform Committee (PCRC) entitled *Parliament's Role in Conflict Decisions* which was published in May 2011.[69]

The PCRC noted that the previous Government had proposed a 'draft detailed parliamentary resolution on war powers in a Green Paper in 2007 and a White Paper in 2008', but that the House 'did not have an opportunity to consider such a motion before the general election in May 2010'. It also noted correspondence from the then Cabinet Secretary, Sir Gus O'Donnell, to the effect that:

> [T]he Government believes that it is apparent that since the events leading up to the deployment of troops in Iraq, a convention exists that Parliament will be given the opportunity to debate the decision to commit troops to armed conflict and, except in emergency situations, that debate would take place before they are committed.

---

the last 12 months, a total of five pilots have been embedded at one time or another with forces conducting strikes over Syria.' HC Deb 20 July 2015, col 1234.

[66] See, eg, HC Deb 20 July, col 1235, where the Shadow Defence Secretary, Vernon Coaker, suggested that Parliament should have been told about the embedded forces. He also asked for a commitment that there would be no further use of embedded UK forces in Syria without parliamentary consent. Concerns about mission creep were also highlighted in September 2015, when it emerged that two British nationals, allegedly fighting for ISIS, had been killed by a British drone strike in Syria. See, eg, 'Islamic State Conflict: Two Britons Killed in RAF Syria Strike' (*BBC Online*, 7 September 2015) www.bbc.co.uk/news/uk-34178998.

[67] C Mills, *Parliamentary Approval for Military Action*, House of Commons Library Briefing Paper 7166 (12 May 2015).

[68] ibid. See also HC Deb 31 January 2013, cols 1054, 1059–60.

[69] Political and Constitutional Reform Committee, *Parliament's Role in Conflict Decisions* (HC 2010–12, 923).

The Committee recalled that during the debate in the context of military action in Libya, under the aegis of United Nations Security Council Resolution 1973, the then Foreign Secretary, William Hague, had indicated that 'we will enshrine in law for the future the necessity of consulting Parliament on military action'. The PCRC saw this as a long-term ambition and recommended that in the interim, 'the Cabinet Manual should include a clear reference to Parliament's current role in decisions to commit forces to armed conflict abroad' and that the Government should 'bring forward a draft detailed parliamentary resolution ... for debate and decision'.[70]

The Government responded to the Committee by way of a letter.[71] It did not address the Committee's recommendation on the *Cabinet Manual*. In relation to the Committee's other recommendations, it said that it could not, at this stage, commit to following the Committee's suggested approach or to meeting the timetable it had proposed, but that it hoped 'to make progress on this matter in a timely and appropriate manner'. Following criticism by the Committee, the Government issued a further response in which it accepted the Committee's recommendation that the Cabinet Manual 'contain a reference to Parliament's current role in conflict decisions'[72] (subsequently, at a Westminster Hall debate in June 2014, Greg Clark MP said that the Cabinet Manual would be updated again to include a reference to the events in the House of Commons on 29 August 2013).[73]

Two further relevant reports were published in the 2010–15 Parliament. The first was by the House of Lords Constitution Committee. It conducted an extensive inquiry and concluded that the existing convention provides the best framework for the House of Commons to exercise political control over, and confer legitimacy upon, such decisions. It argued that the convention was 'flexible, effective and consistent with the existing structure of parliamentary scrutiny of the executive'.[74]

The Lords Committee stated that 'neither primary legislation nor a resolution should be introduced as a means of formalising the role of Parliament in approving deployment decisions', suggesting that much of the impetus for formalising Parliament's role was to make a political statement about where decisions should be taken rather than to correct deficiencies in the legal or military process. It also expressed the view that one of the main obstacles to formalisation (either

---

[70] For additional background, see S Payne, 'Parliament's Role in Conflict Decisions' (*UK Constitutional Law Association Blog*, 2 June 2011) http://ukconstitutionallaw.org/2011/06/02/sebastian-payne-parliament%e2%80%99s-role-in-conflict-decisions.

[71] *Government's Response to the Political and Constitutional Reform Committee* (HC 2010–12, 1477). The *Cabinet Manual*, published in October 2011, indicates at para 5.38 that: 'In 2011, the Government acknowledged that a convention had developed in Parliament that before troops were committed the House of Commons should have an opportunity to debate the matter and said that it proposed to observe that convention except when there was an emergency and such action would not be appropriate.'

[72] *Government's Further Response* (HC 2010–12, 1673).

[73] HC Deb 19 June 2014, cols 157–58WH.

[74] House of Lords Constitution Committee, *Constitutional Arrangements for the Use of Armed Force* (HL 2013–14, 46) para 64.

through legislation or resolution) is that of definition: formalisation would mean specifying the kind of action which would engage parliamentary involvement. The Committee also repeated its earlier concerns that this could lead to the 'risk of rendering deployment decisions justiciable, particularly through applications for judicial review'.[75] There are 'well-established rules that the courts will be very slow to review the exercise of prerogative powers in relation to the conduct of foreign affairs and the deployment of the armed services'[76] (although it is worth noting that the approach taken by the courts is potentially subject to evolution[77] and that, over the last decade or so, they have been willing to trespass into previously forbidden areas).[78]

The Government responded that the Committee's report provided an excellent summary of the case for and against formalisation, and indicated that it would take 'careful note of the Committee's conclusions' that neither primary legislation nor a resolution should be introduced as a means of formalising the role of Parliament in approving deployment decisions.[79]

By contrast, the PCRC, which reported in March 2014,[80] indicated that it ultimately favoured 'Parliament's role being enshrined in law', but stated that it believed that 'agreeing a parliamentary resolution on this subject would serve as a useful interim step by embedding the current convention and clarifying some of the ambiguities that exist under current arrangements'. The report contained a draft resolution perhaps, in part, as the PCRC had protested that the Government had not made progress on the issue 'in a timely manner'. The Committee further indicated that it respectfully disagreed with the Lords Constitution Committee.

The PCRC accepted that 'the question of how to define conflict decisions is central to establishing what decisions Parliament would have to be consulted on, or approve, if the process were formalised'. Yet it argued that 'the current convention is dependent on a shared understanding between Parliament and the Government about which decisions Parliament should have the opportunity to debate'.

---

[75] ibid para 54.
[76] *R v Jones* [2006] UKHL 16, [2007] 1 AC 136 [30].
[77] See, eg, R Joseph, *The War Prerogative: History, Reform and Constitutional Design* (Oxford, Oxford University Press, 2013) 124–56.
[78] See, eg, H Woolf, J Jowell, A Le Sueur et al, *De Smith's Judicial Review* 7th edn (London, Sweet & Maxwell, 2013) paras 3-033–3-034; M Fordham, *Judicial Review Handbook* 6th edn (Oxford, Hart Publishing, 2012); *Council of Civil Service Unions v Minister for the Civil Service* [1985] AC 374; *Lewis v Attorney General of Jamaica* [2001] 2 AC 50; *Campaign for Nuclear Disarmament v Prime Minister* [2002] EWHC 2759 (Admin), [2003] 3 LRC 335; *R (Abassi) v Secretary of State for the Foreign and Commonwealth Office* [2002] EWCA Civ 1598, [2003] UKHRR 76; *R (International Transport Roth GmbH) v Secretary of State for the Home Department* [2002] EWCA Civ 3, [2002] EuLR 225; *R v Jones* [2006] UKHL 16, [2007] 1 AC 136; *R (Gentle) v Prime Minister* [2008] UKHL 20, [2008] 1 AC 1356.
[79] HM Government Response to the Report of the Lords Constitution Committee into Constitutional Arrangements for the Use of Armed Force Published on 24 July, 25 October 2013 (www.parliament.uk/documents/lords-committees/constitution/armedforce/gov-response-to-armed-force-report.pdf).
[80] Political and Constitutional Reform Committee, *Parliament's Role in Conflict Decisions: A Way Forward* (HC 2013–14, 892) 4.

The PCRC also returned to the question of the information available to Parliament when making any decision. It recognised that the current convention makes 'no provision for the advice, regarding matters of fact or law, that is made available to Parliament when a conflict decision is being considered' and stated that this deficiency should be remedied.

Prior to the dissolution of Parliament, in March 2015, the PCRC complained that 'to date the Government has not responded to our latest report'.[81]

D. Analysis

The episodes which occurred over the course of the 2010–15 Parliament certainly appear to have made clear that the convention that Parliament ought to be consulted on the deployment of military forces can no longer be described as 'doubtful'. While the convention was not formalised or codified into a resolution or legislation, it was clearly recognised by the Government.

Gavin Phillipson has argued that the Libya episode 'was perhaps more significant than that of Iraq in 2003' in that, in the case of Libya, 'the Government granted a debate because it believed that a convention required it to do so'.[82] The compliance of the Cameron administration over the Syria vote could simply be seen as a result of political reality. However, it also cemented the view that the political actors were bound by the new convention (and that they themselves accepted that development). Yet the importance of the Syria vote is contested.[83] For example, Louise Thompson has argued that although the vote was 'a crucial one, demonstrating for the first time that Parliament is able to exercise its newfound power over the government in defence and foreign affairs', nonetheless:

> [T]he Commons has since voted yes to air strikes in Iraq; Syria remains the only occasion on which Parliament has said no. Although it was important, we should not focus solely on this when we consider Parliament's role in this important and often overlooked, policy area.[84]

The varying approaches taken by the Brown and Cameron administrations in the 2005 and 2010 Parliaments, and the differing conclusions of the House of

---

[81] Political and Constitutional Reform Committee, *The Work of the Committee in the 2010 Parliament* (HC 2014–15, 1128).

[82] Phillipson (n 38). Here Phillipson is referring to Jennings' classic threefold test for the existence of a convention. First, what are the precedents? Second, did the actors in the precedents believe that they were bound by a rule? Third, is there a reason for the rule? I Jennings, *The Law and the Constitution* 5th edn (London, University of London Press, 1959) 136.

[83] J Rozenberg, 'Syria Intervention: Is There a New Constitutional Convention?' *The Guardian* (2 September 2013).

[84] L Thompson, 'We Shouldn't Focus Solely on the Syria Vote When Assessing Parliament's Power over Military Deployments' (*Democratic Audit Blog*, 30 March 2015) www.democraticaudit.com/?p=12033.

Lords Constitution Committee and the PCRC demonstrate the complexities and challenges that need to be addressed.

As Lord Wallace put it in his evidence to the PCRC:

> This Government, like its predecessor, has discovered as it goes into it that this is a great deal more complex than one thought. The definition of armed conflict and the deployment of forces has all sorts of ragged edges, questions of urgency and secrecy come in.[85]

Certainly, one can conclude that the idea of pursuing a legislative response appears to have receded. Whether a future government will commit to a resolution remains unclear (in spite of the views of the PCRC and some commentators).

The Lords Committee appears to have taken a pragmatic approach having regard to the challenge of reconciling the need to enshrining a convention in a way that is durable and significant on the one hand, but 'flexible enough to deal with what are, by definition, unpredictable circumstances' on the other hand.[86] Yet, as Lord Hennessy has observed, conventions 'can be fragile' and can crumble when confronted by a determined executive.[87]

In one sense, however, the focus on the existence of the convention also highlights the limited role that Parliament may get to play in these types of decisions. For example, what happens if the armed forces get bogged down in a prolonged conflict? There is little opportunity for Parliament to exercise leverage by controlling supply.[88] Furthermore, during the course of the debate, many commentators appeared to accept that a convention might not apply to the deployment of 'advisers' and even special forces.[89] Finally, for obvious reasons, Parliament would probably have no role in circumstances where the Prime Minister considered deploying the nuclear deterrent.[90]

There are also a series of hurdles to be met if the seemingly stalled process to introduce a resolution were to be revived in the 2015 Parliament. These include: the question of definition (discussed above) and whether any such resolution can deal with the wide spectrum of deployment situations; the question of extent (at what point would a government have to seek a fresh mandate and how can what is often referred to as 'mission creep' be prevented); the caveats that would be granted to cover 'urgent' situations (and the question of retrospective approval); access to

---

[85] Political and Constitutional Reform Committee, Oral Evidence, HC 649, 24 October 2013.
[86] *HM Government Response* (n 79).
[87] HL Deb 28 November 2013, col 1613.
[88] Although the expenses must be met by funds voted by Parliament, scrutiny is rather limited.
[89] The limitations of the vote on Syria were demonstrated by the fact that the Government observed that it would be willing to launch further drone strikes in Syria to prevent armed attacks in Britain. See, eg, 'Islamic State Conflict: UK "Would Repeat Syria Drone Strike"' (*BBC Online*, 8 September 2015) www.bbc.co.uk/news/uk-34181475.
[90] See, eg, A Defty, 'Peter Hennessy and the Writing Down of the British Constitution' (*Who Runs Britain Blog*, 13 October 2013) https://whorunsbritain.blogs.lincoln.ac.uk/2013/10/13/peter-hennessy-and-the-writing-down-of-the-british-constitution; P Hennessy, *The Secret State: Preparing for the Worst 1945–2010* (London, Penguin, 2010).

legal advice and intelligence material; and the impact of any new resolution on operational effectiveness and morale.

IV. CASE STUDY 2: PARLIAMENT'S INTELLIGENCE AND SECURITY COMMITTEE

In spite of interest from other select committees, the Intelligence and Security Committee (ISC) is 'the principal mechanism for providing parliamentary oversight of the agencies'.[91]

The ISC was first established by section 10 of the Intelligence Services Act 1994 to examine the policy, administration and expenditure of the Security Service (commonly referred to as MI5), the Secret Intelligence Service (MI6) and the Government Communications Headquarters (GCHQ).

Reforms to the ISC designed to bring it more into line with parliamentary select committees were proposed in the 2007 *Governance of Britain* Green Paper (discussed above) and some (fairly minor) changes were implemented prior to the 2010 General Election.[92]

Thereafter, in October 2011, the Ministry of Justice published the *Justice and Security Green Paper*.[93] The *Green Paper* acknowledged that criticism of the ISC continued, notwithstanding the *Governance of Britain* reforms.[94] These criticisms focused on the fact that the ISC was separate and different from other committees, since it was not a committee of Parliament, but rather a committee of parliamentarians that reported to the Prime Minister. The fact that it answered to the Prime Minister fuelled the impression that it was insufficiently independent. Other criticisms included insufficient knowledge of the operational work of the security agencies, a lack of independent and expert staff, and the fact that the processes by which the ISC was appointed, operated and reported were not transparent.[95]

---

[91] H Bochel, A Defty and J Kirkpatrick, *Watching the Watchers* (London, Palgrave Macmillan, 2014) ch 4 and 'New Mechanisms of Independent Accountability: Select Committees and Parliamentary Scrutiny of the Intelligence Services' (2015) 68 *Parliamentary Affairs* 314, 314.

[92] For more on these, see, eg, House of Commons Library, *Intelligence and Security Committee*, Briefing Note 2178, 29 October 2013; and A Defty, 'Educating Parliamentarians about Intelligence: The Role of the British Intelligence and Security Committee' (2008) 64 *Parliamentary Affairs* 621.

[93] (Cm 8194, 2011). The reforms and subsequent debates primarily related to the reform of court processes rather than parliamentary processes; see I Leigh, 'Rebalancing Rights and National Security: Reforming UK Intelligence Oversight a Decade after 9/11' (2012) 27 *Intelligence and National Security* 722; A Tomkins, 'Justice and Security in the United Kingdom' (2014) 47 *Israel Law Review* 305; C Walker, 'Living with National Security Disputes in Court Processes in England and Wales' in G Martin, R Scott Bray and M Kumar (eds), *Secrecy, Law and Society* (London, Routledge, 2015).

[94] The performance of the ISC was even criticised by the Parliamentary Joint Committee on Human Rights; see, eg, *Allegations of UK Complicity in Torture* (2008–09, HL 152, HC 230) and *Counter-Terrorism Policy and Human Rights (Seventeenth Report): Bringing Human Rights Back* (2009–10, HL 86, HC 111).

[95] House of Commons Library, *Intelligence and Security Committee*, Briefing Note 2178, 29 October 2013.

Many of these criticisms arose in the context of concerns that the security and intelligence services may have been complicit in the rendition and alleged torture of terrorist suspects by third states during the 'war on terror' that had been commenced after 9/11.[96]

The proposals in the Green Paper were welcomed by the then Chair of the ISC, Sir Malcolm Rifkind, who described them as 'significant reforms' (he also noted that the Government had accepted many proposals originating from the ISC itself).[97]

A. The Justice and Security Act 2013

The Justice and Security Act 2013 has repealed section 10 of the 1994 Act and transformed the ISC into the Intelligence and Security Committee of Parliament (albeit not a normal parliamentary select committee) and increased its powers and remit. In addition to the three intelligence and security agencies, the ISC now examines the intelligence-related work of the Cabinet Office, including: the Joint Intelligence Committee (JIC); the Assessments Staff; and the National Security Secretariat. It also provides oversight of Defence Intelligence in the Ministry of Defence and the Office for Security and Counter-Terrorism in the Home Office.

Section 3 of the 2013 Act requires the ISC to make an annual report to Parliament. It can also make any other reports as it considers appropriate concerning any aspects of its functions. This differs from the previous position whereby the ISC made its reports only to the Prime Minister, though section 3(3) still requires prior transmission to the Prime Minister, who can still enforce the excision of materials on security grounds.

The 2013 Act also sets out the new membership criteria (section 1) and the powers of the ISC to call for information (Schedule 1, paragraphs 4–6). In short, although members of the ISC are now appointed by Parliament, they need to be nominated for membership by the Prime Minister (and the Prime Minister is required to consult with the Leader of the Opposition before nominating any person).[98] The Chair of the ISC is chosen by its own members. Its powers to call

---

[96] See, eg, A Horne, 'Security Services under the Microscope' *Criminal Law and Justice Weekly* (3 December 2010).
[97] Intelligence and Security Committee, Press Release, 19 October 2011.
[98] From 1994 to 2008, the Prime Minister appointed members (after consulting the Leader of the Opposition). Parliament got a role in *proposing* some members to the Prime Minister in 2008. From 2004 to 2008, ISC members were appointed by the Prime Minister after consultation with the Leader of the Opposition. The Prime Minister also appointed the chair. This was under s 10 of the Intelligence and Security Act 1994. There was no formal role for Parliament. In 2008, as part of moves to make the appointments process more transparent, a new Standing Order was introduced. The Prime Minister still appointed ISC members under s 10. However, the House could propose 'certain' (not all) members be recommended to the Prime Minister on the basis of a motion from the Committee of Selection. This was under Standing Order 152E.

for information are set out in Schedule 1, as well as powers to take evidence under oath and relevant protections provided to witnesses. The members of the ISC are subject to section 1(1)(b) of the Official Secrets Act 1989 and have access to highly classified material in carrying out their duties.

Yet in spite of these further reforms, there are still calls for change, on the basis that there is a 'perception within Parliament that those appointed to the ISC were too close to the agencies and not the kind of members one would expect to ask difficult or probing questions'.[99] Prior to the 2015 General Election, Andrew Defty noted that 23 of the 39 parliamentarians who have served on the ISC have held ministerial office before being appointed to the Committee, 'with a clear preference for members with ministerial experience in defence, foreign affairs and Northern Ireland'.[100]

These issues were no doubt exacerbated by revelations and allegations around the interception and surveillance programmes operated by the security agencies (following the disclosures by Edward Snowden). The UK's *The Guardian* newspaper was one of a number that published documents provided by Snowden. It identified a series of programmes, including 'PRISM' operated by the National Security Agency in the US (which supposedly secured access to the internal systems of global companies that service the internet) and Tempora (which related to claims that GCHQ had direct taps on transatlantic fibre-optic cables of major telecommunications corporations).[101]

The UK Government (in accordance with a long-standing policy) neither confirmed nor denied the existence of the Tempora programme. Shortly after the Snowden revelations, the ISC issued a perhaps precipitate statement in July 2013.[102] It indicated that it had taken 'detailed evidence from GCHQ' and that it had scrutinised 'GCHQ's access to the content of communications, the legal framework which governs that access, and the arrangements GCHQ has with its overseas counterparts for sharing such information'. Amongst other things, it considered allegations 'that GCHQ circumvented UK law by using the NSA's PRISM programme to access the content of private communications'. The ISC stated that 'from the evidence we have seen, we have concluded that this is unfounded'.

---

[99] A Defty, 'It is Time to Adopt a Different Approach to Appointing Members of the Intelligence and Security Committee' *Democratic Audit* (24 March 2015). See also H Bochel, A Defty and J Kirkpatrick, 'New Mechanisms of Independent Accountability: Select Committees and Parliamentary Scrutiny of the Intelligence Services' (2015) 68 *Parliamentary Affairs* 314.

[100] Defty (n 99). Chairs of the Committee have included the following: Dominic Grieve QC, Sir Malcolm Rifkind, Dr Kim Howells, Margaret Beckett, Paul Murphy, Ann Taylor (now Baroness Taylor of Bolton) and Tom King (now Lord King of Bridgwater).

[101] 'GCHQ Taps Fibre-Optic Cables for Secret Access to World's Communications' *The Guardian* (21 June 2013). See also P Strickland, 'Intelligence Services and the Snowden Revelations' in G Thompson (ed), *Key Issues for the New Parliament 2015* (London, House of Commons Library, 2015).

[102] See www.gov.uk/government/uploads/system/uploads/attachment_data/file/225459/ISC-Statement-on-GCHQ.pdf. These matters remain the subject of legal challenges and forensic investigation before the European Court of Human Rights following the failure to sustain any serious allegation before the Investigatory Powers Tribunal: see *Liberty v UK*, www.liberty-human-rights.org.uk/news/press-releases/liberty-takes-fight-against-mass-surveillance-european-court.

The allegations arose at around the same time as the ISC held its first public evidence session on 7 November 2013. The Committee took evidence from the Directors of GCHQ, MI5 and MI6, and directly addressed some of the Snowden allegations. The then Director of M16, Sir John Sawers, argued that the revelations had been so damaging that 'our adversaries were rubbing their hands with glee' and that the leaks had put 'our operations at risk'.[103]

B. The Impact of the 2013 Reforms

The 2013 reforms have not significantly altered the widespread perception amongst critics of the inadequacies of the ISC. Those critics include the House of Commons Home Affairs Committee, which, reflecting on parliamentary scrutiny as a whole and the ISC in particular, expressed 'concerns that the weak nature of that system has an impact upon the credibility of the agencies accountability, and to the credibility of Parliament itself'.[104] Admittedly, the reforms arrived at the worst of times. Other legislative committees elsewhere in the world have likewise struggled to grapple effectively with the polymorphous and manifold allegations of Snowden. To make matters worse, the ISC Chair, Sir Malcolm Rifkind, had to resign in February 2015 after the *Daily Telegraph* and Channel 4's *Dispatches* programme asserted that he had offered to utilise his position as a senior politician on behalf of a fictitious Chinese company (an obvious potential security risk) in return for substantial financial payments.[105]

As for work undertaken since the reforms, two major reports have appeared. The first was the *Report on the Intelligence Relating to the Murder of Fusilier Lee Rigby*.[106] One of the soldier's killers, Michael Adebowale, had several of his multiple social media internet accounts (later revealed by the media to be operated through Facebook) closed proactively without an official request by the communications service provider (CSP) using an automated process because, according to GCHQ, 'they hit triggers ... related to their criteria for closing things down on the basis of terrorist content'.[107] Facebook also learned, on the completion of a retrospective review of all 11 of his accounts, that Adebowale had also discussed 'in the most explicit and emotive manner' over Facebook's instant messaging service his desire to murder a soldier.

---

[103] 'UK intelligence Work Defends Freedom, Say Spy Chiefs' (*BBC Online*, 7 November 2013) www.bbc.co.uk/news/uk-politics-24847399.

[104] *Counter-terrorism* (HC 2013–14, 231) para 157. See also *Response to the Seventeenth Report from the Home Affairs Committee Session 2013–14 HC 231: Counter-Terrorism* (Cm 9011, 2015).

[105] See N Watt and P Wintour, 'Conservatives Suspend Sir Malcolm Rifkind over Cash-for-Access claims' *The Guardian* (23 February 2015). The House of Commons Standards Committee subsequently cleared Sir Malcolm, concluding that no rules had been broken. See House of Commons Standards Committee, *Sir Malcolm Rifkind and Jack Straw* (HC 2015–16, 472).

[106] Intelligence and Security Committee, *Privacy and Security: A Modern and Transparent Legal Framework* (HC 2014–15, 1075).

[107] ibid para 384.

While the ISC was critical of monitoring procedures by CSPs, serial investigations by the Security Service were excused as sufficiently thorough, especially because, as pointed out even by GCHQ,[108] true intent can be very difficult to discern from online communications. Putting aside other relevant issues around data privacy, accountability for surveillance, the duty of care to users and economic efficiency, if social media companies were to be obliged to proactively monitor and share all postings of a violent extremist nature with the security authorities, the former would have little time or money for anything else and the latter would be deluged with information and likely rendered unable to function on a viable basis. In summary, the ISC's work here was commendable for documenting in detail the failures of security; however, the conclusions drawn might be viewed as at best misplaced and at worst deflecting attention from the security services and their potential shortcomings.

The second report, *Privacy and Security: A Modern and Transparent Legal Framework*,[109] also bore some promising signs of greater transparency, as evidenced by the substantial list of external witnesses invited to make submissions to the inquiry arising from the Snowden revelations. In substance, this report revealed a small number of security staff had been disciplined for misusing their surveillance powers, and it further reassured that mass surveillance is not being conducted. However, the ISC did find that the existing legal powers[110] could be construed as providing the agencies with a 'blank cheque to carry out whatever activities they deem necessary',[111] a belated discovery for a review body which was established under the same legislation. It called for wide scale but largely amorphous legislative reforms. Since the report was published in March 2015, two further reports on investigatory powers were published in the summer of 2015. The first, and much more detailed and precise, report by David Anderson QC, *A Question of Trust*, was presented to the Prime Minister pursuant to section 7 of the Data Retention and Investigatory Powers Act 2014. The second, which had been commissioned by the former Deputy Prime Minister, Nick Clegg, was published by the Royal United Services Institute (RUSI) and was entitled *A Democratic Licence to Operate*. The May 2015 Queen's Speech promised a new Investigatory Powers Bill to 'modernise the law on communications data'. The Draft Bill was published in November 2015.[112] Transparency is significantly advanced by the full explication of 'bulk' surveillance powers and also of some powers of interference (such as with equipment and personal data sets), much as advocated by Anderson. On the other hand, the Draft Bill is far from a comprehensive code on surveillance, and oversight of its powers is not as strong as many critics (including Anderson)

---

[108] ibid para 393.
[109] *Privacy and Security: A Modern and Transparent Legal Framework* (HC 2014–15, 1075).
[110] The Regulation of Investigatory Powers Act 2000, the Security Service Act 1989 and the Intelligence Services Act 1994 provide the main authorisations for surveillance.
[111] *Privacy and Security* (n 109) 117.
[112] Cm 9152.

would wish. The more intrusive powers in the Draft Bill will be overseen by independent Judicial Commissioners, but the recommendation of the ISC that most authorisations should come initially from the Secretary of State to maintain the importance of executive accountability to Parliament has been adopted.

V. CASE STUDY 3: PARLIAMENT'S SCRUTINY OF COUNTER-TERRORISM LEGISLATION

A. The Challenges to Accountability

The accountability of counter-terrorism legislation is emphasised as part and parcel of a wider set of values which might be termed 'constitutionalism'.[113] The meaning of that term extends to insistence upon accountability, observance of the rule of law and respect for individual rights. The concept has been repeated and emphasised throughout the contemporary era of counter-terrorism. For example, Lord Lloyd set four principles against which the legislation should be judged in his 1996 review:

(i) Legislation against terrorism should approximate as closely as possible to the ordinary criminal law and procedure.
(ii) Additional statutory offences and powers may be justified, but only if they are necessary to meet the anticipated threat. They must then strike the right balance between the needs of security and the rights and liberties of the individual.
(iii) The need for additional safeguards should be considered alongside any additional powers.
(iv) The law should comply with the UK's obligations in international law.[114]

The Home Office response to Lord Macdonald's review in 2011 likewise outlined standards relating to effectiveness, freedom, and accountability as follows:

The first duty of Government is to safeguard our national security;
The Government will reverse the substantial erosion of civil liberties and roll back state intrusion;
The Government will introduce safeguards against the misuse of anti-terrorism legislation.[115]

Yet, as was recognised at the outset of this chapter, there are significant obstacles to parliamentary accountability. Some problems are shared with other aspects of national security. These include, first, the sensitivity of the facts and the problem of allowing access to information to parliamentarians whose very function normally requires full transparency and discussion. Most counter-terrorism activity

---

[113] See C Walker, 'Constitutional Governance and Special Powers against Terrorism' (1997) 35 *Columbia Journal of Transnational Law* 1.
[114] *Inquiry into Legislation against Terrorism* (Cm 3420, 1996) para 3.1.
[115] Home Office, *Review of Counter-terrorism and Security Powers* (Cm 8004, 2011) 4.

is not made public, especially those aspects handled by the security agencies. It is reckoned that 80 per cent of the work of the Security Service is devoted to counter-terrorism, and some of the remaining 20 per cent allocated to 'protective security' is also terrorism-related.[116] Mention of protective security raises further inherent problems around accountability. Responses by way of prosecution or executive orders—individuated responses to terrorism—are often viewed as highly emblematic of counter-terrorism. However, contemporary counter-terrorism measures operate overwhelmingly on a collective basis, and individuated treatment is exceptional. This embedded nature of terrorism therefore provokes 'all-risks' security and policing measures,[117] which generally fall within the expansive 'Protect' catalogue of CONTEST (the Government's Countering International Terrorism Strategy).[118] Some 'Protect' measures may be state-operated and conducted in the full glare of the public—stop and search powers may be one controversial example. However, many other aspects of 'Protect' are embedded secretly in operations or designs and, furthermore, are more often than not held in private, not public hands.[119]

Another obstacle to accountability which is shared with national security activities more generally is that counter-terrorism activity is sometimes conducted 'off the books' in the sense that there is no statutory authority for the activity or (in some cases) even any explicit legal authority of any kind. This mode of working may arise because it allows for greater ministerial discretion and reduces opportunity for accountability. Three examples will be briefly related. One is that the independent review system related earlier was not actually specified by law until it was set down in section 36 of the Terrorism Act 2006, even though a reviewer had existed in one shape or another since 1976.[120] The drawbacks of this legal black hole were barely discernible, but they could allow ministers to manipulate resources, access and the timing of publications. The second example concerns the use of the royal prerogative to take away passports. The Home Secretary announced in 2013 that passports will be denied to, or removed from, British citizens 'whose past, present or proposed activities, actual or suspected, are believed by the Home Secretary to be so undesirable that the grant or continued enjoyment of passport facilities is contrary to the public interest'.[121] This prerogative power had only been

---

[116] See www.mi5.gov.uk/home/about-us/what-we-do/major-areas-of-work.html; for the Secret Intelligence Service, see www.sis.gov.uk/about-us/what-we-do/counter-terrorism.html.
[117] See C Walker, 'Neighbor Terrorism and the All-Risks Policing of Terrorism' (2009) 3 *Journal of National Security Law & Policy* 121.
[118] Home Office, *Countering International Terrorism* (Cm 6888, London, 2006), as revised by (Cm 7547, 2009); (Cm 7833, 2010) (Cm 8123, 2011) (Cm 8583, 2013) (Cm 8848, 2014) (Cm 9048, 2015). See C Walker, '"Protect" against Terrorism: In Service of the State, the Corporation, or the Citizen?' in D Jenkins, A Jacobsen and A Henriksen (eds), *The Long Decade: How 9/11 Changed the Law* (New York, Oxford University Press, 2014).
[119] C Nath, *Cyber Security in the UK* (Post Note 389, Houses of Parliament, 2011) 1.
[120] Compare the (Australian) Independent National Security Legislation Monitor Act 2010.
[121] HC Deb 25 April 2013, col 68ws. See further Ministry of Justice, *The Governance of Britain— Constitutional Renewal* (Cm 7342, 2008) para 247; L Jarvis and M Lister, 'Disconnected Citizenship?' (2013) 61 *Political Studies* 656.

used 17 times since 1947, but the growth of 'jihadi tourism' to Syria warranted this development. The choice of the mechanism of the prerogative avoids the bother of prior parliamentary approval.[122] Section 1 of the Counter-Terrorism and Security Act 2015 has granted a further temporary power to seize passports at ports, but the Government ignored all calls for more comprehensive reforms of the laws on passports. The third example of the non-statutory approach is most serious and far-reaching of all, but has also been affected by the Counter-Terrorism and Security Act 2015. Since the time of its unveiling in 2006 until the implementation of Part V of that Act, the 'Prevent' leg of CONTEST was not subject to any statutory basis (or specific legal basis of any kind beyond the grant of supply). This extra-legal status did not rule out a major Home Office review in 2011,[123] nor did it avert attention from several House of Commons select committees.[124] Nevertheless, only in 2014–15, when the Bill was put before Parliament, was there a parliamentary opportunity to debate and challenge fully the principle and detailed contours of the 'Prevent' policy.

Other aspects of parliamentary accountability for counter-terrorism laws and policy diverge from the challenges faced elsewhere in national security accountability. One aspect is the impact of prosecution. As already mentioned, 'Pursuit' of suspected terrorists (to use the term in CONTEST) through arrest and prosecution does not happen very often compared to the tactic of 'Protect' as applied to potentially vulnerable property and processes. Despite the mantra of the Government that 'prosecution is—first, second and third—the government's preference when dealing with suspected terrorists',[125] the rate of arrests resulting in charges is strikingly lower than comparable figures in non-terrorist cases (the average number of arrests per year is around 200 and the rate of charging is around 37 per cent), and so only around 125 terrorist prisoners are held at any one time.[126] But the existence of court cases further hobbles accountability since *sub judice* matters should not be raised,[127] and so discussion regarding controversial cases (such as where almost blanket secrecy is imposed)[128] is hampered. The restraining rules have also caused acute prospective problems with the invocation of draft legislation about police powers of extended detention and Enhanced Terrorism

---

[122] Judicial review still applies: *R v Secretary of State for Foreign and Commonwealth Affairs ex p Everett* [1988] EWCA Civ 7; *R (Atapattu) v The Secretary of State for the Home Department* [2011] EWHC 1388 (Admin).

[123] Home Office, *Prevent Strategy* (Cm 8092, 2011).

[124] See House of Commons Home Affairs Select Committee, *Project CONTEST: The Government's Counter-Terrorism Strategy* (HC 2008–09, 212); House of Commons Communities and Local Government Committee, *Preventing Violent Extremism* (HC 2009–10, 65); House of Commons Home Affairs Committee, *Roots of Violent Radicalization* (HC 2011–12, 1446).

[125] HC Deb 21 February 2008, col 561 (Tony McNulty MP).

[126] See C Walker, *Terrorism and the Law* (Oxford, Oxford University Press, 2011) chs 5–6.

[127] See House of Commons Standing Orders—Public Business (2013) SO 42A and App 1; R Kelly, *The Sub Judice Rule* (SN/PC/1141, House of Commons Library, 2007).

[128] See *Guardian News & Media v Incedal and Rarmoul-Bouhadjar* [2014] EWCA Crim 1861; *R v Incedal* The Times, 27 March 2015, 2.

Prevention and Investigation Measures, whereby it will be almost impossible to explain and justify the need for these contingent powers without reference to the specific cases which warrant their invocation.[129] By contrast, prosecutions for state secrets issues are relatively rare; between 1997 and 2008, there were nine charges and six convictions.[130]

The other special difficulty with parliamentary accountability in the case of counter-terrorism is that, unlike the tectonic plate movements of inter-state national security developments, there is often perceived urgency in dealing with counter-terrorism. This characteristic tempts governments into acting first and answering questions later or, as already noted, demanding that its proposals be treated as 'fast-track' legislation. An example of the latter tendency may be illustrated by the Counter-Terrorism and Security Act 2015. Despite the Prime Minister promising to 'consult Parliament on the draft clauses',[131] between the first announcement of the intention to legislate in the Commons on 1 September 2014 and the actual introduction of the Counter-Terrorism and Security Bill on 26 November 2014, no further details were issued by way of a consultation paper or draft Bill. Instead, both the Prime Minister and the Home Secretary drip-fed additional information via less conventional arenas during November 2014: Cameron in an address to the Australian Parliament[132] and Theresa May in a speech to the Royal United Services Institute.[133] Worse still, when the Bill was introduced into Parliament on 26 November 2014, the 'fast-track' legislative process, designed to truncate parliamentary debate, was adopted.[134] There was considerable parliamentary annoyance that this curtailment followed months of apparent lethargy,[135] but the dreaded 'fast-track' process actually turned out to be 'only semi-fast tracked'.[136] Thus, there followed two solid months of scrutiny (with Royal Assent on 12 February 2015),

---

[129] See Home Office, *Draft Detention of Terrorist Suspects (Temporary Extension) Bills* (Cm 8018, 2011) and *Draft Enhanced Terrorism Prevention and Investigation Measures Bill* (Cm 8166, 2011); Joint Committee on the Draft Detention of Terrorist Suspects (Temporary Extension) Bills, *Report* (2010–12, HL 161, HC 893); Joint Committee on the Draft Enhanced Terrorism Prevention and Investigation Measures Bill, *Report* (2012–13, HL 70, HC 495); H Fenwick 'Designing ETPIMs around ECHR Review or Normalisation of "Preventive" Non-trial-Based Executive Measures?' (2013) 76 *Modern Law Review* 876; C Walker, 'The Governance of Emergency Arrangements' in CP Walker (ed), *Contingencies, Resilience and Legal Constitutionalism* (Abingdon, Routledge, 2015).

[130] L Maer and O Gay, *Official Secrecy* (SN/PC/02023, House of Commons Library, 2008).

[131] HC Deb 1 September 2014, col 25.

[132] House of Representatives, 14 November 2014, 12710-12715, www.gov.uk/government/speeches/australian-parliament-david-camerons-speech.

[133] Theresa May, Speech to the Royal United Services Institute (24 November 2014) www.gov.uk/government/speeches/home-secretary-theresa-may-on-counter-terrorism.

[134] See House of Lords Constitution Committee, *Fast-Track Legislation: Constitutional Implications and Safeguards* (HL 2008–09, 116).

[135] See House of Lords Constitution Committee, *Counter-Terrorism and Security Bill* (HL 2014–15, 92) paras 1–6; Joint Committee on Human Rights, *Legislative Scrutiny: Counter-Terrorism and Security Bill* (2014–15, HL 86, HC 859) paras 1.8, 1.10.

[136] House of Lords Constitution Committee (n 135) para 3.

including several select committee reports[137] and the issuance of an extensive slew of Home Office consultation papers,[138] factsheets[139] and impact assessments[140] mainly in late November and early December 2014. Furthermore, the process of implementation continued post-Assent, owing to the need to devise guidance documents about key parts of the legislation, though, by then, the die had been largely cast.

B. The Record of Accountability

Considering first performance in debates as a mechanism of parliamentary accountability, the main occasion of debates has been in relation to legislative proposals, which have appeared with such regularity and profusion during the past five decades that their history is too lengthy to be recounted in full here.[141] Instead, the following overview will reflect on the quality and impact in relation to the processes of legislating afresh.

As regards quality, there are divergent factors to be considered. As already noted, the curtailment of full engagement (especially of non-parliamentary inputs) caused by fast-track legislation continues to occur (as with the Counter-Terrorism and Security Act 2015). However, 'panic' legislation has generally decreased as a problem compared to earlier times. Four examples will be given.

The most prominent examples with that epithet remain the Prevention of Terrorism (Temporary Provisions) Act 1974 (passed in three days) and the Criminal Justice (Terrorism and Conspiracy) Act 1998 (two days following the extraordinary recall of both Houses of Parliament during the summer recess).[142]

Second, the Prevention of Terrorism Act 2005 came into force on 11 March 2005, just a couple of weeks after it was first introduced into Parliament on 22 February. The exceptionally rapid legislative process was the subject of highly rancorous debate which was said to have 'demeaned' Parliament[143] as well as becoming the catalyst for the most severe bout of disagreement between Houses of Commons

---

[137] See the foregoing, plus: House of Lords Delegated Powers and Regulatory Reform Committee, *Counter-Terrorism and Security Bill* (HL 2014–15, 97 and 110); House of Commons Home Affairs Committee, *Oral Evidence: Counter-Terrorism and Security Bill* (HC 2014–15, 838).

[138] *Prevent Duty Guidance: A Consultation* (December 2014); *Code of Practice for Officers Exercising Functions under Schedule 1 of the Counter-Terrorism and Security Act 2015 in Connection with Seizing and Retaining Travel Documents* (December 2014); *Consultation on Establishing a UK Privacy and Civil Liberties Board* (December 2014).

[139] www.gov.uk/government/collections/counter-terrorism-and-security-bill-factsheets.

[140] www.gov.uk/government/collections/counter-terrorism-and-security-bill-impact-assessments.

[141] See Walker (n 126).

[142] See C Walker, 'The Bombs in Omagh and their Aftermath: The Criminal Justice (Terrorism and Conspiracy Act 1998)' (1999) 62 *Modern Law Review* 879.

[143] HC Deb 28 February 28 2005, col 734 (Dominic Grieve). Most sections were not considered in the committee stage debate, and the Joint Committee on Human Rights had time for just two short reports: *Prevention of Terrorism Bill: Preliminary Report* (2004–05, HL 61, HC 389) and *Prevention of Terrorism Bill* (2004–05, HL 68, HC 334).

and Lords in modern history.¹⁴⁴ In the course of these debates, the Opposition complained that the government had known since December 2004 that replacement legislation was essential, having been forewarned by both the decision of the Appellate Committee of the House of Lords in late 2004 and the report from the Newton Committee in 2003.¹⁴⁵

Third, it is true that the Terrorist Asset-Freezing (Temporary Provisions) Act 2010 was passed in five days in February 2010 following the judgment of the Supreme Court in *HM Treasury v Ahmed*.¹⁴⁶ However, that Act was immediately followed by proposals and debates until the end of that year which resulted in the Terrorist Asset-Freezing etc Act 2010. It was also true that the Counter-Terrorism and Security Act 2015 was formally fast-tracked, though with a paradoxically leisurely timetable which was later conceded to be 'only semi-fast tracked'.¹⁴⁷

Despite these three cases, the more common scenario, which has applied from the Terrorism Act 2006 onwards, is for full debates to occur over a period of some months with full deployment of draft Bill consultation papers and public Bill committees.¹⁴⁸ In this way, the quality of debate has been significantly assisted by well-informed inputs from non-governmental organisations (NGOs) and experts (via public Bill committees and select committees), from reports of independent reviewers or review committees, and from the expertise of Members of Parliament (especially the House of Lords, where retired police and security experts and judges still ply their trade).

As regards impact, a less promising picture emerges in that major alterations to the Government's legislative proposals are uncommon. One might attribute this result as reflective of the prevailing executive dominance and management of Parliament, though a more subtle assessment would also take account of good groundwork and willingness to engage in debate, as noted above. A further factor has been the underlying political consensus that counter-terrorism, along the lines now set out in CONTEST, is justifiable and a high priority.¹⁴⁹ Perhaps the greatest defeat suffered by successive governments has related to the the maximum period of police detention following an arrest under the Terrorism Act 2000. The period stood at 14 days under the Criminal Justice Act 2003, but efforts were made to increase this to 42, 56, or 90 days in the debates around what became the Terrorism Act 2006 and the Counter-Terrorism Act 2008. These attempts were rebuffed

---

¹⁴⁴ The House of Lords sitting of 10 March 2005 actually lasted until 7 pm on 11 March and was claimed to be the longest ever recorded: HL Deb 10 March 2005, col 1059.

¹⁴⁵ See *A v Secretary of State for the Home Department* [2004] UKHL 56; *Privy Counsellor Review Committee, Anti-Terrorism, Crime and Security Act 2001 Review Report* (HC 2003–04, 100).

¹⁴⁶ *HM Treasury v Ahmed* [2010] UKSC 2. See also *HM Treasury v Ahmed (No 2)* [2010] UKSC 5. See Walker (n 32) ch 3.

¹⁴⁷ House of Lords Constitution Committee (n 135) para 3.

¹⁴⁸ See J Levy, 'Public Bill Committees: An Assessment—Scrutiny Sought; Scrutiny Gained' (2010) 63 *Parliamentary Affairs* 534.

¹⁴⁹ See CJ Newman, 'A Chilling Consensus: Political Protest in the "War on Terror"' in J Moran and M Phythian (eds), *Intelligence, Security & Policing Post-9/11* (Basingstoke, Palgrave Macmillan, 2008).

through a mixture of principled rejection based on the value of liberty, doubts concerning proof of factual necessity and the acceptance of the compromise of a doubling of the period to 28 days under the Terrorism Act 2006.[150] The battle over the establishment of control orders by the Prevention of Terrorism Act 2005 was also fierce and affected by unseemly haste, though the Government secured most of its objectives.[151] At best, 'Parliament has been an effective check at times'.[152]

Debates on the considerable corpus of extant counter-terrorism legislation have been even less forceful. Since the Terrorism Act 2000 is a permanent and fully debated counter-terrorism code, in line with the view of the Lloyd Report,[153] there is no requirement for periodic renewal or re-enactment. According to the then Home Office Minister, Charles Clarke:

> We have had so-called temporary provisions on the statute book for 25 years. The time has come to face the fact of terrorism and be ready to deal with it for the foreseeable future. We need to make the powers permanently available, although the fact that those powers are available does not mean that they have to be used.[154]

However, the absence of the trigger of renewal has meant the consequent loss of regular parliamentary debate. The continuance of the Terrorism Act 2000 and most of the subsequent allied legislation has therefore not been the subject of any comprehensive debate, though specific issues arising from operations, court cases or the release of statistics have been raised as parliamentary questions. There was also in February 2010 the *Post-Legislative Assessment of the Prevention of Terrorism Act 2005*, which, by happenstance, fed into debates about what became the subsequent Government's replacement, the Terrorism Prevention and Investigation Measures Act 2011.[155] However, when in 2011 the Home Office produced a *Memorandum to the Home Affairs Committee: Post-Legislative Scrutiny of the Terrorism Act 2006*,[156] even that select committee could not find the time to respond. The only exception in recent years occurred on 21 January 2014, when an Opposition Day motion about Terrorism Prevention and Investigation Measures, which were depicted as fatally weaker than the previous control order regime, produced a two-and-a-half-hour debate followed by a division.[157]

---

[150] The period has now reverted to 14 days: Protection of Freedoms Act 2012, s 57.
[151] See C Walker, 'Keeping Control of Terrorists without Losing Control of Constitutionalism' (2007) 59 *Stanford Law Review* 1395.
[152] D Anderson, *Report on the Operation in 2011 of the Terrorism Act 2000 and Part I of the Terrorism Act 2006* (London, Home Office, 2012) para 11.4. See also M Shephard, 'Parliamentary Scrutiny and Oversight of the British "War on Terror": From Accretion of Executive Power and Evasion of Scrutiny to Embarrassment and Concessions' (2009) 15 *Journal of Legislative Studies* 191.
[153] *Inquiry into Legislation against Terrorism* (Cm 3420, 1996) paras 1.20, 5.15, 17.6. See also Home Office and Northern Ireland Office, *Legislation against Terrorism* (Cm 4178, 1998). The annual review did apply to pt VII, but it was repealed in 2007.
[154] HC Deb 15 March 2000, col 363.
[155] *Post-Legislative Assessment of the Prevention of Terrorism Act 2005* (Cm 7797, 2010).
[156] *Memorandum to the Home Affairs Committee: Post-Legislative Scrutiny of the Terrorism Act 2006* (Cm 8186, 2011).
[157] HC Deb 21 January 2014, col 221. The vote was 236 to 312 against the motion.

It could be argued that the loss of the annual renewal mechanism is not decisive. There is no serious likelihood that any part of the legislation will be struck down or seriously analysed in an hour-and-a-half debate on an affirmative order.[158] It is also logical that there should be no requirement of renewal given the intended permanence of the legislation and the preference for a legislative response which is firmly grounded rather than reactive to emergency. It follows that sunset clauses, insofar as they are mechanisms for potential repeal, are also generally inappropriate for enduring legislation pitched against enduring problems, unless circumstances are radically shifting or are to be shifted as a matter of policy. Those circumstances do apply to the Justice and Security (Northern Ireland) Act 2007, which applies counter-terrorism measures in that jurisdiction over and above those granted by the Terrorism Act 2000 and allied legislation.[159] Yet, while section 40 of that Act provides for an annual reviewer distinct from the Independent Reviewer of Terrorism Legislation, with the report laid before Parliament, the review is confined to sections 21–32 (special police and army powers) and does not apply to the operation of non-jury courts. Furthermore, the legislation is not subject to a fixed life span since the threat may remain 'for a considerable time'.[160] As a result, political accountability for Northern Ireland special powers has been poor compared to the UK-wide Acts. Pre-legislation consultation papers have been confined to juryless trials and private security services. Debates in the parliamentary chambers have been short and poorly attended and, since 2007, few and far between in number. Thus, the main value of annual review is more to underline a presumption against executive powers and to force politicians to take a stance on the issue, to trigger information and to allow the ventilation of research by outsiders or complaints on behalf of constituents than to change the legislation itself. These measures have also been largely ignored by select committees, including the Northern Ireland Affairs Committee, which even failed to respond to the Government's post-legislative scrutiny paper in 2012.[161] The devolving of policing and justice under the Northern Ireland Act 2009 and the Department of Justice Act (Northern Ireland) 2010 could pave the way for closer attention, but the legislation is highly divisive and remains the ultimate responsibility of Westminster. Far more scrutiny has been conducted by the Northern Ireland Policing Board and the Northern Ireland Human Rights Committee than the Northern Ireland Assembly.

There are also doubts about the efficacy of the device of sunset clauses, though, as already noted, it seems to require the legal specification of a post-legislative

---

[158] For the record on control orders, see A Horne and C Walker, 'Lessons learned from political constitutionalism? Comparing the enactment of control orders and terrorism prevention and investigation measures by the UK Parliament' [2014] *Public Law* 267, 282–83.
[159] See Walker (n 32) ch 9.
[160] Hansard (HC) Public Bill Committee, col 147 (18 January 2007), Paul Goggins.
[161] *Memorandum to the Northern Ireland Affairs Committee Post-Legislative Scrutiny Northern Ireland (St Andrews Agreement) Act 2007 Justice and Security (Northern Ireland) Act 2007* (Cm 8400, 2012).

review in order to secure serious attention.[162] This requirement was applied to the Anti-terrorism, Crime and Security Act 2001[163] and it prospectively applies to the Terrorism Prevention and Investigation Measures Act 2011.[164] Yet, radical change probably depends more on a change of political regime rather than on the opportunity for debate. Thus, most recommendations in the report on the Anti-terrorism, Crime and Security Act 2001 have never been the subject of specific debate,[165] though aspects of it dealing with detention without trial were considered in debates on what became the Prevention of Terrorism Act 2005.

In its consultation paper on post-legislative scrutiny, the Law Commission considered the respective merits of review and sunset clauses:

> A review clause may be a useful tool because it is enshrined in statute and therefore has the force of law. It may simply provide for a general review or specify the particular provisions that should be reviewed, the timescale for review and who should carry it out. However, it has been observed that rather than being a pre-planned provision in a Bill, such clauses are often political compromises, representing the price the Government will pay for getting a Bill through Parliament.[166]

The Law Commission contrasted the use of review clauses with sunset clauses, noting the guidance from the Cabinet Office that the use of sunset clauses was a 'way of ensuring that legislation is reviewed, kept up to date, and not left on the statute book after it has served its purpose' and that they were appropriate in circumstances where 'measures extend the power of the state or reduce civil liberties and where measures are taken in the face of considerable opposition'.[167] Nonetheless, the Law Commission recognised that sunset clauses do not 'necessarily ensure that post-legislative review will take place' and that in the case of counter-terrorism, legislation might be used to provide for 'a general debate prior to a decision as to whether to renew the targeted provisions'.[168]

In the absence of the devices of annual renewal or sunset, the level of scrutiny otherwise applied to existing counter-terrorism legislation has declined

---

[162] Post-legislative scrutiny should be a presumption in the case of fast-track legislation according to the House of Commons Political and Constitutional Reform Committee, *Ensuring Standards in the Quality of Legislation* (HC 2013–14, 85) para 64.

[163] See *Privy Counsellor Review Committee, Anti-Terrorism, Crime and Security Act 2001 Review Report* (HC 2003–04, 100).

[164] See s 21 (the Secretary of State's Terrorism Prevention and Investigation Measures powers expire at the end of five years, but may be revived for a period not exceeding five years by affirmative order). Annual review had been a feature of the previous Prevention of Terrorism Act 2005, s 13. See C Walker and A Horne, 'The Terrorism Prevention and Investigation Measures Act 2011: One Thing But Not Much the Other?' [2012] *Criminal Law Review* 421, 436; and Horne and Walker (n 158) 275–76.

[165] But see Home Office, *Counter-Terrorism Powers: Reconciling Security and Liberty in an Open Society* (Cm 6147, 2004).

[166] Law Commission, *Post-Legislative Scrutiny: A Consultation* (Consultation Paper No 178, 2006) para 7.26.

[167] ibid para 7.28.

[168] ibid para 7.29.

further from a relatively low point.[169] The Secretary of State is simply required to lay the report of the independent reviewers before both Houses of Parliament. The system specifies no set parliamentary timetable. However, concentration on debates as a mechanism of accountability does not provide the full picture. While engineering the removal of the annual debate by means of the Terrorism Act 2000, attention did turn briefly towards alternatives and one minister mused upon the possibility of more active select committee scrutiny.[170] This prescient remark has been followed by an outburst of activity by select committees after 2000, and their reports represent a significant portion of parliamentary accountability both for proposed and ongoing counter-terrorism legislation and policy in general. Again, the output is so extensive that only a flavour can be provided here.[171]

The legislative work of select committees has mainly concentrated upon proposed Bills rather than the assessment of operative Acts. The House of Commons Home Affairs Committee and the Joint Committee on Human Rights have been the most active, though important reports have also emanated from the House of Lords Constitution Committee. By contrast, most aspects of the operation of counter-terrorism legislation, including even (allegedly) 'the most fruitful setting' of post-legislative reviews produced by government,[172] have been ignored. Unsurprisingly, the dynamics of review are often fluidly based on political advantage rather than systemic application.[173]

As regards policy or thematic issues, select committees can claim credit only for a handful of systemic reviews unrelated to legislative proposals.[174] None has produced major reforms, but some (especially on stop and search powers) have fed into pending legislative amendments. However, major aspects of counter-terrorism, ranging from the strategic setting of CONTEST to highly controversial measures such as sanctions listings, police arrest and interrogation powers, special offences and court procedures, and the regulation of chemical and biological materials, have largely escaped any attention.

---

[169] See J Oikarinen, 'Parliamentary Oversight of Counter-Terrorism Policies' in AMS de Frías et al (eds), *Counter-Terrorism: International Law and Practice* (Oxford, Oxford University Press, 2012) 939.

[170] Hansard (House of Commons) Standing Committee D, col 315 (8 February 2000), Charles Clarke.

[171] For a full list, see the bibliography to Walker (n 32).

[172] See A Lynch, 'The Impact of Post-Parliament Review on Anti-terrorism Laws' (2012) 18 *Journal of Legislative Studies* 63, 72.

[173] See J Owens, and R Pelizzo, 'Introduction: The Impact of the "War on Terror" on Executive–Legislative relations' (2009) 15 *Journal of Legislative Studies* 119; AW Neal, 'Terrorism, Law-Making and Democratic Politics' (2011) 23 *Terrorism & Political Violence* 557.

[174] See Home Affairs Committee, *Terrorism and Community Relations* (HC 2003–04, 165), *The Home Office's Response to Terror Attacks* (HC 2009–10, 117), *The Roots of Violent Radicalisation* (HC 2010–12, 1446) and *An Inquiry into Counter-terrorism* (HC 2013–14, 231). For the Joint Committee on Human Rights, see *Counter-Terrorism Policy and Human Rights (Seventeenth Report)* (n 94). See also House of Commons Transport Committee, *UK Transport Security* (HC 2005–06, 637); House of Lords Constitution Committee, *Counter-Terrorism Bill: The Role of Ministers, Parliament and the Judiciary* (HL 2007–08, 167).

While these select committees have been able to alert parliamentarians to alleged deficiencies in legislation, they have no power to block or amend Bills. Nonetheless, members of committees have later tabled amendments based on recommendations in committee reports and are often prominent speakers in debates. Furthermore, the Government is obliged by convention to respond to select committee reports (usually within two months).[175] Publication of critical reports can lead to the Government making further information available or adding to the political pressure to make concessions.

C. Analysis

Limited parliamentary accountability of counter-terrorism legislation is regrettable. Extraordinary powers should be subjected to extraordinary scrutiny. This final section will therefore first consider how parliamentary attention and performance could be improved with specific reference to counter-terrorism issues.[176]

First, given that the ongoing work of the Independent Reviewer of Terrorism Legislation might now be bolstered by a Privacy and Civil Liberties Board (under section 46 of the Counter Terrorism and Security Act 2015) and therefore the output from the office can be expected to increase and become even more prominent, the crucial axis to be considered is the relationship between this independent review and Parliament. It was mentioned previously that the Independent Reviewer is appointed neither by nor on behalf of Parliament. But this structural distance should not be allowed to become an impediment to accountability, nor should the absence of an annual renewal be allowed to dull the sensibilities of select committees to the need to monitor counter-terrorism legislation.[177] It would be pointless to strengthen independent scrutiny if its findings fall upon deaf ears. Thus, pronouncements from the Independent Reviewer (or the Board) should be referred not only to the Secretary of State but also to a select committee (the Joint Committee on Human Rights might be a good choice as it is able to feed into the discourses of both Houses, but equally a new Joint Committee could be established for this task);[178] the expectation would be that the select committee will find time to report on the findings and highlight issues to be taken forward for debate. The Secretary of State's attention could be further heightened by adopting

---

[175] Cabinet Office, *Departmental Evidence and Response to Select Committees* (London, TSO, 2005) para 108.

[176] Mechanisms of general application include the importance of pre-legislative scrutiny and statements of compliance under s 19 of the Human Rights Act 1998: Horne and Walker (n 158) 270–72.

[177] Just one review has been held on Terrorism Prevention and Investigation Measures since 2011: Joint Committee on Human Rights, *Post-Legislative Scrutiny: Terrorism Prevention and Investigation Measures Act 2011* (2013–14, HL 113, HC 1014).

[178] At one stage, the House of Commons Home Affairs Committee intended to consider reports from the Police Complaints Authority (HC 1987–88, 583) para 14.

the precedent of the Boundary Commission[179] or by requiring the Secretary of State to provide a statement of reasons for any disagreement from the proposals of the Independent Reviewer.

A second way in which parliamentary scrutiny might be strengthened would be by better structuring, through dividing the counter-terrorism code into different parts, each dependent upon specified standards of justification for their use. In this way, the parliamentary reviewers would be more aware of the tests to be met by the legislation under scrutiny.

At the same time, parliamentary scrutiny should not be viewed as the only available form of accountability or always the most suitable. In connection with counter-terrorism legislation, this chapter has already mentioned the crucial work of the Independent Reviewer of Terrorism Legislation, who enjoys crucial advantages over the parliamentary mechanisms such as greater access to data because of security clearance, greater accumulated expertise, and greater independence from party political influences and constraints. Conversely, as already discussed, there is the disadvantage of political disconnect from Parliament and so no one to 'champion' proposals for reform as against a potentially recalcitrant Home Office. The Independent Reviewer is also subject to limited resources, especially as the work involves not only the counter-terrorism legislation but also invitations to undertake reviews of allied issues such as deportation with assurances and the Data Retention and Investigatory Powers Act 2014.[180] The Counter-Terrorism and Security Act 2015 has made the position both better and worse. On the one hand, section 44 increases the workload by expanding the remit of the Independent Reviewer to cover legislation beyond the Terrorism Acts 2000 and 2006. On the other hand, a more flexible (and less comprehensive) review agenda is allowed under section 45. In this way, there is still an annual report, but no need to review every issue every year. In addition, the creation of a Privacy and Civil Liberties Board under section 46 is intended to support the work of the Independent Reviewer, who will act as chair of the Board. However, details as to how it will work, how many members will be appointed and when it will start are not yet settled; since this idea was thought to derive from Liberal Democrats in the former Coalition Government, the silence may be ominous.

Aside from independent reviewers, another form of accountability to loom large in the field of counter-terrorism law and policy has been the full-scale judicial inquiry.[181] Official commissions which involve taking lawyers outside the courtroom are nothing new, and counter-terrorism in Northern Ireland has been an especially fertile ground for judge-based inquiries, albeit by judges from beyond Northern Ireland. The trend was established early on in the history of the

---

[179] Parliamentary Constituencies Act 1986, s 4.
[180] See HC Deb 21 November 2013, col 60WS; Data Retention and Investigatory Powers Act 2014, s 7.
[181] We distinguish here judicial review in court which is considered in Horne and Walker (n 158) 287–88.

'Troubles' with the Cameron Report[182] and then the Scarman Report,[183] both of which were very wide-ranging inquiries into the origins of violence and responsibilities for it. Subsequent exercises have tended to be more specific and justice-related, but have proven to be no less controversial. These include, for example, Lord Widgery's original inquiry into Bloody Sunday[184] and the inquiries by Lord Parker and Judge Bennett into army and police interrogation practices.[185] Many have addressed the design of the emergency provisions themselves, ranging from the seminal Diplock Report[186] to a regular succession of inquires conducted by lawyers.[187] In recent years, the most prominent example has been the Bloody Sunday Inquiry.[188] Such inquiries have advantages and disadvantages compared to Parliament.[189] The august judicial head is imbued with expertise (especially in terms of forensic and interrogation skills), independence from politics and the ability to deliver well-reasoned reports. The problems include the expenditure and time taken, as well as the aloofness with which the reports are delivered. The judge is usually treated as a Moses-like figure who delivers the commandments, but without duties to enter into any debate or explanation about the crucial stage of implementation.

VI. CONCLUSION

The processing of recent counter-terrorism and state security issues meets most international guidelines,[190] but cannot be claimed to have produced frequent or

---

[182] *Disturbances in Northern Ireland. Report of the Commission Appointed by the Governor of Northern Ireland* (Cmd 532, 1969).

[183] *Government of Northern Ireland. Violence and Civil Disturbance in Northern Ireland in 1969. Report of a Tribunal of Inquiry* (Cmd 566, 1972).

[184] *Report of the Tribunal Appointed to Inquire into the Events on Sunday 30 January 1972 Which Led to Loss of Life in Connection with the Procession in Londonderry on that Day* (HC 1971–72, 220).

[185] *Report of the Committee of Privy Counsellors Appointed to Consider Authorised Procedures for the Interrogation of Persons Suspected of Terrorism* ('Parker Report') (Cmnd 4901, 1972); *Report of the Committee of Inquiry into Police Interrogation Procedures in Northern Ireland* ('Bennett Report') (Cmnd 9497, 1979).

[186] *Report of the Commission to Consider Legal Procedures to Deal with Terrorist Activities in Northern Ireland* (Cmnd 5185, 1972).

[187] See *Report of a Committee to Consider, in the Context of Civil Liberties and Human Rights, Measures to Deal with Terrorism in Northern Ireland* (Cmnd 5847, 1975); *Review of the Operation of the Northern Ireland (Emergency Provisions) Act 1978* (Cmnd 9222, 1984); *Review of the Operation of the Prevention of Terrorism (Temporary Provisions) Act 1984* (Cm 264, 1987); *Review of the Northern Ireland (Emergency Provisions) Acts 1978 and 1987* (Cm 1115, 1990).

[188] Lord Saville, *Report of the Bloody Sunday Inquiry* (HC 2010–12, 29). See also Lord MacLean, *Billy Wright Inquiry Report* (HC 2010–12, 431); Sir M Morland, *Rosemary Nelson Inquiry* (HC 2010–12, 947); Sir D de Silva, *Report of the Patrick Finucane Review* (HC 2012–13, 802).

[189] See C Walker, 'The Commodity of Justice in States of Emergency' (1999) 50 *Northern Ireland Legal Quarterly* 164.

[190] See Special Rapporteur on the promotion and protection of human rights and fundamental freedoms while countering terrorism (New York, A/HRC/14/46 and A/HRC/16/51 United Nations, 2010) paras 19–20.

substantive alterations to government stances. In this way, affirmation is more often given to 'process legitimacy' rather than to 'output legitimacy'.[191] Thus, the merit of parliamentary scrutiny of counter-terrorism has been questioned,[192] with at best 'carefully calibrated concessions'.[193] The key battleground seems to be around the outset of a law or policy: 'if review rarely translates into legislative amendment, then the battle over a law's content should be fought squarely at the point of creation'.[194] Nonetheless, subsequent reviews of legislation and policy can focus the minds of legislators, not least by making them incur higher political costs by having to defend unpalatable legislation in public which may sometimes germinate later changes.

Both the war powers convention and the supervision of the intelligence and security services demonstrate some similar challenges as the scrutiny of counter-terrorism legislation (in relation to the need for secrecy and the potential challenge of urgency). It is still early days for both the new convention and the reformed ISC, although some progress can be seen. In particular, the new public evidence sessions demonstrate a commitment to further openness. The events surrounding the Syria vote suggest that the Government ignores the disquiet of parliamentarians at its peril (and that the appeal that 'something must be done urgently' is not always conclusive). Perhaps both of these issues also demonstrate an increasing reluctance to take the Government at its word.

In broader terms, political constitutionalism, through the operation of Parliament accountability, has been shown to embody advantages and disadvantages. Amongst its advantages are that it can be proactive by shining a light on policy before it becomes politically entrenched. It can engage on a broad front with policy and pose questions which are formulated in broad or political terms, more so than inquiries or courts. It can connect interactively with civil society and the media, thereby performing 'a vital legitimating role'.[195] At the same time, the political setting inherently imposes limits, not least because of the systemic subordination of Parliament by the executive. This control is less strong in the House of Lords, which is one factor why it often shines more brightly in the debates about

---

[191] See F Scharpf, 'Economic Integration, Democracy and the Welfare State' (1997) 4 *Journal of European Public Policy* 18; B Rothstein, 'Creating Political Legitimacy: Electoral Democracy versus Quality of Government' (2009) 53 *American Behavioral Scientist* 311; R Bellamy, 'Democracy without Democracy? Can the EU's Democratic "Outputs" Be Separated from the Democratic "Inputs" Provided by Competitive Parties and Majority Rule?' (2010) 17 *Journal of European Public Policy* 2.

[192] See P Hillyard, 'The Normalisation of Special Powers' in P Scraton (ed), *Law, Order and the Authoritarian State* (Milton Keynes, Open University Press, 1987) 307.

[193] Shephard (n 152) 194. See also F de Londras and F Davis 'Controlling the Executive in Times of Terrorism: Competing Perspectives on Effective Oversight Mechanisms' (2010) 30 *Oxford Journal of Legal Studies* 19, 31.

[194] A Lynch, 'The Impact of Post-enactment Review on Anti-terrorism Laws: Four Jurisdictions Compared' (2012) 18 *Journal of Legislative Studies* 63, 64.

[195] A Neal, 'Terrorism, Lawmaking, and Democratic Politics' (2012) 24 *Terrorism & Political Violence* 357, 362.

counter-terrorism.[196] Furthermore, parliamentary procedures produce markedly uneven performances that are very much affected by circumstances (especially the circumstances of crisis), personalities, timing and time pressures.[197] Political constitutionalism cannot always be counted upon to deliver principled or progressive results, but this chapter has indicated that there are some techniques by which the best possible outcomes can be secured.

---

[196] L Lustgarten, 'National Security, Terrorism and Constitutional Balance' (2004) 25 *Political Quarterly* 4, 8. Other factors may include expertise and a growing sense of legitimacy following reforms: see Shephard (n 152) 195.

[197] Owens and Pelizzo (n 173).

11

Parliament and International Treaties

ARABELLA LANG

I. OVERVIEW

> In constitutional terms, it is a major change, giving Parliament powers it has never had before, but it could be meaningless if you then do not have the mechanism to give effect to that change. (Lord Norton of Louth, 1 July 2008)[1]

AT FIRST SIGHT, Parliament's new statutory role in ratifying international treaties looks muscular: since 2010, the House of Commons has been able to delay indefinitely the Government's ratifying of a treaty. But this power has not yet been used, raising questions of how effective Parliament is at holding the Government's treaty-making to account, and what could improve this.

How is Parliament involved with treaties in practice? It sometimes legislates to bring domestic law into line with proposed treaty obligations and it is notified of all treaties that the Government wants to ratify. The Government's commitment (originally in the informal 'Ponsonby Rule') to lay treaties before Parliament has evolved to include Explanatory Memorandums (EMs) and committee involvement. The Constitutional Reform and Governance Act 2010 (CRAGA 2010) enshrined some of the existing practice and also gave Parliament new powers to delay ratification of treaties. But there are exceptions to these rules, and some types of treaty have their own rules (for instance, some EU treaties require an Act of Parliament or even a referendum).

Has the CRAGA 2010 made much difference? Neither House has yet passed a motion objecting to ratification of a treaty, there are still few debates on treaties (other than EU treaties) in either House, let alone votes or objections, and the Government's duties under the Act might not even be justiciable. But perhaps most importantly, the CRAGA 2010 does nothing new to help Parliament actually scrutinise treaties effectively.

Should there be more reform? Views on this depend on how one balances the Government's freedom to act on foreign relations with Parliament's democratic interest in new obligations and policy. In relation to EU treaties, the pendulum has

---

[1] Joint Committee on the Draft Constitutional Renewal Bill, *Draft Constitutional Renewal Bill* (2007–08, HL 166-II, HC 551-II) Q 751.

swung more towards Parliament than it has for other treaties. There is certainly scope for more debate on other international treaties, whether in government or other time in Parliament, or in public consultations. The Government could be more generous in extending the 21-sitting-day period for which treaties are laid before Parliament. Memorandums of Understanding (MOUs), which are sometimes at least as important as treaties, could have some kind of formal parliamentary scrutiny. And Parliament could be helped by a sifting or scrutiny mechanism for treaties, whether through existing committees or a new treaty committee or sub-committee, or simply a new specialist treaty secretariat. There could even be a formal or informal procedure for involving Parliament when treaties are being negotiated.

This chapter looks at these three questions in turn, using examples from France, Germany, the US, South Africa and Australia to take a comparative approach. It concludes that if there is a desire to give effect to Parliament's new treaty role, a new specialist sifting and scrutiny process is needed to help parliamentarians identify treaties with major implications that need a debate. Parliament is unlikely to gain a formal role in the negotiation of treaties, but a commitment to public consultation on important treaties during their drafting would allow it to be involved if it chose. These measures would go some way towards creating genuine accountability over treaties.

II. HOW IS PARLIAMENT INVOLVED?

A. Treaty-Making is Primarily for the Government

The UK Government signs and ratifies international treaties—currently around 30–40 a year—under the royal prerogative.[2] In 2014, for example, it ratified treaties committing the UK to a new international legal and regulatory framework for the arms trade,[3] allowing the transfer from the US to the UK of submarine nuclear propulsion plants and/or parts and information,[4] and enhancing compensation for sea passengers[5] among others.

The Government's dominant role in making and ratifying treaties reflects the UK's position as a 'dualist' state. In its purest form, this approach means that treaties are seen as creating rights and duties only for the Government under

---

[2] Signing a treaty shows that the Government agrees not to frustrate the object and purpose of the treaty. Ratifying is the main way of binding the Government under international law.

[3] Arms Trade Treaty (adopted 2 April 2013, entered into force 24 December 2014) 52 ILM 988.

[4] Amendment to the Agreement between the Government of the United Kingdom of Great Britain and Northern Ireland and the Government of the United States of America for Cooperation on the Uses of Atomic Energy for Mutual Defense Purposes (adopted 22 July 2014, entered into force 17 December 2014) UKTS 2015 2.

[5] Protocol of 2002 to the Athens Convention relating to the Carriage of Passengers and their Luggage by Sea, 1974 (adopted 1 November 2002, entered into force 23 April 2014) IMO.

international law, rather than automatically becoming a source of domestic law that can be relied on in national courts. Ratifying a treaty therefore does not amount to legislating. Instead, Parliament needs to legislate for treaty provisions to have direct domestic legal effect, and it could in theory pass legislation that conflicts with international treaties. Treaty provisions that are not incorporated into domestic law can, still, have indirect effect: for example, where legislation is capable of two interpretations, one consistent with a treaty obligation and one inconsistent, then the courts will presume that Parliament intended to legislate in conformity with the treaty and not in conflict with it.[6]

This is in contrast to 'monist' countries such as the Netherlands, where the act of ratifying an international treaty immediately incorporates it into national law without the need for any domestic legislation. International law *is* domestic law—indeed, may take precedence over it—and treaties can therefore be enforced by the national courts as soon as they are ratified. This approach usually involves the legislature in the ratification of treaties, as they are another form of domestic law. In some monist countries, direct incorporation applies to all international treaty obligations. Others, such as the US, make a distinction between self-executing treaties (which can be enforced directly by the courts) and non-self-executing treaties (which require implementing legislation).

Outline of Treaty-Making in the UK

— The Government negotiates a treaty, which is often a lengthy process involving a series of inter-governmental meetings.
— The Government signs the finalised treaty.
— Parliament makes any necessary domestic legislative changes.
— The Government lays the signed treaty and an EM before Parliament for 21 sitting days.
— If either House objects, the Government must give reasons why it nevertheless wants to ratify.
— If the House of Commons objects, it has another 21 days to consider the Government's reasons for ratifying, and can object again. This can continue indefinitely, effectively giving the Commons the power to block ratification.
— The House of Lords has only one opportunity to object, and so can only delay ratification briefly.
— If there is no outstanding objection from the Commons, the Government can ratify the treaty.
— The treaty enters into force for the UK, usually once a minimum number of states have ratified it.

---

[6] Lord Bingham of Cornhill, in his maiden speech in the House of Lords, set out this and five further ways in which treaties can have indirect effect in the UK: HL Deb 3 July 1996, vol 573, cols 1465 ff.

But although treaty-making in the UK is primarily the Government's job, Parliament now has a greater say than before. There are several ways it can be involved, including (since 2010) a new power to delay indefinitely the ratifying of treaties.

B. Parliament Sometimes Legislates on Treaties

Where UK law does not conform to a treaty that the Government wants to ratify, Parliament can legislate to bring domestic law into line with the Government's proposed treaty obligations.

The UK's policy is to ensure that domestic law is in line with a treaty before ratifying it, so that the Government is not breaching its new international obligations. When asked to approve such legislation, Parliament therefore looks at how the UK would implement (at least parts of) the treaty, rather than whether the UK should ratify it. Treaties increasingly impose positive obligations on states, which can create room for debate in Parliament—and sometimes the devolved assemblies—about exactly what legislative change is needed to give effect to a new obligation. For example, the Joint Committee on Human Rights (JCHR) looked at whether Parliament should create a new criminal offence of coercive behaviour in order to allow the Government to ratify the Council of Europe Convention on preventing and combating violence against women and domestic violence (the Istanbul Convention).[7]

However, many treaties—even those with major policy implications—require only minor adjustments to domestic law, or none at all: for example, the 2013 Arms Trade Treaty needed only adjustments to secondary legislation. This could leave Parliament's legislating and debating role on the sidelines.

C. Parliament Oversees Treaty Ratification

It is usually accepted nowadays that Parliament has a legitimate interest in treaties, whether or not legislation is needed. Even before the CRAGA 2010 gave it new powers, Parliament debated treaties in several different circumstances and, under the informal 'Ponsonby Rule', the Government alerted Parliament to treaties that it wanted to ratify. But Parliament had no formal role in the ratification of treaties and little power to overcome the will of the executive to ratify a particular treaty unless it required a change in UK legislation or the grant of public money. Parliament could only express disapproval and rely on political pressure to change the mind of ministers or, in extreme cases, withdraw its confidence from them.

---

[7] Joint Committee on Human Rights, *Violence against Women and Girls* (2014–15, HL 106, HC 594) paras 130–40.

i. The Original Ponsonby Rule

The informal 'Ponsonby Rule', under which the Government committed itself to laying any treaty subject to ratification before Parliament so that it could debate it before ratification, took its name from a 1920s Foreign Affairs Minister, Arthur Ponsonby. He gave this three-part undertaking in 1924 during the Commons Second Reading Debate on the Treaty of Peace (Turkey) Bill:

1. Every signed treaty would be laid before both Houses of Parliament for 21 sitting days before ratification and publication.
2. These treaties would be debated in two circumstances:
   (a) the Government would submit 'important' treaties to the House of Commons for discussion within the 21 days;
   (b) for any other treaties, time would be found for debate if there was a formal demand from any party forwarded through the 'usual channels'.
3. The Government would inform the House of Commons of all other 'agreements, commitments and understandings which may in any way bind the nation to specific action in certain circumstances' and which may involve 'international obligations of a serious character, although no signed and sealed document may exist'.[8]

ii. Evolution of the Ponsonby Rule

The Ponsonby Rule gradually crystallised into a constitutional practice, observed in principle by all governments, except in special cases such as emergencies. It evolved to increase the opportunities for scrutiny of treaties, particularly by disseminating more and better information. For example, each treaty subject to ratification (or accession, approval or acceptance)[9] is now published as a Command Paper in one of three series by the Foreign and Commonwealth Office (FCO): the Country Series (for bilateral treaties), the European Communities Series (for treaties between Member States of the European Union (EU)) and the Miscellaneous Series (for multilateral treaties). After they enter into force, all treaties binding the UK are published in a fourth series, the Treaty Series, even if they had previously been published in one of the other series.

Since January 1997—following a Bill tabled by Lord Lester of Herne Hill[10]—the Government has published an EM for every treaty laid before Parliament in order to provide information about the contents of the treaty, the Government's view of its benefits and burdens, and its rationale for ratification. The EMs are drafted by the government department which has the main policy interest in the

---

[8] HC Deb 1 April 1924, vol 171, cols 2000–05.

[9] Accession arises when the Government did not sign a treaty when it was open for signature, but subsequently wants to become a party to it. Approval and acceptance are like ratification, signalling that a state wants to be bound by a treaty; sometimes a state will sign a treaty subject to approval or acceptance respectively in order to give it time to review a treaty after signature without invoking the constitutional procedures which might be required for ratification.

[10] Treaties (Parliamentary Approval) HL Bill 1996. See HL Deb 28 February 1996, vol 569, col 1561.

particular treaty, but are cleared through the relevant legal adviser at the FCO. EMs are also published on the FCO website and so place on public record the name of the minister with primary responsibility for a treaty, its financial implications, the means required to implement it and the outcome of any discussions which have taken place within and outside government. They also describe any UK reservations or declarations.[11]

The Government has undertaken since 2000 to 'normally' accept calls from the relevant departmental select committee (supported by the Liaison Committee) for a debate on treaties with major political, military or diplomatic implications.[12] There have not yet been any such calls, as far as the author is aware.[13]

iii. Committees are Alerted to Treaties in their Area

Parliamentary committees are involved when the Government wants to ratify a treaty in their area. Since November 2000, the FCO has sent a copy of each treaty laid before Parliament to whichever it considers the relevant departmental select committee and/or the JCHR.[14] The committee can decide whether or not to scrutinise the treaty and publish a report, or it can pass the treaty on to another appropriate committee or committees. The Government must respond to any recommendations in select committee reports, but it can choose to reject the recommendations. A report on a treaty would have to be published well before the 21-sitting-day period was over if it was to have any impact, including informing a debate on the treaty.

It is also 'common practice' for ministers to communicate with the relevant select committee prior to signature of a treaty.[15]

But in practice select committee involvement is patchy. The impetus to scrutinise must come from the members themselves, who set their own agenda, so treaties compete with the committee's other priorities and demands on its time. Only the JCHR has shown any real enthusiasm, scrutinising all treaties with a human rights aspect and often reporting on them to Parliament. For instance, it has reported before ratification on human rights treaties, including the Istanbul Convention two protocols reforming the European Court of Human Rights (ECtHR), and the Convention on the Rights of Persons with Disabilities, and on other treaties with human rights implications, including the Council of Europe Convention on the Prevention of Terrorism. The JCHR's report on the Disability Convention was

---

[11] J Harrington, 'Scrutiny and Approval: The Role for Westminster-Style Parliaments in Treaty-Making' (2006) 55 *International and Comparative Law Quarterly* 121, 131–32.
[12] House of Commons Procedure Committee, *Government Response to the Committee: Parliamentary Scrutiny of Treaties* (HC 1999–2000, 990).
[13] See, eg, Ministry of Justice, *The Governance of Britain—War Powers and Treaties: Limiting Executive Powers* (Cm 7239, 2007) para 138.
[14] ibid para 134.
[15] HL Deb 31 January 2008, col 796.

debated in the House of Lords on 28 April 2009, but the Government refused to hold debates in Government time on ECtHR reform despite the JCHR's request.[16]

iv. New Powers in the CRAGA 2010

In 2010, following years of proposals in private members' Bills, a royal commission report, select committee reports, a consultation exercise and a draft Bill, whose proposals on treaties generally met with cross-party support,[17] the CRAGA 2010 gave Parliament new statutory powers on treaties.

Part 2 of the CRAGA 2010 enshrines in legislation the first part of the Ponsonby Rule, committing the Government to laying treaties before Parliament for 21 sitting days before ratification. It also requires the Government to publish EMs for the treaties it lays and allows the 21-sitting-day period to be extended.

These measures simply enshrine the existing practice. But, in a constitutionally bold move, the CRAGA 2010 also gave Parliament a new power to delay ratification of a treaty—indefinitely, in the case of continued objections from the House of Commons. (The Ponsonby Rule had not said what would happen if either House resolved that a treaty should not be ratified.)

However, even when there is a debate and/or a vote, Parliament cannot amend treaties; it can only object to or (either overtly or tacitly) approve whole treaties. This is because it is formally involved only once treaties are signed. Any revision at that stage would require the Government to re-open negotiations with all the other parties to the treaty.

Moreover, the CRAGA 2010 does not cover the second or third limbs of the Ponsonby Rule: it says nothing about making time for parliamentary debates on treaties or informing Parliament about non-treaty agreements. Nor does it say anything about the scrutiny of treaties. Both scheduling debates and setting up new institutional mechanisms for scrutinising treaties were felt to be matters for Parliament to decide internally rather than for legislation.

v. Exceptions and Specific Cases

There are some exceptions to the general rules on parliamentary involvement with treaties, and some types of treaty are specifically excluded.

First, in 'exceptional cases', the Government can ratify treaties without laying them before Parliament for scrutiny, as long as it then publishes the treaty and its reasons for not following the scrutiny rules.[18] There is no indication in the

---

[16] Joint Committee on Human Rights, *Protocol 15 to the European Convention on Human Rights* (2014–15, HL 71, HC 837) para 1.4.
[17] See A Thorp, 'Parliamentary Scrutiny of Treaties: Up to 2010' (House of Commons Library Standard Note SN/IA/4693, 25 September 2009).
[18] CRAGA 2010, s 22.

CRAGA 2010 of what might constitute an exceptional case. Emergencies are likely to be the main examples, but the Government is free to designate anything an exceptional case.

Second, not all treaties are subject to ratification in the international sense, and not all international commitments take the form of a treaty. The UK has, for example, signed many MOUs, which include obligations, but which are not 'binding under international law'.[19] The third limb of the Ponsonby Rule (the commitment to inform the House of Commons of all other binding agreements which involve serious international obligations) has had much less attention.

Third, some specific types of treaties are excluded from the provisions of the CRAGA 2010 on parliamentary oversight—sometimes because their own rules are more extensive:[20]

— EU treaties: those increasing the European Parliament's powers[21] or amending the founding treaties[22] now require an Act of Parliament before ratification, and some also call for a referendum.[23] There is clearly a sense that these treaties are 'important' and therefore need a further level of approval. Treaties concluded by the EU with third parties may be examined by the House of Commons European Scrutiny Committee and may be debated in one of the European Committees or even on the Floor of the House, and also by the House of Lords EU Select Committee or one of its sub-committees.
— Tax treaties: treaties with direct financial implications, which are most commonly bilateral agreements to avoid double taxation, require the assent of Parliament as they affect revenue.
— Treaties concluded by overseas territories, the Channel Islands and the Isle of Man: these governments have the power to conclude treaties only where expressly authorised by the UK Government. Otherwise, the UK may decide to extend the application of a treaty to one or more of them, and would usually consult with the Government concerned.

Fourth, there is no legal requirement to consult the devolved executives or legislatures on treaties, although the UK Government undertakes to cooperate with them on negotiating and implementing treaties. Under devolution arrangements, international relations including treaty-making remain the exclusive responsibility of the UK Government. But it is recognised that the devolved administrations in Northern Ireland, Scotland and Wales need to be involved where a treaty might have implications for devolved areas of responsibility.

Rules governing the cooperation between Whitehall and the devolved administrations are set out in a Concordat on International Relations, which is one of

---

[19] ibid s 25(1).
[20] ibid s 23.
[21] European Parliamentary Elections Act 1978.
[22] European Union (Amendment) Act 2008.
[23] European Union Act 2011.

five concordats supporting an MOU.[24] This is explicitly intended to be binding in honour only rather than in law, but promises cooperation on exchanging information, formulating UK foreign policy, negotiating treaties and implementing treaty obligations. It also provides for ministers and officials from the devolved administrations to form part of UK treaty-negotiating teams and for apportioning any quantitative treaty obligations, as well as imposing penalties should the devolved bodies default on any agreed liability. A recent example is Protocol 15 to the European Convention on Human Rights, on which the UK Government consulted all three devolved administrations before ratifying.[25] Nevertheless, as Joanna Harrington has pointed out: 'It is both implicit and explicit in the nature of the devolved arrangements that Westminster retains the ability to override the actions of any devolved body and it could do so to ensure the State's compliance with its international commitments.'[26]

The Scottish Parliament has a Committee on European and External Relations to monitor developments (though most of its work involves EU scrutiny). Scotland has even acted before Westminster in enacting legislation relating to a treaty: when ratifying the 2000 Hague Convention on the International Protection of Adults, the UK Government made a formal declaration that the convention applied to Scotland alone until implementing legislation was passed for the rest of the UK.

D. Public Consultation

Parliament is not the only forum for scrutinising the Government's treaty intentions. Sometimes the Government organises a public consultation exercise on a treaty before ratification. This can help inform Parliament's legislating or scrutiny roles.

The first example was the public discussion of a draft International Criminal Court Bill in 2000, which led to the International Criminal Court Act 2001 and the ratification of the 1998 Rome Statute of the International Criminal Court. Following the consultation, the Government changed the extradition provisions of the Bill to remove the requirement of dual criminality when a third country seeks extradition over a Rome Statute crime.[27]

---

[24] *Memorandum of Understanding and Supplementary Agreements between the United Kingdom Government, Scottish Ministers and the Cabinet of the National Assembly for Wales* (Cm 4444, 1999), subsequently replaced by *Memorandum of Understanding and Supplementary Agreements between the United Kingdom Government, Scottish Ministers, the Cabinet of the National Assembly for Wales and the Northern Ireland Executive Committee* (Cm 4806, 2000).
[25] Ministry of Justice, *Explanatory Memorandum on Protocol No 15 Amending the Convention on the Protection of Human Rights and Fundamental Freedoms* (Cm 8951, 2014).
[26] Harrington (n 11) 150.
[27] Foreign and Commonwealth Office, *International Criminal Court Bill: Report on the Responses to the Draft Legislation* (Dep 01/165, January 2001) 9. See P Bowers, *The International Criminal Court Bill [HL]* (House of Commons Library Research Paper 01/39, 28 March 2001) 60.

The Government has also consulted during negotiations of a treaty (although this is rare). For example, between April and September 2002, the UK carried out a public consultation on the position to be adopted during negotiations on amending the 1972 Biological and Toxin Weapons Convention. The consultation document expressly sought views from MPs, non-governmental organisations (NGOs) and other organisations and individuals with an interest in the subject.[28]

III. HAS THE CRAGA 2010 MADE MUCH DIFFERENCE?

Whilst the CRAGA 2010 codifies existing procedures for informing Parliament about treaties the Government wants to ratify and gives Parliament its new delaying power, it is hard to see how much difference it has made in practice.

The Public Administration Committee considered the new provisions to be a very weak form of parliamentary safeguard which the Government could in any case short-circuit by declaring a need for urgency, by failing to make time for a debate or by repeatedly asking the House of Commons to reconsider a negative decision.[29] Neither House has yet passed a motion objecting to ratification of a treaty (although the potency of that provision may lie in its existence as much as in its use). And there are still few parliamentary debates on treaties, let alone votes.

There is even a question mark over whether the Government's limited duties to Parliament under the new provisions could actually be enforced.[30] The House of Lords has in the past suggested that prerogative powers 'such as those relating to the making of treaties' are not susceptible to judicial review,[31] and there is no provision in the Act for taking judicial review against the Government for breaching its requirements on treaties. However, following the case of *R (Wheeler) v Office of the Prime Minister*,[32] Jill Barrett argues that a decision to ratify a treaty without statutory approval could in some circumstances be challenged through judicial review:

> The position would therefore seem to be that an alleged breach of Part 2 of the [Constitutional Reform and Governance] Act could, in principle, be justiciable, but courts are likely still to be reluctant to interfere with the exercise of the power when the issue involves policy concerning foreign relations. Much will depend on the particularities of the alleged breach.[33]

---

[28] Foreign and Commonwealth Office, *Strengthening the Biological and Toxin Weapons Convention: Countering the Threat from Biological Weapons* (Cm 5484, 2002).
[29] Public Administration Select Committee, *Constitutional Renewal: Draft Bill and White Paper* (HC 2007–08 499) paras 81–89.
[30] See Joint Committee on the Draft Constitutional Renewal Bill (n 1) 29 (Professor Adam Tomkins).
[31] *Council of Civil Service Unions v Minister for the Civil Service* [1985] AC 374, 418 (Lord Roskill).
[32] *R (Wheeler) v Office of the Prime Minister* [2008] EWHC 936 (Admin).
[33] J Barrett, 'The United Kingdom and Parliamentary Scrutiny of Treaties: Recent Reforms' (2011) 60 *International and Comparative Law Quarterly* 225.

Perhaps most importantly, the CRAGA 2010 does nothing new to help Parliament actually scrutinise treaties effectively. In other words, there is nothing to ensure that Parliament looks at treaties in a systematic way, decides which are significant or controversial and presents its democratic opinions on them to the Government at a point where that could make a difference. This is perhaps surprising given that the aim of the *Governance of Britain* proposals was 'to hold power more accountable'.[34]

Several witnesses to the Joint Committee on the draft Constitutional Renewal Bill in 2008 considered that the Government was focusing on the wrong issue and instead should look at ways of improving parliamentary scrutiny of treaties.[35] Elizabeth Wilmshurst of Chatham House (formerly legal adviser to the FCO) argued that the 'real problem about treaties … is that Parliament does not actually scrutinise them, and the provisions in the Bill do not do anything about that'. She saw the problem as getting Parliament interested in significant treaties, which the Bill does not try to do.[36] Sir Franklin Berman, another former legal adviser to the FCO, suggested that:

> [I]t would be by far more productive for both Parliament and the Executive, in place of the Government's present proposals, to undertake a more thorough and wider-ranging study into the linked questions of the treaty-making process as such and the incorporation of treaty rights and obligations into United Kingdom law.[37]

Sir Franklin considered that such a study might lead to a fresh view of the balance of responsibilities between the Government and Parliament in the treaty-making process, and to a new understanding of the relationship between treaties and domestic law in the UK.

Despite the Joint Committee on the draft Bill saying that its role was to be more assertive on behalf of Parliament,[38] it made few recommendations in this area to substantially increase Parliament's role in the scrutiny of treaties. The one amendment that was made to this part of the Bill was to include a statutory obligation to publish EMs—a proposal earlier made by the Joint Committee on Human Rights.[39]

One practical issue is that parliamentarians might not realise that an important treaty has been laid. They might spot one in the Lords or Commons order papers or on the page on the Parliament website that lists all the treaties that are currently laid before Parliament.[40] Or if they sit on a select committee, they might

---

[34] Gordon Brown, in his first speech to the House of Commons as Prime Minister, HC Deb 3 July 2007, col 815.
[35] Joint Committee on the Draft Constitutional Renewal Bill, *Draft Constitutional Renewal Bill* (2008–09, HL 166 HC 551) para 207.
[36] Joint Committee on the Draft Constitutional Renewal Bill (n 1) 32.
[37] ibid 340.
[38] ibid 22.
[39] See Barrett (n 33) 241–42.
[40] The website www.publications.parliament.uk/pa/cm/cmsilist/section-b.htm includes the number of sitting days remaining for an objection to be made.

be aware that the Government has notified the committee of a treaty it considers to be in the relevant subject area. Alternatively, their own sources, lobbying or the press might notify them of treaties in which they may be interested. But it is easy to imagine that a treaty could complete its 21 sitting days laid before Parliament without being noticed, or at least without its significance being realised.

IV. MORE REFORM?

A. Should Parliament be more Involved in Treaties?

Views on how Parliament should hold the Government to account over new treaty obligations depend on where one stands on the line between giving the Government complete freedom to act on foreign relations, at one end, and, at the other, requiring Parliament's consent to new obligations under international law as a matter of democratic legitimacy.

At the 'government' extreme, one might regret the erosion of the royal prerogative, even given the relatively light touch of parliamentary scrutiny under the CRAGA 2010 and the Government's ability to set aside the new procedures in exceptional cases. In this view, the Government needs to have maximum freedom of action in foreign relations, and is sufficiently accountable to Parliament through its ministers, and to the public through the ballot box. Moreover, where a treaty requires implementing legislation to have domestic effect, Parliament remains the law-maker and debates the most controversial treaties. An elaborate scrutiny mechanism or pre-signature involvement would be too cumbersome, particularly given that most treaties are non-controversial.

At the 'Parliament' extreme, one might welcome the Commons' new power to delay ratification indefinitely, but hold out for further reforms, for instance, on debating treaties or on committee involvement. From this viewpoint, because the volume and scope of treaty-making has grown and now covers a wide range of subjects, often with clear implications for domestic law and policy, the current degree of parliamentary oversight of treaties amounts to a 'democratic deficit'; even the Commons' new power to delay ratification indefinitely is a paper tiger. More treaties should benefit from the level of parliamentary scrutiny already given to some EU treaties. And for Parliament's powers to be effective, more resources, time and mechanisms are needed to help Members fully understand the implications of treaties. Greater parliamentary scrutiny would also result in more information about treaties entering the public domain. Furthermore, where devolved subjects are concerned, devolved governments and legislatures should be more involved in oversight. And for real accountability, Parliament should be able to scrutinise the position taken by the Government in intergovernmental negotiations on a treaty and propose amendments before signature, instead of being presented with a fait accompli which it can only accept or reject in full.

There is plenty of international precedent for giving Parliament a greater role in ratifying treaties (although perhaps paradoxically it is the monist countries—in which treaties automatically have the force of law—which tend to have given their parliaments a greater say in treaty ratification; dualist countries, whose parliaments already need to be involved when legislation is required to give effect to treaty obligations, have not tended to give their legislatures a wider role on treaties). For example:

— France lists in its 1958 Constitution the categories of treaty which can be ratified or approved only with an Act of Parliament: peace treaties, trade agreements, treaties or agreements relating to international organisation, those committing the finances of the state, those modifying provisions which are the preserve of statute law, those relating to the status of persons and those involving the ceding, exchanging or acquiring of territory.[41]
— Germany's basic law states that 'Treaties that regulate the political relations of the Federation or relate to subjects of federal legislation' require federal legislation.[42] In practice, this includes military alliances, treaties of guarantee, treaties on political cooperation, peace treaties, non-aggression pacts and treaties dealing with questions such as disarmament, neutrality and the peaceful settlement of disputes. The vast majority of important international agreements fall within this category.[43] But the executive has considerable discretion over when to submit an international agreement to the Bundestag.
— The South African Constitution takes a slightly different approach, requiring a resolution of both Houses of Parliament for all international agreements, except those of a 'technical, administrative or executive nature' and those which do not require either ratification or accession. The two excepted categories must simply be tabled in Parliament 'in a reasonable time'.[44] Various parliamentary committees in both Houses are involved, and can propose declarations and reservations to treaties.
— In the US, all treaties require the Senate's approval by a two-thirds vote; the Committee on Foreign Relations can propose amendments to a treaty or reject it (or, more often, stall it). Whilst the Senate rarely rejects treaties, many have died in committee or been withdrawn by the President rather than face defeat. The difficulty in obtaining a two-thirds vote has been a cause of the vast increase in the number of international agreements classified in the US as 'executive agreements', which are not subject to Senate approval.
— Australia's all-party Joint Standing Committee on Treaties can inquire into treaties even during the negotiation stage and recommend against ratification, but this does not bind the Government.

---

[41] Constitution of 4 October 1958, art 53.
[42] Basic Law for the Federal Republic of Germany as at November 2012, art 59(1).
[43] J Abr Frowein and M Hahn, 'The Participation of Parliament in the Treaty Process in the Federal Republic of Germany' (1991) 67 *Chicago-Kent Law Review* 2, 367.
[44] Constitution of the Republic of South Africa 1996 (as amended), art 231.

In considering proposals for reform, it is important to think about the purpose of any increased parliamentary involvement: would it be to ensure regularity/constitutionality or to provide legislative/quasi-legislative approval of treaties as a precondition for the UK's assent? Should Parliament be sharing policy-making with the executive (which would really require it to be involved in treaty-negotiation) or simply be given a take-it-or-leave-it power once the treaty had been agreed? If a new committee were created, should it just be a sifting committee or should it have substantive powers to conduct inquiries and make recommendations?

B. More Debates and Votes?

One of the main criticisms of the current provisions is that there are no requirements for a debate or vote on treaties—this is left to 'the usual channels' (ie, the behind-the-scenes arrangements and compromises between the party whips and the leaderships of the Government and opposition parties concerning the running of parliamentary business) and for 'people to make a noise'.[45]

The Government can largely choose whether or not to make time for a debate on a contentious treaty, as it is in charge of most of the parliamentary timetable. Under the Ponsonby Rule, it undertook to submit 'important' treaties to the House of Commons for discussion within the 21 days when they are laid before Parliament. It has also undertaken since 2000 to provide the opportunity for debate of any treaty involving major political, military or diplomatic issues, if the relevant select committee and the Liaison Committee so request.[46] This has not yet happened: certainly, by 2007, the Government had not received any requests for a debate under this procedure,[47] and the author is not aware of any such debates since then.

Otherwise, parliamentarians can use the usual mechanisms for trying to secure a debate, such as (in the Commons) adjournment debates, Westminster Hall debates, topical questions, 10-minute rule Bills, Early Day Motions or the Backbench Business Committee. But none of these results in binding action. Even the Backbench Business Committee controls only a certain amount of time (decided by the Government for any given week), so there is no guarantee of a slot for debating a treaty during the 21 sitting days allowed for objecting to ratification, even if the Committee decides that a debate on a treaty would meet its criteria.[48] Time is of the essence and if a select committee has used some of the 21 days for an inquiry and report, there will be little if any left for a debate.

---

[45] Joint Committee on the Draft Constitutional Renewal Bill (n 1) 331 (Jack Straw, then Lord Chancellor).
[46] House of Commons Procedure Committee (n 12).
[47] Ministry of Justice (n 13) para 138.
[48] See 'How the Backbench Business Committee Works', www.parliament.uk/business/committees/committees-a-z/commons-select/backbench-business-committee/how-the-backbench-business-committee-works.

An example of a treaty debate arranged through the Backbench Business Committee was the over-subscribed one on 'the biggest bilateral trade agreement in the history of the world'—the EU–US trade and investment agreement, or TTIP,—on 18 July 2013.[49] The debate (which was on the floor of the House) came just after the two Governments had begun formal negotiations on the treaty. It aired some information that had not previously come to light, and the European Scrutiny Committee and the House of Lords EU Committee then continued their investigations into negotiating the agreement.

On the other hand, the Westminster Hall debate on the 2014 revision and renewal of the US–UK Mutual Defence Agreement (also in Backbench Business Committee time) was poorly attended.[50] The revised terms of the Agreement extended the existing design cooperation to the nuclear reactors powering the UK's new Trident submarines, leading some to question whether the UK remained sufficiently independent of the US.[51] The debate was secured by the unlikely pairing of Jeremy Corbyn (then a backbench Labour MP) who opposes nuclear weapons and Dr Julian Lewis (a backbench Conservative MP who supports the UK's nuclear deterrent). Despite their opposing views on the substance, the two Members were united in their desire for more debate and were disappointed by the 'struggle' to get more Members to participate.[52] An Early Day Motion that called for the amended Agreement not to be ratified was signed by 57 MPs,[53] but no motion materialised, and there was no debate or vote on the floor of the House, so the Government ratified it.

At one stage, it had seemed as if the 'affirmative resolution' procedure might be introduced for at least some treaties (as in several other countries), meaning that the Government could not ratify until it had a resolution from both Houses.[54] This stronger procedure tends to produce more debates and votes, and debates over which treaties should require active parliamentary approval could in themselves have done an important job of raising awareness. But the procedure did not make it into the CRAGA 2010, so the Government can proceed with ratification unless Parliament is stirred to object.

There have been calls for a formal requirement for a debate or vote if requested by a committee or a well-supported Early Day Motion.[55] Jack Straw (who was then Lord Chancellor and Minister for Justice) also suggested that an appropriate

---

[49] HC Deb 18 July 2013, cols 1342 ff.
[50] HC Deb 6 November 2014, cols 291WH ff.
[51] J Doward, 'Trident Treaty May Be Renewed without Parliamentary Scrutiny' *The Observer* (25 October 2014).
[52] Dr Julian Lewis MP, HC Deb 6 November 2014, col 300WH.
[53] EDM 459 2014–15, tabled 3 November 2014.
[54] Jack Straw introducing the draft Constitutional Renewal Bill, HC Deb 25 March 2008, vol 474, col 32. See also the report of David Cameron's Conservative Democracy Task Force, *Power to the People: Rebuilding Parliament* (6 June 2007) 8, proposing the affirmative resolution procedure for 'significant' treaties.
[55] Joint Committee on the Draft Constitutional Renewal Bill (n 35) para 237.

mechanism might be to make provision in the Standing Orders of each House that if a certain number of Members said they wanted a debate and vote, then this would have to happen.[56] He noted that the Government tends to resist fettering the discretion of the business managers.[57]

Even without increased parliamentary debate, there are precedents and scope for consulting the public more widely on treaties. Building upon this, it may be possible to encourage wider discussion of treaty and international issues in the future.

C. Extending the 21-Sitting-Day Period?

The 21-sitting-day period could be very short for parliamentarians to find out enough about a treaty to decide whether or not to object. Even the most nimble select committee would struggle to conduct an inquiry and publish a report in 21 days, especially if it wants to leave enough time for a debate. It might start an inquiry before the treaty is laid, but in practice is unlikely to begin before an EM is published.

Although the CRAGA 2010 allows the Government to extend the 21-sitting-day period, the Government does not always grant committees the time they feel they need. For example, the JCHR asked for an extension to consider a Prisoner Transfer Agreement with Libya, but was given only a few extra days (despite the controversy over the release of the Lockerbie bomber Abdelbaset al-Megrahi) and therefore could not publish a substantive report.[58] Similarly, it was given only eight extra days to consider a protocol on reform of the ECtHR and secure a Commons debate.[59]

Jill Barrett notes that if a vote is held in either House during an extension of the 21-day period, it will have legal effect only if the Government statement announcing the extension was laid before the original period expired. This creates a different time pressure:

> That means that Parliament will need to present its request to the Government well before the end of the first 21 sitting day period to allow time for the relevant Minister to consider it and lay a statement. If a request is made out of time, the Minister could still decide to postpone ratification of the treaty to allow Parliament further time, but any vote taken out of time will not have legal effect under the [Constitutional Reform and Governance] Act.[60]

---

[56] Joint Committee on the Draft Constitutional Renewal (n 1) 331.
[57] ibid 331.
[58] Joint Committee on Human Rights, *Legislative Scrutiny: Constitutional Reform and Governance Bill; Video Recordings Bill* (2009–10, HL 249, HC 249) para 1.45.
[59] Joint Committee on Human Rights, *Protocol 15 to the European Convention on Human Rights* (2014–15, HL 71, HC 837) paras 1.3–1.5.
[60] Barrett (n 33) 229.

In Australia, the Government has deemed the laying period of 15 sitting days (or, since 2002, 20 sitting days for treaties of major political, economic or social significance) to be enough for the Joint Standing Committee on Treaties to conduct and inquiry and publish a report.[61] That is, however, a specialised committee whose only job is to scrutinise treaties.

D. Widening the Range of Treaties Covered?

Not all treaties or treaty-like documents are covered by the current arrangements.

In 'exceptional' circumstances, the Government can ratify a treaty without laying it before Parliament;[62] this reflects the flexibility of the Ponsonby Rule. There have been some concerns that not all of the instances in which the Ponsonby Rule was avoided were genuinely urgent cases,[63] although recent examples appear to have been uncontroversial.[64] The Government must explain to Parliament why it has taken this step; the Joint Committee on the Bill called for this statement to include detailed information on the nature of the exceptional circumstances.[65] The Government did not accept the Public Administration Select Committee's suggestion that the Bill should either define the circumstances where the usual scrutiny rule would not apply or give Parliament (rather than the Government) the power to waive the requirement.[66] Nor did it follow the Bar Council's proposal that alternative safeguards referred to in the White Paper (consulting Parliament on a shorter timetable, making an oral or written statement to Parliament, and/ or consulting Opposition leaders and others during a recess) should appear on the face of the Bill and be made mandatory.[67] Another suggestion was that the Secretary of State could be required to take all reasonably practicable steps to ensure that no treaty is ratified without the new requirements being followed.[68] As Jill Barrett points out, however, the requirement to lay (not just make) a statement explaining why the 'exceptional circumstances' rule has been or is going to be invoked will ensure greater transparency: 'In future, it should be much easier for Government, Parliament and the public to monitor its use and detect any increase in the frequency of its use.'[69]

---

[61] Australian Department of Foreign Affairs and Trade, *Review of the Treaty-Making Process* (August 1999).
[62] CRAGA 2010, s 22.
[63] Public Administration Select Committee, *Constitutional Renewal: Draft Bill and White Paper* (HC 2007–08, 499) para 87.
[64] See Barrett (n 33) 230–31.
[65] Joint Committee on the Draft Constitutional Renewal Bill (n 35) para 226.
[66] See Public Administration Select Committee (n 63) para 87.
[67] Joint Committee on the Draft Constitutional Renewal Bill (n 1) 69 (General Council of the Bar).
[68] ibid 29–30 (Professor Adam Tomkins).
[69] Barrett (n 33) 231.

The CRAGA 2010 does not widen the range of treaties considered by Parliament. As with the Ponsonby Rule, only treaties requiring ratification, accession, approval, acceptance or other domestic procedures would be covered. A few (but possibly important) treaties provide that consent to be bound is expressed by signature alone, without any need for ratification. MJ Bowman, Director of the University of Nottingham Treaty Centre, describes this as a 'significant loophole'. He cites the example of the 1985 Council of Europe Convention on Spectator Violence and Misbehaviour at Sports Events and in particular at Football Matches, adopted in great haste after the Heysel Stadium disaster. The UK was one of several countries that expressed its consent to be bound by signature alone. Bowman argues that in such circumstances, a treaty might generate unforeseen and unintended implications for civil liberties, so extra scrutiny might be especially important.[70] However, the urgency of that treaty might bring it into the 'exceptional' circumstances category, allowing the Government to avoid laying it before Parliament anyway.

More problematic is the question of 'treaty-like' documents, including MOUs, exchanges of letters between governments and EU common positions, which are excluded from the 2010 Act because they are not 'binding under international law'.[71] These would continue to have no formal parliamentary scrutiny. The Commons Foreign Affairs Committee has suggested that many of these may be more important in their effect than most treaties,[72] and Anthony Aust notes that they are especially important for many defence arrangements (for instance, on the stationing of ballistic missiles) which need to be classified and so cannot be embodied in treaties.[73] Some international lawyers indeed consider MOUs actually to be treaties.[74] In 2008, Jack Straw, then Lord Chancellor, envisaged that such documents could be examined in future by a select committee, in confidence if need be,[75] and the Joint Committee on the draft Bill recommended that the scrutiny of such documents should be enhanced.[76] But there has been no change to the level of parliamentary involvement in such documents.

MOUs that come to Parliament's attention can prompt intense interest and debate. For example, the Labour Government signed controversial MOUs with Jordan and Lebanon on deportation, which aimed to ensure that people could be returned to those countries without being tortured. This prompted several debates in the Commons,[77] arguably showing that parliamentary concerns can be effectively expressed even without statutory scrutiny.

---

[70] Joint Committee on the Draft Constitutional Renewal Bill (n 1) 341.
[71] CRAGA 2010, s 25(1). For a detailed discussion of the definition of 'treaty' in the 2010 Act, see Barrett (n 33) 232–35.
[72] Joint Committee on the Draft Constitutional Renewal Bill (n 1) 371.
[73] ibid 339.
[74] See J Klabbers, *The Concept of the Treaty in International Law* (Leiden, Martinus Nijhoff, 1996).
[75] Joint Committee on the Draft Constitutional Renewal Bill (n 1) 332.
[76] Joint Committee on the Draft Constitutional Renewal Bill (n 35) para 232.
[77] See, eg, HC Deb 19 December 2005, vol 440, cols 2356–57W and HC Deb 15 June 2006, vol 477, col 354WH.

E. New Institutional Mechanisms?

There is currently no institutional mechanism in the UK to ensure that treaties are given adequate parliamentary oversight or scrutiny, whether through select committees, a specific treaty committee or any other method. This makes it harder for parliamentarians to determine which treaties have major implications that need debate.

Perhaps the most popular reform proposal is to create a new treaty committee to help plug the current gaps in the parliamentary scrutiny of treaties.[78] Such a committee could consider all treaties laid before Parliament before ratification and draw attention to any implications that merit parliamentary consideration. It could work with relevant select committees to ensure that those with expertise in the subject could hold an inquiry if they wish and call for a debate and/or a vote. It could also request a debate or an extension of the 21-sitting-day period for parliamentary consideration, and perhaps even undertake inquiries and publish reports itself. Its workload would not be huge—around 18 non-EU treaties a year on average, perhaps at some point expanding to cover MOUs too—but it would require a specialist secretariat. MJ Bowman has argued that committee scrutiny of treaties requires not only expertise on the subject covered by the treaty in question, but also expertise on how the treaty could be used for recognising, protecting and enhancing the relevant interests under international law.[79]

The most obvious example of a parliamentary treaty committee is Australia's Joint Standing Committee on Treaties (JSCOT). Created in 1996 in response to an extensive Senate report,[80] JSCOT is a large all-party committee supported by a small secretariat. It can inquire into and report on any treaty matter, including treaties in the process of being negotiated as well as those that have already been concluded. It can hold public hearings across Australia and review submissions from parliamentarians, NGOs, academics, industry groups and individual citizens. Its reports advise on whether the treaty should bind Australia and on any other issues that emerged during the review process. Usually JSCOT recommends ratification, but on a few very rare occasions, it has recommended unanimously against ratification. More frequently, it criticises the Government for an inadequate National Interest Analysis (required for each treaty) or insufficient consultation. Another of its functions is to make more treaty information available for public scrutiny.[81] It has, however, been criticised for serving as 'a tool for political

---

[78] Joint Committee on the Draft Constitutional Renewal Bill (n 35) para 238.
[79] Joint Committee on the Draft Constitutional Renewal Bill (n 1) 342.
[80] Australian Senate Legal and Constitutional References Committee, *Trick or Treaty? Commonwealth Power to Make and Implement Treaties* (1995).
[81] Harrington (n 11) 131–36.

management' and 'a means by which the executive can channel protest, deflect opposition, and in essence legitimize its own policy preferences'.[82]

Joanna Harrington has set out her opinion of the advantages of large and well-supported treaty committee like Australia's:

> In my view ... a national parliamentary committee comprised of representatives from all parties and all regions specifically dedicated to the task of treaty scrutiny is the best means to achieve greater public awareness as well as democratic accountability. A treaty committee regularizes and institutionalizes the scrutiny function, providing a public home for a wealth of treaty information, while ensuring that parliamentary time is given to the consideration of the future treaty action before the nation is bound. The committee must, however, be of an adequate size if it is to follow Australia's lead and carry out hearings across the nation, and it must be supported by an adequate secretariat capable of nurturing a fruitful relationship with both Government departments and civil society.[83]

One disadvantage of having a dedicated treaty committee is that committees with expertise in the subject matter might then be less likely to consider treaties.

It would be for the Houses themselves to set up any new treaty committee. They have so far been reluctant to do so, despite many calls for one. In early 2000, a Royal Commission on the Reform of the House of Lords[84] proposed that the House of Lords Liaison Committee should consider establishing a new select committee to scrutinise Ponsonby Rule treaties before ratification.[85] The Liaison Committee decided to wait for the Commons Procedure Committee to report before making a recommendation on this;[86] the Commons Procedure Committee's 2000 report on *Parliamentary Scrutiny of Treaties*[87] rejected a new Commons sifting committee for treaties, but did recommend enhancing the role of the existing select committees. Lord Tyler's 2008 Constitutional Renewal Bill[88] sought a joint Treaties Committee of both Houses of Parliament to examine both treaties and treaty-like documents, whose reports on ratification would be an essential part of the scrutiny process. *The Governance of Britain* consultation paper[89] discussed the idea of a new select committee or sifting committee for treaties, which met with some support. In a Lords debate on the proposals, five peers called for a treaty scrutiny committee.[90]

---

[82] Ann Capling and Kim Richard Nossal, 'Square Pegs and Round Holes: Australia's Multilateral Economic Diplomacy and the Joint Standing Committee on Treaties' (annual meeting of the International Studies Association, Chicago, 20–24 February 2001), quoted in H Charlesworth et al, 'Deep Anxieties: Australia and the International Legal Order' (2003) 25(4) *Sydney Law Review* 423, 444.
[83] Harrington (n 11) 158.
[84] Royal Commission on the Reform of the House of Lords (the Wakeham Commission), *A House for the Future* (Cm 4534, 2000) paras 8.37–8.42.
[85] ibid recommendation 56.
[86] HL 1999–2000, 49.
[87] House of Commons Procedure Committee, *Parliamentary Scrutiny of Treaties* (HC 1999–2000, 210) and House of Commons Procedure Committee (n 12).
[88] HL Bill (2008–09) 34.
[89] Ministry of Justice (n 13).
[90] HL Deb 31 January 2008, vol 471, cols 747 ff.

The Joint Committee on the subsequent draft Bill also recommended the creation of a new Joint Committee on Treaties.[91]

Other possible models could be the various committees that sift through and scrutinise EU measures and statutory instruments. Or there could be a new sub-committee of an existing select committee, for instance, the Commons Foreign Affairs Committee. Conceivably, a new 'sifting' secretariat—perhaps connected to the Commons Scrutiny Unit—could give the departmental select committees advice on treaties, helping to inform their decision on whether or not to scrutinise. This would avoid creating a new committee or sub-committee, and would allow treaties to be considered by committees with expertise in the subject, with the help of advice about the substance of the treaty and its legal obligations and implications.

Proponents of a new treaty committee for the UK should beware if they see it as a stepping stone to yet further parliamentary involvement: the Australian Government considers the treaty scrutiny system there to be so effective that there is no need to change to an affirmative procedure which would require Parliament to approve every treaty before it is ratified.[92]

F. Scrutinising Treaties During Negotiations?

There is no formal requirement or mechanism for parliamentary scrutiny before the *signing* of a treaty (ie, when changes could still be made to the text), although ministers do commonly 'communicate with the relevant select committee' before signing a treaty.[93] The powers in the CRAGA 2010 relate only to the ratification of a complete treaty.

Requiring parliamentary scrutiny of treaties during the negotiation stage would allow Parliament to draw attention to future treaty action that has strong opposition and possibly allow it to influence the Government's position in negotiations or even to recommend amendments to the treaty.

The 2003 UK–US Extradition Treaty is an example of where parliamentary concerns might have been more effective if they had been expressed before signature. Ever since it entered into force, there have been widespread political concerns about how it works. Following many parliamentary questions and debates, the Home Affairs Committee published a report into the Treaty.[94] It called on the Government to renegotiate the Treaty to provide the same information requirements for citizens of each country, instead of the 'imbalance' in the wording of the Treaty, which sets a test for extradition from the US but not from the UK and creates a 'widespread impression of unfairness'. Arguably, if parliamentarians had

---

[91] Joint Committee on the Draft Constitutional Renewal Bill (n 35).
[92] Australian Department of Foreign Affairs and Trade (n 61).
[93] HL Deb 31 January 2008, vol 698, col 796.
[94] House of Commons Home Affairs Committee, *The US–UK Extradition Treaty* (HC 2010–12 644).

been able to express this public understanding during the negotiating period, the Treaty might have been worded differently.

But pre-signature scrutiny as a matter of course is not popular. In early 2000, a Royal Commission on the Reform of the House of Lords agreed with the FCO that the large number and variety of treaties, and the political and diplomatic circumstances in which they are negotiated, would preclude a general commitment to compulsory pre-conclusion scrutiny.[95] The Labour Government in 2008 considered that a formal mechanism for scrutinising treaties before signature was neither practical nor workable, 'given the diverse circumstances and timeframes in which treaty negotiations are conducted'.[96]

Treaty texts are usually agreed, revised and finalised by a series of intergovernmental conferences in what can be a very lengthy process. Once they have been finalised and opened for signature and ratification, no individual government or Parliament can amend them. The Government can, however, submit declarations and/or reservations to many treaties when it signs or ratifies them, stating, for example, its understanding of particular treaty provisions or that it does not consider itself bound by a certain provision. Also, treaties can usually be amended by a subsequent treaty or protocol.

Some commentators have called for a non-statutory 'soft mandating' mechanism, allowing Parliament to have some influence on the negotiation of a treaty or at least immediately before signature.[97] This would involve, say, the minister and officials meeting the relevant select committee before international negotiations on a treaty to agree a 'soft mandate' or general bargaining position and desirable outcome. The minister would then report back to the committee and explain any departures from the agreed position.

MJ Bowman suggests that where signature of a treaty is essentially a preliminary to ratification, parliamentary involvement before signature could minimise the risk of disagreements between Parliament and the Government over the desirability of ratification.[98]

Joanna Harrington considers that 'there should be a mechanism that enables Parliament to draw attention to a future treaty action that has strong opposition and this mechanism should not rest on executive goodwill or discretion'. She suggests that a negative resolution procedure could be invoked within the time period assigned for scrutiny, which would 'not overly tie the hands of the executive during treaty negotiation':

> Such a procedure might also encourage greater cooperation between the levels and branches of government to avoid a lobby for triggering the negative resolution mechanism

---

[95] Wakeham Commission (n 84) paras 8.37–8.42.
[96] Ministry of Justice, *The Governance of Britain—Constitutional Renewal* (Cm 7342-I, 2008) para 165.
[97] See Joint Committee on the Draft Constitutional Renewal Bill (n 35) para 236.
[98] Joint Committee on the Draft Constitutional Renewal Bill (n 1) 341.

at a later stage. It is also a middle ground position that balances the various interests at play, admittedly sacrificing some efficiency for some accountability.[99]

On the other hand, Sir Michael Wood, former legal adviser to the FCO, argues that this is not a matter to be dealt with by legislation. Moreover, he points out that treaty negotiations are often conducted in secret, making parliamentary scrutiny at that stage difficult if not impossible.[100]

If done systematically, a general commitment to the public scrutiny of treaty negotiations could give Parliament the opportunity, if it wanted to take it, to scrutinise the Government's position in the negotiations on a treaty. This less formal approach could avoid some of the concerns outlined above.

In the US, the Committee on Foreign Relations can propose amendments to a treaty. The President and the other countries involved must then decide whether to accept the conditions and renegotiate the treaty or to abandon it. According to a Congressional Research Service report:

> Renegotiation of a treaty after Senate consideration is not frequent, and in the case of multilateral treaties is usually considered infeasible because of the number of countries involved and the problems in arriving at the original agreement. Nevertheless, on occasion treaties, particularly bilateral treaties, are renegotiated or negotiated further and amended by protocol as a result of Senate consideration.[101]

The report gives the example of a UK–US tax treaty which had a protocol added to deal with reservations raised by the Committee. Other treaties never entered in force because the Committee's reservations or amendments were not acceptable, either to the President or to the other country or countries that were party to the treaty.

V. CONCLUSIONS

In itself, the CRAGA 2010 does not improve Parliament's scrutiny of treaties. The new power to delay treaties indefinitely sends an important signal, but unless Parliament has a good understanding of the significance of treaties laid before it, how can it use that power effectively?

Possibly the most effective reform in this area was the introduction of EMs for treaties, which are now a statutory obligation. These help readers to identify the handful of treaties each year that have important obligations for the UK, where the public interest legitimately demands some scrutiny of the Government's intentions.

---

[99] Harrington (n 11) 158.
[100] Joint Committee on the Draft Constitutional Renewal Bill (n 1) 434.
[101] Congressional Research Service, 'Treaties and Other International Agreements: The Role of the United States Senate' (US Library of Congress, January 2001) 112.

Whilst there are some parliamentary debates and votes on treaties and other international agreements, and some committee involvement, there is certainly scope for more.

So how could Parliament's identification and scrutiny of treaties be improved, as an important aspect of its job of holding the Government to account? The answer is to make this a specific process, whether by a new parliamentary treaty committee with Members from both Houses, by a sub-committee of the Commons Foreign Affairs Committee or perhaps by expert staff supporting select committees. In any case, Parliament would have to take the initiative and ensure that there was expert advice available. This would be a real breakthrough in creating genuine accountability over treaties and perhaps over some other international agreements such as MOUs too.

If there is a desire to extend some accountability to the negotiating period, perhaps the most acceptable reform would be a commitment to public consultation on important treaties during their drafting. This would give Parliament an opportunity (rather than a cumbersome obligation) to scrutinise at a point where it can make a substantive difference.

12

Sovereignty, Privilege and the European Convention on Human Rights

ALEXANDER HORNE AND HÉLÈNE TYRRELL[*]

I. INTRODUCTION

P ARLIAMENTARY SOVEREIGNTY HAS long been considered the cornerstone of the British constitution. It was most famously defined by the jurist and constitutionalist theorist AV Dicey, who observed that:

> The principle of Parliamentary sovereignty means neither more nor less than this, namely that Parliament ... has, under the English constitution, the right to make or unmake any law whatever: and, further, that no person or body is recognised by the law of England as having a right to override or set aside the legislation of Parliament.[1]

In this context, 'Parliament' refers to the Queen in Parliament, so the sovereignty of Parliament describes what is known as 'legislative sovereignty': UK courts will recognise the supremacy of an Act, which has been approved by both Houses and received Royal Assent.[2] It is a domestic concept. The doctrine does not alter or augment the status of UK legislation in international law or politics.

The origins of the doctrine can be traced back to the Civil War, the Glorious Revolution and the Bill of Rights of 1688, and it was broadly recognised by the constitutional writers of the nineteenth century. Walter Bagehot stated in his 1867 work, *The English Constitution*, that: 'The ultimate authority in the English

---

[*] Thanks are due to Paul Evans, Liam Laurence Smyth, Roger Masterman, Colin Murray and Dawn Oliver for advice and comments upon earlier drafts of this chapter. All errors remain the authors' own.
[1] AV Dicey, *An Introduction to the Study of the Law of the Constitution* 10th edn (Basingstoke, Palgrave Macmillan, 1985 (first published 1959)).
[2] A Bill may also be passed by Parliament without the approval of the House of Lords under the Parliament Act 1911 (as amended by the Parliament Act 1949). Whether such a Bill had been passed by 'Parliament' was the subject of debate in *Jackson v Attorney General* [2005] UKHL 56, [2006] 1 AC 262, in which the majority held that the wording of the the wording of s 2(1) of the 1911 Act clearly provided that legislation made according to its provisions would 'become an Act of Parliament'.

Constitution is a newly-elected House of Commons.'[3] The first edition of *Erskine May*, published in 1844, observed of Parliament that:

> The legislative authority of Parliament extends over the United Kingdom, and all its colonies and foreign possessions; there are no other limits to its power of making laws for the whole empire than those which are incident to all sovereign authority—the willingness of the people to obey, or their power to resist. Unlike the legislatures of many other countries, it is bound by no fundamental charter or constitution; but has itself the sole constitutional right of establishing and altering the laws and government of the empire.[4]

The strength of the doctrine remained evident throughout the mid-twentieth century, often considered to be *the* central tenet of the constitutional settlement. In *The Law and the Constitution*, Sir Ivor Jennings observed that 'the supremacy of Parliament is the constitution',[5] while William Wade described the sovereignty of Parliament as 'the ultimate political fact'.[6] Yet, as Jeffrey Goldsworthy has noted, 'the once popular idea of legislative sovereignty has been in decline throughout the world for some time' as 'a dwindling number of political and constitutional theorists continue to resist the "rights revolution" that is sweeping the globe'.[7] Moreover, domestically, uncertainties have been raised about the impact of both national and international law on Dicey's once apparently inviolable proposition.

The modern challenges to the doctrine of parliamentary sovereignty are well-known and varied and will not be considered in any detail in this chapter. In brief, in addition to 'the ultimate limitations of public consent and of practical constraint',[8] they also include: the UK's accession to the European Union via the European Communities Act 1972 (as recognised by the courts in the case of *Factortame*, the consequences of which are discussed further in chapter 13);[9] devolution;[10] the passage of the Human Rights Act 1998 (which does not challenge directly the legislative sovereignty of Parliament, instead offering a power to read legislation compatibly with the European Convention on Human Rights (hereinafter ECHR

---

[3] W Bagehot, *The English Constitution*, Oxford World's Classics edn (Oxford, Oxford University Press, 2001) 160. Although making no mention of the House of Lords, Bagehot appears to have included legislative sovereignty and later refers more simply to the principle of choosing 'a single sovereign authority'.

[4] Thomas Erskine May, *A Treatise upon the Law, Privileges, Proceedings and Usage of Parliament* (London, Charles Knight & Co, 1844).

[5] I Jennings, *The Law and the Constitution* 5th edn (London, University of London Press 1959) 314.

[6] W Wade, 'The Basis of Legal Sovereignty' [1955] *Cambridge Law Journal* 172, 188.

[7] J Goldsworthy, *Parliamentary Sovereignty: Contemporary Debates* (Cambridge, Cambridge University Press, 2010) 9. For an interesting defence of parliamentary sovereignty, see D Oliver, 'Parliament and the Courts: A Pragmatic (or Principled) Defence of the Sovereignty of Parliament' in A Horne, G Drewry and D Oliver (eds), *Parliament and the Law* (Oxford, Hart Publishing, 2013).

[8] R Rogers and R Walters, *How Parliament Works* 7th edn (Harlow, Pearson 2015), 171 (an interesting example of the former being the repeal of the community charge (or 'poll tax') legislation following mass civil disobedience and non-payment).

[9] *R v Secretary of State for Transport ex p Factortame* [1990] 2 AC 85, [1991] 1 AC 603.

[10] See, eg, M Jack (ed), *Erskine May's Treatise on the Law, Privileges and Usages of Parliament* 24th edn (London, LexisNexis 2011), 186 ff.

or 'the Convention') 'so far as is it possible to do so' under section 3 and the carefully calibrated device of a 'declaration of incompatibility' under section 4);[11] and what has been described as the 'common law radicalism' of certain judges, such as Lord Steyn and Lord Hope.[12] This chapter will focus on the UK's obligation under international law to abide by judgments of the European Court of Human Rights (hereinafter ECtHR or 'the Strasbourg Court') and the impact of that obligation on the doctrine of parliamentary sovereignty.

The issue has been highlighted as a result of the Government's response (or lack of it) to the judgments of the ECtHR in the cases of *Hirst v UK (No 2)*[13] and *Greens and MT v UK*[14]—both of which relate to the contentious issue of prisoner voting and are discussed further below (section II.A). Further questions have developed over the legitimacy of the ECtHR, the application of the Convention as a 'living instrument' and whether the ECtHR has sufficient regard to the margin of appreciation that should be granted to contracting states (section II.B). Section III of the chapter examines a related issue, namely, the impact of the Convention on the internal operations of Parliament (having regard to the potential difficulties that could arise in relation to the constitutional principle of parliamentary privilege).

II. INTERNATIONAL LAW OBLIGATIONS AND HISTORICAL CONTEXT

Compliance with international law is required by the current Ministerial Code[15] and, on a broader level, compliance with international legal obligations has been considered central to the rule of law in the modern constitutional settlement. Lord Bingham wrote that the rule of law in the international legal order required protection through 'the medium of rules, internationally agreed, internationally implemented and, if necessary, internationally enforced'.[16]

---

[11] See, eg, A Young, *Parliamentary Sovereignty and the Human Rights Act* (Oxford, Hart Publishing, 2008).
[12] See, eg, *Jackson v Attorney General* [2005] UKHL 56 [102] and [104]; and *AXA General Insurance v Lord Advocate* [2011] UKSC 46, [2012] 1 AC 868 at [51]. It is worth noting the extra-judicial criticism of any judicial encroachment on the doctrine of parliamentary sovereignty by senior judges such as Lord Bingham (see, eg, T Bingham, *The Rule of Law*, (London, Allen Lane, 2010) and Lord Neuberger (see 'Who are the Masters Now?', 2nd Lord Alexander of Weedon lecture (6 April 2011) http://webarchive.nationalarchives.gov.uk/20131202164909/http:/judiciary.gov.uk/Resources/JCO/Documents/Speeches/mr-speech-weedon-lecture-110406.pdf). For recent commentary on these extra-judicial criticisms, see, eg, F Davis, 'Parliamentary Supremacy and the Re-invigoration on Institutional Dialogue' (2014) 67 *Parliamentary Affairs* 137. A further example is given in the *Moohan v The Lord Advocate (Scotland)* [2014] UKSC 67 [35] (Lord Hodge).
[13] *Hirst v UK (No 2)* (2005) ECHR 681.
[14] *Greens and MT v UK* (2010) ECHR 1826.
[15] The code outlines the duty to 'comply with the law including international law and treaty obligations': Cabinet Office, *The Ministerial Code* (May 2015) para 1.2. See prelim xvii.
[16] Bingham (n 12) 129; see also HWR Wade and C Forsyth, *Administrative Law* 11th edn (Oxford, Oxford University Press, 2014) 155: 'Explicit disobedience by the government to a legal obligation under international law is offensive to the rule of law.'

Nevertheless, the domestic doctrine of parliamentary sovereignty remains unchanged by international legal obligations, insofar as that doctrine dictates the relationship between Parliament and domestic courts. It has long been evident that an Act of Parliament will prevail even in the event of a breach of international law. As Ungoed-Thomas J put it in *Cheney v Conn*:

> What the statute itself enacts cannot be unlawful, because what the statute says and provides is itself the law, and the highest form of law that is known to this country. It is the law which prevails over every other form of law...[17]

Lord Hoffmann reaffirmed this in *R v Lyons*, confirming that it is the courts' duty to apply the law as laid down by Parliament 'whether that would involve the Crown in breach of an international treaty or not'.[18] Where legislation is ambiguous the courts have operated under the presumption that Parliament intends to legislate in conformity with international legal obligations,[19] but the courts are not bound by international law.[20] In the Convention context, the Human Rights Act states only that the UK must 'take into account' the jurisprudence of the Strasbourg Court.[21] It also remains the case that the UK has a dualist legal system: international treaties do not form a part of domestic law unless and until their provisions are expressly incorporated by domestic legislation.[22] As such, the relationship between domestic and international law is primarily an issue for the executive and legislature (as the bodies with legislative initiative and responsibility). The tension created by compliance with international law therefore affects the broader notion of parliamentary sovereignty, insofar as a sovereign state is the ultimate authority over its domestic legal system and legislative scheme.

---

[17] *Cheney v Conn* [1968] 1 All ER 779, 782. It was argued (unsuccessfully) that the validity of parts of the Finance Act were in question because the effect had been to authorise the collection of revenue which might be used for the construction of nuclear weapons, contrary to the Geneva Convention 1957.

[18] *R v Lyons* [2002] UKHL 44, [2003] 1 AC 976 [28]; In this respect, the Westminster Parliament is unique in the UK, as the devolved Parliaments are themselves subject to the Human Rights Act and bound to act compatibly with the Convention: Scotland Act 1998, s 57(2); Northern Ireland Act 1998, s 24(1)(a); Government of Wales Act 2006, s 81(1).

[19] See further C Turpin and A Tomkins, *British Government and the Constitution: Text Cases an Materials* 7th edn (Cambridge, Cambridge University Press, 2011) 61; *R v Secretary of State for the Home Department ex p Brind* [1991] 1 AC 696, 747–48 (Lord Bridge), *cf* 760 (Lord Ackner): 'it is a constitutional principle that if Parliament has legislated and the words of the statute are clear, the statute must be applied even if its application is in breach of international law'.

[20] The majority of the Supreme Court supported this position in *R (on the application of SG and others (previously JS and others) v Secretary of State for Work and Pensions* [2015] UKSC 16. See, eg, Lord Reed at [82]: 'It is firmly established that UK courts have no jurisdiction to interpret or apply unincorporated international treaties.' *cf* Lord Kerr from [252] and Lady Hale from [211].

[21] Human Rights Act 1998, s 2.

[22] See, eg, Lord Woolf, J Jowell, A Le Sueur et al, *De Smith's Judicial Review* 7th edn (London, Sweet & Maxwell, 2013) 268. Treaties are agreed by exercise of the royal prerogative and ratified only after a period of laying before Parliament (Constitutional Reform and Governance Act 2010, s 2). See further ch 11 above in this volume and D Feldman, 'The Internalization of Public Law and its Impact on the UK' in J Jowell and D Oliver (eds), *The Changing Constitution* 8th edn (Oxford, Oxford University Press, 2015).

In relation to the ECtHR, the chief source of tension derives from the international obligation under Article 46 ECHR that the UK (and other contracting states) must 'abide by' judgments of the ECtHR in cases to which it was a party.[23] Such an obligation appears to prescribe the domestic legislative scheme, at least to the extent necessary to ensure Convention compliance.

This tension is not new. Concerns around sovereignty were voiced in the early days of the ECHR.[24] As Bates has noted from the outset, there were warnings that the establishment of a European Court of Human Rights implied the surrender of a very significant amount of sovereignty and the considerable powers of review that a Strasbourg Commission and Court would have over British law.[25] Bates has argued that the manifestation of these concerns made it clear that there was 'a real awareness in 1950 that a European Court could develop into a type of constitutional court for Europe'.[26] Indeed, the supervisory role of the ECtHR was always a feature of the Convention: the provisions of Article 46 ECHR were then found in Articles 32 and 53 (in relation to the Committee of Ministers and the ECtHR, respectively).

In reality, it took time for the Convention system to unfold and there was a degree of uncertainty about the direction in which it would evolve. Bates admits that the full potential of the Convention's influence was difficult to envisage: 'the Convention was simply not viewed in 1950 as a standard setting instrument that was likely to significantly impact on domestic law'.[27] Simpson, too, suspected that the Convention might not have been ratified if the politicians of the time had foreseen its 'intrusiveness into what were once viewed as purely domestic matters'.[28] The early unease about the new system meant that the UK bought into the ECHR system in stages, as the Convention bodies established themselves. The negotiations over the right to individual petition provide an obvious example. During the early drafting stages, the right to individual petition was treated with some suspicion and it was the British drafters who suggested its inclusion on only an optional basis.[29]

Nevertheless, once the UK had opted into this provision (over a decade after ratification), abiding by those judgments soon became the accepted practice. This, Lord Lester has argued, led to the transfer from London to Strasbourg of

---

[23] In *Chester and McGeoch*, Lord Sumption stated that the nature of this obligation was 'in terms absolute': *R (Chester) v Secretary of State for Justice* and *McGeoch v The Lord President of the Council and another* [2013] UKSC 63, [2014] 1 AC 271 [119]. However, it is noted that while the UK Supreme Court found a breach of Protocol 1, art 3, it did not challenge the validity of legislation.

[24] E Bates, *The Evolution of the European Convention on Human Rights* (Oxford, Oxford University Press, 2010) from 77.

[25] ibid 106–07.

[26] ibid 107.

[27] ibid 114.

[28] AWB Simpson, *Human Rights and the End of Empire* (Oxford, Oxford University Press, 2001) 4.

[29] Bates (n 24), 95; Woolf et al (n 22) 655–65; Simpson (n 28).

'the substance, if not the form of parliamentary sovereignty over fundamental rights'.[30] The impact of individual petition was felt through a number of judgments against the UK, beginning in the mid-1970s. By the 1980s,[31] there was evident unease about the perceived threat to the UK's sovereignty, but the right of individual petition was nonetheless renewed each time until the right was made compulsory in 1998 (with the entry into force of Protocol 11 ECHR).[32]

The disquiet about the influence of the Strasbourg Court is not matched by the statistical record. As has been noted elsewhere, relative to the number of applications made, the number of judgments against the UK is small.[33] At the time of writing, the ECtHR had found against the UK in 301 cases out of 22,781 applications received, representing just 2.89 per cent of the total violations found against Member States.[34] The ECtHR's output is heavily balanced towards judgments against a small number of states, stemming in large part from the expansion of membership to the Convention system in the 1990s.[35] Consequently, recent reforms have focused on the management of the Strasbourg Court's caseload. Protocol 14 thus made changes to the admissibility criteria, entering into force in 2010,[36] and the Brighton Declaration adopted in 2012 also focused on reforms to the ECtHR that were designed to address the backlog of cases. The latter document emphasised the subsidiary role of the ECtHR, reiterating that the primary responsibility for protecting Convention rights rests with the (executives and legislatures of) Member States. Protocol 15 adds words to this effect into the text of the preamble to the Convention, framing Member States as the primary guardians of human rights: 'in protecting Convention rights, the Member States 'enjoy a margin of appreciation, subject to the supervisory jurisdiction of the European Court of Human Rights established by this Convention'.[37]

---

[30] A Lester, 'Fundamental Rights: The UK Isolated' [1984] *Public Law* 53, 60. Here it is assumed that Lord Lester refers to parliamentary sovereignty in the wider sense, relating to UK sovereignty in the international legal order, rather than the relationship between Parliament and the courts.

[31] In 1988, the UK Government registered a temporary derogation from art 5(3) ECHR in response to terrorism threats and detention without charge in Northern Ireland.

[32] Bates (n 24) 316–18; David Feldman, 'The European Court of Human Rights and the UK—Why Should Strasbourg Decide on Our Human Rights?' (*UK Constitutional Law Blog*, 7 December 2012) http://ukconstitutionallaw.org/2012/12/07/david-feldman-the-european-court-of-human-rights-and-the-uk-why-should-strasbourg-decide-on-our-human-rights.

[33] A Horne and V Miller, 'Parliamentary Sovereignty and the European Convention on Human Rights' (*Commons Library Blog*, 6 November 2014), http://commonslibraryblog.com/2014/11/06/parliamentary-sovereignty-and-the-european-convention-on-human-rights.

[34] Council of Europe, *ECHR Overview 1959–2014*, www.echr.coe.int/Documents/Overview_19592014_ENG.pdf.

[35] Bates (n 24) 22.

[36] eg, Philip Leach, *Taking a Case to the European Court of Human Rights* 3rd edn (Oxford, Oxford University Press, 2011) 7–9.

[37] Protocol No 15 was laid before Parliament on 28 October 2014: *Protocol N. 15 amending the Convention on the Protection of Human Rights and Fundamental Freedoms* (Cm 8951, October 2014). The supervisory jurisdiction of the Court remains intact, but the additions to the preamble may encourage it to take a step back and, as Fenwick has written, adopt 'a more cautious or nuanced approach … paying greater attention to consistency in its operation of the margin of appreciation doctrine':

The UK Parliament has adopted a number of measures which facilitate compatibility with the Convention. Section 10 of the Human Rights Act 1998 contains a remedial power, enabling a minister to 'make such amendments to the legislation as he considers necessary to remove [an] incompatibility',[38] which may be pursuant to a finding of the ECtHR.[39] The Joint Committee on Human Rights was given a formal role to consider remedial orders and report on compliance with judgments of the ECtHR,[40] in addition to its primary scrutiny function of checking the compatibility of legislative proposals. Nevertheless, these measures do nothing to compromise the ultimate (legal) sovereignty of Parliament over the legislative scheme. Any legislative changes require acquiescence on the part of the legislature, which is more difficult to obtain where the legislative change does not have popular support.

A. The Issue of Prisoner Voting

Few issues better highlight the tensions between Parliament's sovereignty over the domestic legal order and the international obligations under the ECHR than the saga surrounding the (dis)enfranchisement of prisoners.

Prisoners are denied the vote by the Representation of the People Act 1983, as amended by the Representation of the People Act 1985.[41] The ban affects all convicted prisoners, 'irrespective of the length of their sentence and irrespective of the nature or gravity of their offence and their individual circumstances'.[42] In *Hirst v UK (No 2)*, the Grand Chamber of the ECtHR found that the UK's blanket ban on prisoner voting was in breach of Protocol 1, Article 3 ECHR, which provides for 'free elections … under conditions which will ensure the free expression of the

---

H Fenwick, 'Prisoners' Voting Rights, Subsidiarity, and Protocols 15 and 16: Re-creating Dialogue With the Strasbourg Court?' UK Constitutional Law Blog (26 November 2013), http://ukconstitutionallaw.org/2013/11/27/helen-fenwick-prisoners-voting-rights-subsidiarity-and-protocols-15-and-16-re-creating-dialogue-with-the-strasbourg-court. See also Joint Committee on Human Rights, *Protocol 15 to the European Convention on Human Rights* (2014–15, HL 71, HC 837) paras 3.9–3.11.

[38] Human Rights Act 1998, s 10(2).
[39] ibid s 10(1)(b).
[40] See generally A Donald and P Leach, 'The Role of Parliaments Following Judgments of the European Court of Human Rights' in M Hunt, H Hooper and P Yowell (eds), *Parliament and Human Rights: Redressing the Democratic Deficit* (Oxford, Hart Publishing, 2015).
[41] Although prisoners were not able to vote for some time prior to that Act as one consequence of the rules governing land ownership under the Forfeiture Act 1870. See further *Voting Rights of Convicted Prisoners Detained within the United Kingdom: The UK Government's Response to the Grand Chamber of the European Court of Human Rights Judgment in the Case of Hirst v. the United Kingdom* (Consultation Paper, CP29/06, 2006). A historical background to the ban on prisoner voting falls outside the scope of this chapter. A detailed explanation of the ban on prisoner voting is given in A Horne and I White, *Prisoners' Voting Rights*, House of Commons Library Standard Note SN/PC/01764, 11 February 2015. See also C Murray, 'A Perfect Storm: Parliament and Prisoner Disenfranchisement' (2013) 66 *Parliamentary Affairs* 511, who has pointed out that the debate has been skewed by the 'mythologised view' that denying prisoners the vote has been a 'long-standing' feature of the legislative framework (at 552).
[42] *Hirst v UK (No 2)* (n 13) [82].

opinion of the people in the choice of the legislature'.[43] The ECtHR found that 'a general, automatic and indiscriminate restriction on a vitally important Convention right must be seen as falling outside any acceptable margin of appreciation, however wide that margin might be'.[44]

While Strasbourg jurisprudence is not binding on domestic courts,[45] Article 46(1) ECHR provides that a state is bound to abide by decisions of the Strasbourg Court to which it was a party. *Hirst* was such a case and the UK came under an international obligation to address the blanket ban.

There was, however, little enthusiasm for following the judgment of the Strasbourg Court and successive governments have resisted legislative change. The lack of urgency is hardly surprising given the supposed popularity of the current ban among the electorate. Even a partial repeal of the blanket ban is unlikely to be a vote-winner. Jack Straw was explicit about the delay in his autobiography:

> In my last ministerial post as Justice Secretary I'd made many decisions about many things; but I'd also spent three years ensuring that the government took no decision in response to a judgment by the European Court of Human Rights that the UK's ban on convicted prisoners being able to vote was unlawful. I'd kicked the issue into touch, first with one inconclusive public consultation, then with a second.[46]

The failure to address the issue gave rise to a large body of applications to the Strasbourg Court and, a few months after the 2010 General Election, the Strasbourg Court handed down a further judgment: *Greens and MT v UK*.[47] In *Greens*, the ECtHR repeated the conclusions from *Hirst* that the blanket ban was incompatible with the Convention, but also repeated its subsidiary role; the UK Government had been given a wide discretion as to how to comply with the *Hirst* judgment and it was not 'appropriate' for the Court to be prescriptive about 'the content of future legislative proposals'. Given the 'lengthy delay' on the issue, the Court imposed a timetable for action, concluding that the UK Government should introduce legislative proposals within six months of the final judgment.[48] In doing so, the Court reiterated the Article 46 ECHR requirement to comply with judgments of the Court to which a state is party. It stated that the UK Government was therefore 'required to enact the relevant legislation within any time frame decided by the Committee of Ministers, the executive arm of the Council of Europe, which supervises the execution of the Court's judgments'.[49]

---

[43] ibid.
[44] ibid.
[45] Section 2 of the Human Rights Act 1998 requires that domestic courts 'take into account' relevant Strasbourg jurisprudence.
[46] J Straw, *Last Man Standing* (London, Macmillan, 2012). See also Joint Committee on Human Rights, *Monitoring the Government's Response to Court Judgments Finding Breaches of Human Rights* (2006–07, HC 728, HL 128) para 77: 'the Government would be taking a generally unpopular course if it were to enfranchise even a small proportion of the prison population'.
[47] *Greens and MT v UK* (n 14).
[48] ibid [115].
[49] ibid [115]; Press Release no 328, European Court of Human Rights, 12 April 2011.

A month after the judgment in *Greens*, the Government announced that it would 'act to implement the judgment of the European Court of Human Rights'.[50] It did so while emphasising that it would implement the *Hirst* judgment in a way that meets the UK's legal obligations, 'but does not go further than that'.[51] The statement was followed by two debates. A Westminster Hall adjournment debate was held on 11 January 2011, where a general opposition to legislative change was made clear.[52] One month later, the Backbench Business Committee also allotted parliamentary time to the issue. As Nicol has noted, that debate was replete with references to the doctrine of parliamentary sovereignty as well as to the rule of law and the separation of powers.[53] The motion for debate was:

> That this House notes the ruling of the European Court of Human Rights in *Hirst v the United Kingdom* in which it held that there had been no substantive debate by members of the legislature on the continued justification for maintaining a general restriction on the right of prisoners to vote; acknowledges the treaty obligations of the UK; is of the opinion that legislative decisions of this nature should be a matter for democratically-elected lawmakers; and supports the current situation in which no prisoner is able to vote except those imprisoned for contempt, default or on remand.[54]

David Davis opened the Backbench Business Committee debate by asking whether 'the requirement to give prisoners the vote [is] sensible, just, right and proper' and whether the decision should be made by the ECtHR or by 'this House on behalf of the British people'.[55] Other commentators have noted that the MPs made heavy reference to key constitutional principles. Perhaps for this reason, Turpin and Tomkins have described the debate as 'high quality, thorough and (generally) well-informed'.[56] Those who supported the motion made numerous references to the democratic accountability of the legislature, arguing that the issue boiled down to an attempt by unaccountable judges at the ECtHR to undermine the sovereignty of Parliament.[57] Few MPs were prepared to openly oppose the motion and Nicol has pointed out that the debate was not well-attended by backbenchers willing to register their support for the principle of compliance with the Strasbourg jurisprudence.

The motion was carried (on a free vote) by 234 votes to 22.[58] It was suggested a number of times that the issue was not about whether prisoners should have the

---

[50] HC Deb 20 December 2010, col 151WS. The proposals were to include the provision of votes for offenders sentenced to a term of imprisonment of less than four years, although the sentencing judge would be able to remove that right. However, no timetable was given for these changes.
[51] ibid.
[52] HC Deb 11 January 2011, col 1WH.
[53] D Nicol, 'Legitimacy of the Commons Debate on Prisoner Voting' [2011] *Public Law* 681.
[54] HC Deb 10 February 2011, col 493.
[55] ibid.
[56] Turpin and Tomkins (n 19).
[57] See, eg, HC Deb 10 February 2011, col 575 (Ms Priti Patel); HC Deb 10 February 2011, col 547 (Mr Rehman Chishti); HC Deb 10 February 2011, col 531 (Ms Anne Main).
[58] HC Deb 10 February 2011, col 584, Div 199.

right to vote, but about the right of the House of Commons to legislate on the subject. It was said that the ECtHR was seeking to extend its powers, described as a case of 'mission creep' through which it has 'undermined the authority of [the House of Commons]'.[59] It was also argued that the ECtHR was overreaching itself: 'through the decision in the *Hirst* case and some similar decisions, the ECtHR is setting itself up as a supreme court for Europe with an ever-widening remit'.[60] More simply, some Members contended that the ECtHR had developed requirements in the Convention that were not intended by the drafters or signatories. The sentiment was put this way by Jack Straw and David Davis, in an article for the *Daily Telegraph*:

> [W]e now find ourselves in a situation where the Court is trying to impose judgments on Britain which would have astonished those who signed the Convention … [I]n attempting to overrule British law on prisoner voting rights, Strasbourg judges have exceeded the limits of their proper authority.[61]

The language of that article runs to the heart of the issue. The Strasbourg Court is said to be 'impos[ing] judgments' on the UK Parliament, 'overul[ling] British law'. The Prime Minister himself put it this way when he declared that the matter was for Parliament to decide, 'not a foreign court'.[62]

Such is the strength of criticism levelled at the ECtHR that one might imagine that the Grand Chamber in *Hirst* had instructed the UK Parliament to give all or most prisoners the vote. The Grand Chamber did not ask for such a change or even find that there was no rational basis for the current ban. It simply found that the UK's blanket ban on prisoner voting was disproportionate.[63] In fact, the most obvious of the Grand Chamber's concerns in *Hirst* was not about the legislative scheme itself, but about the lack of substantive debate within the UK legislature on the justification for 'maintaining such a general restriction on the right of prisoners to vote'.[64]

Having held debates on the issue, the UK Government referred the *Greens* judgment to the Grand Chamber, effectively appealing the six-month deadline

---

[59] ibid col 507 (Mr Gary Streeter). The language of 'mission creep' was repeated in the Conservative Party Manifesto in the run-up to the 2015 General Election: Conservative Party Manifesto 2015, *Strong Leadership, a Clear Economic Plan, a Brighter, More Secure Future*, www.conservatives.com/manifesto.
[60] HC Deb 10 February 2011, col 502.
[61] D Davis and J Straw, 'We Must Defy Strasbourg on Prisoner Votes' *Daily Telegraph* (24 May 2012). Similar points were made during parliamentary debates; see, eg, HC Deb 10 February 2011, col 504.
[62] HC Deb 23 May 2012, col 1127.
[63] *Hirst v UK (No 2)* (n 13) [84].
[64] ibid [79]; Murray (n 41) 523; T Lewis, '"Difficult and Slippery Terrain": Hansard, Human Rights and *Hirst v UK*' [2006] *Public Law* 209, 212. While s 19 of the Human Rights Act 1998 requires that ministers make a declaration about the compatibility of legislation with the ECHR, there is no obligation or process in place to examine pre-Human Rights Act legislation for Convention compatibility. In another context, Lord Reed expressed unease about judicial scrutiny of the legislative process, feeling that an argument that such scrutiny 'impinges upon long-established constitutional principles governing the relationship between Parliament and the courts': *R (on the application of HS2 Action Alliance Ltd) v Secretary of State for Transport* [2014] UKSC 3, [2014] 1 WLR 324 [78].

for legislative proposals. The request was dismissed. The Government requested a further extension to the deadline pending the outcome of another ECtHR case on prisoner voting, *Scoppola v Italy (No 3)*, which was granted. The judgment in *Scoppola* confirmed the conclusion in *Hirst* that a blanket ban on prisoner voting constituted a violation of Protocol 1, Article 3 ECHR. The Court recognised that it would be for Member States to decide how to amend the indiscriminate bans.[65] The Grand Chamber also rowed back from an earlier decision of the First Section of the Court in the case of *Frodl v Austria*, which would have constrained the margin of appreciation of Convention Member States far more significantly.[66] Far from requiring the repeal of the ban altogether, it was therefore open to the UK to restrict the ban to prisoners convicted of particularly serious criminality or to those serving sentences for particular classes of offence.[67]

Nevertheless, when the Draft Voting Eligibility (Prisoners) Bill was presented, it included, alongside proposals for reform, an option to retain the current blanket ban. The Council of Europe's Committee of Ministers reflected on the UK's legislative proposals and pointed out that the option to retain the blanket ban on voting by prisoners 'cannot be considered compatible with the European Convention on Human Rights'.[68] The Joint Committee on the Draft Voting Eligibility (Prisoners) Bill also expressed its disappointment 'that the Government itself should be proposing to Parliament an option that it knows to be unlawful'.[69] But the inclusion of this option was, to a certain extent, inevitable. It presented an opportunity to do more than simply ignore the Strasbourg jurisprudence—it provided Parliament with the option to positively defy it.[70]

In his statement following the introduction of the Draft Prisoner Voting (Eligibility) Bill, the then Lord Chancellor, Chris Grayling, stressed that 'it remains the case that Parliament is sovereign' and that the ban on prisoner voting 'passed by

---

[65] Although see, eg, E Bates, 'Analysing the Prisoner Voting Saga and the British Challenge to Strasbourg' (2014) 14 *Human Rights Law Review* 503, 509. Bates notes the dissenting judgments in *Hirst* and the reality that 'only two reform options were available: restore the vote to prisoners in the post-tariff phase of detention (in cases such as *Hirst*, the tariff part of the sentence relating to the minimum period to be served for retribution and deterrence), or amend domestic law such that only judges could disenfranchise prisoners as part of sentencing'.

[66] See *Frodl v Austria* (2011) 52 EHRR 5 [28], where the court ruled that: 'Disenfranchisement may only be envisaged for a rather narrowly defined group of offenders serving a lengthy term of imprisonment; there should be a direct link between the facts on which a conviction is based and the sanction of disenfranchisement; and such a measure should preferably be imposed not by operation of law but by the decision of a judge following judicial proceedings.'

[67] *Hirst v UK (No 2)* (n 13) [84]; Murray (n 64), 523; Bates (n 65) 509 fn 36: 'Contracting States [had] adopted a number of different ways of addressing the question of the right of convicted prisoners to vote.' Thus, Strasbourg 'confined itself' to concluding that UK law was outside 'any acceptable margin of appreciation, leaving it to the legislature to decide on the choice of means for securing the rights' in question.

[68] Decision of the Committee of Ministers, 1157th Meeting (DH), 4–6 December 2012.

[69] Joint Committee on Draft Voting Eligibility (Prisoners) Bill, *Report* (2012–13, HL 103, HC 924) para 234.

[70] Bates (n 65) 504. As Bates has written, that would be without precedent in the ECtHR history and could have major ramifications for the Convention system.

Parliament remains in force unless and until Parliament decides to change it.' The Lord Chancellor attempted to support this point by reference to Lord Hoffmann's dicta in *ex p Simms*: 'Parliamentary sovereignty means that Parliament can, if it chooses, legislate contrary to fundamental principles of human rights.'[71]

As Turpin and Tomkins have pointed out, the rule in *Simms* is subject to some qualification, including a requirement that Parliament 'has squarely confronted what it is doing' and that the rights implications of the legislation have not 'passed unnoticed'.[72] Neither could be said to have applied in the case of prisoner voting. Moreover, as the Joint Committee recognised, the *Simms* case addressed domestic law (the Human Rights Act 1998) rather than the UK's international law obligations under the Convention itself.[73] The Committee noted that the distinction was set out in a 2011 lecture delivered by the current President of the Supreme Court, Lord Neuberger of Abbotsbury:

> [U]ltimately, the implementation of a Strasbourg, or indeed a domestic, court judgment is a matter for Parliament. If it chose not to implement a Strasbourg judgment, it might place the United Kingdom in breach of its treaty obligations, but as a matter of domestic law there would be nothing objectionable in such a course. It would be a political decision, with which the courts could not interfere.[74]

Lord Neuberger continued:

> While, in a sense, legal sovereignty is fettered so long as Parliament is required to implement a decision of the Strasbourg court, the fetter is however akin to that imposed by the European Communities Act 1972: neither is permanent. Any such fetter remains only so long as the Treaty obligation itself remains valid, but any country can withdraw from the Treaty, and that demonstrates that whatever limit membership imposes on legal sovereignty, it is a fetter which endures only whilst our membership endures—i.e. only while Parliament wants it to endure.[75]

The then Attorney General, Dominic Grieve, spoke in similar terms when giving evidence to the Justice Committee:

> [I]t is entirely a matter for Government to make proposals but ultimately for Parliament to determine what it wants to do. Parliament is sovereign in this area; nobody can impose a solution on Parliament, but the accepted practice is that the United Kingdom observes its international obligations.[76]

The last quoted sentence was important. Grieve had explained to the Justice Committee that: 'Parliament gives and can take away; Governments can leave the Council of Europe if they choose to do so.'[77]

---

[71] *R v Secretary of State for the Home Department ex p Simms* [2000] 2 AC 115, 131.
[72] Turpin and Tomkins (n 19) 81.
[73] Joint Committee on Draft Voting Eligibility (Prisoners) Bill (n 69) para 89.
[74] Lord Neuberger (n 12) [56].
[75] ibid.
[76] HC Deb 22 November 2012, col 745.
[77] Oral evidence to the Justice Committee, 24 October 2012.

In a speech made the following day, Grieve stressed that the UK Parliament had not been made 'subservient to the Strasbourg Court';[78] rather, observing the judgments of the Strasbourg Court was 'an international legal obligation arising by Treaty'.[79] It was therefore 'possible for Parliament to take no action on the judgment'.[80] Explicit disobedience of this kind would ignore the well-established requirement for executive actors to respect the decisions of independent tribunals with jurisdiction over them and,[81] as Wade and Forsyth have suggested, would be 'offensive to the rule of law'.[82] The practical consequence would be to breach the Treaty and make the Government 'liable to criticism and sanctions from the Council of Europe by its fellow signatories and to damages awarded by the Court'.[83]

The matter came before the UK Supreme Court in *R (Chester) v Secretary of State for Justice* and *McGeoch v The Lord President of the Council and another*.[84] Both cases concerned prisoners convicted of murder and sentenced to life imprisonment, who had been denied the vote in UK parliamentary and European elections. The prisoners attracted little sympathy from the Justices of the Supreme Court, who dismissed both appeals. While the Prime Minister declared the judgment to be a 'victory for common sense',[85] the Supreme Court did not disagree with the Strasbourg Court about the incompatibility of a blanket ban. It refused to make a further 'declaration of incompatibility' only on the basis that it was unnecessary, owing to an existing declaration of incompatibility on the issue (made in *Smith v Scott*)[86] and the fact that the matter was currently under review in Parliament (the Court made specific reference to the publication of the draft Bill and the establishment of the Joint Committee to examine it).[87] The domestic doctrine of parliamentary sovereignty thus remained intact: although recognising the incompatibility of the blanket ban, the Supreme Court in *Chester* did not set out to challenge the legislation and left the issue of Convention compliance to Parliament.

In Strasbourg, the most recent instalments in the saga have been by way of the decisions in *Firth v UK* and *McHugh v UK*.[88] *Firth* concerned a number of prisoners who had been denied the vote in European parliamentary elections. The ECtHR considered the domestic progress on the issue, including the publication of a draft Bill. Since the legislative position remained unchanged, the Court

---

[78] Dominic Grieve, speech to the BPP Law School on Parliament and the judiciary, 25 October 2012.
[79] ibid.
[80] ibid.
[81] *M v Home Office* [1994] 1 AC 377.
[82] Wade and Forsyth (n 16) 155.
[83] ibid.
[84] *R (Chester)v Secretary of State for Justice and McGeoch v The Lord President of the Council* (n 23).
[85] HC Deb 16 October 2013, col 736.
[86] *Smith v Scott* 2007 SC 345.
[87] *R (Chester) v Secretary of State for Justice* and *McGeoch v The Lord President of the Council* (n 23) [19].
[88] *Firth and others v UK* [2014] ECHR 874; *McHugh v UK* Application No 51987/08, European Court of Human Rights, 10 February 2015.

inevitably followed its earlier judgment in *Greens*, finding that there had been a violation of Protocol 1, Article 3 ECHR. Interestingly, the Court nevertheless denied the applicants' claim for compensation and legal costs. It was said that lodging an application in relation to this matter was by now straightforward and should not incur costs relating to legal assistance.[89] The Court came to the same conclusion in the *McHugh* case, also denying 1,015 applicants compensation for the violation of their rights under Protocol 1, Article 3 ECHR.[90]

The UK Parliament nonetheless remains under a duty to implement the Strasbourg jurisprudence on prisoner voting, pursuant to the Article 46 ECHR duty to abide by decisions of the Strasbourg Court, to which it is a party. Lord Judge reflected on the consequences of this obligation in a lecture given at University College London:

> [I]n our constitutional arrangements Parliament is sovereign. It can overrule, through the legislative process, any decision of our Supreme Court. In relation to the Strasbourg Court, and the Convention, is this principle negatived by our accession to the treaty obligation contained in Art 46? Do we, can we, accept the obligation ... that when a UK case arises, our Parliament must take 'general measures in its domestic legal order to put an end' to the violations found by the European Court? Can that possibly be required if Parliament disagrees? For me the answer is, of course not. But these observations clearly indicate the intended route, and the future is long as well as short.[91]

The matter is at a curious impasse. Without the prospect of successful compensation claims, it is difficult to envisage the motivation for legislative change. Aside from the political fallout from implementing an unpopular legislative scheme, any government that moves to repeal or amend the current ban risks a far more powerful critique (correct or not): that it is bowing to the authority of the Strasbourg Court and admitting that the UK Parliament no longer has the final say. Indeed, the Coalition Government kicked the matter firmly back into touch when it published a Command Paper (in December 2014) indicating that prisoners would not be granted the vote ahead of the 2015 General Election.[92] The current Conservative Government was elected in May 2015 on a manifesto which claimed to have prevented giving prisoners the vote and included a commitment to 'break the formal link between British courts and the European Court of Human Rights',[93] making it unlikely that implementing the Strasbourg judgments will be a priority.

---

[89] *Firth and others v UK* (n 88) [21].

[90] It is not assumed that all applicants in these cases would have been successful in arguing an infringement of their rights under the Convention. The Strasbourg Court has frequently repeated the possibility that the right to vote could be subject to some limitations, short of the full blanket ban.

[91] Lord Judge, 'Constitutional Change: Unfinished Business' (*UCL*, 4 December 2013) www.ucl.ac.uk/constitution-unit/constitution-unit-news/constitution-unit/research/judicial-independence/lordjudgelecture041213.

[92] *Responding to Human Rights Judgments 2013–14* (Cm 8962, December 2014).

[93] Conservative Party Manifesto 2015 (n 59) 62. Breaking the formal link between the British courts and the ECtHR would presumably involve a treaty alteration in order to remove the right to individual petition. It was not clear at the time of writing how such a change would be implemented.

The consequences of inaction are not altogether clear. Dominic Raab MP (appointed Parliamentary Under Secretary of State at the Ministry of Justice, with responsibility for Human Rights, in May 2015) has previously argued that the practical repercussions of a UK refusal to address the issue would be 'negligible', since the Strasbourg machinery 'cannot enforce its own judgments or compensation awards':[94]

> The worst that can happen is that the unimplemented judgment will sit—with hundreds of others—on the Committee of Ministers' list for review. There is no prospect of a fine, let alone Britain being kicked out of the Council of Europe. Despite egregious human rights abuses, military dictatorship in Greece and Russian atrocities in Chechnya, no state has ever been voted out of the Council of Europe.[95]

Yet inaction on the part of the Council of Europe would surely undermine the force of the international obligation enshrined by Article 46. As one commentator has pointed out, it would also 'effectively introduce a democratic override by the back door'.[96] 'It would be saying to other states that as long as a bill was put before a national Parliament ... that would be enough to "abide by" judgments of the court.'[97]

In the meantime, the UK continues to deny all prisoners the vote, in breach of the Convention and in defiance of its obligations under Article 46(1). Moreover, as the ECtHR made clear in another case, *McLean and Cole v UK*,[98] further complaints will be admissible with each election that passes if amending legislation is not brought into force.[99]

B. The Legitimacy and Jurisdiction of the ECtHR

The tension created by the pressure to comply with decisions of the Strasbourg Court is aggravated by concerns surrounding the legitimacy and jurisdiction of the ECtHR as an institution in itself.

Lord Hoffmann made a number of points on this front in a well-known paper entitled 'The Universality of Human Rights'.[100] He was sceptical about the

---

[94] D Raab, 'What Happens if We Defy Europe? Nothing' *Daily Telegraph* (2 February 2011).
[95] Dominic Raab was appointed as a junior minister in the Ministry of Justice in the incoming Conservative Government after the 2015 General Election, potentially with the brief to introduce the Bill to repeal the Human Rights Act.
[96] A Wagner, 'No-one Should Be under Any Doubt—Prisoners are Not Getting the Vote under this Government' (*UK Human Rights Blog*, 18 November 2012) http://ukhumanrightsblog.com/2012/11/18/no-one-should-be-under-any-doubt-prisoners-are-not-getting-the-vote-under-this-government.
[97] ibid.
[98] *McLean and Cole v UK* (2013) 57 EHRR SE95.
[99] ibid [37].
[100] Lord Hoffmann, 'The Universality of Human Rights', Judicial Studies Board Annual Lecture, 19 March 2009 (subsequently published at (2009) 125 *Law Quarterly Review* 416).

Strasbourg Court's position as an international arbiter at all,[101] adding that the primary mechanism through which the Strasbourg Court protects the principle of subsidiarity—the margin of appreciation doctrine—is an inadequate safeguard:

> In practice, the Court has not taken the doctrine of the margin of appreciation nearly far enough. It has been unable to resist the temptation to aggrandise its jurisdiction and to impose uniform rules on Member States. It considers itself the equivalent of the Supreme Court of the United States, laying down a federal law of Europe.[102]

He took the view that the fact that the Strasbourg Court could aggrandise its jurisdiction was particularly objectionable because, unlike the Supreme Court of the United States or, indeed, the Court of Justice of the European Union (CJEU) in Luxembourg,[103] the Strasbourg Court 'lacks constitutional legitimacy'. This is said to be primarily a result of the imbalance in judicial appointments (caused by large Council of Europe states such as the UK, Germany and France being afforded the same representation on the Court's bench as the smallest states, such as Luxembourg and San Marino) and the process by which judges are elected.[104] Without that legitimacy, Lord Hoffmann argued that the Strasbourg Court should be 'particularly cautious in extending its reach'.[105]

A number of other senior judges have since added their comments on the role of the ECtHR and relationship between it and the domestic legal system.[106] A few months after Lord Hoffmann's speech, Lady Justice Arden delivered a lecture in which she suggested that the Strasbourg Court ought to develop the subsidiarity principle, leaving less important cases to be dealt with by domestic courts,

---

[101] ibid [23].
[102] ibid [27].
[103] ibid [39].
[104] ibid [38]. The disquiet about the election process is ironic, given that other critical commentators often refer to the 'unelected European judges' when referring to the deficiencies of the ECtHR. See, eg, Adam Wagner, 'Unelected Judges Dictating Our Laws etc. etc.' (*UK Human Rights Blog*, 11 February 2011) http://ukhumanrightsblog.com/2011/02/11/unelected-judges-dictating-our-laws-etc-etc.
[105] Lord Hoffmann (n 100) [39].
[106] Lady Justice Arden, 'Peaceful or Problematic? The Relationship between National Supreme Courts and Supranational Courts in Europe' (Sir Thomas More Lecture, 10 November 2009); Lord Neuberger (n 12); Baroness Hale, 'Beanstalk or Living Instrument? How Tall Can the ECHR Grow?' (2011 Barnard's Inn Reading, 18 June 2011); Lord Carnwath, 'The Subsidiary Role of the European Court of Human Rights in the UK Judicial System' (Seminar on Subsidiarity in Supranational Jurisdictions, Rome, 20 September 2013); Lord Sumption, 'The Limits of Law' (27th Sultan Azlan Shah Lecture, Kuala Lumpur, 20 November 2013); Lord Justice Laws, 'The Common Law and Europe' (Hamlyn Lecture III, 27 November 2013); Lady Hale, 'What's the Point of Human Rights?' (Warwick Law Lecture 2013, 28 November 2013); Lord Judge, 'Constitutional Change: Unfinished Business' (UCL, 4 December 2013); Lord Mance, 'Destruction of Metamorphosis of the Legal Order' (World Policy Conference, Monaco, 14 December 2013); Lord Dyson, 'The Extraterritorial Application of the European Convention on Human Rights: Now on a Firmer Footing, But is it a Sound One?' (Essex University, 30 January 2014); Lord Neuberger, 'The British and Europe' (Cambridge Freshfields Annual Law Lecture, 12 February 2014); Lord Justice Moses, 'Hitting the Balls out of Court: Are Judges Stepping over the Line?' (Creaney Memorial Lecture, 26 February 2014); Lady Justice Arden, 'An English Judge in Europe' (Neill Lecture, Oxford, 28 February 2014); Lord Dyson, 'Are the Judges Too Powerful?' (2014 Annual Bentham Association Presidential Address, 12 March 2014).

'without further recourse to the Strasbourg court even if the litigant is dissatisfied with the result':[107]

> [T]he margin of appreciation is not solely about the protection of rights. It is also about the competence of national institutions. The margin of appreciation ought not to be just about cases where there is no consensus in the contracting states. It is also about comparative institutional competence. This aspect of the doctrine of the margin of appreciation should be recognised and developed.[108]

A connected issue relates to the status of the ECHR as a 'living instrument'.[109] The concept provides that the scope of the Convention evolves over time, taking into account evolving social conceptions common to the Member States. There is therefore another inevitable tension with the sovereignty of Parliament in the sense that the Convention rights may evolve in directions that were not anticipated or intended by the domestic legislatures ratifying the instrument. Lord Sumption made these sorts of criticisms in a lecture given towards the end of 2013:

> The treatment of the Convention by the European Court of Human Rights as a 'living instrument' allows it to make new law in respects which are not foreshadowed by the language of the Convention and which Parliament would not necessarily have anticipated.[110]

Lord Sumption is not alone in expressing concern. Prior to his appointment, Justice Minister (and former international lawyer) Dominic Raab described the 'living instrument' doctrine as a 'judicial coup', which 'represents a naked usurpation, by a judicial body, of the legislative power that properly belongs to democratically elected law makers'.[111] The prisoner voting issue (discussed above) was an obvious example, Raab argued, since a clear right to prisoner voting had not been present in the text of the ECHR, but was 'fabricated by judicial innovation, contrary to the express terms of the ECHR and the intentions of its architects'.[112]

---

[107] Lady Justice Arden, 'Peaceful or Problematic?' (n 106). A change of this sort would presumably require an amendment to the treaty in relation to individual petition. The authors are grateful to Paul Evans for this observation.

[108] ibid 16–17. However, Lady Justice Arden also pointed out the value of having a court with ultimate authority to interpret the Convention, especially alongside the doctrine of parliamentary sovereignty: 'an international system of human rights has considerable advantages for the United Kingdom. It subjects the institutions of the state to outside scrutiny, and that is particularly important when, as in the United Kingdom, there is a strong doctrine of parliamentary sovereignty ... The existence of supranational courts, establishing human rights principles, also empowers the domestic judiciary and strengthens their independence as against other institutions of their own state'. ibid 10.

[109] *Tyrer v UK* (1978) 2 EHRR 1 [31].

[110] Lord Sumption (n 106) 11.

[111] D Raab, *Strasbourg in the Dock: Prisoner Voting, Human Rights & the Case for Democracy* (London, Civitas 2011), 9.

[112] ibid xiii, 5–6. Similar sentiments have been repeated elsewhere. See, eg, M Pinto-Duschinsky, *Bringing Rights Back Home* (London, Policy Exchange, 2011), 11: the Strasbourg Court 'tended to stretch the original text of the European Convention on Human Rights to fit situations well outside the expectation of those who drafted and ratified it'. See Joint Committee on the Draft Voting Eligibility (Prisoners) Bill (n 69) paras 31–37 and 77–87.

In a 2015 lecture for Policy Exchange, Jeffrey Goldsworthy made reference to theories of interpretation commonly called 'living constitutionalism' having the consequence of 'ratcheting up' or 'upping the ante' in terms of rights protection.[113] Even Baroness Hale (who has generally spoken in favour of the Convention) has voiced her fear that the approach would 'lead to a narrowing of the margin of appreciation'.[114]

In the *Chester* and *McGeoch* cases before the Supreme Court,[115] Lord Sumption expressed explicit dissatisfaction with the Strasbourg Court's approach in the prisoner voting cases. In his Lordship's view, absent the Strasbourg jurisprudence, the question of how serious an offence has to be to warrant temporary disenfranchisement would be 'a classic matter for political and legislative judgment and that the United Kingdom rule is well within any reasonable assessment of a Convention state's margin of appreciation'.[116] Nevertheless, he concluded that there was 'no realistic prospect that further dialogue with Strasbourg will produce a change of heart'. The decisions of the ECtHR were 'an adjudication by the tribunal which the United Kingdom has by treaty agreed should give definitive rulings on the subject. The courts are therefore bound to treat them as the authoritative expositions of the Convention'.[117] But this does not give binding force to the jurisprudence of the Strasbourg Court or mean that Parliament's actions are prescribed by the judgment. Following his retirement as Lord Chief Justice of England and Wales, Lord Judge commented that:

> The force of Treaty obligations and the authority of the Strasbourg Court on the correct interpretation of the Convention, and the rights established by it, are well understood. The adoption by our Supreme Court of Convention principles identified by the Strasbourg Court normally follows. The respect owed by Parliament to the views expressed by that Court is embodied in the Human Rights Act itself. But ... the imposition of those views on Parliament represents a dramatic and unconstitutional extension of judicial authority.[118]

Parliament retains ultimate sovereignty over the domestic legal order. The courts apply limited pressure to the doctrine through findings of Convention incompatibility, but have neither developed nor been afforded a power to alter (or force alteration of) the legislative scheme. The related but distinct tension between the

---

[113] J Goldsworthy, 'Losing Faith in Democracy: Why Judicial Supremacy is Rising and What to Do about it', Launch of Policy Exchange Judicial Power Project (9 March 2015) 5–6.

[114] Baroness Hale (n 106) 18.

[115] *R (Chester) v Secretary of State for Justice and McGeoch v Lord President of the Council* (n 23).

[116] ibid [137].

[117] ibid [121]. Not all commentators agree that art 46 requires such a conclusion. Lord Justice Laws spoke on the subject in the 2013 Hamlyn Lectures, noting that 'this is an obligation which sounds in public international law; it forms no part whatever of our domestic law'. J Laws, *The Common Law Constitution* (Cambridge, Cambridge University Press, 2014) 80.

[118] Lord Judge, 'A View from London' *Counsel Magazine* (October 2014) www.counselmagazine.co.uk/articles/view-london.

ECtHR and the legislative sovereignty of the UK Parliament is strictly a matter of international law.

Given the potency of issues such as prisoner voting, it is not surprising that this tension has received some political attention. In 2014, the Conservative Party published a short document outlining 'the Conservatives' proposals for changing Britain's human rights laws'. It was stated at the start of that document that:

> The European Court of Human Rights has developed 'mission creep'. Strasbourg adopts a principle of interpretation that regards the Convention as a 'living instrument'. Even allowing for necessary changes over the decades, the ECtHR has used its 'living instrument doctrine' to expand Convention rights into new areas, and certainly beyond what the framers of the Convention had in mind when they signed up to it. There is mounting concern at Strasbourg's attempts to overrule decisions of our democratically elected Parliament and overturn the UK courts' careful applications of Convention rights.[119]

The document set out reforms to alter the legal status of ECtHR decisions and to repeal the Human Rights Act, replacing it by 'put[ting] the text of the original Human Rights Convention into primary legislation'.[120]

The 2015 Conservative Party Manifesto formalised some of the points made in that earlier document,[121] repeating plans to 'reverse the mission creep that has meant human rights law being used for more and more purposes, and often with little regard for the rights of wider society'.[122] On that basis, the Conservative Party proposed to 'scrap' the Human Rights Act and 'introduce a British Bill of Rights which will restore common sense on the application of human rights in the UK'.[123] It was said that the new Bill of Rights would 'remain faithful to the basic principles of human rights, which we signed up to in the original European Convention on Human Rights'.[124] Crucially, the Bill of Rights would 'break the formal link between British courts and the European Court of Human Rights, and make our own Supreme Court the ultimate arbiter of human rights matters in the UK'.[125]

---

[119] Conservative Party, *Protecting Human Rights in the UK: The Conservatives' Proposals for Changing Britain's Human Rights Laws*, www.conservatives.com/~/media/files/downloadable%20Files/human_rights.pdf, 3.

[120] ibid 5.

[121] ibid.

[122] Conservative Party Manifesto 2015 (n 59) 73.

[123] ibid. The concern about the impact of the ECtHR on parliamentary sovereignty was not shared by all political parties. The Labour Party devoted very little space to the issue in its 2015 Manifesto, stating simply that a Labour Government would 'stand up for citizens' individual rights, protecting the Human Rights Act and reforming rather than walking away from the European Court of Human Rights': Labour Party Manifesto 2015, *Britain Can Be Better*, www.labour.org.uk/manifesto, 67; The Liberal Democrats went the furthest, writing that 'the Human Rights Act will remain' and that a Liberal Democrat Government would 'take appropriate action to comply with decisions of UK courts and the European Court of Human Rights': Liberal Democrat Party Manifesto 2015, *Stronger Economy. Fairer Society. Opportunity for Everyone*, www.libdems.org.uk/manifesto, 14 and 114.

[124] ibid.

[125] ibid 60. The UK Independence Party's position was similar to the Conservative Party. Interestingly, it also included a statement about making 'our own Supreme Court … the final authority on matters of Human Rights'. UK Independence Party Manifesto 2015, *Believe in Britain*, www.ukip.org/manifesto2015, 53.

The last of these statements is curious; Parliament would presumably retain ultimate sovereignty since it could always overrule a judgment of the Supreme Court by enacting legislation to that effect. Breaking the formal link would presumably also involve a revision of the ECHR, at least in respect to the mandatory right to individual petition.

Shortly after its election in May 2015, the new Conservative Government put forward a Queen's Speech that promised to 'bring forward proposals for a British Bill of Rights'. An Explanatory Memorandum published on the same day indicated that the intention was to 'replace the Human Rights Act', 'reform and modernise our human rights legal framework and restore common sense to the application of human rights laws'. At the time of writing, it was not clear whether this would result in another consultation exercise, a draft Bill or primary legislation at some later date.

Opposition to any move to leave the ECHR amongst some members of the Conservative Party led some commentators to speculate that the prisoner voting issue would, once again, be kicked into the long grass until the parliamentary arithmetic could be made to add up in favour of some sort of reform. In the meantime, the issue may yet return to the UK courts in a different context. At the time of writing, the case of *Thierry Delvigne v Commune de Lesparre Médoc and Préfet de la Gironde* had just been determined by the CJEU, sitting as a Grand Chamber. It also concerned the prisoner voting issue. The CJEU concluded that it was possible to maintain a ban which, by operation of law, precluded persons convicted of a serious crime from voting in elections to the European Parliament, but that such a ban had to be proportionate to the aim pursued. The Court determined that the ban to which Delvigne was subject was proportionate insofar as it took into account the nature and gravity of the criminal offence committed and the duration of the penalty. It is not immediately clear what impact the judgment will have on the UK's 'blanket ban' on prisoners voting. While the Strasbourg jurisprudence is not binding on UK domestic courts, the decisions of the CJEU are.[126]

III. THE ECHR, PARLIAMENTARY PRIVILEGE AND PROCEDURES

In addition to the issues relating to legislative sovereignty and law-making discussed above, the ECHR can also have a potential impact on the internal operations of Parliament.

Neither the House of Commons nor the House of Lords falls within the definition of a public body for the purposes of the Human Rights Act 1998 and, in the domestic sphere, they are broadly protected by Article 9 of the Bill of Rights 1688.[127] Article 9 has been recognised as a significant constitutional provision

---

[126] European Communities Act 1972, s 2(1).

[127] Which provides, in modern parlance, that 'the Freedom of Speech and Debates or Proceedings in Parliament ought not to be impeached or questioned in any Court or Place out of Parliament'.

by the UK courts[128] and the Bill of Rights can be seen to underpin Parliament's sovereignty (and the domestic courts' unwillingness to challenge the validity of legislation).[129]

Nonetheless, Parliament still has to have regard to the jurisdiction of the Strasbourg Court. This is because, unlike the domestic courts, the ECtHR is not constrained by parliamentary privilege and the prohibition on questioning or impeaching parliamentary proceedings under Article 9.[130] One example of this is the way in which the ECtHR feels able to review the debate in the UK Parliament. As mentioned above, this could be seen in the case of *Hirst (No 2)*, where the Grand Chamber noted the fact that the domestic legislation was adopted without relevant debate on the point.[131] The Grand Chamber went further in the case of *Animal Defenders International*, where it examined the quality of parliamentary pre-legislative scrutiny in some detail and indicated that it had attached 'considerable weight' to the exacting and pertinent review conducted by, inter alia, the UK Parliament when judging the proportionality of the prohibition on political advertising on television and radio imposed by the Communications Act 2003.[132]

The most obvious cases of concern are circumstances where Members seek to rely on absolute privilege under Article 9 (freedom of speech cases)[133] or where Parliament's select committees are perceived to be acting oppressively or abusing their powers.[134]

In relation to privilege and freedom of speech, the point was well-illustrated in the case of *A v UK*.[135] The case involved an MP who had called the family of a constituent 'neighbours from hell', naming the constituent and giving her precise address in the Chamber. The ECtHR found by a majority of 6:1 that the inability of the constituent to sue for defamation was a justified and proportionate means of promoting the legitimate aims of protecting free speech in Parliament and maintaining the separation of powers between the legislative and the judiciary. Oonagh Gay and Hugh Tomlinson QC have suggested that, having regard to the

---

[128] See, eg, *Thoburn v Sunderland City Council* [2002] EWHC 195 (Admin), [2003] QB 151; and *R (HS2 Action Alliance Ltd) v Secretary of State for Transport* [2014] UKSC 3, [2014] 1 WLR 324.

[129] See, eg, *Edinburgh and Dalkeith Railway Co v Wauchope* (1842) 8 Cl & Fin 710; and *British Railway Board v Pickin* [1974] AC 765. See also the comments of Drewry in ch 13 below.

[130] In the domestic sphere, see, eg, *Pepper v Hart* [1993] AC 593; *Prebble v Television New Zealand Ltd* [1995] 1 AC 321; *R v Chaytor and others* [2010] EWCA Crim 1910, [2010] 2 Cr App R 34.

[131] This has been the subject of some debate (on the basis that where a provision has cross-party support in the UK Parliament, there is not necessarily a substantive debate on the merits or proportionality of the provision).

[132] *Animal Defenders International v UK* (2013) 57 EHRR 21 [114]–[116].

[133] See, eg, O Gay and H Tomlinson, 'Privilege and Freedom of Speech' in Horne, Drewry and Oliver (n 7).

[134] See, eg, R Gordon and A Street, *Select Committees and Coercive Powers—Clarity or Confusion* (London, Constitution Society, 2012).

[135] *A v UK* (2003) 36 EHRR 51. See also M Jack et al (eds), *Erskine May's Parliamentary Practice* 24th edn (London, Butterworths 2011) 301.

dissenting judgment in the case of Judge Loucaides, 'it is possible that in a future, more serious case, the "absolute" immunity in Art 9 will be found to be disproportionate and in violation of the Convention'.[136]

A more recent example of the sort of issue that can arise involved the former MP and Defence Secretary, Geoff Hoon. On 21 March 2010, the *Sunday Times* published the results of a joint investigation which it had carried out with Channel 4's *Dispatches* programme. An undercover journalist had secretly interviewed nine MPs, including Mr Hoon. All the Members were planning to leave the House at the 2010 General Election. Mr Hoon had allegedly told a journalist posing as a company representative that he wanted to make use of his international knowledge and contacts in a way that 'makes money'.[137]

The Parliamentary Commissioner for Standards investigated a complaint under the Code of Conduct against Mr Hoon. The Commissioner concluded that Mr Hoon had breached the MPs' code of conduct and had brought the House of Commons into disrepute. The Commissioner's report was considered by the (then) Commons Standards and Privileges Committee, which took evidence from Mr Hoon. The Committee recommended that 'for committing breaches of the Code of Conduct, one of which was a particularly serious breach, Mr Geoff Hoon apologise to the House through this Committee in writing and that his entitlement to a Parliamentary photo pass be suspended for five years, with effect from 1 January 2011'.[138] The Report from the Committee on Standards and Privileges, covering the Hoon case and a number of similar allegations against other former Members, was debated on 15 December 2010. The House imposed the sanctions recommended by the Committee.

Mr Hoon pursued a series of complaints before the ECtHR.[139] Amongst other things, he alleged a number of violations of Article 6(1) ECHR (in respect of the decisions of the Commissioner, as endorsed by the Committee and the House of Commons). He also complained about the denial of access to a court to challenge, by way of appeal, the legality of the parliamentary proceedings conducted against him and the sanctions imposed.

The Fourth Section of the Strasbourg Court concluded that Mr Hoon's case was inadmissible because the parliamentary proceedings in question, which were concerned with investigating possible breaches of the Code of Conduct of Members of Parliament, did not attract the application of Article 6(1) ECHR, since they did not determine, or give rise to, a dispute as to the applicant's 'civil' rights for the purposes of that Article. In relation to the admissibility of a second complaint in relation to Article 8, the Court's Fourth Section determined, inter alia, that

---

[136] Gay and Tomlinson (n 133).
[137] 'European Court rejects Geoff Hoon's Human Rights Complaint' (*BBC Online*, 4 December 2014) www.bbc.co.uk/news/uk-politics-30326629.
[138] House of Commons Committee on Standards and Privileges (HC 2010–11, 654-I).
[139] *Hoon v UK* [2014] ECHR 1442 (13 November 2014).

the procedure followed gave the applicant 'a fair opportunity to put his case and defend his interests, as regards both his status as a public-office holder and as regards his private reputation'. It also noted that he had an avenue of recourse open to him 'in the form of a legal action against the newspaper in question and the television company. Consequently, the applicant was not entirely without means of redress'. Significantly, the Court's Fourth Section displayed no inhibition in considering a case that would have been out of bounds for a court subject to the Bill of Rights 1688.[140]

A. Parliament's Response

There has been some movement on these issues on the part of Parliament. The report of the Joint Committee on Parliamentary Privilege, which was published in July 2013, made a number of suggestions for fair procedures for witnesses,[141] which were subsequently approved by the Liaison Committee to adopt as guidelines for select committees in order to test how they worked in practice.[142] The House of Lords developed new procedures in 2010 to allow individuals (apart from ministers) who are the subject of criticism in a select committee report to see the report in draft and have the opportunity to make representations.[143]

There is a related issue around the sanctions that either House is able to impose. Although either House may theoretically have the power to fine or imprison in respect of a contempt of the House,[144] these sanctions appear to have fallen into disuse in the UK, and any attempt to resurrect them may fall foul of the ECHR. This could become an issue in circumstances where, for example, an individual refused a select committee summons or lied to a select committee

---

[140] For an even more striking assertion of the Court's jurisdiction over the internal proceedings of national parliaments, see the 2014 decision in *Karàcsony* (Application No 42461/13), where the Court's Second Section decided that the Hungarian Parliament's right to regulate its own proceedings did not outweigh the freedom of expression of a handful of MPs who flouted protocol by displaying slogans on placards during a debate. See *Karàcsony and others v Hungary* [2014] ECHR 939.

[141] Joint Committee on Parliamentary Privilege, *Report of Session 2013–14* (2013–14, HL 30, HC 100).

[142] Formal Minutes of the Liaison Committee, 2013–14 session, 27 November 2013.

[143] The recommendation in the Fourth Report of 2009–10 of the House of Lords Committee for Privileges and Conduct was agreed by the House of Lords on 27 July 2010.

[144] 'The Houses' power to punish non-members for contempt is untested in recent times. In theory, both Houses can summon a person to the bar of the House to reprimand them or order a person's imprisonment. In addition, the House of Lords is regarded as possessing the power to fine non-members. The House of Commons last used its power to fine in 1666 and this power may since have lapsed.' HM Government, *Parliamentary Privilege* (Green Paper, Cm 8318, 2012) para 252. For more on the limitations on select committee powers, see, eg, R Kelly, 'Select Committees: Powers and Functions' in Horne, Drewry and Oliver (n 7) 190–93.

(giving false evidence to a committee under oath is a different matter: the Perjury Act 1911 provides for those making false statements under oath to be tried in the courts).[145]

The Government has noted that if either House were to seek to codify its powers to reprimand, fine or imprison, it would need to review its procedures for punishing non-members to ensure that safeguards were in place so that those individuals received a fair hearing.[146] The Joint Committee on Parliamentary Privilege[147] acknowledged that the ECHR is an 'impediment' on either House 'imposing its will on a contemnor', stating that:

> While domestic courts may be unable to consider proceedings in Parliament, the European Court of Human Rights has asserted its jurisdiction, relying on Article 6 of the European Convention on Human Rights which provides for the right to a fair trial 'by an independent and impartial tribunal'.

Yet the Joint Committee rejected the approach of criminalising specific contempts, arguing that this would entail 'a radical shift of power between Parliament and the courts', 'would introduce delay' and 'would increase uncertainty about how contempts which were not covered by criminal statute could or should be dealt with, and remove the flexibility which is the chief advantage of the current system'.

The Joint Committee instead concluded that the first and most important challenge was 'to assert the continuing existence of each House's jurisdiction over contempt'—contending that the power to fine (based on the power possessed by the UK House of Commons) had only recently been asserted and used in New Zealand. The Joint Committee recognised that the second challenge was to devise a system that complied 'with modern expectations of fairness and due process, which are very different to those which applied in the late nineteenth century'.

Given the fluid and dynamic nature of some select committee proceedings[148] and the varying approaches to witnesses handling taken by different Chairs and committee members, this may be easier said than done, although any guidance to improve the standard of fairness for normal committee inquiries is likely to be welcomed by witnesses.

---

[145] See, eg, R Gordon and A Street, *Select Committees and Coercive Powers—Clarity or Confusion?* (London, Constitution Society, 2012); Jack et al (n 135) 115 and 763; A Horne, 'Evidence under Oath, Perjury and Parliamentary Privilege' (*UK Constitutional Law Blog*, 29 January 2015) http://ukconstitutionallaw.org/2015/01/29/alexander-horne-evidence-under-oath-perjury-and-parliamentary-privilege. Where evidence is not given upon oath, it is still punishable as a contempt of the House.

[146] HM Government (n 144). A previous Joint Committee on Privilege which reported in 1999 had recommended that a statutory power to fine non-Members should be transferred to the High Court; see Joint Committee on Privilege, *First Report* (1998–99, HL 43, HC 214-I) paras 309 and 324.

[147] Joint Committee on Parliamentary Privilege (n 141).

[148] An example of this in the 2010–15 Parliament was the decision of the Public Accounts Committee to examine the (then) General Counsel and Solicitor of HMRC under oath—see Public Accounts Committee, *HM Revenue and Customs Accounts 2010–11* (HC 2010–12, 1531) Q294.

IV. CONCLUSION

The doctrine of parliamentary sovereignty remains central to the constitutional settlement. The doctrine, insofar as it regulates the relationship between the legislature and the courts, is not altered by membership of the Council of Europe and the Convention system. As with all international legal obligations, courts may continue to interpret ambiguous legislative provisions according to the presumption of compliance with international law, but the final word remains with Parliament. Moreover, Parliament has itself prescribed the nature of the courts' powers in relation to the Convention and the Strasbourg Court's jurisprudence. The Human Rights Act 1998 thus provides that the Strasbourg jurisprudence must be 'take[n] into account' (not followed), that legislation must be read compatibly 'so far as is possible to do so' and that courts may declare legislation to be incompatible (but not strike it down). In all instances, Parliament retains the power to overturn judicial decisions or to enact Convention-incompatible legislation.

There are, nevertheless, obvious tensions between the pressure to comply with international law and the legislative sovereignty of Parliament. In relation to the ECtHR, the most obvious source of tension has arisen from the obligation contained in Article 46 ECHR to abide by the final judgments of the Strasbourg Court to which it is a party. It has been argued in this chapter that this is an obligation in international law, with no direct bearing on the domestic doctrine of parliamentary sovereignty. The UK maintains a dualist legal system, meaning that any legislative changes required as a result of judgments that fall within the scope of Article 46 still require acquiescence on the part of the legislature.

So what should happen in circumstances where the Government of the day feels unable to accept a judgment of the ECtHR, such as on the issue of prisoner voting? Assuming that the Government accepts the clear guidance from the Joint Committee on the Draft Voting Eligibility (Prisoners) Bill—that by being a signatory to the Convention system, 'we incur obligations that cannot be the subject of cherry picking'—there are a number of options available.[149]

A first option is simply to denounce the Convention. This is an outcome that the Joint Committee recognised: it concluded that it could not countenance withdrawal from the Convention 'in respect of an issue of modest practical importance'.[150] Withdrawal by the UK would clearly have a significant and deleterious impact on the entire Convention system. Although under Article 65(2) ECHR, denunciation does not have retrospective effect (and hence legally the obligation under Article 46 ECHR would remain), as the Joint Committee observed: 'In practice, were the UK to decide to leave the entire Convention system ... the continuing obligation to comply with the *Hirst* judgment, could become largely academic, politically if not legally.'[151]

---

[149] Joint Committee on Draft Voting Eligibility (Prisoners) Bill (n 69) para 112.
[150] ibid para 229.
[151] ibid para 107.

A second option is for the contracting states concerned to effect compliance in a modest and pragmatic fashion, and see whether that satisfies the Court. In the case of prisoner voting, the Joint Committee suggested a compromise solution: namely, to return to the situation that pertained when the UK entered into the Convention. Some would see this as a climbdown that would result in a perceived loss of sovereignty; others would see it as a sensible compromise.

A final option is to examine further the idea of some form of democratic override mechanism. Such an option may look unlikely in practice given the diplomatic sensitivities involved. Moreover, to be acceptable in rule of law terms, it would probably require the override to be exercisable only in circumstances where the Committee of Ministers at the Council of Europe determined that the ECtHR had erred in its interpretation of the Convention (rather than allowing individual Member States to try to opt out of judgments that they found unsatisfactory). Given that it is already open to contracting states to amend the Convention itself, this may not be such a radical innovation. It could certainly avoid a disavowal of the Convention system, although the compromise may be at the cost of certainty and of the Strasbourg Court's authority over the interpretation of the Convention.

13

Euroscepticism and Parliamentary Sovereignty: The Lingering Shadows of Factortame *and* Thoburn[1]

GAVIN DREWRY

If the supremacy within the European Community of Community law over the national law of Member States was not always inherent in the EEC Treaty, it was certainly well-established in the jurisprudence of the Court of Justice long before the UK joined the Community. Thus, whatever limitation on its sovereignty Parliament accepted when it enacted the European Communities Act 1972 was entirely voluntary. (Lord Bridge, *Factortame No 2*)[2]

[T]he doctrine of parliamentary sovereignty clearly means something very different from what it meant before Britain entered the European Community in 1973. It remains in form, but not in substance. In practice, therefore, if not in law, parliamentary sovereignty is no longer the governing principle of the British constitution. (Vernon Bogdanor)[3]

I. INTRODUCTION

AS THIS CHAPTER was being completed, in the aftermath of the 2015 General Election, backbenchers on the 'Eurosceptic' wing of the Conservative Party—under the banner of 'Conservatives for Britain'—were girding their loins for a vigorous 'leave' campaign in the in-out referendum on UK membership of the European Union (EU) promised in their party's election manifesto. One of their key demands was 'the right for Britain to veto EU laws'—to which

---

[1] Parts of this chapter have been adapted from a previously published article by the author: G Drewry, 'The Jurisprudence of British Euroscepticism: A Strange Banquet of Fish and Vegetables' (2007) 3(2) *Utrecht Law Review* 101.
[2] *R v Secretary of State for Transport ex p Factortame (No 2)* [1991] AC 603, 658.
[3] V Bogdanor, *The New British Constitution* (Oxford, Hart Publishing, 2009) 283.

the Foreign Secretary, Philip Hammond, responded as follows, in a BBC television interview with Andrew Marr:

> If you were talking about the House of Commons having a unilateral red card veto—that is not achievable, that's not negotiable, because that would effectively be the end of the EU. What we are looking for is a system where a group of national parliaments could operate a red card.[4]

The core of the Eurosceptic position has targeted the provisions of the European Communities Act 1972 that affirm the supremacy of European law over domestic legislation enacted by the Westminster Parliament. Thus, section 2(1) of the Act provides that (in respect of European legislative instruments, such as Community regulations, that have direct effect):

> All such rights, powers, liabilities, obligations and restrictions from time to time created or arising by or under the Treaties, and all such remedies and procedures from time to time provided for by or under the Treaties, as in accordance with the Treaties are without further enactment to be given legal effect or used in the United Kingdom shall be recognised and available in law, and be enforced, allowed and followed accordingly; and the expression 'enforceable EU right' and similar expressions shall be read as referring to one to which this sub-section applies.

Section 2(2), which applies to other European measures—for the most part directives—that do not have direct effect, makes it possible to give effect to such measures by secondary legislation; moreover, section 2(4) further provides that such secondary legislation can amend an Act of Parliament, since the delegated legislative power includes the power to make such provision as might be made by an Act of Parliament.

Bearing in mind these issues and the controversies surrounding them, this chapter looks back at some key elements of the continuing debate about the constitutional relationship between a supposedly supreme or sovereign Westminster Parliament and the judiciary: a judiciary that (according to established constitutional orthodoxies) stands aloof from political controversy and is respectful of the will of Parliament, but is charged with the crucial task of interpreting and applying the relevant statutory provisions and doing so in a context in which the Treaties of the EU have acquired a quasi-constitutional status. The chapter focuses on two juristic causes célèbres which brought into sharp focus some of the constitutional realities of EU membership—the *Factortame* case (or, more accurately, cases) and *Thoburn*, the so-called Metric Martyrs case. Both cases were played out at the end of the last century, but their significance lingers on.

---

[4] Broadcast on 7 June 2015, www.bbc.co.uk/programmes/articles/3hshxFhHM4dKd3px6Q3NzRF/transcripts.

II. SOVEREIGNTY: A MULTI-LAYERED CONCEPT

Sovereignty is a ubiquitous and much-debated word in the lexicon of constitutional discourse, and it has proved to be a highly emotive term in the context of the never-ending debates about the EU. The term has various nuances of usage—two, in particular, both of which are of relevance to the theme of this chapter.

At one level, sovereignty connotes the definitive autonomy of post-Westphalian, 'sovereign', nation states—autonomy that has, in modern times, been challenged by globalisation, in all its manifestations, and by the proliferation of supranational institutions and treaty obligations, including those establishing the terms of EU membership for its 28 Member States.

At another level, in the UK, we find, in constitutional sources going back to the seventeenth century, recurrent reference to a narrower conception of sovereignty, qualified by the adjective 'parliamentary'—referring to the status of Parliament as the supreme and ultimate source of law. In his dissenting judgment in the Supreme Court 'black spider letters' case (involving the disclosure of correspondence between the Prince of Wales and a government minister) in March 2015, Lord Wilson referred, in somewhat hyperbolic terms, to the 'precious constitutional principles' that had been invoked in this case by the Court of Appeal—'the most precious of which is parliamentary sovereignty, emblematic of our democracy'.[5] Bogdanor has, using more measured language, interpreted the principle to mean that 'the British Constitution could … be summed up in just eight words: "What the Queen in Parliament enacts is law"'.[6] However, as he further points out, in the passage cited as an epigraph to this chapter, parliamentary sovereignty may not be quite 'the governing principle' that its champions might wish to claim for it.[7] And its claims to being 'emblematic of our democracy' might equally be open to some dispute.

Both these variants of the term 'sovereignty' have featured strongly in the UK debates—inside and outside Westminster—about the nature and development of the EU and about the UK's membership thereof. In some contexts, references to sovereignty in its 'national autonomy' sense have been conflated with parliamentary sovereignty—a reflection both of the slipperiness of the concept and perhaps also of a solipsistic tendency for Parliament to equate its own legislative supremacy with the sovereign autonomy of the nation state of which it is the legislative branch.

III. WESTMINSTER SOVEREIGNTY: THE DICEYAN MODEL AND ITS CRITICS

As noted in chapter 12 above, the modern evolutionary history of the constitutional principle of parliamentary sovereignty in England dates back to the Glorious

---

[5] *R (Evans) v Attorney General* [2015] UKSC 21, [2015] 2 WLR 813 [168].
[6] Bogdanor (n 3) 13.
[7] *cf* the opening words of Lord Hope's speech in *Jackson v Attorney General* [2005] UKHL 56 [104].

Revolution of 1688. Two hundred years later, AV Dicey enunciated what came to be regarded as the 'classical' formulation of the principle: in essence, the unlimited right of Parliament to make or unmake any law (a right that extends to all parts of the Queen's dominions) and the principle that no person or body has a right to override or set aside the legislative enactments of the sovereign Parliament. There is no codified constitution that gives special status to entrench statutes that have special constitutional significance, and no Parliament can bind its successors.

The Diceyan doctrine has subsequently been critically re-examined by many modern jurists, some of whom have pointed out that Dicey's doctrine was formulated in the heyday of the British Empire, when the Westminster Parliament legislated not only for the UK but also for numerous British colonial territories. When these territories gained their independence in the second half of the twentieth century, some major weaknesses of the 'classical' model of parliamentary sovereignty were exposed. As Adam Tomkins has put it: '[I]f Parliament cannot bind its successors, what is the legal effect of Parliament in (say) 1950 declaring that a particular colony is independent if a later Parliament in (say) 1960 decides to revoke that acknowledgement of independence and to resume its former imperial task of legislating for the territory?'[8] And he continues: 'if post-colonial independence generated one set of problems for the Diceyan conception of parliamentary sovereignty, the United Kingdom's accession ... to the [EU] gave rise to another'.[9]

IV. PARLIAMENTARY SOVEREIGNTY AND EUROPEAN LAW

Many modern variations on the theme of parliamentary sovereignty can be found in the controversies surrounding the UK's relationship with 'Europe' (the inverted commas being a reminder that, while this chapter is mainly about the EU, the debates have spilled over into, and sometimes been bracketed with, issues surrounding the European Convention on Human Rights—see chapter 12). They have featured explicitly and implicitly in the ebb and flow of the Manichean disputes between 'Eurosceptics' and 'Europhiles' that lie at the heart of present-day political controversies, but the story goes back a long way—at least as far back as the enactment of the European Communities Act 1972.

The actual word 'sovereignty' has sometimes been bandied about in these debates in both of the senses noted above, but, even when it is not explicitly articulated, its spirit lurks between the lines of much Europe-related discourse—as in the opening of the debate on the second reading of the European Communities Bill in February 1972, when Labour Opposition spokesman, Peter Shore MP, claimed that 'over a wide area of our affairs Parliament is inevitably doomed to become a spectator of legislative events'.[10]

---

[8] A Tomkins, *Public Law* (Oxford, Clarendon Press, 2003) 94.
[9] ibid.
[10] HC Deb 15 February 1972, col 295.

It is interesting to note, however, that much of the early debate in Parliament about membership of the European Communities seems to have paid surprisingly scant regard to the constitutional implications. Anthony King has observed that in the debate in 1961 arising out of the Macmillan Government's (as it turned out ill-fated) decision to seek membership of the European Communities, the emphasis, on both sides of the House of Commons was on the implications of joining an *economic* community:

> The House debated the issue twice that summer ... On neither occasion were constitutional considerations remotely to the fore. The prime minister in his initial statement made no reference to them; neither did the leader of the opposition, Hugh Gaitskell. ... Addressing the ... question of (in Macmillan's own words) 'what has often been called sovereignty', the prime minister insisted that joining the EEC would have few if any implications along these lines, and he likened membership of the Common Market to Britain's membership of other international organisations such as the North Atlantic Treaty Organisation and the Organisation for European Economic Cooperation.[11]

This observation strongly echoes those of Danny Nicol in his study of what he saw, in the years leading up to the new millennium, as the growing 'juridification' of British politics.[12] Nicol took issue with the use of the phrase 'entirely voluntary' by Lord Bridge in *Factortame (No 2)* (see the epigraph to this chapter), with reference to Parliament's supposed awareness of the sovereignty implications of joining the European Communities. His examination of the parliamentary debates of the 1960s and 1970s led him to cast serious doubt on whether many MPs (or even ministers) fully appreciated the constitutional implications of membership. In particular, there was little overt recognition of the pivotal role of the European Court of Justice (ECJ): MPs were much more worried about the *legislative* functions of the Commission and the Council of Ministers, and the threat that they might usurp the law-making role of the Westminster Parliament. And only very gradually did it seem to dawn on them, after *Factortame* and the *EOC* case,[13] and in the run-up to the ratification of the Maastricht Treaty in 1992, that the UK courts themselves, empowered by key rulings of the ECJ, would regard it as part of their function to enforce EC law, even in the face of primary Westminster legislation.

Having examined the debates in 1971 on the principle of entry, Nicol suggested the following explanation for MPs' seeming lack of awareness of the constitutional implications:

> Perhaps the most convincing explanation is the constitutional milieu in which parliamentarians functioned. During the preceding sixty years the courts had not only respected the doctrine of parliamentary sovereignty but had (at least until the late 1960s) adopted a

---

[11] A King, *The British Constitution* (Oxford, Oxford University Press, 2007) 93.
[12] D Nicol, *EC Membership and the Judicialization of British Politics* (Oxford, Oxford University Press, 2001).
[13] *R v Secretary of State for Employment ex p Equal Opportunities Commission* [1995] AC 1, discussed below.

restrained attitude to judicial review. The fact that the judiciary had for so long operated only on the fringes of the political arena meant that for parliamentarians the world of public law was alien territory. They were accustomed to working within a politics-based constitution largely untouched by legal concerns. Their inability to appreciate the likelihood that Community membership would entail a shift in power from Parliament to the judges stemmed in no small measure from their unfamiliarity with having to grapple with legal doctrines.[14]

And, in the concluding section of his book he reiterated the point that politicians in those early days were simply not accustomed to the idea of courts playing such an important constitutional role:

> MPs were so unfamiliar with a prominent judicial role that they were in no position to debate it until they had experienced it. Even those MPs who were previously barristers or solicitors seemingly divested themselves of their legal baggage once they entered the political arena.[15]

Thus, the crucial metamorphosis—the 'juridification', to adopt Nicol's terminology—of a 'politics-based' constitution, in which the courts had hitherto been willing to accept without much question the sovereign prerogatives of Parliament, into a 'law-based' constitution in which legislators find themselves circumscribed by a higher level of constitutional norms which the courts are ready and willing to apply, even in the face of primary legislation, seems to have happened without Parliament realising what it was signing up to.

V. PARLIAMENTARY SOVEREIGNTY AND JUDICIAL DISEMPOWERMENT

Parliamentary sovereignty requires the judiciary to apply statute law strictly in accordance with the will of Parliament. In practice, this may be easier said than done. As already indicated, much of the controversy about sovereignty in relation to the EU ultimately has to do with the relationship between Parliament and the courts.

From the earliest days of the UK's membership of the European Communities, the British courts have recognised that, in Lord Denning's words, 'rights or obligations created by the Treaty are to be given legal effect'[16] and this principle—an inescapable consequence of EC membership—has regularly been reaffirmed in subsequent cases (notably in *Factortame*, discussed below). It has been noted that, in the UK, issues of Community law 'arise in many different types of proceedings in diverse courts and tribunals including prosecutions in magistrates' courts and the Crown Court, in ... proceedings for judicial review, in industrial tribunals and in civil actions for damages and other remedies against both public

---

[14] Nicol (n 12) 75.
[15] ibid 254.
[16] *HP Bulmer Ltd v J Bollinger SA* [1974] Ch 401.

bodies and commercial organisations'.¹⁷ The most familiar device for challenging the non-compliance of public authorities with EU obligations is to apply for judicial review in the Administrative Court.¹⁸ Part 68 of the Civil Procedure Rules enables the civil courts in England and Wales to apply to the ECJ for preliminary rulings under Article 267 of the Treaty on the Functioning of the European Union (previously Articles 234 and 177 of the Treaty Establishing the European Communities).¹⁹ Similarly, the UK Supreme Court may make references under rule 42 of the Supreme Court Rules 2009.

There is, indeed, an important set of issues about the behaviour of national courts in the latter context—the question when and when not to refer an issue to the ECJ. It has been noted, for instance, that UK courts have become more willing to make preliminary references (as happened, as we shall see, in Factortame, but not in the *Thoburn* case or the more recent *HS2* case) and have eased the restrictive criteria for so doing that were originally laid down in 1974 by Lord Denning in the case of *Bulmer v Bollinger*.²⁰ Paul Craig has suggested several explanations for this, one being that 'the very fact of referral may enable the national court to have some input into the substantive doctrine which is being developed by the ECJ'.²¹ It has also been suggested that the capacity of courts that are lower in the judicial hierarchy to make references can enable them 'to circumvent higher court jurisprudence', as well as earning their decisions a higher profile among legal commentators.²²

VI. THE PRIMACY OF EU LAW: BEFORE *FACTORTAME*

Long before the UK became a member of the European Communities, the ECJ had sent out clear messages about the supremacy of European law over the domestic laws of Member States. In the *Van Gend en Loos* case (1963), it spoke of 'a new legal order of international law for the benefit of which the [member] states have limited their sovereign rights, albeit within limited fields'. And in *Costa v ENEL* (1963), it held that 'the terms and spirit of the Treaty [of Rome], make it impossible for the

---

¹⁷ A Le Sueur and M Sunkin, *Public Law* (Harlow, Longman, 1997) 684.
¹⁸ For an extensive discussion of the nature of judicial review as applied in relation to issues of EC law, see H Mercer, 'European Union Law' in M Supperstone et al (eds), *Judicial Review* 5th edn (London, LexisNexis, 2014) ch 15.
¹⁹ ibid paras 15.8.1–15.8.16.
²⁰ *HP Bulmer Ltd v J Bollinger SA* (n 16).
²¹ P Craig, 'Report on the United Kingdom' in A-M Slaughter et al (eds), *The European Court and National Courts: Doctrine and Jurisprudence* (Oxford, Hart Publishing, 1998) 195, 221.
²² K Alter, 'explaining National Court Acceptance of European court Jurisprudence: A critical Evaluation of Theories of Legal Integration', in Slaughter et al (n 21) 227, 242. For further discussion of these and related issues, see K Alter, 'The EU's Legal System and Domestic Policy: Spillover or Backlash?' (2000) 54 *International Organisation* 489; C Carrubba, 'Legal Integration and the Use of the Preliminary Readings Procedure in the European Union' (2005) 59 *International Organisation* 399.

states ... to accord precedence to a unilateral measure over a legal system accepted by them on a basis of reciprocity. Such a measure cannot therefore be inconsistent with that legal system'. So the basic constitutional picture was (or should have been) clear to Parliament when it debated and passed the 1972—and if it was not clear, then the penny should certainly have dropped with the ECJ's decision in *Simmenthal* (1978),[23] a case which (in Alan Page's words) 'first alerted many UK lawyers to the constitutional significance of membership'.[24] In that case, relating to a law enacted by the Italian Parliament, the ECJ held that: 'In accordance with the principle of the precedence of Community law, the relationship between provisions of the Treaty and directly applicable measures of the institutions on the one hand and the national law of the Member States on the other, is such that those provisions and measures not only by their entry into force render automatically inapplicable any conflicting provisions of current national law.'

Soon afterwards came the opening chapters of the *Factortame* saga, involving the rights of Spanish fishing companies under the European Common Fisheries Policy (CFP). In the first of a sequence of cases stretching over some 12 years, the House of Lords, having made a reference to the ECJ on the legality of part of the Merchant Shipping Act 1988 (an attempt by the Government to side-step the UK's Treaty obligations under the CFP), confirmed the supremacy of EC law over national law in areas where the Communities have competence. In a further phase of the litigation (*Factortame ((No2)*), the ECJ held that the relevant provisions of the 1988 Act had to be disapplied by the UK courts if they were incompatible with the Treaty. Further rulings confirmed that Member States could be liable in damages for breaches of EC law.

We turn now to look in more detail at this saga—significant much less for its outcome (which was more or less inevitable) than for its revelatory impact on those who had hitherto failed to recognise the juridical significance of EU membership for Diceyan parliamentary sovereignty.

VII. THE *FACTORTAME* SAGA

'EC "rewrites" British Constitution' thundered *The Independent* (20 June 1990); 'Landmark Ruling Gives EC Power over UK Law' murmured *The Times*. Both newspaper headlines signalled the shockwaves generated by the ruling of the ECJ, and associated decisions of the House of Lords, in *Factortame Ltd v Secretary of State for Transport (No 2)*.[25] Many cases with at least as much actual or potential relevance to the UK had been decided by the ECJ since the UK joined the

---

[23] Case C-106/77 *Simmenthal II* [1978] ECR 629.
[24] A Page, 'Balancing Supremacy: EU Membership and the Constitution' in P Giddings and G Drewry (eds), *Britain in the European Union* (Basingstoke, Palgrave Macmillan, 2004) 49.
[25] Case C-213/89 *Factortame Ltd v Secretary of State for Transport (No 2)* [1991] 1 AC 603.

European Communities in January 1973, but the *Factortame* saga still has a special place in the political history of Britain's love-hate relationship with the Community and the EU which that Community later became. The saga unfolded more or less exactly at the point that the tide of opinion in Mrs Thatcher's Conservative Government was turning strongly in a Eurosceptical direction—signalled by the Prime Minister's famous speech to the College of Europe in Bruges in September 1988. The ECJ's decision, and the UK's courts' rulings that followed from it, was—to most lawyers at least—inevitable and unsurprising. But to many non-lawyers, it highlighted with hindsight the magnitude of the constitutional implications of the European Communities Act 1972, which had given statutory effect to the UK's decision to sign up to the European Treaty.

The legal and constitutional ramifications (particularly the 'parliamentary sovereignty' implications) of the *Factortame* litigation and other cases related to it have been subjected to exhaustive analysis elsewhere,[26] and only an outline, with no more than a (non-lawyer's) sketch of the complex technicalities, will be offered here. Its background lies in the CFP, initiated in 1970 by the six founding Member States of the EC, nearly three years before Britain joined the Communities in January 1973.[27]

The British fishing industry is economically important and politically vocal, and its voice was heard in the background to the debates in the Westminster Parliament in the run-up to entry. (It has, incidentally, been noted that one of many grievances raised by anti-market MPs in those debates was the fact that British accession to the CFP was announced in Parliament in December 1971, two months *after* the House of Commons had debated and agreed in principle to join the Communities.)[28]

In 1983, a new 'Total Allowable Catches' regime was introduced to conserve fish stocks through the imposition of national quotas. Spain, which joined the EC in 1986, did badly in the quota allocation, and a number of Spanish fishing companies—Spanish fishermen seem to have been every bit as politically vocal

---

[26] Every UK public law textbook or treatise published since the first *Factortame* judgments has included substantial discussion of the case (but coverage in political science textbooks has been very patchy and generally superficial; see below). There are also numerous case notes in UK (and some overseas) legal journals. See, in addition: Tomkins (n 8) 212; Nicol (n 12); N Gravells, 'Disapplying an Act of Parliament Pending a Preliminary Ruling: Constitutional Enormity or Community Law Right?' [1989] *Public Law* 568; D Oliver, 'Fishing on the Incoming Tide' (1991) 54 *Modern Law Review* 442; P Craig, 'Sovereignty of the United Kingdom Parliament after *Factortame*' (1991) 11 *Yearbook of European Law* 221; Craig (n 21); HWR Wade, 'What Has Happened to the Sovereignty of Parliament?' (1991) 107 *Law Quarterly Review* 1; J Drexl, 'Was Sir Francis Drake a Dutchman?—British Supremacy of Parliament after *Factortame*' (1993) 41 *American Journal of Comparative Law* 551; I Loveland, 'Parliamentary Sovereignty and the European Community: The Unfinished Revolution?' (1996) 49 *Parliamentary Affairs* 517; D Morris, 'The Scope for Constitutional Challenge of Westminster Legislation' (1991) 12 *Statute Law Review* 186; C Harlow, 'Disposing of Dicey: From Legal Autonomy to Constitutional Discourse?' (2000) 48 *Political Studies* 356.

[27] For a comprehensive overview of the history and rationale of the CFP, see M Wise, *The Common Fisheries Policy of the European Community* (London, Methuen, 1984).

[28] Nicol (n 12) 80.

as their British counterparts—sought to obtain part of the British quota either by purchasing fishing boats already registered as British (under a statute of 1894) or by re-registering their own boats in Britain, establishing subsidiary companies in the UK for the latter purpose. The UK Government (lobbied by disgruntled British fishermen) tried to prevent this 'quota hopping' by introducing new requirements of nationality and residency for the crews of British shipping vessels, together with a requirement that the vessels operated from British ports. These measures were challenged in the ECJ and proved, in any case, difficult to enforce, so the decision was taken to legislate against the subsidiary companies. Provisions were included in the Merchant Shipping Act 1988 to prevent the registration of vessels as British unless they were owned by resident British citizens or by companies, three-quarters of whose shareholders were resident citizens.

The European Commission then brought an enforcement action against the UK in the ECJ, challenging the nationality requirement as an apparent breach of EC law.[29] But the more significant litigation in the context of the present discussion began with an application for judicial review brought by a number of Spanish companies, including Factortame Ltd, in the High Court, claiming that the conditions laid down in the 1988 Act were in breach of various articles of the Treaty of Rome and thus infringed their rights under Community law. The UK Government contended that the requirements of the Act were fully compatible with EC law and were merely intended to ensure that ships registered in Britain had a bona fide residency basis for being allowed to do so.

In March 1989, the Divisional Court then referred the issue to the ECJ under Article 177 (subsequently renumbered as Article 234) of the Treaty Establishing the European Communities, meanwhile granting the applicants an interim injunction temporarily requiring the British Government to allow the ships to remain on the register pending the ECJ's substantive ruling. The Government successfully appealed against this injunction, the House of Lords holding that English courts could not grant interim relief that had the effect of disapplying an Act of Parliament and that, in any event, according to section 21 of the Crown Proceedings Act 1947, interim injunctions could not be granted against the Crown in civil proceedings.[30] However, their Lordships then referred the matter to the ECJ.

In June 1990, the ECJ (ruling in advance of a substantive decision on the original reference by the Divisional Court) reaffirmed the by now well-established principle[31] that national courts are required to set aside any provisions of national law that prevents a directly applicable Community law from having full effect. The case then came back to the House of Lords, which now accepted that it was empowered to grant interim injunctions against ministers where an issue of Community law is involved.[32] In reaching this decision, it made clear that it was exercising a

---

[29] Case C-246/89R *Commission of the European Communities v UK* [1989] ECR 3125.
[30] *Factortame Ltd v Secretary of State for Transport* [1990] 2 AC 85.
[31] See in particular *Simmenthal II* (n 23).
[32] Case C-213/89 *Factortame Ltd v Secretary of State for Transport (No 2)* [1991] 1 AC 603.

jurisdiction expressly conferred on it by the UK Parliament under section 3(1) of the European Communities Act 1972, which provides that:

> For the purpose of all legal proceedings any question as to the meaning or effect of any of the Treaties, or as to the validity, meaning or effect of any EU instrument, shall be treated as a question of law (and, if not referred to the European Court, be for determination as such in accordance with the principles laid down by and any relevant decision of the European Court).

So, whatever critics may have thought to the contrary, this was no illicit or revolutionary usurpation of parliamentary supremacy by an English court.[33] The UK Government issued an Order in Council to amend the relevant part of the 1988 Act. In July 1991, the ECJ ruled on the substantive issue, holding that the 1998 Act was indeed incompatible with Community law.[34]

This was no means the end of the *Factortame* story, the political controversies surrounding which rumbled on through the 1990s, not least when a further ECJ ruling rubbed salt into the wound by confirming (by extension from its earlier decision in *Francovich v Italy*)[35] that the UK must pay financial compensation to the Spanish companies that had been denied the right to fish.[36] Even as late as 2002, the Court of Appeal was called upon to address a technical case relating to the payment of fees to a firm of forensic accountants who had prepared and submitted the earlier claims for damages.[37] And, of course, the case remains as one of many black marks in the ledger of Eurosceptic grievances, albeit now somewhat faded by time—marking the point at which the courts suddenly entered public and political consciousness as the allies of Brussels and the upholders of a new constitutional-legal order against the old order of unquestioned Diceyan parliamentary sovereignty.

A number of commentators have discussed the *Factortame* cases in juxtaposition with the subsequent, and equally important, ruling of the House of Lords in *R v Secretary of State for Employment ex p Equal Opportunities Commission*.[38] In this case, which involved the employment rights of part-time workers under the Equal Pay Directive, the House of Lords felt quite confident about disapplying provisions of a UK statute without first referring the matter to the ECJ. Danny Nicol, who describes this case as 'the natural follow up to *Factortame*',[39] observes

---

[33] See Tomkins (n 8) 117.
[34] (Case C-221/89) *R v Secretary of State for Transport, Ex parte Factortame Ltd (No 3)* [1992] QB 680 ('Factortame II'), 25 July 1991.
[35] *Francovich and Bonifaci v Italy* [1991] ECR I-5357, [1993] 2 CMLR 66.
[36] Joined Cases C-46/93 and C-48/93 *Brasserie du Pêcheur v Germany* and *R v Secretary of State for Transport ex p Factortame* [1996] ECR I-4845. See also *R v Secretary of State ex p Factortame Ltd (No 5)* [2000] 1 AC 524.
[37] *Factortame v Secretary of State for the Environment, Transport and the Regions (No 2)* [2002] 4 All ER 97.
[38] *R v Secretary of State for Employment ex p Equal Opportunities Commission* [1995] AC 1.
[39] Nicol (n 12) 196.

that 'no longer did the United Kingdom's highest court feel compelled to refer statutory provisions to the ECJ whenever it believed them to be incompatible with Community law. Now it was prepared to override them itself'.[40] He quotes an editorial in *The Times* around the time of the decision (5 March 1994) as saying that 'by its methods in the EOC case the House of Lords has given Britain its first taste of a constitutional court'. The newspaper anticipated a heated debate in Parliament, though in the event, as Nicol observed, the case received only tangential parliamentary attention. The House of Lords also made clear that its ruling of incompatibility was directly effective without the need for any amendment of the legislation.

VIII. THE METRIC MARTYRS

Metrication is one of those symbolic issues that seem to arouse an astonishing degree of nationalistic sentiment among British citizens, much of it seemingly out of proportion to the subject's substantive importance. The debate about metrication in Britain long pre-dates the establishment of the EC (there were numerous official reports and parliamentary debates on the subject throughout the nineteenth century) and a decision in principle to move towards the replacement of imperial units of measurement by metric ones was taken by the Wilson Government in the 1960s, several years before the enactment of the European Communities Act 1972.[41]

The 'Metric Martyrs' case that so agitated Eurosceptic sentiments concerned four food retailers, in different parts of the country, who had fallen foul of UK weights and measures legislation that had given effect to an EU metrication directive (80/181/EEC). An important feature of this legislation was to require traders who continued to use imperial measures to display the metric equivalents as well. The defendant whose case attracted the most attention then, and has continued to do so since, was Steven Thoburn, a greengrocer from the city of Sunderland in the north of England, who was determined to continue to display his goods marked only with imperial weights and to use only weighing machines calibrated accordingly. Three of the cases (including Thoburn's) had involved successful criminal prosecutions; the fourth case arose from magistrates' rejection of an appeal against conditions that had been attached by a local authority to the renewal of a trading licence. The four cases were conjoined in appeals by way of case stated (procedurally not quite the same as a judicial review, though often of similar effect) from magistrates' courts to the Queen's Bench Divisional Court.

The main substantive issue in the case was whether legislation passed after the enactment of the European Communities Act 1972 could be said to have impliedly

---

[40] ibid 198.
[41] See G Drewry, 'Metrication: An Interim Review' (1976) 47 *Political Quarterly* 332.

repealed section 2(2) of the 1972 Act. The latter—cited at the beginning of this chapter—had conferred a so-called Henry VIII power[42] to enable primary legislation to be amended by means of subordinate legislation for the purpose of implementing any Community obligation in the UK. The Weights and Measures Act 1985 had been amended by this means to give effect to the EC Units of Measurement Directives. The appellants argued that this Henry VIII power could only be used in respect of legislation already on the statute book at the time the 1972 Act had been passed and that the amendments to the 1985 Act, which were the basis of the appellants' convictions, were unlawful.

The details of the case can be found in an immensely detailed and learned judgment by Laws LJ, who ruled against the appellants.[43] The essence of his finding was that there can be no limitation on the use of a Henry VIII clause. The principle of parliamentary sovereignty means that no Parliament can bind its successors, and this means that Parliament cannot dictate the form of future legislation. He also ruled that there was a distinct category of *constitutional* statute—of which the European Communities Act 1972 is one important instance—to which the principle of implied repeal (overriding previous statutory provisions merely by contradicting those provisions in a subsequent Act of Parliament) did not apply. A constitutional statute can only be repealed in express terms. This echoes Craig's comment in the late 1990s on the significance of *Factortame* that, at the very least, it 'means that the concept of implied repeal ... will no longer apply to clashes concerning Community and national law'.[44] The relevant passage in Laws LJ's judgment is as follows:

> We should recognise a hierarchy of Acts of Parliament: as it were 'ordinary' statutes and 'constitutional' statutes. The two categories must be distinguished on a principled basis. In my opinion a constitutional statute is one which (a) conditions the legal relationship between citizen and State in some general, overarching manner, or (b) enlarges or diminishes the scope of what we would now regard as fundamental constitutional rights. (a) and (b) are of necessity closely related: it is difficult to think of an instance of (a) that is not also an instance of (b). The special status of constitutional statutes follows the special status of constitutional rights. Examples are the Magna Carta, the Bill of Rights 1689, the Act of Union, the Reform Acts which distributed and enlarged the franchise, the Human Rights Act 1998, the Scotland Act 1998 and the Government of Wales Act 1998. The [European Communities Act 1972] clearly belongs in this family. It incorporated the whole corpus of substantive Community rights and obligations, and gave overriding domestic effect to the judicial and administrative machinery of Community law. It may be there has never been a statute having such profound effects on so many dimensions of our daily lives. The [European Communties Act 1972] is, by force of the common law, a constitutional statute.[45]

---

[42] A term used, usually pejoratively, with reference to the sixteenth-century monarch's autocratic reputation for legislating by royal decree.
[43] *Thoburn v Sunderland City Council* [2002] EWHC 195 (Admin), [2003] QB 151.
[44] P Craig, *Administrative Law* 4th edn (London, Sweet & Maxwell, 1999) 302.
[45] *Thoburn v Sunderland City Council* (n 43) 185.

This passage—much discussed subsequently by constitutional lawyers—encapsulates the same kind of message that came as such a shock to those observers of the *Factortame* case whose heads had been buried in the sand about the extent of the constitutional revolution consequent upon UK membership of the EC. The idea of there being a sub-species of 'constitutional statute', treated as something distinctive by the courts, as identified by Laws LJ, would have been unthinkable in the pre-EC era a generation or so ago.[46] The absence of a codified British constitution has meant that we in the UK—lawyers and non-lawyers alike—have had to climb a very steep learning curve to get to grips with new ways of talking and thinking about constitutional matters[47] (and these issues were to be revisited a decade later in the *HS2* case, considered below).

The Divisional Court refused the appellants leave to appeal to the House of Lords, but certified that a point of law of general public importance was involved; the House of Lords itself subsequently refused leave to appeal. A campaign was launched to secure a free pardon for Mr Thoburn and an application, backed by the civil liberties pressure group Liberty, was subsequently lodged with the applications committee of the European Court of Human Rights (ECtHR), but in February 2004, the committee declared the application inadmissible.[48] A few days after learning about this decision, Mr Thoburn died of a heart attack, but his 'martyrdom' was immortalised on numerous campaigning websites. Eventually, he (posthumously) and his supporters were to be vindicated. In September 2007, the Commission announced that it was reversing its policy and that the UK would not be required to go metric by 2009. EU Commissioner Verheugen told the BBC: 'I organised a huge consultation, and the result was that industry told us there was no problem with the existing system. I want to bring to an end a bitter, bitter battle that has lasted for decades and which in my view is completely pointless. We're bringing this battle to an end.'[49] So an apparent defeat in the courts had given a lot of additional momentum to a political campaign—one that eventually proved successful.

It should be noted, moreover, that the courts in which this battle was fought were not the ECJ in Luxembourg, but the UK's own domestic courts. Luxembourg's jurisprudence has empowered the UK courts, and the latter have had no hesitation in accepting their role as upholders of European law, without the need for constant external prompting by their ECJ colleagues. This provides further food for Eurosceptic thought—as does another area of recent and continuing controversy, considered in the next section.

---

[46] Though, by convention, the House of Commons has tended to treat constitutionally significant Bills, such as the European Communities Bill, in a particularly formal and inclusive way, eg, by holding the committee stage, where the Bill is considered in detail, clause by clause, on the floor of the House rather than in a much smaller public Bill committee.

[47] But see the cautionary comment on the implications of Sir John Laws' judgment in an editorial note in (2007) 28(2) *Statute Law Review* iii–v.

[48] *Thoburn v UK* App No 30614/02.

[49] http://news.bbc.co.uk/1/low/uk/6988521.stm.

IX. THE EU CHARTER OF FUNDAMENTAL RIGHTS: ANOTHER CUE FOR EUROSCEPTIC OUTRAGE

On 12 November 2013, the *London Evening Standard* published an article entitled 'Top Judge "Surprised" that Controversial EU Laws that We Blocked are Now Legally Binding'. On the following day, the front page of the *Daily Mail*—a Eurosceptic tabloid newspaper always on the lookout for fresh examples of supposed assaults on UK sovereignty at the hands of the EU—displayed the headline 'Dozens of EU Human Rights are Smuggled into the UK: Grayling Attacks Brussels after Claims by Top Judge'.

These stories were prompted by remarks made by Mostyn J in *R (AB) v Secretary of State for the Home Department*,[50] in which a claimant had sought to assert a right (to the protection of personal data) not available under the Human Rights Act 1998, but contained in the EU Charter of Fundamental Rights. Referring, obiter, to the *NS* case, decided earlier in the year by the ECJ,[51] which he interpreted to mean that the Charter held the potential to expand the scope of human rights protection into areas beyond the scope of the Human Rights Act, the judge opined that:

> The constitutional significance of this case can hardly be overstated. The Human Rights Act 1998 incorporated into our domestic law large parts, but by no means all, of the European Convention on Human Rights. Some parts were deliberately missed out by Parliament. The Charter of Fundamental Rights of the European Union contains, I believe, all of those missing parts and a great deal more. Notwithstanding the endeavours of our political representatives at Lisbon it would seem that the much wider Charter of Rights is now part of our domestic law. Moreover, that much wider Charter of Rights would remain part of our domestic law even if the Human Rights Act were repealed.

Given that Conservative ministers in the Coalition Government had been talking about repealing the Human Rights Act and adopting a British Bill of Rights, designed to reduce the influence of the ECtHR, it was perhaps not surprising that the judge's remarks were quickly denounced by one of the most vocal proponents of that position, the then Secretary of State for Justice, Chris Grayling. Mr Grayling duly responded to the *Evening Standard* story by promising to challenge Mostyn J's ruling in the courts 'as soon as possible'.

But although, particularly in Eurosceptic circles, arguments about the scope of the EU Charter of Human Rights have tended to become entangled with controversies about the Human Rights Act and the role of the ECtHR, the status of the Charter is quite different from that of the European Convention on Human Rights. The latter (discussed in chapter 12 above) is a creation of the Council of Europe;

---

[50] *R (AB) v Secretary of State for the Home Department* [2013] EWHC 3453 (Admin).
[51] Joined Cases C-411/10 and C-493/10 *NS v Secretary of State for the Home Department* [2013] QB 102. The decision of the ECJ was in response to references to it by the Court of Appeal and the High Court of the Republic of Ireland.

the former is part of the legal order of the EU. The EU Charter was approved at the Nice Summit in December 2000, but its legal significance began with the coming into force of the Lisbon Treaty on 1 December 2009, which amended Article 6(1) of the Treaty on the European Union to include EU recognition of the Charter, which, it proclaimed, 'shall have the same value as the Treaties'. Noting the ambiguity of wording that does not actually make the Charter part of the Treaties, but, at the same time, attributes to it 'the same legal value' as those Treaties, Dorota Leczykiewitcz observes that:

> In that sense it should be regarded as part of 'primary law of the EU' with which EU legislation should be in compliance. Equally, the Charter should form part of the concept of 'the Treaties' as referred to by the European Communities Act 1972 [as amended]. This means that all rights to which the Charter gives rise to, if in accordance with EU law they are meant to be given legal effect, 'shall be recognised and available in law, and be enforced, allowed and followed' accordingly in the UK.[52]

In the run-up to the signing of the Lisbon Treaty, the Governments of the UK and Poland negotiated the addition of a protocol (Protocol 30), Article 1(1) of which states that the 'Charter does not extend the ability of the Court of Justice of the European Union, or any court or tribunal of Poland or of the United Kingdom, to find that the laws, regulations or administrative provisions, practices or actions of Poland or of the United Kingdom are inconsistent with the fundamental rights, freedoms and principles that it reaffirms'. Article 1(2) further provides that the Title IV of the Charter, which deals with economic and social rights, does not create justiciable rights, unless Poland and the UK have provided for such rights in their national laws. In the *NS* case (above), the Luxembourg Court held that Article 1(1) of Protocol 'explains Art 51 of the Charter with regard to the scope thereof and does not intend to exempt the Republic of Poland or the United Kingdom from the obligation to comply with the provisions of the Charter or to prevent a court of one of those Member States from ensuring compliance with those provisions'.

On 19 November 2013, the Chair of the Commons European Scrutiny Committee, Bill Cash MP (himself a long-standing Eurosceptic), tabled an Urgent Question, asking the Government for a statement on the status in the UK of the EU Charter following the ruling of Mostyn J in the *AB* case. In his reply, Mr Grayling, the Justice Secretary, said that:

> The judge's view was that the Luxembourg court had, in the case of NS, held that the charter could create new rights that apply in the UK. It is important to be very clear to the House: we do not agree with that analysis of the NS case … It is no secret in this House that I would not personally have chosen to sign up to the Lisbon Treaty or to the Charter of Fundamental Rights. However, it is also important to say that the charter's effects are limited to EU law within the UK, and I have not seen any evidence that it goes beyond

---

[52] D Leczykiewicz, 'The EU Charter of Fundamental Rights and its Effects' (*UK Constitutional Law Blog*, 4 August 2011) http://ukconstitutionallaw.org.

that. I would be very concerned if there was any suggestion that the charter did in fact create new rights.[53]

In reply to some Labour frontbenchers who claimed in the debate that the UK had an opt-out from the Charter, the Secretary of State said that Protocol 30 'does not enable us to opt out of the charter. We are still subject to it in EU matters'.[54]

Soon afterwards, the Commons European Scrutiny Committee embarked upon an inquiry into the 'state of confusion' surrounding the application of the Charter in the UK. Its Report was published in April 2014.[55] Having taken extensive evidence, some of it from academic constitutional experts, the Committee concluded that there were many 'blurred' areas that a legal challenge in the courts (hitherto the preferred approach of the Government) could not satisfactorily resolve. The Committee expressed concern about what it saw as an inevitable growth in the jurisdiction of the ECJ 'with increasingly unintended consequences' and recommended that primary legislation be introduced to amend the European Communities Act 1972 'to exclude, at the least, the applicability of the Charter in the UK'—as some had claimed, wrongly, Protocol 30 would do.

In its response to the Report,[56] the Government promised to 'continue to monitor both ECJ and domestic proceedings on the interpretation of Charter rights and on the boundaries of the Charter's scope of application to Member States, and will intervene in cases where appropriate'. It confirmed that 'as long as the UK is a member of the European Union, it has a duty to implement all EU law that applies to it'. Therefore, 'any decision to disapply legislation, including the Charter, which has the same status as the Treaties, would no doubt have political, legal and diplomatic consequences'—which no doubt it would.

Mostyn J's concerns about the constitutional threats posed by the ECJ's judgment in the *NS* case may have been somewhat over the top. But his remarks did serve a useful purpose in giving a preliminary airing to issues around the Charter which will no doubt continue to feature, from time to time, in pro- and anti-EU discourse.

X. EPILOGUE: THE *HS2* CASE

This chapter began by considering the tricky and elusive concept of parliamentary sovereignty with reference to the long-running political debate about the UK's relationship with the EU—the most recent episodes of which have taken place in the shadow of a promised in-out referendum on UK membership. A lot of water has flowed beneath the bridge in the two decades since the *Factortame* and the

---

[53] HC Deb 19 November 2013, col 1087.
[54] ibid col 1089.
[55] House of Commons European Scrutiny Committee, *The Application of the EU Charter of Fundamental Rights in the UK: A State of Confusion* (HC 2013–14, 979).
[56] Cm 8915, July 2014.

Thoburn decisions, but, winding the clock forward to the present, we find continuing echoes of both cases, notably in the UK Supreme Court's judgments in the *Action Alliance* appeal decided in January 2014,[57] in which both cases were cited and distinguished.

The appeal concerned the intended use of the parliamentary hybrid Bill procedure as the statutory basis for authorising the successive stages of the proposed 'HS2' high-speed rail network. Although this procedure provided for select committee hearings in both Houses, at which parties directly affected by the project would be able to present evidence and air their objections, the appellant objectors, seeking judicial review, argued that this did not meet the procedural requirements of a 2011 EU directive on Environmental Impact Assessment—in particular, because of the exclusion of issue of principle from the select committee hearings and because the proceedings would be subject to whipped party discipline.

Thus, apart from the intrinsic complexity and political controversiality of the subject matter of the litigation, the courts were being asked to look at—among other things—some aspects of the legislative process itself, a task that surely risked bringing the judiciary into close, potentially constitutionally conflictual engagement with fundamental aspects of parliamentary sovereignty.

In unanimously dismissing the appeal, the seven-judge Supreme Court, giving multiple, mutually complementary, judgments, duly recognised the constitutional issue, but steered a careful course around the dangerous constitutional rocks. The Justices also decided that this was not an occasion that required a reference to the Luxembourg Court.

On the issue of parliamentary sovereignty, here is a key passage from the judgment of Lord Reed:

> I am mindful of the importance of refraining from trespassing upon the province of Parliament or, so far as possible, even appearing to do so. The court can however consider the effect of the Directive under EU law without in my opinion affecting or encroaching upon any of the powers of Parliament. The Parliamentary authorities have not thought it necessary to seek to intervene in these proceedings, although the court was told that they have been kept informed of the parties' cases. No bill or draft bill has been placed before the court. Nothing the court does or says at this stage will affect the supremacy of Parliament in respect of any bill presented to it; nor will it affect the power of the Secretary of State, or any other Member of Parliament, to present to Parliament whatever bill he thinks fit. Nor is it necessary for the court to express any view, let alone take any action, concerning any decision to lay any bill before Parliament or concerning Parliament's approving such a bill. The court can in my opinion resolve the issue raised by the appellants by performing its ordinary duty to interpret legislation.[58]

---

[57] *R (HS2 Action Alliance Ltd) v Secretary of State for Transport* [2014] UKSC 3, [2014] 1 WLR 324.
[58] ibid [95].

And here is another passage, from the jointly written judgment of Lord Neuberger and Lord Mance, echoing, and adding a gloss to, Sir John Laws' affirmation in *Thoburn* that 'ordinary' statutes can be distinguished from those having a distinctively 'constitutional' status:

> The United Kingdom has no written constitution, but we have a number of constitutional instruments. They include Magna Carta, the Petition of Right 1628, the Bill of Rights and (in Scotland) the Claim of Rights Act 1689, the Act of Settlement 1701 and the Act of Union 1707. The European Communities Act 1972, the Human Rights Act 1998 and the Constitutional Reform Act 2005 may now be added to this list. The common law itself also recognises certain principles as fundamental to the rule of law. It is, putting the point at its lowest, certainly arguable (and it is for United Kingdom law and courts to determine) that there may be fundamental principles, whether contained in other constitutional instruments or recognised at common law, of which Parliament when it enacted the European Communities Act 1972 did not either contemplate or authorise the abrogation.[59]

Readers are referred to an interesting analysis by Mark Elliot of the constitutional significance of the *HS2* case, with particular reference to these comments of Lord Neuberger and Lord Mance.[60] However, the main significance of the case for the theme of this chapter has rather less to do with the substantive content of the subtle and learned arguments of the Supreme Court Justices and those of the judges in the courts below than with the fact that—unlike *Factortame* and *Thoburn* and, more recently, the *AB* case, which raised issues relating to the EU Charter of Fundamental Rights—it attracted few if any headlines in the non-legal media, or indeed much audible intake of breath by Eurosceptic politicians. What media interest there was had to do with the political impact of the case as another episode in the long-running and continuing debates about the impact and policy merits of the *HS2* decision itself. Apart from legal commentaries, hardly any attention was given to the fact that the UK courts were engaging in the interpretation and application of EU law in relation to the legislative process—and thereby (albeit incidentally) testing the scope of parliamentary sovereignty. As it turned out, the decision duly genuflected towards Diceyan orthodoxy by reaffirming the law-making prerogatives of Parliament, albeit with some comments along the way that might pave the way for some interesting constitutional developments in the future.

Factortame and *Thoburn* had, in their day, given a sharp and salutary reality check about the constitutional implications of EU membership—no doubt an uncomfortable, even shocking one to some Eurosceptics with their heads in the sand who had not been following the clearly defined pattern of previous cases

---

[59] ibid [207].
[60] M Elliot, 'Reflections on the HS2 Case: A Hierarchy of Domestic Constitutional Norms and the Qualified Primacy of EU Law' (*UK Constitutional Law Blog*, 23 January 2014) http://ukconstitutionallaw.org.

affecting other EU Member States. But the passage of time has relegated these cases from the main pages of constitutional commentary to the status of important historical footnotes and those strident newspaper headlines and editorials about those cases now look, in hindsight, rather silly. The main legacy of the two cases derives simply from their reaffirmation of the new constitutional order that flowed inevitably from the European Communities Act 1972. Euroscepticism seems, in the last few years, to have shifted much of its attention in the direction of European human rights and the Strasbourg Court, but that is another story and, for this book, another chapter.

Index

Accommodation Decisions 187–88
Accountability
 see also **Lobbyists; National security; Scrutiny**
 association with reforms 64
 civil servants 182
 counter-terrorism
  challenges to accountability 226–30
  need for reform 236–38
  record of accountability 230–36
 impact of Wright Committee reforms 157–59
 importance of giving reasons behind Bills 72
 rights implications 76
 role of MPs 29
 scrutiny of EU legislation 104
Ad hoc committees
 European Committees 97–98
 post-legislative scrutiny 118, 128, 136
 pre-legislative scrutiny (PLS) 44–45
'agenda initiative' 154–55
All-party parliamentary groups 168–70
Amendments
 backbenchers 135
 government response 67–68
 House of Lords procedure 119–20
Automated decision-making
 concluding remarks 202
 constitutional questions
  delegation of power 194–95
  enhanced compliance with rule of law 191–92
  importance 190
  legal basis 193–94
  no-go areas 196–97
  right to object to decisions 195–96
  shift towards rule-bound decision-making 192–93
 examples
  'Employment Status Indicator' (ESI) tool 186–87
  Suitability of Accommodation Decisions 187–88
 meaning and scope 184–86
 need for Select Committee inquiry 197
 organisational change in Parliament 199–200
 overview 183–84
 requirement for new 'law' 201
 scrutiny 198–99
 statutory provisions 188–90

Backbench Business Committee (BBCom) 143–48, 254–55
Backbenchers
 amendments 135
 automated decision-making 197
 concessions in House of Commons 135
 Euroscepticism 291
 government response to amendments 68
 Select Committee on Reform of the House of Commons 140
 speakers in House of Lords 123
Bill of Rights 1688 11, 158, 163, 205, 265, 284, 303, 309
Bill of Rights (proposed) 2, 88, 283–85, 305
Bills
 government Bills 118–24
 hybrid Bills 308–10
 importance of giving reasons behind Bills 72
 'portmanteau' bills 51
 Private Members' Bills
  practical effect 22
  scrutiny as means of legitimising change 29
 Private Peer's Bills
  House of Lords procedure 125–26
  practical effect 22
  selection for PLS 42–43

Civil servants
 Bill Team attendance 56
 decision-making 190
 ethical standards 182
 European scrutiny 94
 regulation of lobbyists 170–72, 177
Command Papers 46, 245, 278
Committees
 see also **Select committees**
 ad hoc committees
  European Committees 97–98
  European policy committees 97–98
  post-legislative scrutiny 118, 128, 136
  pre-legislative scrutiny (PLS) 44–45
 Backbench Business Committee (BBCom) 143–48, 254–55
 Commons Liaison Committee 44, 206
 Constitution Committee
  benefits of applying constitutional standards 71
  House of Lords reform 136
 Grand Committee 120–21
 House of Lords procedure 124–25

impact of reform in House of
  Commons 149–53
Intelligence and Security Committee (ISC)
  effect of Justice and Security Act
    2013 222–24
  establishment and role 221–22
  impact of 2013 reforms 224–26
Joint Committee on Human Rights
  benefits of applying constitutional
    standards 71
  part of general process of scrutiny 35
Joint Committee on the Draft Voting
  Eligibility (Prisoners) Bill 273, 281, 289
Modernisation Committee 40, 42, 54,
  58, 59
part of general process of scrutiny 35
Political and Constitutional Reform
  Committee
  benefits of applying constitutional
    standards 72–73
  benefits of PLS 58
  selection of Bill for PLS 43
pre-legislative scrutiny (PLS)
  advantages and disadvantages of particular
    committees 44–45
  allocation of draft Bills to committees 44
  choice of procedure 45–46
  engagement and evidence 46–48
  expert support 48–49
Public Bill Committees 40, 69–70
ratification of treaties 246–47
Standing Committees 40
Wright Committee *see* **Select Committee on
  Reform of the House of Commons**
Commons Liaison Committee 44, 206
Compatibility with human rights
  concluding remarks 289–90
  devolved powers 268
  general approach to sovereignty 271
  prisoners' rights 273–79
Constitution Committee
  benefits of applying constitutional
    standards 71
  House of Lords reform 136
Constitutional matters
  see also **Good practice (rules and standards);
    Sovereignty; Supremacy of EU law**
  automated decision-making
    delegation of power 194–95
    enhanced compliance with rule of
      law 191–92
    importance 190
    legal basis 193–94
    no-go areas 196–97
    right to object to decisions 195–96
    shift towards rule-bound
      decision-making 192–93
  benefits of sampling 32

code of constitutional standards
  advantages and examples 80–87
  concluding remarks 87–88
  work of Constitution Committee since
    2001 77–80
deployment of armed forces 207
evaluation of legislative scrutiny
  case for improved standards 65–66
  House of Commons 67–71
  House of Lords 66–67
growing public debate 71–75
importance in the field of human
  rights 75–76
need for improved standards 63–65
Parliament
  exercise of legislative power 19
  failure of separation of powers 18–19
  sovereignty as cornerstone of British
    constitution 265–67
  war-making powers 219–21
Counter-terrorism
  accountability
    challenges to accountability 226–30
    need for reform 236–38
    record of accountability 230–36
  concluding remarks 238–40
  selection of Bill for pre-legislative
    scrutiny 43
Courts
  disquiet at influence of ECtHR 269–71
  impact of ECtHR decision on PLS 48
  judicial disempowerment 296–97
  legitimacy and jurisdiction of the
    ECtHR 279–84
  search for certainty 25

Debates
  'agenda initiative' 154–55
  foreign policy and war 206–07
  House of Lords 119
  ratification of treaties 254–56
  scrutiny of EU law
    procedure 98
    scheduling of debates 113–14
    strengths of Commons scrutiny 105
    weaknesses of Commons scrutiny 106–07
Defamation 47–48, 285
Delegated powers
  see also **Secondary legislation**
  automated decision-making 194–95
  Delegated Powers and Regulatory Reform
    Committee
    benefits of applying constitutional
      standards 71
    part of general process of scrutiny 35
Democratic legitimacy *see* **Legitimacy**
Devolved powers
  coordination of statute and policy 47

Index

EU scrutiny 94
human rights compatibility 268
lobbyists 174, 182
parliamentary privilege 163
treaty ratification 248–49, 252
Digital technology
   automated decision-making 183–84
     concluding remarks 202
     constitutional questions 190–97
     example—'Employment Status Indicator' (ESI) tool 186–87
     example—Suitability of Accommodation Decisions 187–88
     meaning and scope 184–86
     need for Select Committee inquiry 197
     organisational change in Parliament 199–200
     overview 183–84
     requirement for new 'law' 201
     scrutiny 198–99
     statutory provisions 188–90
   e-petitions 155–57
   impact of ISC reforms 224
   records of internet browsing 50
   secured access to global companies 223
Direct applicability of EU law 90
Direct effect of EU law 90
Draftsmanship
   benefits of PLS 58
   pragmatic role for Parliament 30
Dualism 90

E-petitions 155–57
'Employment Status Indicator' (ESI) tool 186–87
English Votes for English Laws (EVEL) xxv, 88
European Convention on Human Rights
see **Human rights**
European Union
   characteristics of EU law 90
   concluding remarks 115
   effect of ECA 1972 91
   European Scrutiny Committee of House of Commons
     activities 2006–14 96
     debates 98
     inquiries 98
     membership and staff 96–97
     powers 97
     terms of reference 95–96
     three ad hoc European Committees 97–98
   government action on scrutiny obligations
     block opt-out 114
     opt-in decisions 112–13
     scheduling of debates 113–14
     Scrutiny Reform Report 113
   impact of UK membership on sovereignty 291
   impact on UK legislation
     House of Commons Select Committee on European Community Secondary Legislation 91–92
     Select Committee on Procedures for Scrutiny of Proposals for European Instruments 92–93
   judicial disempowerment of UK courts 296–97
   monitoring compliance with subsidiarity
     legal challenges 103
     parliamentary procedure 103
     reviewing legislation 101–02
   opt-in decisions 103–04
   procedures common to both Houses
     documents and EMs 93–94
     scrutiny reserve resolution 95
   Scrutiny Reform Report
     earlier engagement 108
     European Committees 109
     mainstreaming 108–09
     oral questions 108
     revision of Standing Order No 143 107
     scrutiny reserve 108
   Select Committee on the European Union of the House of Lords
     inquiries 101
     membership and staff 99
     responsibilities 99–100
     scrutiny process 100
     sub-committees 100
     terms of reference 99
   strengths of Commons scrutiny
     breadth of scope 104–05
     debates 105
     influence 105
   strengths of Lords scrutiny system
     experience 110
     influence 111
     inquiries 110–11
     Pre-European Council Evidence Sessions 111
     sifting process 110
     size 109
     wider engagement 109
   supremacy of EU law 296–97
     acceptance by UK 291
     before *Factortame* 297–98
     Factortame and the 're-writing of the British constitution' 298–302
     key characteristic of EU law 90
     'Metric Martyrs' case 302–04
   weaknesses of Commons scrutiny
     debates 106–07
     lack of detailed scrutiny 105–06
     mainstreaming 106
   weaknesses of Lords scrutiny system 111–12

314 Index

Euroscepticism
  aftermath of 2015 General Election 291–92
  issues surrounding sovereignty
    heart of Eurosceptic debate 294–96
    multi-layered concept 293
    response to EU Charter of Fundament
      Rights 305–07
Executive see Government
Expenses scandal
  general impact 139–40
  impact on Labour Party 180
  select committee inquiry 147
  Select Committee on Reform of the House
    of Commons 141–43
Explanatory notes 48, 73, 86, 123, 178

Fair trial (Art 6) 85, 163, 286, 288
Filibustering 59, 207
Freedom of speech
  absolute privilege 285
  Bill of Rights 1688 284
  importance 163

General standards see Good practice
  (rules and standards)
Good law initiative 3
Good practice (rules and standards)
  automated decision-making
    need for organisational change in
      Parliament 200
    shift towards rule-bound
      decision-making 192–93
  code of constitutional standards
    advantages and examples 80–87
    work of Constitution Committee since
      2001 77–80
  growing call for reform 71–75
  importance in the field of human
    rights 75–76
Government
  control of parliamentary time 21
  influence over PLS 44, 46
  ministerial obligations to observe
    international law
      general principles 267–71
      Ministerial Code vii
      prisoners' rights 271–79
  political reality of elected government 20–21
  ratification of treaties 242–44
  regulation of lobbyists 170–72
  response to legislative amendments 67–68
  response to scrutiny of EU legislation
    block opt-out 114
    opt-in decisions 112–13
    scheduling of debates 113–14
    Scrutiny Reform Report 113
Government Digital Service Unit 185, 199
Grand Committee 120–21

Hansard Commission the Legislative
  Process 39
House of Commons
  constitutional standards 67–71
  European Scrutiny Committee of House
    of Commons
    activities 2006–14 96
    debates 98
    inquiries 98
    membership and staff 96–97
    powers 97
    strengths 104–05
    terms of reference 95–96
    three ad hoc European Committees 97–98
    weaknesses 105–07
  government control of parliamentary
    time 21
  MP's individual accountability 29
  reform
    Backbench Business Committee
      (BBCom) 143–48
    House Business Committee 148–49
    impact of expenses scandal 139–40
    impact on accountability 157–59
    public participation 153–57
    Select Committee on Modernisation of the
      House of Commons 140–41
    Select Committee on Reform of the House
      of Commons 141–43
    select committees 149–53
  scrutiny
    House of Lords distinguished 17–18
    political reality of elected
      government 20–21
    separation of powers 19
House of Lords
  composition 129–31
  constitutional standards 66–67
  lobbyists 166–68
  MP's individual accountability 29
  need for reform 136
  scrutinizing process
    committee assessment 124–25
    government Bills 118–24
    impact on legislation 131–36
    post-legislative scrutiny 128–29
    Private Peer's Bills 125–26
    secondary legislation 126–27
  scrutiny
    House of Commons distinguished 17–18
    separation of powers 19
  Select Committee on the European Union of
    the House of Lords
    inquiries 101
    membership and staff 99
    responsibilities 99–100
    scrutiny process 100
    strengths 109–11

sub-committees 100
terms of reference 99
weaknesses 111–12
Human rights
Eurosceptic response to EU Charter of Fundamental Rights 305–07
importance of constitutional standards 75–76
international law obligations
general approach to sovereignty 268–71
prisoners' rights 271–79
parliamentary privilege
impact of ECHR 284–87
reform proposals for Bill of Rights 287–88
role of Scrutiny Unit lawyers 49
Hybrid Bills 308–10

Impact assessments 73, 94, 178, 230
Information technology *see* **Digital technology**
Intelligence and Security Committee (ISC)
effect of Justice and Security Act 2013 222–24
establishment and role 221–22
impact of 2013 reforms 224–26
International law obligations
general principles 267–71
Ministerial Code vii
prisoners' rights 271–79
International treaties
opt-in decisions 112, 114
ratification
concluding remarks 263–64
impact of reform 250–52
need for more reform 252–63
overview 241–42
parliamentary involvement 242–50
public participation 249–50
relationship with sovereignty
concluding remarks 289–90
general approach 267–71
prisoners' rights 271–79
supremacy of EU law 291, 297–301, 306

Joint Committee on Human Rights
benefits of applying constitutional standards 71
part of general process of scrutiny 35
Judicial disempowerment 296–97

Law-making
see also **Legislation**
benefits of PLS 54–59
constitutional model based on separation of powers 19
influence of members of parliament 21–22
Legislation
see also **Law-making**

English Votes for English Laws (EVEL) 88
as tool of government policy
formation of policy 24–25
general acceptance of position 22–23
inconsistent underlying assumptions 23–24
need for legitimacy 25–26
part of scheme for change 26–27
political constraints 24
search for certainty 25
Legitimacy
ECtHR 279–84
importance of elected MPs 70
legislation as tool of government policy 25–26
role of PLS 53–54
scrutiny as means of legitimising change 27–28
Lobbyists
all-party parliamentary groups 168–70
ban on paid advocacy 164–65
current rules 165–66
House of Lords 166–68
ministers and civil servants 170–72
organic part of Parliament 161–62
Parliamentary regulation
background 162–63
reform proposals
Coalition Government proposals 172–74
implementation 179–82
Trade Union Administration Act 2015 174–78
Lords Constitution Committee 35

Members of Parliament
see also **Backbenchers**
accountability 29
expenses scandal
general impact 139–40
impact on Labour Party 180
select committee inquiry 147
Select Committee on Reform of the House of Commons 141–43
growing rebelliousness 67–68
individual accountability 29
influence over law-making 21–22
marginalisation 68–69
Ministerial Code xviii, 170–71, 182, 267
Modernisation Committee 40, 42, 54, 58, 59

National security
counter-terrorism
challenges to accountability 226–30
concluding remarks 238–40
need for reform 236–38
record of accountability 230–36
selection of Bill for PLS 43
historical background 205–10

316 Index

Intelligence and Security Committee (ISC)
  effect of Justice and Security Act 2013 222–24
  establishment and role 221–22
  impact of 2013 reforms 224–26
  overview 203–05
  war-making powers
    impact of Iraq War 211–14
    overview 210–11
    prerogative in 2010–15 Parliament 214–19
    reinforcement of constitutional convention 219–21

Opt-in decisions 103–04, 112–13, 114

Parliament
  as constitutional institution
    exercise of legislative power 19
    failure of separation of powers 18–19
    implicit requirement for reform 19–20
    political reality in House of Commons 20–21
  pragmatic role 28–36
Parliamentary Counsel
  influence on work of Parliamentary attention 30
  role 16
Parliamentary privilege
  Bill of Rights 1688 284
  human rights
    impact of ECHR 284–87
    reform proposals 287–88
  lobbyists 163
Participation *see* **Public participation**
Pilot 'public readings' 155
Policy
  allocation of priorities 31–32
  coordination of statute and policy with devolved powers 94
  legislation as tool of government
    formation of policy 24–25
    general acceptance of position 22–23
    inconsistent underlying assumptions 23–24
    need for legitimacy 25–26
    part of scheme for change 26–27
    political constraints 24
    search for certainty 25
  two-stage analysis 34–35
Political and Constitutional Reform Committee
  benefits of applying constitutional standards 72–73
  benefits of PLS 58
  selection of Bill for pre-legislative scrutiny 43
'Ponsonby Rule' 245–46

'Portmanteau' bills 51
Post-legislative scrutiny
  see also **Pre-legislative scrutiny (PLS)**
  House of Lords 128–29
  part of general process of scrutiny 36
Pre-legislative scrutiny (PLS)
  see also **Post-legislative scrutiny**
  agreement on positive effects over time 40–41
  beneficial outcomes 54–59
  defined 40
  future developments 59–62
  history of effectiveness 39–40
  increasing volume of draft legislation 43–44
  ineffectiveness 51–53
  legitimacy role 53–54
  part of general process of scrutiny 36
  preconditions for effectiveness 49–51
  purpose 42
  role of committees
    advantages and disadvantages of particular committees 44–45
    allocation of draft Bills to committees 44
    choice of procedure 45–46
    engagement and evidence 46–48
    expert support 48–49
  selection of Bills 42–43
Prisoners' rights
  international law obligations 271–79
  pre-legislative scrutiny (PLS)
    expert support 48
    impact of ECtHR decision 48
    selection of Bill for PLS 43
Private Members' Bills
  practical effect 22
  scrutiny as means of legitimising change 29
Private Peer's Bills
  House of Lords procedure 125–26
  practical effect 22
  scrutiny as means of legitimising change 29
Privilege *see* **Parliamentary privilege**
Programme motions 119
Public Bill Committees 40, 69–70
Public participation
  see also **Lobbyists**
  impact of reform in House of Commons
    'agenda initiative' 154–55
    calls for government action 153–54
    e-petitions 155–57
  inquiries
    European Scrutiny Committee of House of Commons 98
    Select Committee on the European Union of the House of Lords 101
  pre-legislative scrutiny (PLS)
    beneficial outcomes 55–56
    engagement and evidence 46–48
  ratification of treaties 249–50

Ratification of treaties
  concluding remarks 263–64
  impact of reform 250–52
  need for more reform
    debates and votes 254–56
    extension of 21-day sittings 256–57
    increased scope of treaties
      covered 257–58
    new institutional mechanisms 259–61
    relationship between government and
      Parliament 252–54
    scrutiny during negotiations 261–63
  overview 241–42
  parliamentary involvement
    committees 246–47
    exceptions 247–49
    government role 242–44
    legislation on treaties 244
    new statutory provisions 247
    'Ponsonby Rule' 245–46
  public participation 249–50
Reform
  automated decision-making
    need for Select Committee inquiry 197
    organisational change in
      Parliament 199–200
    requirement for new 'law' 201
    scrutiny 198–99
  constitutional standards 71–75
  counter-terrorism 236–38
  House of Commons
    Backbench Business Committee
      (BBCom) 143–48
    House Business Committee 148–49
    impact of expenses scandal 139–40
    impact on accountability 157–59
    public participation 153–57
    Select Committee on Modernisation of the
      House of Commons 140–41
    Select Committee on Reform of the House
      of Commons 141–43
    select committees 149–53
  House of Lords 136
  implicit requirement of law-making 19–20
  legislation as tool of government
    policy 26–27
  lobbyists
    Coalition Government proposals 172–74
    implementation 179–82
    Trade Union Administration Act
      2015 174–78
  parliamentary privilege 287–88
  pragmatic role for Parliament 30
  pre-legislative scrutiny (PLS) 40, 59–62
  ratification of treaties
    debates and votes 254–56
    extension of 21-day sittings 256–57
    impact 250–52

    increased scope of treaties
      covered 257–58
    new institutional mechanisms 259–61
    new statutory provisions 247
    relationship between government and
      Parliament 252–54
    scrutiny during negotiations 261–63
  scrutiny as means of legitimising
    change 27–28
  scrutiny of EU legislation
    earlier engagement 108
    European Committees 109
    mainstreaming 108–09
    oral questions 108
    revision of Standing Order No 143 107
    scrutiny reserve 108
Report stages
  effectiveness 36
  House of Commons 69, 141
  House of Lords 122–26
  lobbyists 174
Rippon Commission 39
Robot government *see* **Automated
  decision-taking**
Rule of law
  challenges to counter-terrorism
    legislation 226
  code of constitutional standards 77
  enhanced compliance with automated
    decision-taking 191–92
  implementation of human rights 273,
    277, 290
  international obligations 267
  legislative processes 83–86
  normativity of the UK constitution 75–76
  ordinary and constitutional statutes
    distinguished 309
Rules *see* **Good practice (rules and standards)**

Salisbury-Addison Convention 1945 82, 119
Sampling
  benefits of new approach 31–32
  need for organisational change in
    Parliament 200
  specialist committees 36
Scrutiny
  see also **European Union; Pre-legislative
    scrutiny (PLS)**
  automated decision-making 198–99
  counter-terrorism legislation
    historical background 207–09
  effectiveness
    concluding remarks 36–37
    difficulties of measurement 16–17
    exercise of legislative power 19
    House of Commons and Lords
      distinguished 17–18
    implicit requirement for reform 19–20

influence of members of parliament   21–22
overview   15–16
House of Lords
  committee assessment   124–25
  government Bills   118–24
  impact on legislation   131–36
  post-legislative scrutiny   128–29
  Private Peer's Bills   125–26
  secondary legislation   126–27
  two-dimensional problem   117–18
inconsistent underlying assumptions   23–24
as means of legitimising change   27–28
pragmatic role for Parliament   28–36
ratification of treaties   261–63
Secondary legislation
House of Lords procedure   126–27
Select Committee on Procedures for Scrutiny of Proposals for European Instruments   91–92
Security *see* **National security**
Select committees
automated decision-making   197
European Community Secondary Legislation   91
impact of reform in House of Commons   149–53
Modernisation of the House of Commons   140–41
national security
  historical background   205–06
  Intelligence and Security Committee (ISC)   221–26
  outcome of Iraq War   207
Procedures for Scrutiny of Proposals for European Instruments   92–93
Reform of House of Commons   59–60, 141–43
Separation of powers
code of constitutional standards   77
debate on prisoner voting   273
failure as constitutional model   18–19
role of privilege   285
vesting of executive power   21
Sovereignty
see also **Supremacy of EU law**
concluding remarks   289–90
cornerstone of British constitution   265–67
Diceyan model and its critics   293–94
Factortame and the 're-writing of the British constitution'   298–302
heart of Eurosceptic debate   294–96
impact of UK membership of EU   291
intended use of the parliamentary hybrid Bill   307–10
international law obligations
  general approach   267–71
  prisoners' rights   271–79

judicial disempowerment   296–97
legitimacy and jurisdiction of the ECtHR   279–84
'Metric Martyrs' case   302–04
multi-layered concept   293
role of PLS   50
undermining by ECtHR   285
Standards *see* **Good practice (rules and standards)**
Standing Committees   40
Standing Orders
e-petitions   156
English Votes for English Laws (EVEL)   xxv
initiation of legislation   21
Private Members' Bills   125
rules governing procedure   45
Scrutiny Reform Report   107
Third Readings   122
Strathclyde Review   xvii
Subsidiarity
legal challenges   103
parliamentary procedure   103
reviewing legislation   101–02
Sunset clauses
constitutional standards   74, 82
efficacy   233–34
Prevention of Terrorism Acts   209
purpose   79
Supremacy of EU law
see also **Sovereignty**
acceptance by UK   291
before *Factortame*   297–98
Factortame and the 're-writing of the British constitution'   298–302
key characteristic of EU law   90
'Metric Martyrs' case   302–04

Technology *see* **Digital technology**
Terrorism *see* **Counter-terrorism**
Treaties *see* **International treaties**

War-making powers
impact of Iraq War   211–14
overview   210–11
prerogative in 2010–15 Parliament
  ISIS/ISIL/Islamic State   215–16
  Libya   214
  Mali   216
  reports from parliamentary committees   216–19
  Syria   xxv, 215
reinforcement of constitutional convention   219–21
West Lothian Question   xxv
Wright Committee *see* **Select Committee on Reform of the House of Commons**